CLIVE JONES
TORE T. PETERSEN
(*editors*)

Israel's Clandestine Diplomacies

HURST & COMPANY, LONDON

First published in the United Kingdom in 2013 by
C. Hurst & Co. (Publishers) Ltd.,
41 Great Russell Street, London, WC1B 3PL
© Clive Jones, Tore T. Petersen and the Contributors, 2013
All rights reserved.
Printed in India

The right of Clive Jones, Tore T. Petersen and the Contributors to
be identified as the Author of this publication is asserted by them
in accordance with the Copyright, Designs and Patents Act, 1988.

A Cataloguing-in-Publication data record for this book
is available from the British Library.

ISBN: 978-1-84904-233-8

www.hurstpublishers.com

CONTENTS

CONTENTS

ACKNOWLEDGEMENTS

The chapters in this edited collection were originally presented as papers at the international conference 'From the Centre to the Periphery: Israel, Clandestine Diplomacy and the Modern Middle East', held at the Norwegian University of Science and Technology (NTNU), Trondheim, between 9 and 10 May 2011. We thank all those who participated in the conference, but in particular the editors gratefully acknowledge the assistance and support of Professor Kathrine Skretting, dean of the Faculty of Arts and Humanities, NTNU, who supported this endeavour from the outset. We also express our profound gratitude to the conference coordinator, Elise Hov, who combined considerable organisational flair and efficiency with good grace and humour, and Anne Haug, who so ably dealt with all the travel arrangements of the conference participants. We are also deeply indebted to Mr Leslie Silver, OBE, whose financial support helped to cover much of the costs of what proved to be such a memorable event. Finally, the editors thank Michael Dwyer of Hurst Publishers for all his help and assistance.

CONTRIBUTORS

Dr Yoav Alon is a senior lecturer in the modern history of the Middle East at Tel Aviv University specialises in Jordanian history and politics, the British Empire in the Middle East, the Palestine Mandate and tribal societies in the modern Middle East. He is the author of *The Making of Jordan: Tribes, Colonialism and the Modern State* (2007) as well as articles which have been published in journals such as the *International Journal of Middle Eastern Studies*, the *British Journal of Middle Eastern Studies*, the *Journal of Imperial and Commonwealth History* and *Die Welt des Islams*. Email: yalon@post.tau.ac.il

Dr Amnon Aran is a senior lecturer at City University, London. His work focuses on the international relations of the Middle East, with special reference to the Arab–Israeli conflict and the foreign policy of Middle Eastern states. His publications include *Israel's Foreign Policy towards the PLO: The Impact of Globalization* (2009), and (with Chris Alden) *Foreign Policy Analysis: New Approaches* (2011). Email: amnon. aran.1@city.ac.uk

Uri Bialer is emeritus professor of international relations at the Hebrew University, Jerusalem, and holder of the Maurice B. Hexter Chair in International Relations–Middle Eastern Studies. His publications include *The Shadow of the Bomber; The Fear of Air Attack and British Politics 1932–1939* (1980), *Between East and West; Israel's Foreign Policy Orientation 1948–56* (1990), *Oil and the Arab–Israeli Conflict 1948–63* (1999) and *Cross on the Star of David: The Christian World in Israel's Foreign Policy 1948–67* (2005). Email: msbialer@gmail.com

ix

CONTRIBUTORS

Dr Ahron (Ronnie) Bregman teaches at the Department of War Studies, King's College London, where he focuses on the Arab–Israeli conflict and the Middle East peace process. He is the author of *The Fifty Years War: Israel and the Arabs* (1998, with Jihan el-Tahri), the companion book to a six-part BBC/PBS television documentary and its sequel, *Elusive Peace: How the Holy Land Defeated America*, the companion book to a three-part BBC/PBS television documentary, *A History of Israel* (2002), and *Israel's Wars: A History Since 1947* (2000, 2002, 2010). His book *Occupation* is forthcoming. Email: ahronbregman@gmail.com

Dr Jacob Eriksson was awarded his PhD by the School of Oriental and African Studies (SOAS), London, in October 2011 for his thesis 'Swedish Mediation of the Israeli–Palestinian Conflict: a Study of the Utility of Small-State Mediation and Track II diplomacy'. He received his BA in war studies and history and his MA in international peace and security from the Department of War Studies at King's College London. His research interests include the Israeli–Palestinian conflict and the wider Arab–Israeli conflict, conflict resolution, Middle Eastern politics and security and Islamic terrorism. Email: bjjeriksson@gmail.com

Professor Clive Jones holds a Chair in the School of Government and International Affairs at the University of Durham. He was previously Professor of Middle East Studies and International Politics at the University of Leeds. He specialises in the Arab-Israeli conflict and Gulf Security. His publications include *Britain and the Yemen Civil War* (2004/2010), *Soviet Jewish Aliyah 1989–92* (1996) with Emma Murphy, *Israel: Challenges to Democracy, Identity and the State* (2002), and is co-editor with Ami Pedahzur of *The al-Aqsa Intifada: Between Terrorism and Civil War* (2005) and with Sergio Catignani, *Israel and the Hizbollah: An Asymmetric Conflict in Historical and Comparative Perspective* (2010). Email: clive7738@yahoo.com

Dr Zach Levey is senior lecturer and chair of the Division of International Relations, Department of Political Science at the University of Haifa where he specialises in the history of the Arab–Israeli conflict and Israeli foreign policy. His publications include *Israel and the Western Powers: 1952–1960* (1997), *Britain and the Middle East* (edited with Elie Podeh) and *Israel in Africa: 1956–1976* (Brill, Martinus Nijhoff and Republic of Letters, forthcoming). Email: zachl@poli.haifa.ac.ul

CONTRIBUTORS

Professor Rory Miller is director of Middle East and Mediterranean studies at King's College London, where he specialises in European and US intervention in the Middle East and the role of small states in the region. He is the author of three books, *Divided against Zion: Opposition to a Jewish State in Palestine, 1945–48* (2000), *Ireland and the Palestine Question, 1948–2004* (2005) and *Inglorious Disarray: Europe, Israel and the Palestinians since 1967* (2011). He has edited or co-edited five books including *Ireland and the Middle East: Trade, Society and Peace* (2008) and *Britain, Palestine and Empire: The Mandate Years* (2010). Email: rory.miller@kcl.ac.uk

Tore T. Petersen is professor of international and American diplomatic history at the Norwegian University of Science and Technology (NTNU), Trondheim, Norway. He is the author of *Richard Nixon, Great Britain and the Anglo-American Alignment in the Persian Gulf and Arabian Peninsula: Making Allies out of Clients* (2009); *The Decline of the Anglo-American Middle East, 1961–1969: A Willing Retreat* (2006); *The Middle East between the Great Powers: Anglo-American Conflict and Cooperation, 1952–1957* (2000) and is the editor of *Challenging Retrenchment: The United States, Great Britain and the Middle East, 1950–1980* (2010) and *Controlling the Uncontrollable: The Great Powers in the Middle East* (2006). Email: tore.petersen@ntnu.no

Yehudit Ronen is associate professor of political studies at Bar-Ilan University. She is the author of numerous academic journal articles and books including *Qaddafi's Libya in World Politics* (2008) [in Hebrew], *Sudan in Civil War: Between Africanism, Arabism and Islam* (1995) and *The Maghrib: Politics, Society and Economy*. Professor Ronen is also the author of a novel—*Carob Whiskey*—which won two prestigious literary prizes in Israel. Email: yronen@post.tau.ac.il

Dr Noa Schonmann is a lecturer in the politics and international relations of the Middle East at the University of Oxford, and a fellow in politics at Pembroke College. Her book, *Israel's Phantom Pact: Foreign Policy on the Periphery of the Middle East*, will be published by I.B. Tauris in 2013. She completed a DPhil at Oxford's Oriental Institute, and holds a master's and a bachelor's degree in modern Middle East history from Tel Aviv University. Email: noa.schonmann@politics.ox.ac.uk

CONTRIBUTORS

Dr Yigal Sheffy is senior lecturer at the Program for Diplomacy Studies, Tel Aviv University, where he specialises in the modern military history of the Middle East and intelligence studies. His publications include *The Intelligence Dimension of the Palestine Campaign, 1914–1918* (1998) and *Early Warning Countdown: The "Rotem" Affair and the Israeli Security Perceptions, 1957–1960* (2008, in Hebrew) and is co-editor with Shaul Shai of *The First World War: Middle Eastern Perspective* (2000) and with Haim Goren and Eran Dolev of *Palestine and the First World War—New Perspectives* (2012 forthcoming). Email: sheffy@post.tau.ac.il

Dr Shlomo Shpiro is deputy head of the Political Studies Department at Bar-Ilan University, Israel, and chairman of the International Intelligence History Association (IIHA). He specialises in intelligence, terrorism and security. His recent publications include co-editing the two-volume series *Handbook of Global Security and Intelligence* (Praeger 2008), 'Israeli Intelligence and Al Qaeda' (*International Journal of Intelligence and Counter-Intelligence*), 'KGB Human Intelligence Operations in Israel' (*Intelligence and National Security*), 'Commissions of Inquiry as Agents of Change in the Israeli Intelligence Community', in Stuart Farson and Mark Phythian (eds), *Commissions of Enquiry and National Security* (2011). Email: sshpiro@yahoo.com

Dr Asaf Siniver is a senior lecturer in international security in the Department of Political Science and International Studies at the University of Birmingham. He specialises in the Arab–Israeli conflict, international mediation and US foreign policy, and holds a Leverhulme Research Fellowship (2011–13). He is the author of *Nixon, Kissinger and US Foreign Policy: The Machinery of Crisis* (2008 and 2011), and is the editor of *International Terrorism post 9/11: Comparative Dynamics and Responses* (2010 and 2012). Email: a.siniver@bham.ac.uk

ENDNOTE ACRONYMS

BBC—SWB	British Broadcasting Corporation—Summary of World Broadcasts
CZA	Central Zionist Archives
FRUS	Foreign Relations of the United States
HA	Haganah Archive (Tel Aviv)
IDFA	Israel Defence Force and Defence Establishment Archives
ISA	Israel State Archives
IWM	Imperial War Museum (UK)
LBJ	Lyndon Baines Johnson Presidential Library
NAI	National Archives of Ireland
NARA—CIA	The National Archives and Records Administration—Central Intelligence Agency
TNA	The National Archive (UK)

INTRODUCTION

THEMES AND ISSUES

Clive Jones

On 29 November 2010, the respected Israeli newspaper *Ha'aretz* ran a story titled 'Wikileaks Blows Cover of Israel's Covert Gulf States Ties'. Based on leaked diplomatic cables between the US embassy in Tel Aviv and Washington, the story detailed the 'good and personal relationship' said to have developed between the then Israeli foreign minister, Tzipi Livni, and her counterpart from the United Arab Emirates, Shaykh Abdullah Ibn Zayed, despite the absence of formal diplomatic ties between the two states. The shared suspicion towards the regional designs of Tehran that undoubtedly underpinned these ties even extended, it was alleged, to a secret dialogue between Israel and Saudi Arabia, conducted under the auspices of the former head of the Mossad, Meir Dagan.[1]

Such reports would normally be treated with circumspection, but the veracity of this account was never denied by the parties involved. Indeed, despite the absence of formal diplomatic ties, such 'clandestine' or 'secret' diplomacy is of a piece with the long-standing attitudes, practices and strategies of successive Israeli governments towards both state and non- or substate actors in a region once described by Binyamin Netanyahu as a tough neighbourhood. While it is easy to dismiss such an aphorism as glib, it nonetheless highlights the extent to which a real-

1

ist paradigm, informed by a profound sense of the few against the many in a largely hostile region, has come to shape the dominant perception of Israeli diplomacy where the enemy of my enemy is my friend. To this end, the WikiLeaks disclosure of ties, however tentative, with other Gulf states is but the latest in a long tradition of Israeli clandestine ties which have helped Jerusalem not only surmount its regional isolation, but also help frame security agendas that pose equally complex and often damaging dilemmas among erstwhile foes. Thus secret support for the royalist forces in the Yemen Civil War in the 1960s, the Christian Phalange movement in Lebanon, the Kurds in Iraq in the 1970s and the Anyanya rebel movement in southern Sudan in the 1980s are some of the more well-known instances of Israel's pursuit of a 'periphery doctrine' designed to achieve strategic advantage.[2]

But Israel's clandestine diplomacy is of course more than just secret support for irredentist groups in far-off lands—the so-called periphery. Indeed, at a time when the legitimacy of Israel—if not its very legality—has been subject to unprecedented scrutiny and criticism across the globe, how Israel has used secret diplomacy, what constitutes its essence and the extent to which it might be seen more as a manifestation of bureaucratic rivalries than a response to external challenges and opportunities are areas that remain underexplored. In short, is a view formed by realpolitik sufficient to explain recourse to a level of 'secret diplomacy' which, as Ahron Klieman has suggested, is perhaps unique in the contemporary era?[3]

To begin with, we should acknowledge the methodological difficulties associated with the very term 'clandestine diplomacy' or indeed 'secret diplomacy'. By definition, most diplomacy remains largely hidden, or rather the debates that inform the defining of interests and the means to achieve them—as opposed their practical outcome—are shielded from public scrutiny as governments seek to protect both sources and reputations. Equally, with its clear inference of the role played by intelligence agencies, it would be all too easy to assume that such diplomacy remains an adjunct of secret service. As the intelligence historian Len Scott has noted:

Although clandestine diplomacy is a neglected area of enquiry, there are a number of examples of where intelligence services are used to engage in secret and deniable discussions with adversaries. One question is whether clandestine diplomacy can be conceived as a form of covert action intended to influence an adversary or whether it is distinct from covert action because it involves conscious co-operation with the adversary and potential disclosure of the officers involved.[4]

Such debates certainly have resonance in any informed discussion of Israel's foreign intelligence service. For example, the Mossad reportedly retains a particular unit under its auspices—Tevel—which is responsible for liaising with intelligence services and foreign ministries across the world, many of whom publicly shun more formal relations with Israel.[5] In the case of Israel at least, the intelligence services have exercised an influence (and some would add that they have cast a shadow) over how a particular Israeli diplomatic tradition has developed since the founding of the state in 1948. This points to a tension in the role that intelligence services play in the furtherance of foreign policy objectives, a tension that is not unique to the State of Israel. Again as Scott notes:

One further and important distinction needs to be drawn, between intelligence services acting as diplomatic conduits, and intelligence services acting as quasi-independent foreign policy makers. While it may be difficult to distinguish between the two, the use of intelligence services by governments to conduct negotiations is distinct from where intelligence agencies have their own agendas and priorities. Various accounts of CIA and SIS activity in the Middle East in the 1950s, for example, suggest that both organisations were pursuing their own foreign policies at variance with their foreign ministry colleagues.[6]

But as several contributors to this volume argue, Israel has not been immune from such variances. Indeed, the Israeli approach to diplomacy was shaped by the pre-state institutions of the Jewish community in Palestine or Yishuv, where, conscious of its material and demographic limitations but nonetheless fired by the need to realise statehood, the Jewish Agency learnt how best to maximise their resources and manipulate their interlocutors, be they tribes across the Jordan or their British overlords in Mandate Palestine in pursuit of Zionist aspirations. The extent to which this culture continued to shape and dominate Israeli approaches towards international affairs when perhaps more formal diplomatic strategies might have been equally effective in securing defined foreign policy objectives remains prescient. Research by Ahron Bregman suggests, for example, that on the eve of the June 1967 war, the Israeli Cabinet under Levi Eshkol was presented with two differing assessments by Foreign Minister Abba Eban, and the then head of the Mossad, Meir Amit, following two separate visits to the White House over the extent to which Washington would indulge Israeli unilateral action. The more belligerent assessment of the spy chief won out.[7]

This in turn suggests that clandestine diplomacy may not always be the result of sober appreciation of an external environment where antipathy towards Israel has determined diplomatic strategies. In short, we need to understand the bureaucratic rivalries and domestic pressures that have seen both public and secret diplomacy run parallel together but driven by often conflicting motives albeit bound by a desire to achieve the same ends. Israel's vexed relationship with Germany, particularly in the 1950s and 1960s, would certainly appear to conform to such a pattern. Moreover, clandestine diplomacy can also encompass 'signals', both of intent and capability, which can be used to send discreet yet loaded messages over redlines that should not be crossed or, by contrast, opportunities that might be explored in lieu of more formal government approval. We cannot, for example, have a full account of Israeli–Egyptian relations in the 1960s without accounting for such signals, while equally, the contacts between Israeli academics and representatives of the PLO were crucial in laying the groundwork for the more formal exploratory talks between Israeli diplomats and their Palestinian counterparts that led to the Oslo process.

Such talks were of course shrouded in secrecy and could easily again fall under the rubric of clandestine or secret diplomacy. However, it is more appropriate to see such negotiations as a subset of this kind of diplomacy. For while recognising the need for secrecy in order to progress towards mutually satisfactory goals, such diplomacy rarely escapes for long the attention of the media or indeed interested parties—both state and non-state—who have a stake in the eventual outcome. Here, and where the pattern of negotiations, coupled with the interests to be pursued, determine the extent to which Israel has indeed wanted the detail of such discussions to remain 'below the radar', it is perhaps best to refer to 'discreet diplomacy'. For example, in the aftermath of the Camp David negotiations in 2000, Ehud Barak proved remarkably quick to blame his Palestinian interlocutors for the breakdown of the negotiations, an event which presaged the outbreak of the al-Aqsa intifada and the emergence of increasingly bitter narratives regarding culpability.[8]

But we should not forget that while secret or discreet diplomacy might often have been subordinated or subsumed by security interests, secret diplomacy has also had an intrinsic value in its own right, not least when it comes to Israel's relations with the Jewish Diaspora. From Operation Magic Carpet, which brought Jews from the mountains of Yemen to Israel in 1948, through to the rescue of over 1000 Jews from war-torn Sarajevo in the 1990s, aliyah—Jewish migration to Israel—remains, as Michael Brecher noted some four decades ago, a foreign policy value for Israelis and not just another objective.[9] Indeed, while some in Israel doubt the continued efficacy of the 'Law of Return' as physical space (excluding the occupied territories) and natural resources, most notably water, diminish exponentially, aliyah remains integral to state identity despite the emergence in recent years of debates among some Israelis over the continued relevance of Zionism.[10]

The lengths Israel has been prepared to go towards this endeavour have inevitably stretched the resources of the state, but equally policy-makers in Jerusalem have been more than adept at using Israel's close ties with Washington to act as a kind of 'diplomatic courier' for third parties anxious to improve ties with the United States but who are constrained from doing so openly. Israel's relations with some African states, most notably Sudan, certainly fall within this category. Equally, in an episode that still begs more questions than have ever been answered, the Israeli role in the 'arms for hostages' affair in the 1980s around the selling of American weapons to Iran in return for the release of US citizens held captive by the Hezbollah in Lebanon demonstrates the fine line that can exist between pursuing defined foreign policy objectives and allegations of nefarious activity.[11]

The contributors to this volume touch on many of the themes and issues outlined above in a series of original and often controversial chapters. Perhaps at the end of this volume, readers might feel that the essence of Israel's clandestine diplomacy is easier to 'feel' empirically than define conceptually beyond a base commitment to ensuring the security and indeed survival of the Jewish state. Yet the richness and diversity of the chapters would have been lost if constricted by a rigid conceptual framework, the concern being that the authors might have had to engage in forms of intellectual contortion if their respective contributions were to 'fit' a particular methodological approach. Even so, each chapter does, in full or in part, address key questions and themes about the nature and diversity of Israel's clandestine diplomacies. These are:

1. Does Israel have a culture of 'covert diplomacy rooted in its pre-state past'?

2. Have the very tools used to pursue the 'periphery doctrine'—designed to help Israel break the animus of a predominantly Arab–Muslim Middle East—actually helped or hindered the Jewish state achieve its foreign policy objectives and goals?

3. Has the preference for covert diplomacy been as much driven by internal bureaucratic rivalries as by the need to observe external sensitivities?

4. What weight should be ascribed to individuals in policy formation and the utility of 'covert diplomacy' in achieving defined goals and ends?

5. How effective has 'signalling' been as a form of covert diplomacy through the threatened or actual use of military power?

6. How have Israel's interlocutors and close allies come to view its use of secret (or, as some might prefer, 'discreet') diplomacy in shaping both the process and desired outcomes of peace negotiations? Has the very emphasis upon securing 'hard' power objectives helped/hindered the achievement of those self-same security goals?

7. In this era of globalisation and WikiLeaks it would be all too easy to dismiss the importance of 'covert diplomacy'. Even so, soft power and public diplomacy have increasingly come to dominate popular diplomatic discourse. What does this mean for Israel's use of clandestine diplomacy in the future, and can such diplomacy remain immune from the wider eddies of change across the wider Middle East?

These themes and questions are not mutually exclusive and some will be of more relevance to particular chapters than to others. They nonetheless capture the diversity of the subject area in its broad historical context, providing in the process a sense of perspective in understanding Israel's use (and in some cases abuse) of clandestine diplomacy over nearly eight decades. Finally, all the contributions, which have been arranged chronologically, have been informed by extensive use of primary sources, with much of the material on which individual chapters are based being made public for the very first time. Even so, particularly with those chapters dealing with Israel's relations with the Arab world, the editors acknowledge what some might see as a paucity over the use of Arab sources, particularly in the period after 1948. Yet even in these more enlightened times, ties with Israel, clandestine or otherwise, still remain taboo areas for many regimes and actors across the Arab world.

INTRODUCTION: THEMES AND ISSUES

Unless or until Arab state archives and other primary sources are made available for public scrutiny, the story of Israel's secret ties to a range of Arab actors will necessarily remain partial. This should not detract however from the insights and original material presented by the contributors to a volume that ultimately, deals first and foremost with Israel's conduct of clandestine diplomacy.

In Chapter 1, Amnon Aran places these debates over the use of clandestine diplomacy within a wider historical context and in particular focuses upon three determinants that have shaped Israel's foreign policy: statism or *mamlachtiyut*, the emergence of ethno-nationalism and finally globalisation. The need to establish a secure state amid a hostile environment and with access to finite natural resources and a limited population base certainly shaped Israel's immediate foreign policy agenda. Thus the role of the individual was shaped by the demands of the collective, which reached its apogee in Israel's remarkable military triumph in June 1967.

This in turn, however, unleashed the forces of ethno-nationalism, which redefined both Israel's domestic political landscape, and by extension, its foreign policy agenda. With *mamlachtiyut* a declining currency of political exchange in Israel, Aran puts forward the argument that the scope and direction of Israel's foreign policy from the mid 1980s onwards became a function of the interplay between ethno-nationalism on the one hand, and Israel's embrace of globalisation on the other. Such interplay, Aran concludes, has implications for the continuing utility of secret diplomacy as an adjunct of wider Israeli foreign policy.

Yet it is easy to forget that in the initial process of state-building, the Jewish Agency, that quasi-governmental body that represented the Yishuv, embraced clandestine diplomacy almost as the means to curry grace and favour with key actors across the region. Thanks to the work of Avi Shlaim and Uri Bar-Joseph, we now know a great deal about the contact between King Abdullah and the leaders of the nascent Israeli state that effectively divided Palestine between the newborn Jewish state and the Hashemite dynasty following the Arab–Israeli war of 1948–9.[12] Less well known, however, is the true extent of contacts between the East Bank tribes and emissaries from the Jewish Agency during the inter-war period. Based upon the mutual gain to be had from joint commercial ventures, such ties stood out, as Yoav Alon notes in Chapter 2, in marked contrast to the growing regional antipathy and violence that marked wider pan-Arab sentiment towards the Zionist endeavour.

Indeed, the scope and warmth of these relations alarmed the British who, fearful of the wider unrest such relations might provoke, eventually exerted pressure on Abdullah to forego such ties.

Equally, however, the British were not averse to calling upon the services of the Jewish Agency when immediate need triumphed over longer-term regional interest. Chapter 3 therefore explores the often-vexed relationship between the British intelligence community in Palestine and the Jewish Agency during the Second World War. While clearly the junior partner, this proved far removed from a normal patron–client relationship, something which Reuven Zaslany, later to become the first head of the Mossad and a man who figures prominently in several other contributions to this volume, exploited to the full. Indeed, the role of Zaslany (who later adopted his *nom de guerre* 'Shiloah' as his official surname) highlights the importance of cultivating individual relationships with key interlocutors, a vital facet of Israel's secret diplomacy where more formal relations were conspicuous by their absence.

This is certainly a theme that informs Chapter 4. Facing an Arab oil embargo that threatened to strangle the Jewish state almost at birth, Jerusalem established covert ties with a range of actors, both state and non-state, who could help avert an energy crisis. In the case of developing ties with Iran—an early manifestation of the periphery doctrine—this also included courting the services of a US diplomat with strong connections to Israel in helping to expedite the flight of Jews from Baghdad amid a rising tide of anti-Semitism across Iraq. As Uri Bialer explains, both the need to secure oil supplies and the flow of Jews from the Arab Diaspora were not just foreign policy goals for the newborn state, but were actually existential values central to the very survival of the state itself. The periphery doctrine and with it the idea of wider regional acceptance and legitimacy is at the core of Chapter 5 by Noa Schonmann. In her detailed exposition of Turkish–Israeli relations, Schonmann highlights how Israel hoped that 'back-door diplomacy' might eventually yield more tangible diplomatic ties, the hope being that the de facto recognition of the Jewish state by Ankara would evolve into de jure recognition with attendant economic, political and strategic benefits to be had by both parties. In this endeavour, however, Jerusalem was only partially successful, for as Schonmann argues using the metaphor of an illicit affair, Israel as the mistress was far too eager to please her Turkish husband for the latter to leave his Arab wife.

And that Arab wife appeared to be becoming more strident in her demands. In particular, buoyed by the outcome of the Suez Crisis of 1956 and seemingly convinced by a regional dialectic that promised the eventual triumph of Arab nationalism, President Gamal Abd al-Nasser of Egypt appeared to present a substantial strategic threat to Israel. How Israel, and in particular military intelligence, read these signals and how in turn they impacted upon decision-making prior to the June 1967 war forms the core of Chapter 6 by Yigal Sheffy. Noting that secret overtures to Cairo made by David Ben-Gurion in the early 1960s had been rebuffed, Israel's military and political leadership worked on the assumption that Egypt eventually wished to confront the Jewish state, but that it lacked the military wherewithal to do so. Ensuring this remained the case, Jerusalem sought to exacerbate Cairo's regional difficulties, not least in providing covert aid to royalist forces in Yemen who were fighting against a republican government backed at one point by over 50,000 Egyptian troops. Equally, Israel itself was not immune from escalating tension with its other Arab neighbours, most notably Syria, who it feared was looking to disrupt the head waters of the Jordan River and disrupt the construction of Israel's national water carrier. By drawing on hitherto closed sources in the Israel Defence Force archives, Sheffy concludes that the outbreak of war in June 1967 came about not because it was desired by either Jerusalem or Cairo, but because misjudgement and the inability to signal clearly actual intent drove the parties to conflict.

An alternative perspective on the events leading to the outbreak of the June 1967 war and the role played by both personality and bureaucracy is provided by Asaf Siniver. In Chapter 7 he discusses the role of Abba Eban, one of Israel's most noted statesmen, in the crises. A man more admired overseas than in his own country, Eban as foreign minister always favoured diplomacy over military action, a position that often sat uncomfortably with the more hard-line positions of Cabinet colleagues. While sincere in his attempts to broker a peaceful resolution to the crisis, Eban eventually succumbed to the more belligerent mood among members of Levi Eshkol's Cabinet, knowing full well that these ministers had been persuaded by the more direct (if secret) talks that the then head of the Mossad, Meir Amit, had had with officials in Washington. If this chapter highlights one key theme, it is the extent to which Israel's Ministry of Foreign Affairs has often become little more than an emasculated bureaucracy, its role limited to explaining and 'selling' policy decisions over which it exercised little influence and which, behind closed doors, it often expressed profound doubts.

Such bureaucratic disagreements certainly inform Chapter 8, an examination of Israeli involvement in Uganda between 1962 and 1972. This involvement was of a piece with the periphery doctrine, but equally, as Zach Levey notes, the means by which Israel hoped to exert influence over an increasingly wayward regime in Kampala created dissonance between the Mossad and the IDF military mission to Uganda on the one hand, and Foreign Ministry officials on the other who felt that recourse to arms sales purchased little in the way of longer-term influence. Indeed, the hubris of the Mossad and the IDF regarding their ability to influence the Ugandan leader was exposed by the erratic behaviour of Idi Amin, who looked increasingly towards the Arab world to secure a regime whose regional ambitions far exceeded its capabilities.

But if engagement with Uganda ultimately brought few rewards, Israel's covert engagement with other African states certainly proved more rewarding, not least because both parties understood that the very basis of the relationship was grounded in realpolitik. From the mid-1950s onwards, Israel had nurtured ties with a newly independent Sudan whose welcome independence from British rule was soon matched by concern over Egypt's intentions towards Khartoum. A series of military coups and the outcome of the June 1967 war saw Sudan publicly located once again within the Arab fold. Indeed, in an effort to undermine successive Arab Muslim regimes in Khartoum, Jerusalem had established covert ties with the predominantly Anyanya Christian tribes of southern Sudan who, from the late 1960s onwards, launched a long and bitter struggle for independence. Needless to say, in an echo of its involvement in Yemen, Israel was quick to offer military support.[13]

However, fidelity to Arab unity took second place to regime survival. Wracked by a civil war that exacerbated a myriad of religious, ethnic, tribal and sectarian cleavages, by the early 1980s President Gaafar Muhammed Numayri looked to Washington to save his regime. As Yehudit Ronen explains in Chapter 9, this created an opening for discreet engagement with Israel to be resumed in the hope that this would be looked on favourably in Washington. To this end, Numayri allowed Sudan to be used as a transit point for the mass evacuation of Ethiopian Jews to Israel fleeing the twin effects of famine and war in their homeland. Again, the extent to which Israel was willing to go to expedite this

10

particular aliyah with its biblical overtones is extraordinary. Equally, whatever benefits the hapless Sudanese president hoped to accrue by his alliance with 'little Satan' proved short-lived: he was to be removed in a coup d'état in the spring of 1985, the disclosure of his involvement in this particular exodus certainly helping to expedite his enforced exile in neighbouring Egypt.

Chapters 10 and 11 focus upon the clandestine nature of Israel's relations with two European states: West Germany and Ireland. Taking as his point of departure the legacy of the Holocaust, Shlomo Shpiro moves beyond the well-known debates over reparations that shaped early engagement between Bonn and Jerusalem to focus upon the intelligence and military cooperation between the two states that had a profound impact upon their respective defensive capabilities. In particular, he outlines the extent of this secret collaboration in providing key technical intelligence on Soviet radar systems under operation CERBERUS. The success of this operation was, he notes, as much determined by the close personal relations that developed between key individuals as by any procedural agreements. Such warmth, however, was never replicated in ties between Dublin and Jerusalem despite the best efforts of the latter. As Rory Miller notes in Chapter 11, on the surface this is somewhat surprising given the vibrant Jewish community in Dublin that was often influential in republican circles and the shared experience of indigenous underground organisations fighting British imperialism.

Yet while granting de facto recognition of the state, Dublin proved remarkably reluctant to extend de jure recognition, a function of its dependence on Arab oil. Thus despite discreet (and often secret) entreaties from Israeli diplomats in London, it was not until the early 1990s and largely in response to the Oslo peace process that Ireland finally allowed an Israeli diplomatic mission to open in Dublin. This episode perhaps highlights the difficulties involved in conducting diplomacy where preconceived notions of the national interest determine competing bureaucratic positions. By contrast, Chapter 12 explores how 'Track II diplomacy' was used by former Israeli deputy foreign minister, Yossi Beilin, in an attempt to overcome the increasingly fractious relations between Israeli and Palestinian negotiators that had emerged in the wake of the initial euphoria that had surrounded the signing of the Oslo Accords in 1993. As Jacob Eriksson notes, Track II diplomacy involved 'non-officials' of the conflicting parties in secret talks designed to identify creative solutions to borders, refugees and settlements. Such talks were perhaps unique in that Beilin entrusted them to academics rather than to trained diplomats who were kept out of the loop. Indeed, these talks were highly compartmentalised, with even Shimon Peres, Beilin's immediate superior in the Israeli Foreign Ministry, unaware of their scope and content. Eventually leaked, the proposals developed never had a chance to enjoy wider dissemination among the Israeli public given the national mood in the wake of the assassination of Premier Yitzhak Rabin in November 1995.

Yet national mood remains a powerful, if often, overlooked variable in understanding the ability of Israeli leaders to take risks for peace. In the final chapter of this volume, Ahron Bregman provides a fascinating insight into how close Damascus and Jerusalem came to concluding a peace agreement at the turn of the millennium. With the devil very much in the details, it is as much a tale of loss of nerve in secret negotiations as it is a missed opportunity for a wider regional peace. Indeed, under domestic political pressure and sensitive to the often fickle mood of the Israeli electorate, the evidence presented by Bregman suggests that the then Israeli prime minister, Ehud Barak, bears considerable responsibility for the ultimate failure of these negotiations.

Finally, a health warning. The reader should note that this volume does not claim to be an exhaustive treatment of Israel's use of clandestine diplomacy or an exercise in either opprobrium or approbation in how the Jewish state has conducted the more secretive elements of its foreign relations. Particular episodes of Israeli clandestine diplomacy have been the subject of extensive studies elsewhere, not least Israel's ties to various Christian and Druze groupings in neighbouring Lebanon.[14] Rather, through exploring these hitherto little-known examples of how Israel has conducted clandestine relations, this volume seeks to explain the context and course of this hidden diplomacy from both a historic and a comparative perspective. If, in the process, it sheds new light upon both the process and impact of Israel's clandestine diplomacy over nearly seven decades, then that in itself will have proved a fruitful endeavour with immense intrinsic value in understanding Israel's contemporary place among the nations in the twenty-first century.

1

ISRAELI FOREIGN POLICY
IN HISTORICAL PERSPECTIVE

STATE, ETHNO-NATIONALISM, GLOBALISATION

Amnon Aran

Introduction

In order to both contextualise and inform the analysis of Israel's use of
clandestine diplomacy from the birth of the state onwards, this chapter
adopts what might be termed a periodic approach towards analysing
Israel's foreign policy, using the concepts of state, ethno-nationalism, and
globalisation, as its analytical tools. It argues that Israeli foreign policy
encompasses three major periods: statist (1948–73), ethno-nationalist
and statist (1973–85), and globalisation, ethno-nationalism and declining statism (1985 to the present). Of course, the analytical concepts of
state, ethno-nationalism and globalisation cannot explain every decision
and action in Israel's foreign policy since 1948. However, these concepts
can be considered ideal types that capture the salient trends in Israel's
foreign policy in relation to three issues: the composition of the domestic
arena, the social make-up of the foreign policy elite and the conflicting
approaches that shape the conduct of Israel's foreign affairs. Analysis of

Israel's changing external environment is conspicuously absent not because it is unimportant, but because the underlying assumption in this chapter is that the effects produced by changes in the external environment depend on how domestic actors interpret and comprehend them. Therefore, this chapter is informed by an emphasis on *innenpolitik*, understood to be the primacy of domestic factors in explaining foreign policy, and by extension, Israel's use of clandestine diplomacy.

In examining Israel's foreign policy, this chapter also attempts to account for change in the inner formulation of Israeli foreign policy. Drawing on the work of Stephen Krasner and others, the chapter is informed by the assumption that there is an intimate link between crisis and institutional change.[1] In particular, two crises are considered significant for explaining changes in Israeli foreign policy: the 1973 October war and its aftermath, and the economic crisis that resulted in the adoption of the Economic Emergency Stability Plan (EESP) in 1985. Finally, the framework is used to prompt some reflections upon the linkage between trends in Israeli foreign policy and its covert diplomacy.

Contrasting Approaches to Israeli Foreign Policy

The framework proposed to explain continuity and change in Israeli foreign policy since 1948 is situated in relation to three alternative analytical approaches. The 'regional' approach, which explains Israel's foreign policy in terms of the political and military make-up of the Middle East, comprises two strands. Some scholars, such as Efraim Inbar, emphasise the unremitting hostility of the Middle East towards the very idea of Israel's existence. It is argued that this compelled Israel to predicate its foreign policy on military force and subordinate it to its defence requirements. Accordingly, the eventual realisation by Egypt, Jordan and finally the Palestinian Liberation Organization (PLO) that Israel could not be eradicated by force enabled a reformulation of Israeli foreign policy vis-à-vis these entities.[2] However, the regional approach has also produced studies of a different nature. While conceiving of the military and political make-up of the Middle East as the key determinant of Israel's foreign policy, scholars such as Benny Morris see the impact as more complex. While they acknowledge that the Middle East's political and military make-up presents Israel with formidable challenges, they conceive of Israeli foreign policy as having more latitude than scholars such as Inbar would concede. In these accounts Israel's foreign policy is seen as a mixed bag of successes and missed opportunities.[3]

The second approach explains Israel's foreign policy in terms of domestic factors. The key players identified include the political parties—especially the Labour Alignment and Likud[4]—as well as the settler movement[5] and the Israeli Defence Force (IDF).[6] Those using this approach argue that each of these actors, to varying degrees, manipulated Israeli foreign policy and its implementation. Explaining Israeli foreign policy in terms of a Zionist ideology or identity constitutes the third approach.[7] The most cogent account in this strand is Avi Shlaim's work, which explains Israel's foreign policy in terms of Ze'ev Jabotinsky's doctrine of the iron wall, which advocated the erection of an iron wall of Jewish military force against the perceived implacable Arab hostility to the Zionist project. Shlaim and his followers offer a 'revisionist interpretation of Israel's foreign policy towards the Arab world during the first fifty years following statehood'.[8] They argue that establishment of military force and its deployment has become an Israeli foreign policy end, which contrasts with Jabotinky's doctrine of attaining military supremacy as a means for enabling political engagement with the Arab side and an end to conflict.

The Statist Period

What follows is an examination of Israeli foreign policy from 1948 to the present in terms of the state, ethno-nationalism and globalisation. The concept of the state in this chapter borrows heavily from a neo-Weberian institutional approach in which the state is seen as 'a set of administrative, policing and military organisations headed, and more or less well coordinated, by an executive authority'.[9] In this formulation the state is an 'actual organisation' possessing relative autonomy and the capacity to act in the internal and external spheres. The state's relative autonomy in both contexts derives from its unique positioning to deal with the exigencies imposed by international security competition, an ongoing need to extract finance, for example through taxation to fund its endeavours, and its capacity for surveillance. States use surveillance of civil society to both pacify and mobilise its resources. The state–civil society relationship is therefore one of competition in which the state has relative autonomy.[10]

In Israel, the salience of the state in determining foreign policy from 1948 to 1973 was reflected and advanced by the predominant ideological edifice of *Mamlachtiyut*.[11] The contours of *Mamlachtiyut*—a form of political and social development that privileged the state—first emerged among the pre-state Jewish community in Palestine (the Yishuv) but came to be most closely associated with David Ben-Gurion, Israel's first prime minister when he was leader of the ruling centre-left party, Mapai. Mapai led every coalition and dominated the premiership until it merged with Ahdut Ha-Avoda on the eve of the 1965 elections to form the Labour Alignment. Constructing the state around the notion of *Mamlachtiyut* was a very political act that identified the state with Mapai. Ben-Gurion and Mapai used the notion of *Mamlachtiyut* to realign internal politics and delegitimise political rivals such as Menachem Begin's Herut party.

Mamlachtiyut, however, was more than a product of and part of Ben-Gurion's and Mapai's political agenda. It portrayed the state as the epitome of Jewish historical revival; it elevated the state to a supreme symbol, making it and its institutions the objects of loyalty and identification. *Mamlachtiyut* introduced values and symbols that emphasised state legitimacy and the shift from parochial interests (characteristic of Yishuv) to a collective interest (typifying the statist era).[12] For instance, the political economy of Israel derived from a collectivist ethos highlighting the challenges of arming and defending the country, settling the waves of new immigrants, penetrating the frontier regions where Arabs were living or which bordered Arab countries and developing an economic infrastructure to cope with the immigrants and eventually eliminate Israel's dependence on charity and loans.[13]

Mamlachtiyut, therefore, endowed an aura of supreme political universality to a state with interests beyond politics, which rendered competing social and political-bureaucratic actors powerless to challenge its authority. The state mobilised the citizenry to serve its goals, presented as the common good, through what Moshe Lissak termed 'regimented voluntarism'.[14] The IDF ethos of the warrior (*lochem*) was the ultimate individual 'voluntaristic' act above all other forms of individual activity in the political, economic, social and cultural spheres.[15] The IDF was central in the ideological construct of *Mamlachtiyut* and its espoused regimented voluntarism. Consequently, although the initial development of *Mamlachtiyut* was geared towards consolidating Ben-Gurion's and Mapai's power, over time it became associated with the institutions of the state at the expense of identification with a political party.

The significance of *Mamlachtiyut* and the centrality it afforded to the state in relation to society had some important implications for Israel's foreign policy. First, it left little room for societal actors such as political lobby groups, political parties, the media or financial players to challenge the state, generally or specifically, on foreign policy issues. It was also an obstacle to external actors making inroads into Israeli foreign policy. It allowed the state—especially the IDF and the Prime Minister's Office—to develop relative autonomy from society and the external sphere in formulating and implementing foreign policy.[16] Second, as Baruch Kimmerling argues, for three decades Israel was led by a distinguishable elite—Ashkenazi, secular, nationalist men—that perceived its duty as presiding over the Zionist project.[17] *Mamlachtiyut* encompassed its credo of creating new Jews, sabras and warriors in Eretz Israel, which had the effect of legitimising the elite's leadership and expanding the already wide space for manoeuvre to conduct Israel's foreign affairs.

It would be a mistake, however, to regard Israel's leadership during the statist phase as unified. From the early 1950s on, Israel's foreign policy exhibited rivalry between the activist approach represented by David Ben-Gurion, and the non-activist stance represented by Moshe Sharett. The activist school was based on the assumptions of Israeli self-reliance; vigorous and repeated use of military force as the key foreign policy tool; and deep suspicion towards the international community. The non-activist school was predisposed towards a more restrained use of military force, a greater willingness to rely on diplomacy and a recognition that both in the definition and pursuit of Israel's foreign policy interests the international community was important.[18]

The third impact produced by *Mamlachtiyut* should therefore be understood against the backdrop of these contrasting approaches. The key tenets upon which *Mamlachtiyut* was predicated, especially the centrality of the IDF and the ethos of *lochem*, created a state structure that supported domination of the Ben-Gurion-led activist approach over Sharett's non-activist stance. This had significant implications for Israel's foreign policy behaviour during this period. For example, the response to infiltrations across the borders from the Gaza Strip and Jordan was generally not confined to tit-for-tat raids. Rather, reprisals tended to be disproportionate and often came at the expense of exploring diplomatic initiatives. This dynamic can be seen in the events sur-rounding the Gaza raid, Operation Kineret, and the run up to and outbreak of the 1956 war.[19] From the perspective of this chapter, the mutually reinforcing relationship between *Mamlachtiyut* and the activist approach certainly determined Israel's more aggressive approach towards its external environment. Consequently, the institutions under the con-trol of the activists, such as the Prime Minister's Office and the IDF, gained greater influence over Israel's foreign policy-making than the Ministry of Foreign Affairs, which was dominated by Sharett, the cham-pion of non-activism.

A number of interesting connections between Israel's covert diplomacy and the evolution of Israeli foreign policy during the statist period might be suggested at this point. First, covert or clandestine diplomacy, like foreign policy-making more broadly, was crafted and implemented within the state, which possessed a relative autonomy from its society and the external environment. Second, Israel's covert diplomacy was largely a matter dealt with by the foreign policy elite and the intelligence community in particular and was often informed by the tension between the two dominant foreign policy schools of thought: activist and non-activist. Arguably, the conduct of such diplomacy formed part of the state capacity and nation-building in the early formative years of the State of Israel. This is perhaps demonstrated most visibly in Israel's ties with France throughout the 1950s, ties which helped the Jewish state to develop its own nuclear research reactor at Dimona in the Negev desert.[20]

The Rise of Ethno-Nationalism

Rather than regarding the state as the main political vehicle for organis-ing the community, ethno-nationalists believe that a political commu-nity derives from what is perceived to be a homogenous descent group. Its members bear the distinct markers of a nation—culture, history, language, attachment to a particular territory—which are inscribed into their identities. From this perspective, community and state are not seen as separate: the community is expressed in and embodied by the state and in this case a Jewish state.[21] Ethno-nationalism was never wholly absent from Israel's foreign policy, but at least up to the 1967 war its impact was secondary to the state factor embodied in *Mamlachtiyut*. Israel's spectacular military victory in the 1967 war triggered the process that would ultimately shift the balance between state and ethno-nationalism. The victory provoked an eruption of nationalistic feeling in the Israeli Jewish public who saw it as the return of the Jewish people to their biblical cradle: Judea, Samaria and most notably Jerusalem.[22] At the same time, however, the spectacular performance of the state in the 1967 war reinforced some of the key tenets of *Mamlachtiyut*—centrality of the IDF, the warrior ethos and the notion of the state as a focus for citizens' loyalty. This hampered the ability of domestic actors to translate the eruption of ethno-nationalist sentiment after the 1967 war into a political force that could challenge the state.

The conditions favouring a domestic challenge to the state and the centrality of *Mamlachtiyut* were created by the crisis prompted by the 1973 war. This development is in line with the link between institutional change and crises described earlier. Although Israel was ultimately victorious, the 1973 war was perceived as a massive blunder and it resulted in close scrutiny of the state and its political-military elite from the public, rival generals and politicians and, finally, the government-appointed Agranat Commission, which was charged with investigating the war.[23] The combined effect of the military and economic price to Israel of the 1973 war, the public protest against the state and the overt conflict within the state's military-political circles severely dented *Mamlachtiyut* and the leadership it upheld. The state was unable to maintain an image of being 'beyond politics' or its status as a focus for citizen loyalty and regimented voluntarism, which undermined *Mamlachtiyut* and its statist ethos. This is not to argue that *Mamlachtiyut* and the institutional edifice it supported, at whose centre was the IDF, became insignificant, but to show that the weakening of *Mamlachtiyut* was a key political development in the process that shifted the balance from the state towards ethno-nationalism in foreign policy.

This had implications in terms of the changes and continuities to the three aspects of Israel's foreign policy outlined previously: Israel's foreign policy elite, the domestic actors affecting Israel's foreign policy and conflicting approaches to the conduct of Israel's foreign relations. Israel's foreign policy elite changed from being dominated almost exclusively by Ashkenazi, secular, nationalist, males, to an elite bearing the imprint of ethno-nationalism. This shift can be seen most strongly in the inroads made by the Jewish settler movement to the locus of Israel's foreign policy-making: the Prime Minister's Office and the IDF.[24] The concurrent weakening of *Mamlachtiyut* created the political conditions for societal actors other than the Jewish settler movement to exert their influence on Israel's foreign policy. Against this backdrop emerged the 'Peace Now' movement, which levelled a powerful critique against Likud's settlement policy and the 1982 invasion of Lebanon. The movement's impact should be seen not so much in material terms but as an alternative ideational framework to that of Likud. For instance, Tamar Hermann shows that the two-state paradigm to end the conflict with the Palestinians grew steadily to become the preferred option among the Israeli centre-left. By presenting this alternative political framework, Peace Now made an important contribution to the ideational foundations for subsequent negotiation with the PLO.[25]

The extent of these changes certainly impacted upon the conduct of Israel's foreign policy. If the period 1948–73 was characterised by conflict between the activist and non-activist stances, that between the June 1967 and 1973 wars, and with it the rise of ethno-nationalism, now saw the emergence of differences between approaches to peace defined as either 'hawkish' or 'dovish'. In some respects the divide between hawks and doves reflected the debate between activists and non-activists over the balance Israel should strike between diplomacy and use of military force to achieve foreign policy goals. The doves, like the non-activists, wanted more active peace initiatives from the Israeli government towards the Arab states. The hawks, like the activists, maintained that military force should continue to be the central Israeli foreign policy tool. The election to power in 1977 of a right-wing Likud-led coalition under Menachem Begin now produced a government that enjoyed greater manoeuvrability to apply more hawkish policies. Untainted by the national political fallout over Israel's unpreparedness for the October 1973 war and reaping the electoral benefits of a shift in Israel's demographic makeup, Begin proved more than willing to use military force to eliminate what he saw as existential threats to the state as well as using such force to redraw the political geography of the region in Israel's favour. But while the destruction of the Iraqi nuclear reactor at Osirak in June 1981 was successful,[26] the invasion of Lebanon exactly one year later, designed to destroy the PLO as a military threat and as a political symbol of Palestinian national aspirations, proved disastrous. Not only did Israel become mired in a long and costly guerrilla war, but any hopes that a pro-Israeli Christian government in Lebanon could be imposed upon a largely sectarian polity through force of arms proved illusory. Indeed, while Israel may have vanquished the PLO, the emergence of Hezbollah, a direct consequence of Israel's invasion, only emphasised the limitations of this epitome of Clauswitzian logic.[27]

Change was apparent in other respects too, most notably in the debate over the degree of Israel's self-reliance, which perhaps most strongly reflected the enduring (though increasingly secondary) influence of *Mamlachtiyut*. From the perspective of the state two events during the October 1973 war demonstrated that in the political and military context of the cold war, Israel no longer had the capacity, assumed after its overwhelming victory in June 1967, to 'go it alone'. These two events were: (1) the massive airlift by the US air force to Israel of munitions and spare parts that enabled the IDF to launch successful counteroffensives against Egypt and Syria which altered the course of the war in Israel's favour, and (2) the worldwide nuclear alert issued by Washington in the final two days of the war in order to deter the Soviet Union from intervening on the sides of Egypt and Syria.[28]

Subsequent events illustrate that the activist stance of self-reliance had indeed become problematic. This was reflected most clearly in the attitude of successive Israeli governments, be they Labour Alignment or Likud-led coalition governments, to consolidate the relationship with the United States. Consequently, successive memoranda were signed between Jerusalem and Washington. The first was signed in 1975 during the first premiership of Yitzhak Rabin as part of the Sinai II agreement with Egypt. Under the Likud coalition government led by Begin, this memorandum was upgraded as part of the formal Israeli–Egyptian peace agreement of 1979 which led directly to full Israeli withdrawal from the Sinai Peninsula. Finally, with Ronald Reagan's election to the White House in November 1980, Israel came to be seen as a 'formidable strategic asset'[29] within the wider context of the cold war, leading to a memorandum of understanding on strategic cooperation being signed between Washington and Jerusalem on 30 November 1981. While this was suspended in December after Israel annexed the Golan Heights, it was reactivated in 1983.[30]

The significance of these memoranda in the context of this chapter lies in the political, military and economic support guaranteed to Israel and in their globalising effects. Previously, Israel could only achieve secondary and tertiary alliances or ties that ensured a continuing and

21

adequate flow of weapons and strategic materials and which provided parallel efforts that coordinated Israel's efforts to contain Arab states. Israel's alliances with France in the 1950s and the Kennedy administration in the early 1960s are testament to this.[31] The deepening strategic relationship with the United States after 1973 was more than a mere secondary or tertiary alliance, however. The memoranda effectively embedded Israel into what has been termed a global cluster of states, built around the Western alliance against the USSR. Israel's military and political incorporation into this global cluster is reflected in its agreement to deploy the IDF to missions unrelated to the defence of Israel and the description of the USSR in Israeli official documents as a confrontation state.[32] Israel, therefore, like other states in the global cluster, no longer had an exclusive monopoly over the use of the means of violence. Its state authority and use of legitimate monopoly over the use of political force was pooled within the global cluster, at least in terms of its use in the external sphere. In this respect, the consecutive memoranda had the effect of inducing a process of military and political globalisation for Israel.

Settlement of the debate over Israel's self-reliance constituted a significant change compared to the disagreement between the activists and non-activists on this issue. However, the most significant difference between pre- and post-1973 debates on the conduct of foreign policy was the disagreement over the significance of territory. The doves were willing to relinquish almost all the territories captured in 1967 in exchange for real peace with the Arabs. They opposed the assumption of a fait accompli in the territories because it limited future options for peace. The most extreme hawks reflected the rise of ethno-nationalism and demanded annexation of all the territories captured in the 1967 war. Although this goal was not attained, the influence of the hawkish stance was significant. The hawks were instrumental in allowing government agents and private entrepreneurs to acquire Arab lands in the occupied territories to facilitate the defreezing of their ownership and permit the establishment of Jewish settlements in the territories—the first step towards establishment of sovereignty over the area.[33] This meant that from the hawkish perspective the land occupied in the 1967 war, especially the West Bank and the Gaza Strip, could not be collateral for peace. As a result, the territorial factor hampered the prospects of realising the Labour Alignment's preferred option to deal with the

Palestinians: the Jordanian option. It also impacted on the peace negotiations with Egypt, resulting in Israel refusing to relinquish its control
over the Gaza Strip.[34]

What might the shift from the statist-era to the ethno-nationalist and
statist period have entailed as far as Israeli secret diplomacy is concerned?
In some respects, such as building state capacity, the role of Israeli secret
diplomacy remained constant in relation to the previous period. However, some changes occurred. First, the conduct and implementation of
Israeli covert diplomacy was informed by the dove–hawk rivalry, not the
activist and non-activist debates. Second, because domestic actors had a
greater impact than before on foreign policy-making, there was a greater
chance that covert diplomacy would become public knowledge. In fact,
in some cases secret diplomacy that became public knowledge constituted part of the political rivalry between the hawks and the doves. This
was strongly exemplified as the public gained insights into Israeli covert
diplomacy in Lebanon, particularly from the late 1970s onwards as
Israel looked to redraw the Lebanese political map by imposing a pro-
Israel Christian-Maronite dispensation.[35] Third, in exercising clandestine
means by which to pursue distinct foreign policy objectives, Israel had
to take into account the opinions and position of Washington to a far
greater degree than before.

Enter Globalisation

Although the term 'globalisation' has been in academic use since the
1970s, no serious attempts were made to theorise it until the late 1980s.
By the end of the 1990s the hyper-globalist, global sceptic and transformational theses defined the debates surrounding globalisation.[36] More
recently, a fourth approach to globalisation—the mutually constitutive
thesis—has been proposed, which includes two critiques of the debate
on globalisation that are relevant to this chapter.[37] The first is against the
hyper-globalist and transformational view of globalisation solely in
terms of economics, technology or the impact of spatio-temporal factors. This conception underestimates the role politics and, by extension,
foreign policy might play in globalisation.[38] Instead, argues the mutually
constitutive thesis, globalisation should be considered a multi-centric,
multidimensional and dialectical process constituted of political and
military factors alongside other factors including economic, technologi-

cal, ecological and social elements. Thus, globalisation can be defined as a multidimensional contested process that involves the increasing embedding of political, military, economic, social and cultural activities in politically unified (quasi-)global spheres of activity.[39]

The second critique is on the globalisation–state relationship. Hyper-globalists see the state rendered increasingly irrelevant by globalisation; transformationalists take the more moderate view that it compels states to transform. Thus hyper-globalist and transformationalist theses converge around the assumption that the state is external and counterpositioned to contemporary globalisation. This conceptualisation is rejected by the mutually constitutive thesis that conceives of globalisation as 'predicated on and producing state transformations'.[40] In other words, globalisation, the state and, by extension, foreign policy, are in a mutually constitutive relationship. The rise of globalisation as a vital factor in understanding Israel's foreign policy builds on the argument that changes to its foreign policy were linked closely to the growing crisis in the economy following the October 1973 war. The crisis was provoked by the state acting as the central pivot of the economy. This resulted in it becoming increasingly indebted to powerful actors in the internal sphere, including the burgeoning bureaucratic sector, workers' committees in the employ of the state and the powerful Histradrut trade union federation. Economic policy became increasingly undisciplined, allowing excessive public sector deficit spending, frequent recourse to corrective devaluations and government-lending policies that favoured borrowers over the state. For example, during 1973–85 inflation rose to 440 per cent annually; GNP rose by an average 0.81 per cent per annum and from 1981 to 1986 by only 2 per cent; in 1973 to 1985 the import surplus grew from $1.5 billion to $3.97 billion; and state foreign indebtedness rose by a factor of six between 1970 and 1986.[41] Thus, by 1985, 'the economic crisis had come to pose tangible threats to the state itself—its fundamental legitimacy and its economic viability'.[42]

The then Likud–Labour national government of the mid-1980s responded to this crisis by launching its Economic Emergency Stabilisation Plan (EESP), which involved shedding state obligations to social groups and economic sectors and devolving responsibility to the market. This wilful withdrawal of the state was compounded by measures that embedded various spheres of the Israeli economy in global arenas.[43] Most significant for this discussion was the globalisation of trade, finance and capital markets. Before the EESP the private sector was dependent on government-allocated credit which, as Gershon Shafir and Yoav Peled observe, ultimately rendered it 'for all practical purposes another branch of government'.[44] However, the globalisation of trade and finance allowed Israeli businesses to obtain capital from the global economy, greatly reducing their dependence on state- and government-allocated credit.[45] Indicatively, 'the share of direct or indirect government loans to the private sector fell from 57.6% to 29.7% in just three years, from 1987 to 1990'.[46]

A large body of research agrees that the EESP was much more than an economic measure; in hindsight, it triggered the globalisation of Israel's economy, society and culture.[47] The implications of this process for Israeli foreign policy-making were profound. Its domestic make-up changed as new societal actors encroached on Israel's foreign policy-making. For instance, the vibrant Israeli business community became independent of the state and more influential. Businessmen joined the inner circle of the decision-makers, most notably those of the successive governments of Ariel Sharon and Ehud Olmert.[48] The business community had an impact on Israeli policy (e.g. supporting the Rabin government during the early years of the Oslo process and cementing relations with the rising powers in Asia: India and China).[49]

The media also became more influential in Israel's foreign policy-making. The availability of multiple local and global media channels affected Israel's foreign policy-making in a number of ways. Israeli national media organisations felt they were losing in the commercial competition with the global news corporations that characterised the media landscape and also the discrepancies between the Israeli and global news coverage was damaging the former's credibility. Therefore, there were demands for a revision of the censorship agreements, resulting in new accords being signed in 1989 and 1996 which progressively relaxed the censorship rules.[50] This more open and competitive environment reduced the government's ability to set the agenda for foreign policy debate and promoted media leaks. In turn, the risk of a leak affected Israel's decision-making structures. For instance, when testifying to the Winograd Commission, set up to investigate the poor performance of the IDF during the 2006 war with Hezbollah, Prime Minister Olmert admitted that he had established a forum of seven individuals responsible for decision-making during war. This structure was set up to avoid decisions of what in effect became an inner Cabinet being leaked to the media.[51]

Finally, the ability of government to use the IDF as a foreign policy tool was rendered more difficult. Although the media still carried patriotic and jingoistic statements about the military, these were increasingly complemented by damning reports about the army's activities. The army was portrayed as an inefficient and wasteful, unprofessional organisation, damaging to civil society, chauvinistic towards female soldiers and not sufficiently sensitive to the needs of combatants. These reports significantly weakened the social and political status of the IDF[52] and, by implication, complicated the use of the IDF as a foreign policy tool. This was compounded by the growing pervasiveness of images transmitted globally. Almost two decades earlier Shimon Peres had succinctly captured the impact of using the military as a foreign policy tool in today's media environment:

In contemporary wars, there is no longer a need for Trojan horses because the media provides 'real time coverage' of wars to every house in 'our global village'. Every one of us therefore has a Trojan horse in their private backyard. This may shorten the time that is available for small and medium states—which are situated in regions in which world powers have vested interests—to use military force. International pressure or military intervention will be swiftly employed, in order to put an end to any attempt to destabilize the system.[53]

It would be wrong, however, to think that the domestic make-up of Israel's foreign policy was subsumed to the forces driving Israel's globalisation. In fact, the steady rise of ethno-nationalism since 1973 proved enduring. From the early 1990s the ongoing impact of the Jewish settler movement and Likud was compounded by the emergence of two other political actors: Shas, the Sephardi ultra-orthodox party, and Yisrael Beiteinu (Israel Our Home), a predominantly hard-line nationalist if secular party. The scope of this chapter does not allow in-depth examination of the rise of these political actors; suffice to say that they enabled the Sephardi-observing Jews and immigrants from the former Soviet Union to produce political representatives from their own ranks.[54] The Jewish settler movement, Likud, Shas and Yisrael Beiteinu came to comprise an ethno-religious–nationalist coalition. They opposed the concessions Israel made towards the PLO and, later, the Palestinian Authority (PA). The religious elements of the coalition opposed the growing impact of globalisation, seeing this as an attack on Jewish tradition, and the roots and the Jewish character of the state, which could lead to the assimilation of Israel into the gentile world.[55]

The rise of societal actors supporting the globalisation of Israel and the enduring importance of ethno-nationalism raises questions about the degree to which statism remains influential. The Israeli state was not undermined as a result of global trends on the one hand and ethno-nationalist–religious trends on the other. Yet these forces certainly eroded the key tenets of *Mamlachtiyut*—collectivism, the warrior ethos and the status of the state as the focus of identification. Thus the impact of the state is currently derived from its unique position to deal with the ongoing security challenges faced by Israel—from terrorism to the prospect of a nuclear Iran. The ability of the state to deal with these exigencies retains its influence, primarily via Israel's security network.[56] But the aforementioned trends in the societal arena have affected the social make-up of Israel's foreign policy elite. From the late 1990s Israel's political leadership increasingly reflected the increased influence of societal actors such as businessmen, Shas and Yisrael Beiteinu, exemplified in the nomination of Avigdor Lieberman for foreign minister, all indicative of the trend towards the demise of the Ashkenazi, secular, nationalist male elite. This shift is the most significant change in the social make-up of Israel's foreign policy-making since the victory of Likud in the 1977 elections.

In light of both the range and impact societal actors and their actual make-up have had on the conduct of Israeli foreign policy, both change and continuity now shape Israel's foreign policy behaviour. Clearly, security as articulated by the government of the day, as well as the IDF, determines Israel's foreign policy behaviour.[57] Equally, however, globalisation with security has become a key variable in explaining and understanding Israel's foreign policy. Thus the decision by Yitzhak Rabin and Shimon Peres to recognise the PLO and sign the Oslo Accords in 1993 was inextricably linked to the perception that these steps would further embed Israel into political, military and economic spheres of global activity.[58] In turn, Ariel Sharon linked the unilateral withdrawal from Gaza with deepening Israel's economic integration with global frameworks and maintaining its political and military global standing. His comments, delivered to an important annual gathering of Israel's economic elite at the Caesarea Conference on 30 June 2005, are illuminating:

I believe that Disengagement will be one of the most successful, economically influential steps carried out in Israel. It is sufficient to examine the influence which the Disengagement has had on the growth of the Israeli economy even before it is carried out. I believe that your experts estimated that benefits of Disengagement at 2% GNP per annum. There is no doubt that the dramatic increase in tourism, foreign investment and consumption originate primarily in optimism in the political arena. It is no accident that in the past two years [since 2003] we have seen renewed growth and the return of foreign investors.[59]

Unlike Rabin, Peres and Sharon, Benjamin Netanyahu did not attribute much significance to the interrelationship between foreign policy change and globalisation. In *A Place Among the Nations*, which is widely considered to be the blueprint of Netanyahu's beliefs, he devoted little attention to the interrelationships between foreign policy and globalisation.[60] Indeed, when asked whether he shared Peres' vision of a new and globalised Middle East, he replied that 'the notion was characteristic of people who live under continuous siege and want to change what is happening beyond their walls by imagining a different reality'.[61] Thus, rather than being propelled by a drive towards globalisation, both the first and second Netanyahu governments were characterised by what might be termed the ethno-nationalism–security nexus. This factor was key in the first Netanyahu government's efforts to unpick the Oslo process. In Netanyahu's second term, the ethno-nationalism–security nexus was a central contributing factor to ongoing stalemate with the Palestinians.[62]

Nonetheless, the rise of globalisation as an influential factor in Israeli foreign policy, alongside the ongoing salience of ethno-nationalism and declining statism, has not changed the role of Israeli secret diplomacy in the broader matrix of Israeli foreign policy. Employing secret diplomacy as a way to increase Israeli state capacity is as important today as it was during the previous periods examined in this chapter, particularly where it is designed to meet defined strategic goals. However, the context in which it is employed is different in a number of ways. The combination of new means of technology and global media communications means that it is much more difficult than before to avoid decisions taken within government forums—including those referring to secret diplomacy—from being leaked. The WikiLeaks episode mentioned in the Introduction to this volume illustrates this point most clearly. Consequently, Israeli covert diplomacy has greater global material implications than in erstwhile periods. The debates over whether or not Israel would attack Iran, and the alleged clandestine diplomacy and direct covert action Israel is alleged to have used to deny Tehran a nuclear weapons capability—cyber attacks, assassinations, sabotaging Iranian installations—epitomise the trend of Israeli covert diplomacy 'going global'.[63] Concurrently, as the state has increasingly retreated from the erstwhile roles it played in the economy, society and culture, covert diplomacy plays less of a role in Israeli identity formation (if not state consolidation) than in the past. Indeed, other forces that are religious, economic and ethnic in character have now largely replaced the salient role once given over to clandestine diplomacy in the process of nation-building and consolidating the physical reality of the state.

Conclusion

This chapter outlined a historical-analytical framework to examine Israel's foreign policy, based on the state, ethno-nationalism and globalisation as determinants of Israel's foreign policy. It accounts for changes in Israel's foreign policy by linking it to crises: the political-military crisis following the 1973 war, and the economic crisis faced by Israel in 1985. The degree of change is explored in relation to the nature and impact of societal actors on Israel's foreign policy, the social make-up of the foreign policy elite and shifts in the contours defining Israel's foreign policy. Although this approach privileges the domestic over the external sphere, this is justified by acknowledging the significance afforded to domestic factors in determining how external change might be interpreted. This approach is contrasted with those approaches that place emphasis only on regional and ideological factors. Certainly, this chapter does not determine what to understand in Israel's foreign policy to the same degree of specificity as suggested by these approaches. This is readily acknowledged. However, this limitation is compensated for by a framework which has outlined how to understand Israeli foreign policy and its episodic shifts.

To this end, three key points need to be emphasised. First, the approach in this chapter underlined the rise of new actors in distinct historical periods and how their waxing and waning are linked to changes in the conflicting approaches to Israel's foreign policy. It examined the role of domestic actors in creating inroads into Israel's foreign policy-making, at the expense of the salience of the state. Second, the chapter focused upon how to explain change and especially the role of crises in shifting the focus of Israel's foreign policy. In particular, the effects generated by the crises of 1973 and 1985 were highlighted as the most apposite examples. The concern for security has remained constant in Israel's foreign policy but from the 1948–73 activist/non-activist debate to the 1973–85 hawk–dove debates, and from these to the debate on globalisation versus ethno-nationalism, crises have been pivotal to the changes examined. Thirdly, the chapter suggests such trends in Israeli foreign policy that may have influenced the crafting and conduct of Israeli secret diplomacy. Most notably, this included the decline in the relative autonomy of the state in its ability to employ covert diplomacy given the impact of globalisation as well as the declining role secret diplomacy has come to play in Israeli identity formation. This is not to suggest that covert diplomacy will ever disappear entirely from Israel's foreign policy repertoire. After all, such diplomacy remains an accepted part of international statecraft writ large. Even so, in an era of globalisation, its influence in determining national identity, let alone as a means to achieve defined objectives, is likely to be diminished.

2

FRIENDS INDEED OR ACCOMPLICES IN NEED?

THE JEWISH AGENCY, EMIR ABDULLAH AND THE SHAYKHS OF TRANSJORDAN, 1922–39

*Yoav Alon**

Introduction

From the beginning of the 1930s and through to the outbreak of the Second World War, the Jewish Agency—established in 1929 as a quasi-governmental authority to help further the goal of Jewish statehood in Palestine—deliberately set out to cultivate close relations with the Transjordanian political elite. Against the background of increasingly strained relations between Jews and Arabs west of the Jordan River, the Zionists found more forthcoming interlocutors in the East Bank. Constant and extensive communications resulted in political coordination, business transactions revolving around land and natural resources and even personal friendships.

This relationship entailed the potential of important benefits to both parties. Never satisfied with the Emirate of Transjordan that he established with British patronage in 1921, Abdullah bin Hussein coveted

*This research was supported by The Israel Science Foundation

Palestine, alongside parts of Greater Syria, as part of his territorial dispensation. He hoped he could enlist the support of the Zionists to achieve this goal. However, not only would the Jewish Agency refuse to agree to anything less than Jewish sovereignty west of the Jordan River, the very *raison d'être* of Zionism, but they also hoped to incorporate within their national project the more fertile parts of Transjordan.

Despite these contradictory long-term goals, in the short term at least both sides found it beneficial to maintain cordial, if not always discreet ties. Abdullah's political and financial dependence on the British and his growing rivalry with the leaders of the Palestinian national movement made him amenable to Zionist overtures and indeed their occasional financial support. Similarly, the economic crisis that hit Transjordan in the first part of the 1930s prompted a group of landowning tribal leaders to offer the lease or sale of their land to the Jews. The negotiations on the land seemed like a way to facilitate Zionist colonisation in Transjordan, but even after the land option was no longer pursued from the mid-1930s, the Zionists saw Transjordan as a political asset. With the escalation of the conflict between Jews and Arabs in Palestine, Abdullah and the Transjordanian political elite stood out in their willingness to maintain and project cordial relations with the Zionist movement. All these served as the foundation of the long relationship which has been described by superlatives such as an 'adversarial partnership', a 'tacit alliance', a 'political alliance', or purely 'symbiotic'.[1]

The diplomacy across the Jordan was sometimes secret but often became common knowledge. Abdullah made no effort to conceal his dealings with the Jews, while on other occasions it was the officials of the Jewish Agency who wished to trumpet their diplomatic success in Transjordan. Ultimately neither secrecy nor publicity had much effect on the success of this diplomacy. More than anything else, the outcome of the interaction across the Jordan reflected the political and economic interests of both parties as well as the severe constraints under which they operated. In particular, Abdullah remained wholly dependent upon his British patrons and, despite his best efforts, remained beholden to their financial largesse.

At the same time, however, he and the shaykhs enjoyed extensive autonomy vis-à-vis the Transjordanian public, and therefore were not seriously undermined by the exposure of their relations with the Jewish Agency. Nevertheless, and despite much dealing across the river, the gaps between the two sides remained profound. Consequently, apart from general feelings of friendship, some coordination, as well as the financial support which the Zionists granted Abdullah—in itself a remarkable phenomenon in light of fierce Arab hostility towards Zionism—very few tangible deals were reached between the parties during the Mandate years.

This study explores the tension between open and clandestine diplomacy during the period in which the leaders of the Jewish community in Palestine (the Yishuv) and the Hashemite leaders in Transjordan looked to secure their respective polities. Its aim is twofold: firstly, it highlights the public dimension of the relationship, and secondly, it explores other factors that accounted for fluctuations in the fortunes of these ties. In so doing, the chapter sheds light on a relatively underexplored period in relations between the political leadership of the Yishuv and Transjordan, between 1922 and 1939, one that has traditionally been overshadowed by the period between 1945 and 1951 and the armed conflict over Palestine. Indeed, as this chapter argues, any understanding of the relationship that emerged between Transjordan and the newly declared State of Israel after 1948 has to take account of ties between the Jewish Agency and Emir Abdullah, ties that came to shape both the perceptions and expectations of officials in Amman and Jerusalem.

As such, this chapter begins with a preliminary account of the early phase of the relationship between the Jewish Agency and the Transjordanian potentate during the 1920s, outlining the basic attitudes of both sides which came to determine relations in the period under discussion. The early 1930s, explored in detail in the next section, saw the intensification of this relationship, as well as its expansion beyond the Hashemite court in Amman to include Transjordanian tribal leaders. The negotiations during this period mainly revolved around Jewish land purchases. Finally, the outbreak of the Arab Revolt in Palestine in 1936 presented new opportunities for close coordination between Abdullah and the Zionists, and the last section analyses the reasons why, despite the shared interests involved, such cooperation never came to be realised.

The Early Contacts

Early contacts between Abdullah and the Zionists in Palestine began in 1922 when Abdullah was visiting London where he held talks with

Chaim Weizmann, president of the World Zionist Organization. What started as secret diplomacy quickly became common knowledge after information had been leaked, provoking criticism of both leaders from their respective constituencies. While the talks came to nothing, they at least served to establish the first link between the parties.[2]

In retrospect, however, one could see that the gap between the ambitions of the two parties was too wide to be bridged by such diplomacy. In the meeting Abdullah suggested recognising the Balfour Declaration—exactly as his brother Faisal had done when he signed the conditioned agreement with Weizmann in 1919. In return, the ruler of Transjordan expected the Zionists to recognise his future sovereignty over Palestine and urged them to use their influence with the British government to effect such an outcome. With only slight modifications, this proposal would repeat itself over the next three decades. However, the Zionists could agree to nothing short of an independent Jewish state in Palestine, a stance that despite disputes within the Yishuv over the exact borders of the state, remained constant until the establishment of Israel in 1948.

However, even without definite agreements, the parties needed each other to achieve short-term goals. The Zionists found in Abdullah a moderate and friendly interlocutor. As the opposition to Zionism from the Arabs of Palestine grew, especially after the 1929 riots at the Western (Wailing) Wall and the massacre of Jews in Hebron, Abdullah's friendship stood out and grew in importance. For Abdullah, the Zionists seemed to be an avenue to relieve his pressing political and economic dependence on the British position in Transjordan. He also entertained hopes that they would help him to expand his rule, either to Palestine or to Syria. In later years, when Abdullah fell out with the leaders of the Palestinian movement, much of the friendship's *raison d'être* was based on the struggle with a common enemy. It was very much a case of 'my enemy's enemy is my friend'.

In many ways Abdullah's personality facilitated such a cordial relationship. As Avi Shlaim has written, Abdullah's basic approach towards the Jews had a great impact over the relationship he cultivated with the Zionists. His worldview was first and foremost shaped by his experience of the Ottoman Empire, for prior to his arrival in Transjordan he had lived a large part of his life in Istanbul where he and his family were part of the Ottoman elite surrounding Sultan Abdulhamid II. As Shlaim notes, 'To his early contacts with the Zionists Abdullah brought the self-confidence and flexibility in dealing with minorities that he had acquired under the Ottoman regime.'[3] Shlaim goes on to explain that Abdullah viewed the Jews as 'fabulously wealthy and skilled in the way of the modern world', an outlook which was the result of his contact with Jewish physicians, merchants and financiers in Istanbul.[4] One could add that Abdullah's incredible patience, his innate optimism and naïveté also allowed the maintenance of relations, which apart from financial gains, lucrative as they were, proved quite fruitless. For their part, the Zionist leaders were impressed by his moderation, pragmatism and most likely his somewhat aristocratic and engaging personality.[5] Against the uncompromising and hostile approach of the Palestinian leaders, Abdullah was seen as a potentate worth courting if Zionist aspirations were to be realised.

After the initial meetings with Weizmann in London, there were several more opportunities for an open dialogue between the parties in the course of the 1920s. In 1924 an official Zionist delegation came to Amman to greet Abdullah's father, Sharif Hussein bin Ali. Two years later, Weizmann and Colonel Frederick Kisch, head of the Palestine office of the Zionist Executive, met Abdullah in Amman to discuss economic cooperation. The cordial nature of these talks encouraged the Zionist leader in his view that there was a real chance to reverse the 1922 White Paper that severed the eastern part of the Mandate from the Jewish national home. A few days after he returned from Amman, Weizmann was quick to articulate the Jewish policy towards Transjordan in a public rally in Tel Aviv. Although the Zionists had just recorded another political success by persuading the British government to admit Jews to the newly established Transjordan Frontier Force, Weizmann stressed other means of Jewish–Arab cooperation: 'We see in Transjordan the eastern part of *Eretz Israel*. However, we shall not build the bridge across the river Jordan with soldiers—we shall make our way by Jewish labour, with the plough and not with the sword.'[6]

Weizmann's vision was partly implemented in the late 1920s when highly visible projects of Transjordanian–Zionist cooperation were established east of the river. Obviously, these projects could not have been concealed from public eye. In 1927 the Jewish engineer Pinhas Rutenberg received the concession to establish a hydroelectric power plant in Naharayim, where the Yarmuk and Jordan rivers joined within Transjordanian territory. It was Abdullah himself who 'ceremonially started up the turbines at the official opening of the plant'.[7] Similarly, in 1929 the Jewish-owned Palestine Potash Company obtained a concession to extract the rich chemical resources of the Dead Sea. Moreover, as early as 1927 a group of young Jews had tried to settle in Amman and help rebuild the city that was badly damaged in an earthquake. Although such events stirred some opposition in Transjordan, and a much more vociferous outcry among Palestinian Arabs who feared the consequences of such encroachment, Abdullah for the most part remained unmoved by demonstrations.

Plans for Jewish Colonisation

The early 1930s saw an intensification of relationships. Land became the major issue of discussion in the first half of the 1930s and the circle of Transjordanian interlocutors expanded to include a group of large landowners, most of whom were tribal shaykhs. This intensification was the result of several factors. For the Zionists, Transjordan and its moderate leadership gained more importance following the 1929 riots in two major respects. First, the deterioration of relations with the Palestine Arabs necessitated cultivating relations with other Arab figures. The moderate Abdullah and the tribal elite which supported him served this purpose. Second, the 1930 British White Paper threatened to restrict Zionist land purchase in Palestine, prompting the Jewish leaders to explore the possibility of Jewish settlement east of the river. In Transjordan, the dire economic situation that badly affected the country from the late 1920s until the mid-1930s meant that Abdullah and the landowners had to look for foreign capital by selling, leasing or developing their land, much of which was left uncultivated because of drought conditions and financial constraints.[8] Abdullah had just become a landowner himself as the British had granted him a large estate in the Jordan Valley. The emir was always short of money due to strict British supervision of the emirate's budget and the modest civil list which was allocated to him by the British Exchequer. As such, the Zionist influx made sound financial sense.

Accordingly, in the early 1930s the interests of the two political elites seemed to be converging. In September 1930 Abdullah issued an invitation to the Zionist leadership to resume the dialogue. In February 1931, Kisch, now in his capacity as the director of the Jewish Agency's Political Department, went to Amman to meet the emir. Reporting on the visit, the Hebrew daily *Davar* presented it merely as a social visit to Abdullah's ageing father, Hussein, in Amman whom—it reminded its readers— Kisch had already met in 1924. This version later appeared in the Jewish Agency's statement. Despite this official Zionist attempt to play down the visit's political significance, the Palestinian newspaper *Al-Karmal* vehemently attacked Abdullah and Kisch. The Palestinian *Filastin* and the Egyptian *Al-Ahram* speculated that the parties had discussed the transfer of Palestinians into Transjordan and the Jewish purchase of land there.[9]

In the same year the Jewish Agency began to explore the Transjordanian option. It sent agents and experts to gather information about settlement options and political tendencies among the local population. This intensified activity that now took place beyond the gates of Abdullah's palace soon became common knowledge. In a small country such as Transjordan with a small population and a tiny capital—Amman in the early 1930s had less than 10,000 residents[10]—secrecy and discretion soon proved rare diplomatic commodities.

These early forays caught the attention of several Transjordanian shaykhs who offered to do business with the Jews. A case in point was Shaykh Mithqal Pasha al-Fayiz, the paramount leader of the Bani Sakhr tribal confederation. The largest landowner in the country was heavily indebted and found it difficult to make his vast land profitable. In December 1930 he approached, via an intermediary, Nahum Pfefer, a Zionist official from the Palestine Land and Development Company. At the time Pfefer conducted the first thorough agrarian survey of Transjordan on behalf of the Jewish Agency. After his intermediary received a negative answer to the proposal to sell 30,000–35,000 dunums, Mithqal al-Fayiz emerged from the shadows and invited Pfefer to his village. In the summer of 1931 Mithqal repeated his proposals and was persuaded by Taysir Dawji, the Jewish Agency's principal agent in Transjordan, to approach the Zionists directly. Mithqal duly did so and repeated his offer in a meeting with Haim Kalwarisky, the director of the Zionist Executive's Arab Bureau.[11]

Mithqal's new proposals paralleled a change of personnel in the Jewish Agency that had significant policy implications. In August 1931 Chaim Arlozoroff replaced Kisch as the head of the Political Department. According to Yoav Gelber, this personality change gave 'fresh impetus' to Zionist attempts to infiltrate into Transjordan.[12] Arlozoroff set two objectives: to exploit the economic difficulties in Transjordan in order to facilitate Jewish colonisation, and to cultivate political bonds with the local elite.[13] Therefore, Arlozoroff favoured a positive response to Mithqal's offers. However, the matter dragged on inconclusively for another year due to lack of funds and initial concern among the leadership of the Jewish Agency over undertaking such a huge and potentially problematic project on the East Bank of the Jordan. Nevertheless, the negotiations continued and in November 1932 during a visit to Jerusalem, Mithqal met his most senior Zionist official to date, the president of the World Zionist Organisation, Nahum Sokolov. In that meeting Mithqal repeated his offer of land sales to the Jews on the East Bank of the River Jordan.[14]

Mithqal's direct contact with the Jews soon became public, which gave rise to angry reactions from the Palestinian leadership and press as well as Arab nationalists in Transjordan. His contact with the Zionist movement was particularly painful because the same nationalist circles in Palestine hailed Mithqal in 1929–31 as an Arab national leader. He earned this reputation when he opposed the Anglo-Transjordanian treaty of 1928. He was also considered to be a member of the opposition to the Transjordanian government in his capacity as an elected member of the Legislative Council.[15] Indeed, only shortly before his contacts with the Jews became public, the Jaffa-based *Filastin* went so far as to feature Mithqal's visit to Palestine on its front page, printing his picture and describing him as 'the great Arab leader' and 'one of the heroes of Arabism' (*batal al-'uruba*).[16]

Far from acting as a deterrent, the publicity of Mithqal's dealings with the Jews only served to prompt other landowners to put forward similar offers. At the end of 1931 and the beginning of 1932 Jewish land dealers, mediators and officials contacted the notables of Karak, including the two leading families, the Majali and Tarawneh, and received offers to sell land to Jews in the Karak area and around the shore of the Dead Sea and to develop their land with Jewish capital and expertise.[17] The increased contacts between the Jews and the notables soon reached the attention of nationalist circles and provoked fierce reaction. In 1932 the Transjordanian Arab Congress, an umbrella opposition body, met in Amman to discuss a number of issues including 'the Zionist enterprises in Transjordan'. During the conference a dispute erupted between the nationalists and several shaykhs, among them Mithqal, who ultimately withdrew from the meeting.[18]

Nevertheless, the chiefs were eager to do business with the Jews and assured the Jewish Agency that they could deliver the goods and confront the opposition. Many of them, Mithqal in particular, enjoyed such high stature and political clout that they could easily face even the most vocal opposition, as long as it came from outside their own tribal constituency. Mithqal himself assured Pfefer at an early stage of their negotiations while anticipating the public outcry that, '[T]he Pasha, with his influential position in Transjordan and his personal friendship with the Emir, could undertake to get the *kushan* [title deed] registered in the name of any owner designated to him in the teeth of any opposition that might arise.'[19]

Despite the public row during the summer and autumn of 1932 the number of offers to sell land all over Transjordan grew steadily. Alongside Mithqal's proposal, Arlozoroff reported with great satisfaction at the end of 1932 that offers were received from some of the more prominent tribal shaykhs and landowners. Offers were received from several of the Majali shaykhs, from Sultan al-'Adwan, the paramount leader of the Balqa tribal confederation, from Rashid al-Khuza'i, the tribal leader of the Jabal 'Ajlun subdistrict and from Sa'id Pasha Abujaber, a large Christian landowner and merchant. Later on the Agency received more proposals but had to turn them down outright because of lack of funds and the uncertainty of the entire endeavour.[20]

But for a while it seemed as if the Transjordanian frontier was opening for the Zionists. Following the activity of the Zionist institutions, private Jewish businessmen travelled to Transjordan looking for business partners and government officials to facilitate economic cooperation. It was again Weizmann, now temporarily without an official capacity, who publically and enthusiastically articulated the meaning of such development: 'Today, the Jewish merchant is invited to set up his factory in Transjordan. Today, one can begin to talk about Transjordan.'[21]

While Mithqal and other shaykhs were negotiating with the Jews, Abdullah too was intensifying his contacts with Jewish officials in Palestine. Indeed, at this time, he made no secret over his contacts with Zionist emissaries. For example, in March 1932 he publically received Chaim Arlozoroff in his palace. When news of this visit was published in the Arab press, the subsequent wave of protest in Palestine was such that British officials in London, Amman and Jerusalem openly expressed their opposition to any moves likely to promote Jewish ambitions in Transjordan.[22]

But while such official approaches brought no tangible political results for either side, in late September 1932 two members of the Jewish Agency's Executive affiliated with the Revisionist movement—a rival faction to the socialist-dominated Zionist leadership—conducted secret negotiations with Abdullah over leasing some 70,000 dunams of his land at Ghur al-Kibd in the Jordan Valley. At the end of the year they came to an agreement with Abdullah, presenting Arlozoroff with a fait accompli. Indeed, on 3 January 1933 Abdullah granted a leasehold option on his land for six months in return for £500. Despite the efforts of both parties to keep the deal under wraps, this too soon became public following exposure in the Arab and Palestinian press.[23] The outcry that ensued so alarmed the British authorities that London now advised Abdullah against concluding such a deal. The combined pressure of Arab nationalists on the one hand and the British on the other now prompted Abdullah to deny the very existence of the transaction. However, behind the backs of the British, Abdullah continued to engage in a game of diplomatic subterfuge by extending the option of land sales three more times. For example, in 1935 he received £3,500 for a four-year extension to the lease of land while his confidant Muhammad al-Unsi received a payment from the Jewish Agency of £1,800 for his part in negotiating the deal on behalf of Abdullah. While the actual lease never materialised, Shlaim notes that the Ghur al-Kibd deal nevertheless 'provided a thin veneer of legitimacy for what could otherwise be construed as the payment of a political subsidy'.[24]

Parallel to events surrounding Ghur al-Kibd, negotiations with Mithqal had been ongoing and indeed were close to a conclusion. But the leadership of the Jewish Agency now realised that they had neither the funds nor the political approval of the British Mandatory authorities to purchase land and settle Jews east of the river. However, after constant pressure from Mithqal and in an attempt not to alienate a man whose 'Arab' credentials could help legitimise more defined Zionist ambitions within Palestine, Arlozoroff now agreed to alleviate some of the shaykh's continued financial difficulties. He accepted Mithqal's offer to pay a mortgage on land in the Transjordanian village of Barazayn, owned by the cash-strapped shaykh. In effect, the mortgage was a loan. In the wake of the Ghur al-Kibd scandal, however, Arlozoroff got cold feet, feeling that perhaps the Jewish Agency would incur the wrath of the British while doing little to assuage tensions with the Arabs of Palestine.

He asked Mithqal to postpone the deal lest it gave Arab nationalists more ammunition to advance their anti-Zionist campaign. Mithqal was upset about that delay, but in recompense he received £200 in advance. In April 1933 Moshe Shertok and another Jewish official, Joseph Stromza, eventually went to Transjordan and registered a mortgage on the land, paying Mithqal the rest of the loan, a total of £675. Although the Agency conducted contacts and negotiations with many shaykhs, this was the only deal done with Transjordan's landowners which actually came to completion.[25]

Taking heart from this deal, Mithqal went on to attempt a more ambitious plan involving cooperation with the Jews. He now took it upon himself to facilitate the flow of Jews into Transjordan. The idea was to convince the landowning shaykhs and notables of the technical benefits to be had from Jewish expertise in agriculture as well as the prospects of Jewish capital investment. This tactic was also designed to exert pressure on the British authorities to be more forthcoming in their subsidies towards the tribes knowing full well that London could ill-afford political unrest. Certainly, this approach of 'divide and benefit' enjoyed the support of Abdullah. Throughout 1933, Mithqal was busy in extensive political campaigning to realise his scheme, and worked closely with the Jewish Agency which in turn advanced him finance to support his activity. While some of the coordination between Mithqal and the Agency remained confidential, for the most part it amounted to nothing less than an outright political campaign.

Indeed, in January 1933 Mithqal had already presented to the Agency his idea of convening a conference of landowners who wished to sell land to the Jews. An informal meeting in his house led to a more formal gathering in February which resulted in telegrams being sent to the emir and the British high commissioner in Palestine, Arthur Wauchope, protesting over the depth of the economic crisis and demanding the development of the country and capital investment, a clear reference to Jewish money.[26] Moreover, this position had been cleared with Abdullah beforehand. Prior to the gathering at his home, a delegation of shaykhs and notables closely associated with Mithqal had visited Abdullah to offer him encouragement and support in his dealing with the Jews and to act as a counterweight to the Arab nationalist Istiqlal party, which opposed any concessions to the Zionists.[27]

Mithqal kept his allies in Jerusalem informed about his progress while continuing to ask for financial help. Attempts at discretion on the part of Jewish Agency officials who remained acutely aware of the sensitive nature of these ties were not always reciprocated. In one visit to Mithqal, Aharon Cohen, secretary of the Arab Bureau of the Jewish Agency, came disguised as an Arab, yet three weeks later he was introduced by his host to a gathering of tribal elders and other notables as 'Dr. Arlozoroff's official'.[28] Several months later *Filastin* reported that Mithqal used the money received from 'Harun the Jew' to induce some tribal leaders to join another conference he was attempting to organise.[29] Mithqal eventually went as far as forming a political party, Hizb al-Tadammun al-Urdunni (the Jordanian Solidarity Party), which was openly in favour of Jewish immigration to Transjordan. The party was named by *Filastin* as the Arab Zionist Party (Al-Hizb al-'Arabi al-Sahyuni).[30] Yet the party failed to attract a critical mass of support, and it soon fragmented with most of its members being absorbed into another, equally ephemeral party of shaykhs and notables formed to support Abdullah.

Even so, Mithqal's activity had served the Jewish Agency well, not least because it had offered the Zionists a political mechanism to circumvent British opposition to any Jewish colonisation in Transjordan. It was important for the Zionists to prove that there was indeed Arab support for the idea of settlement on the East Bank of the River Jordan, and to this end the Jewish Agency organised a public reception in honour of Mithqal and his associates in the King David Hotel in Jerusalem in April 1933. The shaykhs met Weizmann and other senior Zionist officials and exchanged speeches praising the new bond of friendship between the two parties. The use of Mithqal's friendship for propaganda needs was also realised in the publication in the Hebrew press of his letter of condolence to the widow of Chaim Arlozoroff following the latter's murder on the Tel Aviv beachfront in June 1933 in circumstances that still remain politically controversial.[31]

But notwithstanding the efforts of Mithqal, the notables, Abdullah and the Jewish Agency, the aim of getting the British to endorse Jewish colonisation in Transjordan was never realised. After intensive contacts between senior British and Zionist officials in the first months of 1933, the former finally came out with a clear message. In May 1933, during a meeting in London, both Colonial Secretary Philip Cunliffe-Lister and Wauchope expressed to Sokolov, Weizmann, Rutenberg and two leading Jewish dignitaries, Lord Rothschild and Lord Reading, their sympathy for the idea of future Jewish settlement in Transjordan, but stressed that for the moment, it remained unrealistic.[32]

Now, as Gelber argues, the focus on land purchases shifted from Transjordan to Palestine. Although for a while the Zionists still entertained the hope of receiving British approval for settlement in Transjordan after 1935 the issue was no longer discussed.[33] Accordingly, from the perspective of the Jewish Agency, relations with the shaykhs now lost much of their political value, and as such, Mithqal was effectively abandoned by Jewish Agency officials.[34]

Abdullah, the Jewish Agency and Arab Revolt

The outbreak of the Arab Revolt in Palestine brought about a new phase in Zionist–Hashemite relations. The great challenge imposed by the Palestinian resistance and fresh British thinking about the best solution for Palestine made Abdullah a necessary ally for the Jews. From Abdullah's point of view, the British and Zionists' predicaments in Palestine seemed a good opportunity to stress his claim over Palestine. In order to realise his ambitions he now needed the consent of the Zionist movement.

These contacts were kept confidential. It seems that, for Abdullah, the intensity of the Palestinian struggle and the heightened emotions in Palestine and the region at large made open contacts with the Jews politically unpalatable. Instead, close contact with the Jewish Agency was maintained between the parties either by direct meetings or more frequently through Abdullah's trusted confidant, Muhammad al-Unsi. Although the relationship was beneficial to both parties, its secrecy could not make up for the fundamental incompatibility between the parties' interests. Nevertheless, both were careful to maintain a friendship driven by instrumental need.

The outbreak of the revolt in 1936 made Abdullah an important player in the politics of Palestine. Faced with a general strike and an outburst of violence directed against the Jewish Yishuv and Mandate authorities, Wauchope asked the emir to use his influence among the Palestinian leadership in an effort to persuade them to call off the strike. For their part, the Palestinian leaders, who hitherto had been suspicious of Abdullah's intentions and had rejected his attempts to intervene in Palestinian affairs, now saw him as a useful mediator to broker negotiations with the Mandate authorities.[35]

On 1 May the Arab Higher Committee went to Amman to enlist Abdullah's support in trying to reach an accommodation with the British.

The Jewish Agency also now sought the good offices of Abdullah with Moshe Shertok asking him to use his influence among the Palestinian leadership to call for moderation. Two weeks later al-Unsi came to Jerusalem. He briefed the Jewish Agency on the Palestinian demands and Abdullah's own proposal for ending the violence. The emir wanted the Jews to accept his idea of suspending Jewish immigration to Palestine for several years, a position softened somewhat by his own offer to accept Jewish migration to Transjordan instead. It seems that this idea was not as altruistic as it first appeared, since Abdullah saw this as a means to an end: to unite Palestine and Transjordan under his reign. But he also asked for financial assistance from the Jewish Agency in order to help ensure political quiescence among the tribes across Transjordan. In the event, the Agency would agree only to a payment of £500, hardly an exercise in financial largesse for longer-term political gain.[36]

Indeed, it became apparent that a clear gulf existed between the positions of Abdullah and the Jewish Agency. According to Gelber, this was '[T]he lowest ebb to which Abdullah's relationship with the Jews sunk until May 1948.'[37] Even so, the two parties maintained a regular and frequent dialogue with each other. During the first months of the revolt al-Unsi and Cohen maintained close contacts either by telephone or through the frequent visits of al-Unsi to Jerusalem. They exchanged information about such topics as British and Arab positions, Palestinian activities across the Jordan and the attempts to rally support among the tribes and developments in Palestine. Al-Unsi carried persistent requests from his master for the Jewish Agency to compromise. At minimum, Abdullah requested that the Zionists agree to the temporary suspension of Jewish immigration and allow the Palestinian leadership a face-saving solution as a precursor to the halting of the general strike afflicting economic hardship across Palestine. Al-Unsi also asked for more financial help. Angry at a suggestion that cut to the very core of the Zionist state-building enterprise in Palestine, the Jewish Agency now demanded clarification of Abdullah's request that Jewish immigration be suspended.[38]

Again, a political agreement could not be reached between the parties, yet the Zionists did grant Abdullah several thousand pounds. This was a significant sum in light of Abdullah's modest means and at a time when his annual gratuity from the civil list amounted to £12,000.[39] Abdullah used the money together with a special grant from the British government to cultivate the loyalty of some influential shaykhs, in effect a form of coup-proofing that ensured the fidelity of the tribes by providing insurance against the revolt spilling over to the East Bank of the River Jordan.[40] By the end of 1936 what later came to be seen as the first phase of the revolt had begun to falter, a direct result of Britain's draconian counter-insurgency strategy that pushed Palestinian Arabs to the point of exhaustion. Indeed, Abdullah's influence on events across the river was marginal. Even so, the brief hiatus in hostilities allowed space for what became known as the Peel Commission of Inquiry to begin work on the causes of the violence and to suggest prescriptive measures that would ameliorate the conditions that had occasioned the revolt. Against this background discussions between the Zionists and Abdullah once again ensued. The talks were informed by shared suspicions over the designs of the Arab national movement in Palestine which had been given increasingly effective voice under the leadership of the mufti of Jerusalem, Haj Amin al-Husseini.

As the Peel Royal Commission was nearing its deliberations, news about the plan to partition Palestine between Arabs and the Jews was leaked. David Ben-Gurion authorised Pinhas Rutenberg to try and reach an agreement with Abdullah on the partition of Palestine and Jewish settlement in Transjordan. This, he argued, would elicit substantial Jewish investment in the country. However, in his meeting in London in May 1937 with senior Zionist officials Abdullah remained non-committal and suggested that both sides wait for the official British decision.[41]

The Commission's recommendation for the partition of Palestine, and with it the annexation of 80 per cent of western Palestine by Transjordan under Abdullah's reign, seemed to fulfil most of the emir's ambitions and he now set out to secure the support of all relevant parties. However, he was only able to enlist no more than a qualified commitment from the Jews while the Palestinians rejected the report outright. These reactions and the resumption of the revolt convinced the British government that the recommendations of the Peel Commission were unworkable. In May 1939, with war threatening in Europe and mindful of the need to placate Arab and Muslim opinion across the Middle East if British forces were to be released for operations elsewhere, the government under Neville Chamberlain published the White Paper. With its rejection of partition in favour of a unitary state to be granted independence after ten years and its call for severe restrictions on Jewish land purchase and immigration, the policy effectively ended the prospects for a Jewish–

Transjordanian understanding, though contacts, albeit intermittently, were maintained throughout the duration of the Second World War. Only with the end of hostilities in Europe, the realisation over the scale of the mass slaughter visited upon European Jewry and finally the unilateral British decision to terminate its Mandate in Palestine by May 1948 was the door opened for a new and more significant phase of clandestine diplomacy across the river.

Conclusion

Drawing on the extensive scholarship on Zionist–Transjordanian relations, archival sources and the Hebrew and Arabic press in Palestine, this chapter has explored the question of clandestine diplomacy and its effect on the outcome of these prolonged and multifaceted relations. Although some of the contacts were kept secret many soon became public knowledge. This in itself deserves attention. In the context of the consolidation of the Arab national movement in the interwar period and the growing tension between Jews and Arabs in Palestine, the Transjordanian political elite stood out in its willingness and ability to maintain open and friendly relations with the Zionist movement.

Throughout, Abdullah exercised a relatively free hand in his dealings with the Jewish Agency. Lacking anything like an informed political consciousness, public opinion in Transjordan had yet to mature or become radicalised by the heady mix of Arab nationalism or Palestinian irredentism. Indeed, by the time of the unification of both banks of the River Jordan in 1950, the total population of Transjordan was not much greater than 400,000, most of them nomads or peasants. The country lacked developed urbanisation on a grand scale, with only the capital Amman recognisable as a major population centre. The printed media, often seen as another precondition for the emergence of nationalism, remained in its infancy with only two newspapers—both under the complete control of Abdullah—in limited circulation. Moreover, levels of literacy in the country remained low as the limited education system produced only a small group of young and politically aware intellectuals. While they came to cohere around an Arab nationalist agenda and felt great sympathy with the plight of their Arab brothers in Palestine, their small numbers as well as Abdullah's ability to co-opt them prevented such intellectuals from acting as an effective nationalist opposition.[42]

This young and modern aspiring elite therefore remained marginal, a position in sharp contrast to that group of people whose support Abdullah needed most: the landowning tribal shaykhs. Loyal to themselves and to their tribes, they were indifferent to national ideology and had few reservations about dealing with the Zionists or supporting the emir's overtures towards the Jews if it served their interests.

Still, despite Abdullah's ability to maintain his diplomacy vis-à-vis the Jewish Agency, the result of these contacts amounted to very little. It was the constraints imposed by the British, such as over the issue of Jewish land purchases and settlement, the reluctance of the Zionist leadership to compromise over the issue of immigration and the wide gap between the parties' political interests that prevented a wider deal ever being realised. Even the tacit agreement dividing Palestine that was apparently agreed in secret on the eve of the 1948 war was of a piece with the negotiations of the 1930s: vague, general, flexible and subjective and therefore open to differing interpretations.[43] Ultimately, what shaped events on the ground was the balance of power between the parties, their interests and the limitations imposed by the British and the international community on the realisation of parallel yet competing national projects.[44]

3

INFLUENCE WITHOUT POWER?

BRITAIN, THE JEWISH AGENCY
AND INTELLIGENCE COLLABORATION, 1939–45

Clive Jones

Introduction

This chapter explores intelligence collaboration between Britain and the Jewish Agency during the Second World War. Most accounts of this period highlight the functional nature of this collaboration, an approach that many historians regard as a trade-off between immediate expediency on the one hand and concerns that such help in the longer term would undermine Britain's post-war position in Palestine on the other. The argument that the overall pattern of intelligence relations was overshadowed and ultimately determined by the pro-Arab and anti-Jewish views of officials in the Foreign Office and Colonial Office in London and Jerusalem has a powerful resonance, not least in the implicit overtones of betrayal from a power whose adherence to the strictures of the 1939 White Paper enforcing severe limitations over Jewish immigration to Palestine placed imperial interests over moral imperative.[1] When viewed through the prism of the Holocaust, the prevailing sense is that

Britain offered too little too late in using its clandestine assets to help rescue some of the remnants of European Jewry.

While intelligence collaboration was undoubtedly shaped by wider British policy across the Middle East, this chapter argues that intelligence liaison and collaboration at an operational level was more nuanced and less conditioned by adherence to stated British government policy. Equally, having developed its own indigenous intelligence capability but with only limited access to both financial and material resources, the clandestine relationship with key British intelligence officials allowed the Jewish Agency to develop and strengthen its transnational links, magnify the importance of their contribution to the Allied war effort at both a practical and symbolic level beyond the actual numbers of people involved, while developing a reservoir of expertise and experience that was to prove invaluable in the struggle for statehood.

The Context of Collaboration

In November 1944, speaking before a closed meeting of the Jewish Agency Executive, Reuven Zaslany, the head of intelligence and security affairs for the Political Department of the Jewish Agency, made this assessment of intelligence collaboration with the British:

We [the leadership of the Jewish Agency] told ourselves there is a war with Hitler, and we have a desire to defend *Eretz Yisrael* and that there is a clear British interest in allowing us to do so ... But they remained suspicious of us and they said, 'These Jews have their own general interests and we do not interest them. The Jewish Agency only want to exploit the relationship in the name of gathering information on the authorities and in order to steal weapons and in order to do this you will send us your people who will eventually rise up against Britain.'[2]

Accusations of perfidy on the part of London and the Mandate authorities have long informed analysis of British relations with the Jewish Agency during the Second World War. For despite the integration of the productive capacity of the Yishuv in support of the British war effort—particularly in the manufacture of textiles, the production of electric cables and the other paraphernalia of war required to equip and supply the British Armed Forces—the attitude of the Mandate authorities towards the leadership of the Jewish Agency, which represented the nascent structures of a state-in-waiting, remained decidedly cool.[3] In a conflict that was to see 30,000 Palestinian Jews serving in the British Armed Forces, the apparent ingratitude of London appeared of a piece with concerns that future British policy in Palestine remained hostile to the very idea of Zionism and Jewish statehood.[4] For David Ben-Gurion, the leader of the Jewish Agency, and his colleagues such official British attitudes seemed ingrained from the outset of the war despite their stated desire to become fully integrated into the British war effort.[5]

Certainly, attitudes among colonial officials in London and Jerusalem towards the Jewish Agency were often strained. Indeed, the British High Commissoner in Palestine, Sir Harold MacMichael, advocated the dismemberment of the Jewish Agency and for Palestine to become a Crown Colony as the first step in overseeing the implementation of the 1939 White Paper.[6] But outside the immediate antagonism surrounding the political future of the Palestine Mandate, a more productive relationship between Britain and the Jewish Agency did develop around the shadowy world of intelligence and covert operations, particularly where such operations were external to Palestine. In explaining how this relationship emerged three factors need to be born in mind.

First, such relations rarely conformed to a patron–client relationship since the 'patron', the British intelligence community in this instance, rarely acted in a coherent manner towards the Jewish Agency. This was partly the result of function. Three of the British intelligence organisations with which this chapter concerns itself, the Secret Intelligence Service (SIS or MI6), the Special Operations Executive (SOE) and MI9, were essentially 'foreign' agencies responsible for prosecuting operations in distant theatres, rather than being unduly concerned with the volatile mix of local politics in Palestine. By contrast, the Criminal Investigation Division (CID) of the Palestine Police as well as the Security Intelligence Middle East (SIME), the regional cover name of MI5, were concerned with the threat of Jewish subversive activity, most notably from the right-wing Irgun Zvai Leumi and Lehi as well as the main underground militia of the Jewish Agency, the Haganah. While the machinery for intelligence-sharing between these secret British organisations certainly existed, it was often haphazard and on several occasions led to interdepartmental turf wars.

Second, the demands of total war meant that there was a rapid expansion in the numbers recruited into the SIS, SOE and MI9. This meant recruiting a range of talented individuals from civilian life whose main concern was to help 'win the war', rather than necessarily be constrained by the eddies of local politics. Such attitudes were not, however, restricted to wartime recruits. Lieutenant Colonel Anthony Simonds who oversaw MI9 operations across the Mediterranean and the Balkans was a professional soldier noted for his pro-Zionist sympathies who played an intrinsic part in overseeing the so-called 'paratroopers mission', now part and parcel of Israeli folklore.[7] This was in marked contrast to those officers working for the CID who continued to run intelligence-led operations against targets in both the Jewish and Palestinian Arab communities. The assassination of the leader of the Lehi, Avraham Stern, by members of the CID in Tel Aviv at the beginning of 1942 when the position of Britain in the Middle East was far from secure is testament to this disconnect as was the arrest of members of the Haganah, the mainstream militia group who were actually working for the SOE.[8]

Third, even if a client, the Jewish Agency was often in the advantageous position of having more to 'sell' to the patron. By the outbreak of war in 1939 it had its own dedicated intelligence service, the Sheruth Ha-Yediot Ha-Artzit or SHAI (Information Service). While this had been tasked with penetrating the Palestine Police and monitoring the activities of right-wing Zionist militants, it had also nurtured and developed networks of agents and assets both among the Palestinian Arab community and the wider Middle East.[9] Moreover, as a largely immigrant society with members representing virtually every community across the Diaspora, the Yishuv offered linguistic expertise that proved highly attractive to British intelligence. Alongside Mossad Le'Aliyah Bet, which was responsible for the illegal immigration of Jews to Palestine, the Jewish Agency had in fact developed an intelligence capacity whose covert experience of working with the British intelligence community was to prove of immeasurable value in securing a sovereign Jewish state in Palestine after 1945. Indeed, a typology of intelligence collaboration is discernible, from the hard and functional that was driven by immediate expediency, to more normative types of collaboration determined by personal relationships and immune from the wider eddies of war. By examining the relationships that existed between the main external British intelligence agencies and the leadership of the Jewish Agency, a theme emerges that certainly came to influence Israel's use of clandestine diplomacy: that the absence of constructive ties with recognised state authorities need never inhibit the exercise of influence with its constituent organs through other, more clandestine means.

Intelligence Collaboration: The Early Years

Irrespective of the state of relations between the leadership of the Yishuv and the Colonial Office, the Jewish Agency had in fact been quick to make contact with the SIS on the outbreak of war. In September 1939 a meeting between Dr Chaim Weizmann and Major Lawrence Grant of Section 'D' of the SIS resulted in a quid pro quo agreement being reached. This allowed the Jewish Agency access to the SIS communications network between London, New York and Jerusalem, while the service would provide the necessary documentation for operatives of the Jewish Agency, many of whom hailed originally from Central and Eastern Europe, to travel back to their countries of origin in order to undertake intelligence work for the allies.[10]

This arrangement was met with deep distrust by officials in Whitehall and Jerusalem who regarded the primary role of SIS as actually being to gather intelligence against the Jewish Agency in the wider struggle against illegal Jewish immigration to Palestine, the belief being that such immigration could be used by German military intelligence, the Abwehr, to infiltrate agents into Palestine.[11] The SIS largely resisted this pressure. While sensitive to the security issues surrounding Jewish aliyah, the SIS never saw their role as constrained by the demands of the Mandate authorities, and indeed, when approached by the Jewish Agency to collaborate over intelligence work, the head of station in Cairo, John Shelley, readily accepted these overtures, alerting his colleague in Jerusalem, Major John Teague, to the possibilities that could now be exploited in gathering information on Italian activities across the Mediterranean and further afield. This soon expanded to other areas of the continent. With few if any viable assets in East and Central Europe and certainly none that could provide timely and reliable information on the volatile politics of the Balkans, circumstance determined a more open approach towards the Jewish Agency.[12]

The Jewish Agency extolled the virtues of Zionist organisations in Eastern Europe that could be harnessed towards wider British strategy in the Balkans. Section 'D' of SIS was charged with fermenting sabotage and political subversion in those countries whose proximity to the Axis powers made them particularly vulnerable to their entreaties. The Balkans and Hungary came under subsection D/H of Section 'D' whose particular interest lay in denying the Germans use of the Ploeşti oilfields in Romania as well disrupting the transport of raw material—including iron ore—that was crucial to the German war effort by blocking the Danube at the 'Iron Gates' where the river formed a boundary between Romania and Yugoslavia.[13]

By now, Section 'D' were dealing not only with Zaslany, but also his immediate superior, the director of the Political Department of the Jewish Agency, Moshe Shertok, and David Hacohen, a senior member of the Haganah, an organisation likened in one SIS report as equivalent 'to the I.R.A of Palestine'.[14] Accordingly, by the end of March 1940, discussions between the Jewish Agency and the secret service to send men into Eastern Europe had reached a fairly advanced stage of planning. A memorandum from Section 'D' outlined the extent of this collaboration:

They [the Jewish Agency] will pick out 100 qualified men … to work as crews on the various vessels which we now control on the Danube and which are being organised to protect British interests in the event of a German excursion down the river … The other side of their work will be the recruitment of a batch of 5 qualified men to go to Roumania [sic] in an apparently, innocent normal way, and when they get there to work with HaCohen, in cooperation with our people there. HaCohen will build up in Roumania an organisation, composed partly of local recruits with whom he will get in touch through Zionist circles, and partly of the men he will bring from Palestine.[15]

The SIS was anxious that the involvement of both Shertok and Hacohen in this endeavour should remain above reproach from the Mandate authorities since it was felt that any prolonged absence from Palestine on their part would raise suspicions in Jerusalem that they might be engaged in illegal immigration activities.[16] But wary of empowering the Jewish Agency, it was now suggested by the Mandate authorities that the SIS might find suitable recruits themselves from the Yishuv, thereby circumventing the Jewish Agency and avoiding the inevitable concerns over the loyalty and reliability that serving two masters among those recruited would inevitably raise.

The SIS, however, knew that this was unrealistic. In an unmarked despatch of 17 April, but which was probably drafted by Teague, it was noted that '[C]o-operation of the Jewish Agency in the matter of obtaining intelligence could not be adequately secured by using a cut out' and that, accordingly, any attempt to do so 'might well jeopardise the whole [Romania] scheme by suggesting that we do not trust them'.[17] In the event, the scheme foundered on wider Foreign Office objections. At a time when more conventional forms of diplomacy were felt more likely to secure a pro-British policy across the Balkans and Eastern Europe, any disclosure that London was prepared to sanction clandestine activity on the soil (and waters) of erstwhile friendly states was deemed anathema.[18] Still, by the later spring of 1940, firm ties had been established with the leadership of the Jewish Agency or 'The Friends' as they were now referred to in SIS reports. While fully aware that the Jewish Agency wanted to use the resources of British intelligence to ensure contact remained with their own organisations across the Balkans, one report in late May noted that, 'There really is no doubt that if they got down to it they could be extraordinarily useful from this point of view [intelligence gathering in Eastern Europe] as their connections are widespread and their organisation and intelligence service very efficient.'[19]

However, at the very point when collaboration between the SIS and the Jewish Agency appeared set to enter a more productive phase, the collapse of France, and with it the bloody eviction of the remnants of the British Army from the continent of Europe, brought about a restructuring of British intelligence sanctioned by the new British prime minister, Winston Churchill. Anxious to promote subversion and resistance among the occupied peoples of Europe, Section 'D', with its emphasis upon sabotage, was separated from the SIS and amalgamated with a small research department in the War Office specialising in the study of irregular warfare, (MI)R, and a semi-covert propaganda office attached to the Foreign Office known as 'Electra House'. With its emphasis upon sabotage and irregular warfare within a secret service many felt that the location of Section 'D' was the very antithesis of the patient, unobtrusive collection of clandestine information which supposedly defined an efficient intelligence organisation. The result was the formation of Special Operations Executive or SOE in July 1940, an organisation whose struggles against the Axis powers were more than matched by the bitter bureaucratic rivalry among its own employees as well as with the SIS.[20] The 'Friends' still continued to deal with the SIS in Palestine and Cairo, a relationship that actually intensified after 1943, by which time the SIS had come to adopt the regional cover name of the Inter-Services Liaison Department (ISLD). Nonetheless, for the next two years it was the SOE which was to take the dominant lead in dealing with the 'Friends'.

The SOE and the 'Friends'

While the SOE emerged as a defined bureaucratic organisation with discreet functions in London, inter-service rivalries at GHQ Cairo meant that Section 'D' and MI(R) continued to operate as distinct entities until a merger was forced through by London in the summer of 1941. Ostensibly under the command of General Sir Archibald Wavell in Cairo and directly responsible to the deputy director of Military Intelligence, Brigadier Sir Iltyd Clayton, their relationship was antagonistic with little coordination between the two regarding operational planning. Such turf wars did nothing to dampen the ardour of the Jewish Agency towards working with this new clandestine service, but it hardly helped smooth the process of liaison. Shertok and Ben-Gurion had, for example, already alerted the SIS in the spring of 1940 to the danger of an increase in German espionage activity in Palestine, a danger they felt had not been taken seriously by the Mandate authorities because the 'civil administration ... are too prejudiced against them'.[21] This was certainly the view of Lieutenant Colonel Anthony Simonds. In July 1940, while serving as a staff officer under Wavell, he was approached by a member of MI(R) who suggested that a party of Palestinian Jews under his command might infiltrate Lebanon and destroy the pipeline linking the Kirkuk oilfields to the port of Tripoli. While sympathetic, he replied that the Mandate authorities and the Palestine Police in particular would not condone such an operation, and indeed the CID, despite the fall of France, continued to maintain close ties with their Vichy counterparts.[22]

But the Jewish Agency remained alert to the wider eddies of Axis intrigue in Lebanon, Syria and Iraq. As early as January 1940, the Jewish Agency had been sending back reports from its own sources inside Syria and Lebanon under Tuvia Arazi warning of growing Nazi intrigue inside Damascus.[23] For example, in March 1941, a report was forwarded by Zaslany to Clayton in Cairo, giving details of a conference convened in Damascus between agents of the German Abwehr and pro-Nazi Arabs. It gave precise details of the Arab delegates (but not the German participants) involved and claimed that stated German policy was to see the abolition of British and French rule across the Middle East and 'the inclusion of Lebanon and Palestine in the Arab Empire'.[24] Similar worse-case scenarios informed Zaslany's reports on conditions inside Syria on the eve of the British invasion in June 1941. In another missive to Clayton outlining the extent of German intrigue inside Syria, he noted that unless Britain intervened soon, much of the goodwill harboured by many Arabs towards the British would be sacrificed on the altar of political expediency if they sensed that pro-Axis forces would remain in the ascendency.[25]

However, by May 1941 it was events in neighbouring Lebanon that now shaped the scope of covert collaboration. Having been separated from the SIS, Section 'D' and MI(R) now sheltered uneasily together under the umbrella of Special Operations 2 (SO2) of MO4, the recently assigned regional cover name for SOE. Unaware of the rivalry that still prevailed between the two elements of SO2, Zaslany and his colleagues agreed to recruit twenty-three men from the Haganah, all experienced seamen trained in irregular warfare who, under the command of a British officer, Major Sir Anthony Palmer, were tasked with sabotaging the oil refineries at the coastal port of Tripoli in Lebanon. This mission, codenamed 'Boatswain', was highly sensitive, not least because Britain had yet to engage in formal hostilities against the Vichy regime in Damascus. But having set sail from Haifa on board a converted coast guard launch, *Sea Lion*, on the night of Sunday, 18 May 1941, contact was soon lost. At first adverse weather conditions were blamed, but in the absence of any radio communication suspicions of a more bloody fate began to emerge. Even today, the exact course of events remains unclear but it would appear that a heightened state of alert among the Vichy French along the coast led to the detection of the mission. While *Sea Lion* probably reached Tripoli, it was surprised by French coastal defences, resulting in the deaths of some of the party and the capture of others. Their subsequent fate is still unclear although the strong suspicion remains that they were executed following interrogation by Vichy Authorities.[26]

Eldad Harouvi has argued that Operation Boatswain, planned in haste and with little operational intelligence of the target, was driven less by strategic imperative and more by the need for MO4 to justify its existence to an increasingly sceptical GHQ in Cairo exasperated at the bureaucratic malaise surrounding SOE and its operations in the Middle East.[27] Equally, however, the exigencies of war, not least the stated aim of denying an oil-refining capacity of benefit to the nationalist regime in Baghdad, determined the risk worthwhile. Moreover, given the dire warning issued by Zaslany and Shertok over German intrigue across the

Middle East, the Jewish Agency hardly proved to be reluctant participants in this venture.[28]

But if Boatswain was an unmitigated disaster, the actions of the men of the Plugot Machatz or Palmach (Strike Companies) of the Haganah proved quite the reverse. Under the leadership of Yitzhak Sadeh, the Palmach had, by 1941, begun to develop subunits defined as much by their language abilities as martial prowess who could infiltrate behind enemy lines. These units included a 'German platoon' (Ha'Machlaka Ha'Germanit) as well as a 'Syrian platoon' (Ha'Machlaka Ha'Surit) whose members played a key role in the reconnaissance of Vichy French positions up to and including the Anglo-Australian invasion of Syria and Lebanon on 8 June 1941. Contrary to some accounts, these units of the Palmach had received limited training from the SOE in guerrilla warfare prior to the invasion of Syria and Lebanon, their linguistic skills and knowledge of the border with Lebanon only being called upon by SOE through force of circumstance: a small group of Arabs already trained and tasked with cutting the Vichy lines of communication deserted on the eve of the invasion. Only a last minute approach to Shertok by a young SOE officer saved the situation, leading to the deployment of members of the Syrian platoon in advance of the main Allied invasion force to secure bridges.[29]

By late summer of 1941 the SOE had established a training school, designated STS 102, in the grounds of an old monastery, close to the summit of Mount Carmel with its commanding view of Haifa bay. Many of the teaching staff, such as the classics scholar Nicholas Hammond, already had first-hand experience of fighting behind enemy lines in Greece, and while this experience was now utilised in developing a curriculum, the emphasis was very much upon guerrilla warfare rather than intelligence. This is important because by the spring of 1942 soldier-scholars such as Hammond and Christopher Woodhouse, who had developed a deep sympathy for Zionist aspirations, were not only imparting the finer points of demolitions or map-reading to Greeks, Yugoslavs and others destined for Eastern Europe, but also to some members of the Palmach and the Haganah who had now been recruited with the blessing of the Jewish Agency for what was termed training 'post-occupational duties' should Axis forces emerge triumphant in Egypt and push onwards towards Palestine.[30]

With its emphasis upon irregular warfare, the skills taught by SOE instructors to their students at places such places as Kibbutz Mishmar

Ha'emek in the Jezreel Valley were easily transferable to other members of the Palmach and the Haganah once they had graduated, skills that in turn could later be turned against the Mandate authorities. In the winter of 1941 and despite pressure being brought to bear by the Jewish Agency, such arguments had determined strict quotas on the number of Jews recruited for 'post-occupational' work, but the spring and summer of 1942 brought about a radical rethink in Jerusalem. The failure to deny the Japanese access to the tin and rubber of the Malay Peninsula was seen as a major setback, which could at least have been partially alleviated by organised stay-behind networks. When combined with the success of Axis forces in North Africa, the 'Palestine Scheme' had an immediacy that pushed to one side the more parochial concerns of the Mandate authorities.

The implications were not lost on the hierarchy of SOE. In April 1942 the British high commissioner in Palestine, Sir Harold MacMichael, was subject to a request from the Jewish Agency for the expansion of what MO4 termed the 'Friends Scheme' from thirty recruits to 180. Those recruited were to be infiltrated into surrounding Arab states, most notably Syria and Lebanon, and with an emphasis upon wireless communications, they were to set up a network of 'stay-behind' agents in the event of wholesale British retreat from the region. In the event, some forty recruits were trained and covertly deployed into Syria.[31] Still, having trained 400 Jews for post-occupational work by June 1942, it was noted that '[W]hile the employment of individual Jews may be necessary, the preparation of further Jews in anything approaching large numbers for post-occupational activities should, for political reasons, only be resorted to in the future in the face of a serious and immediate threat.'[32]

Instead, the emphasis was placed upon establishing post-occupational wireless networks with the suggestion that 150 specially trained radio operators, divided into twenty-five cells under five regional commanders would be distributed across Palestine.[33] These networks were trained and ready to be deployed by the late summer of 1942. But even here, British officials, including MacMichael, remained suspicious of the 'post-occupational scheme', suspicions they were keen to impress upon the new head of mission at SOE Cairo, Lord Glenconner, whose appointment in September 1942 saw him keen to become acquainted with his new 'parish' as quickly as possible. A constant complaint among British officials was that the Jewish Agency not only appeared to be tacitly condoning the wholesale theft of weapons and equipment from British Army depots across Palestine, which was said to be costing over £100,000 per week, but that they now sought to gain maximum advantage from the post-occupational scheme devised by SOE, despite the clear limits placed by the British on the type of paramilitary skills to be imparted. Attention was drawn, for example, to the arrest of six members of Haganah in Tel Aviv who were caught red-handed training as radio operatives. Despite Hacohen's insistence that they were being trained for post-occupational work in Syria, the Mandate authorities had no knowledge of those arrested and certainly their names did not appear on any agreed manifest.

But the SOE knew they were in no position to pick a fight with the Agency if the post-occupational schemes across the Middle East were to pay future dividends. All knew that the first loyalty of those recruited was to the Jewish Agency and 'We have never, therefore, been more than a junior partner and our control over the man [Hacohen] must depend on maintaining good relations with their [the arrested operators] masters.' Even so, it led Glenconner to conclude that SOE had been taken 'for suckers' by the Jewish Agency and the future collaboration should be on the basis of the SOE retaining the upper hand 'and they did what they were told'.[34]

But with Rommel's defeat at El Alamein and the threat to Palestine lifted, MacMichael insisted that clear water now emerge between the SOE and the Jewish Agency. The nadir was perhaps reached when, in March 1943, members of the Haganah disguised as British servicemen raided the arsenal of STS 102.[35] From that moment onwards, senior officers in SOE maintained a distance from the Jewish Agency that was to remain for the rest of the war despite attempts by Zaslany and others in the spring and summer of 1944 to lobby for the despatch of up to 100 'Palestinian civilians' to be sent to Hungary to disrupt the mass deportations of Hungarian Jews. The plan was ostensibly shelved for geopolitical reasons—it being accepted that Hungary would most likely fall under Moscow's sphere of influence as the war drew to a close and Jewish agents working for SOE would hardly assuage Soviet suspicion of British intrigue.[36] Senior officers had, however, come to the conclusion that SOE had been so thoroughly penetrated by the Jewish Agency that any meaningful relationship based overwhelmingly on realising British interests in Palestine, let alone the Balkans, was impossible.[37]

60

INFLUENCE WITHOUT POWER?

ISLD, MI9 and the Jewish Agency

If discord marked the relationship between the SOE and the Jewish Agency by the summer of 1943, relations with ISLD and MI9 proved to be more cordial. In the summer of 1940 and with help from the SIS station in Jerusalem, an interrogation centre in Haifa was established in conjunction with members of the SHAI to process refugees and immigrants entering Palestine. Not only did it allow the Mandate authorities to develop an impressive screening system, but it also allowed ISLD access to recent immigrants from Europe able to provide valuable information regarding German industrial and economic activity throughout Eastern Europe.[38] Equally, ISLD had not forgotten the ability of the Agency to find individuals whose background and language skills met a particular operational requirement. For while the threat from Nazi Germany dominated the immediate intelligence horizons of the British, plans were drawn up in May 1941 to penetrate the Soviet Union by planting an agent among Jewish communities close to the major naval ports of Sevastopol and Nicolaeff in the Crimea. Given the subsequent German invasion of the Soviet Union in the following month, it is unknown if this gambit ever went beyond the planning stage. Even so, it is indicative of the value placed on the external networks controlled by the Jewish Agency that ISLD officers maintained contact with Zaslany and Shertok, despite the undoubted concerns of the CID and wider Colonial Office policy.[39]

Their functional role as external covert organisations—ISLD was tasked with the gathering of military intelligence against Axis targets in Central and Eastern Europe while MI9 aimed to abet the escape of Allied servicemen on the run behind enemy lines and help prisoners of war to fashion their own escape—determined the scope of their activities. On the surface at least these had little to do with enhancing the capabilities in irregular warfare of the Palmach or the Haganah. The Balkans once again had become the focus of British intelligence activity, and with the successful invasion of Italy in September 1943 the ISLD was looking to expand the number of missions attached to partisan groups across Eastern Europe. One British recruit, Owen Reed, described the ISLD as 'Very Oxford: Christchurch Dons and British Council types ... Very unmilitary and unregimental. Most of them clapped into uniform as experts in strange fields ... [R]ampant individualists with a passion for truth.' For while an innate conservatism determined the political outlook of the more established SIS officers, Reed observed more radical proclivities among those recruited purely for the duration of the war. These tended to favour the communist partisans across the Balkans, a sentiment born in no small measure from the fact that they seemed to be killing more Germans.[40] Reed was eventually parachuted in to join a mission on Slovenia, but however good the intelligence and inter-personal skills of these officers, they lacked sufficient fluency in the local languages. Not unnaturally, ISLD turned to Shertok and Zaslany to redress this paucity.

Both men had already shown a keenness to work with ISLD but on the understanding that those recruited and trained as wireless operators would be openly serving two masters. As early as the beginning of 1942, reports reaching the Jewish Agency regarding the fate of European Jewry had made Zaslany determined to send operatives into Eastern Europe to ascertain the true extent of the unfolding horror. One such scheme had already foundered in the spring of 1942, it being alleged that the pressure from the Mandate authorities had scuppered the operation, although tempestuous relations between those recruited and their British instructors hardly helped matters. On 25 February 1943 Zaslany wrote to Squadron Leader Smith Ross of the ISLD Cairo in an attempt to resurrect the scheme and highlighting the continued existence of Zionist underground cells in Bulgaria, Romania and Hungary and that Jewish Agency 'envoys' could be infiltrated through Istanbul, an important hub for SIS missions into Eastern Europe in an attempt to exploit such cells. Once in position, their dual role could then be realised. Such was the urgency behind this request that Zaslany offered to subsidise the training of those recruited by providing his own wireless instructors.[41] Teething problems, however, still existed among those recruited to the ISLD. Some refused to be inducted into the British Armed Forces, despite the British, rightfully, seeing this as necessary precaution for maintaining an agent's cover. Others demurred over the need to undergo parachute training, insisting instead that they be smuggled into Europe via Turkey.

In the event some twenty-five Palestinian Jews were recruited by the ISLD as W/T operators and dropped behind enemy lines as part of wider missions, sometimes in collaboration with the SOE and MI9 across Yugoslavia, Bulgaria and Romania.[42] While these missions were tasked primarily with providing intelligence on Axis forces, they also provided insights into the wider political context that determined partisan planning and operations. It was also fully understood by ISLD that where such agents happened upon 'Jewish refugees who are in possession of information that might be useful to us, they should be given the facilities to pass this information on to us [the Jewish Agency]'.[43] One such recruit, Dan Laner (Gatoni), who was a member of the German platoon of the Palmach, was dropped into Slovenia close to the Austrian border. In the winter of 1944 his mission was overrun by the Germans near Stajerska. Separated from the rest of the partisans in his group who were immediately executed, Laner expected the same fate after being interrogated. Only a momentary lapse in concentration on the part of his guards allowed him to escape. He later went on to enjoy a successful military career in the Israel Defence Forces, reaching the rank of major-general.[44]

Despite instructions from the Jewish Agency, however, few of these ISLD agents were able to provide anything more than token assistance to Jewish refugees or indeed provide accurate information regarding the location of Nazi death camps inside Austria. Those that were able to do so were usually part of joint missions run with MI9, the least well known of Britain's external intelligence agencies but one which perhaps enjoyed the most productive relationship with the Jewish Agency. This was due in no small part to Anthony Simonds, whose association with Zaslany dated back to 1935. Set up as a department of the War Office in December 1939, the role of MI9 was to harness intelligence gleaned from escaped or repatriated prisoners of war (POWs) and to help incarcerated servicemen to escape either by prior training given before capture or through the smuggling of escape aids into prison camps.[45] Simonds was appointed head of the Balkans and Middle East Section of IS9 (M.E) in 1941, the regional cover name for MI9. Those recruited as agents joined 'A' Force, another evasive title designed to further obscure MI9 activity. Simonds had already taken advantage of his contacts with Zaslany and others in the latter part of 1942 to arrange the so-called 'Three Names Scheme' whereby any Allied serviceman on the run behind enemy lines in the Balkan countries could contact these named sources who, using networks of underground Zionist movements, could then be evacuated via Turkey. Focused primarily on Hungary and Romania, details of the contacts were smuggled into selected Allied personnel in POW camps in Eastern Europe.[46]

This arrangement was developed further in February of 1943 with the signing of a tripartite agreement between Simonds, Zaslany and a leading member of the Haganah, Ze'ev Shind, codename 'Dany'. This became known as the Tony and Dany agreement. Simonds knew that with the air attacks on Ploeşti increasing as Germany's only reliable source of oil came within range of Allied bombers, an incremental rise in the number of downed air crew would be the inevitable result. The insertion of 'A' Force agents with the appropriate language skills was deemed necessary because the 'Three Names Scheme' would be unlikely to be able to cope with the sheer volume of personnel on the run. In return, Simonds agreed that those recruited from the Yishuv could help in the rescue of European Jewry and use the capabilities of MI9 to this end. The agreement, condoned personally by Winston Churchill, was signed in February 1943 but it was not until October that it was formally activated. In the event, twenty agents were recruited into 'A' Force, many of whom, such as Hannah Szenes, were to become something akin to national icons in Israel after 1948.

These agents were careful not to reveal their true identities to IS9 officers, partly to prevent SIME from compiling dossiers upon them and partly to protect any relations or acquaintances of agents still living in Axis-held territory. All were, however, 'enlisted' into the British Armed Forces and given formal service records to enhance their cover if captured in uniform, cover that might be enough to spare their lives. In several cases it did. In truth, the 'dual use' value of these missions into Romania, Hungary, Bulgaria and along the Yugoslav–Austrian border was never fully realised. The 'Cobweb Mission' dropped close to the Hungarian–Yugoslav border in March 1944 oversaw the successful evacuation of over 120 airmen in a seven-month period. By contrast, operations into Romania proved disappointing, the codename given to a succession of such missions, 'Operation Anticlimax-Lyon' or 'Operations Anticlimax-Blue', being a rather apt summation of realities on the ground when in August 1944 Romania abandoned its former German ally for the Soviets. The infamous mission which cost Szenes her life, 'Operation Chicken', was in fact a joint 'A' Force/ISLD mission where it was hoped the agents involved would develop both intelligence and escape networks across Hungary and Romania. A native of Budapest, Szenes seemed ideal for the job, but happenstance, not least the full German occupation of Hungary in March 1944, and in truth a mixture of poor field security and eventual betrayal, led to her capture, interrogation and execution by the Nazis in November 1944.[47]

Simonds acknowledged the apparently meagre returns from these missions, but noted in his reports that in light of the physical distances involved, a largely cowed or hostile population across these countries and the ever-changing geopolitics of the region that the number of Allied servicemen eventually rescued, 150 in total, was no mean achievement.[48] But even the assessment of the Political Department of the Jewish Agency concluded that only in a few cases was the work of 'A' Force of any use. All too often, agents, both Jewish and non-Jewish, were sent on missions that were already superfluous, often resulting from information that had a limited sell-by date. For example, however good the intelligence received from the Haifa interrogation centre was, it was often redundant regarding local conditions by the time any particular group of refugees had reached Palestine and their information processed. Yet when the scale of the tragedy that had befallen European Jewry had become known by the end of 1944, not least the deportation and mass murder of 400,000 Hungarian Jews at Auschwitz-Birkenau in the space of three months, a sense of betrayal began to permeate the subsequent summaries of collaboration with Allied intelligence agencies in general and the British in particular. For example, a report from Zaslany's own department summarising the scope of intelligence collaboration with the British noted that 'Despite all the efforts of the Jewish Agency to send reinforcements to help groups of Jewish resisters who stood alone, the Allied powers did not lend a hand to establish a Jewish resistance movement in the Nazi Diaspora.'[49]

But harsh as it may sound, even if the British had wanted to instigate and support Jewish resistance movements across Eastern Europe, it is doubtful that even by the winter of 1943, and despite the continued existence of underground Zionist movements, the flames of rebellion could have been ignited more widely. Only in Albania and Yugoslavia where coherent partisan organisations existed was British and Allied help, mainly through the despatch of SOE missions, ever sanctioned on anything like an operational scale to support partisan operations. Such propitious conditions simply did not exist in the rest of the Balkans and Eastern Europe. In short, the human terrain in Hungary, Romania and Bulgaria was for the most part fallow and resistant to most attempts to plant the seeds of rebellion. To this extent, the importance of the 'parachutists' mission' is widely acknowledged to be in its symbolism as a physical act that the Yishuv had not forsaken the fate of European Jewry.

Conclusion

Realpolitik certainly determined the attitude of some within the wider British intelligence community in Palestine towards realising cooperation with the Jewish Agency. Moreover, the closeness and intensity of the relationship undoubtedly paralleled the wider fortunes of war, and accusations of disloyalty on both sides, particularly with regards to the position of senior SOE personnel, continue to resonate. But such liaison was often beholden to a Mandate authority who feared that the bureaucratic entropy among and between the ISLD, SOE and MI9 would only advantage a Jewish Agency whose organisation and efficiency among the Yishuv set it apart from its Arab Palestinian and indeed most other nationalist and anti-colonial movements seeking independence from British rule. Indeed, given the strictures of the White Paper, the level and intensity of intelligence liaison was surprisingly close and much of this can be attributed to an influx of amateurs into secret service whose overall sentiment was determined by a need to 'get the job done', rather than be hamstrung by the often opaque concerns of wider British policy. In turn, this allowed Zaslany, Shertok and Hacohen in particular to exact a level of cooperation from the British which, in truth, their finite resources at times hardly warranted. It was the drive by the Jewish Agency to deploy their limited resources to best effect and the lessons derived from doing so, not least with British intelligence, which helped shape Israel's use of clandestine diplomacy in the decades following the end of the Second World War.[50]

4

THE POWER OF THE WEAK

ISRAEL'S SECRET OIL DIPLOMACY, 1948–57

Uri Bialer

Introduction

During the first twenty years of Israel's existence, petroleum was the
only practical source of energy for its rapidly growing population and an
ever-expanding and modernising economy. As such, ensuring secure
access to this most precious resource was no less a basic existential problem as the supply of armaments. However, despite almost crippling
financial limitations, the chief constraints in obtaining crude oil and its
refined products were political. Governments and the major oil companies, primarily British and American (but later the Soviets and Iranians
too), viewed the issue predominantly from the perspective of the Arab–
Israeli conflict. Nevertheless, Israel pursued an ambitious oil policy
whose aims extended well beyond the supply of minimal civilian and
military requirements. It sought to re-establish the Haifa oil refinery—a
British-run enterprise in operation since 1939—as the supplier for
domestic consumption and to promote a newly established petrochemical industry in the hope that it would become the source of much-
needed foreign exchange earnings.[1]

To this end, it was hoped that the pipeline from Iraq to Haifa could be reactivated and/or the Suez Canal opened for tankers serving Haifa. Moreover, the Israeli government repeatedly tried to break the monopoly over price structure imposed on the domestic oil market during the British Mandate regime, and to abolish the tax-exempt status of foreign oil companies. Although not all these goals were achieved, Israel's oil diplomacy between 1948 and 1957 can be viewed as highly successful. It managed to diversify Israel's oil supplies by closing independent deals with Russia and Iran, and to make incremental improvements in its relations with the foreign companies operating inside Israel itself. Above all it secured supply agreements with Iran which not only became the main source of oil but also helped to develop the Red Sea port of Eilat into a major oil depot. Pipelines were eventually laid all the way from there to Haifa, thus opening a new oil supply route (for Iranian crude and of Haifa-refined products) to Europe. This chapter examines the reasons for the successes of Israel's oil diplomacy, which can justifiably be termed 'Statecraft in the Dark'. Given the breadth and depth of the subject area, this chapter concentrates on three major achievements of Israel's secret oil diplomacy which until the late 1990s remained little known even in Israel. These achievements were (1) keeping the British in between 1949 and 1950; (2) the secret diplomatic entry into Iran in 1950; and (3) the hidden diplomacy that secured the supply of Iranian oil to Israel between 1955 and 1957.

Keeping the British In

Among the most injurious results of the War of Independence between 1948 and 1949 was Israel's near total disconnection from sources of natural energy. Mandatory Palestine, and later the State of Israel, were totally dependent on imported oil since none existed in the country (in 1955 a negligible amount was discovered near Ashkelon), while the use of coal had been almost entirely discontinued by the late 1930s. Until the British evacuation of Palestine in 1948, oil for local consumption had been imported under unfavourable financial conditions because the British government had granted a near monopoly to four oil companies, one of them American.[2] This monopoly prevented wider competition and allowed these companies to enjoy exclusive rights over prices. Even though the oil was coming from the Middle East, its cost was exceptionally high, being based on the value of imports from the Gulf of Mexico. Although the British-owned refineries in Haifa had been operating since 1939, and there was a pipeline carrying crude oil from Kirkuk in Iraq to the refineries, the prices worked to the distinct disadvantage of the local population. Nevertheless, oil was obtainable as long as Britain ruled Palestine. This situation changed following the end of the Mandate in 1948.

Prior to its final withdrawal, however, Britain had gradually realised that the refineries would have to be shut down, mainly through fear that the belligerents, especially the Arabs, would sabotage the installations. When, at the outbreak of hostilities leading to the War of Independence, Iraq halted the passage of oil to Haifa, broader geopolitical considerations contributed to London's decision to close the refineries. Not wishing to be seen as helping the Jews, whose control of Haifa was virtually assured by April 1948, the British placed a de facto embargo on oil shipments to Israel, a move that threatened to paralyse the state during the first months of the War of Independence.[3] Israel's tactical success in preventing this was achieved through the integration of a strictly controlled use and storage of limited oil imports, and the threat to nationalise the refineries in order to convince the British to continue the limited flow of petroleum.

After the war, all international efforts to secure the opening of the Iraqi pipeline to the Haifa refineries, or to import Iraqi or Iranian Persian crude oil via the Suez Canal, failed. The Arabs remained committed to the boycott of Israel; the British proved reluctant to pressure Iraq or Egypt, while Washington remained unsupportive of British commercial efforts to find an alternative supply route. Israel, for its part, rebuffed every attempt to challenge its sovereignty in Haifa and the oil refineries—an Iraqi and Egyptian precondition to negotiations. The cumulative effect of these conflicting positions led Great Britain to decide to close down the Haifa refineries by early 1950.

However, due mainly to the seriousness with which Israel's threat to nationalise the refineries was taken in London, this decision was postponed. Britain feared such nationalisation for two important reasons. Firstly, there were increasing concerns that across the Middle East the position of British oil companies was coming under threat from nationalist movements, and London feared that Israel's threatened action could set an uncomfortable precedent.[4] Indeed, such fears came to be realised in 1951 when, under the leadership of Mohamed Mossadegh, Iran nationalised the assets of the Anglo-Iranian Oil Company, the forerunner to British Petroleum (BP). Second, the British came to realise that the Suez Canal could be used as a passageway for oil supplies to the Haifa refineries after all. This operation, codenamed 'Operation Vasco da Gama', was designed to bring Persian Gulf oil to Israel via the Cape of Good Hope, and then return with empty tankers via the Suez Canal. In retrospect it seems that the Egyptians either turned a blind eye to the scheme or remained unaware of its existence. Whatever the case, the operation granted the refineries a reprieve and they continued to process oil whose price justified the circuitous operation. This was important for proving the profitability of the refineries, especially in light of the persistent claim of British oil companies that the price of petroleum and its transportation from Venezuela (the only realistic alternative source of crude oil to the Middle East) had turned the Haifa refineries into a money-losing enterprise.[5]

An agreement was eventually reached between London and Jerusalem in May–July 1950, which stipulated that the refineries would operate only for local consumption and not for export (which would have required the British to organise the large-scale transportation of Middle East oil to Haifa, a prospect regarded as completely out of question for political reasons). The result of these developments was that for eight critical years Israel came under the aegis of the British oil companies which continued to control two-thirds of the local market. In agreeing to such terms, Israel was greatly influenced by the desire to avoid having to import oil independently while concurrently retaining links to the international oil companies. Such Anglo-Israeli cooperation over oil stood in stark contrast to the overwhelming trend now sweeping across the Middle East by the early 1950s: the emergence of national movements that regarded the control and exploitation of their energy sources by foreign companies as of a piece with Western imperialism and one that had to be utterly eradicated. Against this background Israel's decision to allow foreign oil companies an operating monopoly over the Haifa oil refineries deserves further analysis.

Israel rejected the wholesale nationalisation of its energy production for several reasons.[6] Firstly, such an act would bring Israel into a head-on clash with the oil companies over importing, refining and marketing rights since all the companies were involved in these branches. Such a confrontation also came with some risk because, legally, Israel's claim against the Mandate's oil concessions was essentially weak. Even if Jerusalem was to win in the international courts, it would almost certainly be called on to pay a considerable amount in compensation, sums of money that it sorely lacked at the time. Furthermore, the nationalisation of the energy market was likely to be regarded as an ominous threat to foreign investors—existing or potential—as well as to investors in energy supplies and oil drilling, of dealing with Israel.

Moreover, the expulsion of foreign companies would undoubtedly provoke a harsh reaction that would be very damaging to Israel. Indeed, it was uncertain whether Israel would be allowed to purchase oil within the framework of the domineering international cartel after it had ejected the leading companies. It was also doubtful whether it could guarantee the transportation of oil because in this area, too, the world tanker market was controlled by the big companies. Even if Israel were to reconcile itself to the closure of the refineries this would be unacceptable because the state would have to forgo the development of its petrochemical industry and import refined oil at a high cost. Financing was also a weighty problem. It was clear that, following any nationalisation of the refineries, London would either withhold or completely suspend Israel's sterling reserves, which would prove disastrous for the Jewish state in light of the near total depletion of its foreign currency reserves. By contrast, the continued connection with the British oil companies would guarantee the use of these reserves for the purchase of oil. Furthermore, any action against foreign oil companies would include the ouster of 'Socony Vacuum', the most active American oil concern in Israel, and would probably destroy Israel's chances of receiving economic aid from Washington.

Above all, it should be remembered that Israel had just come into existence and lacked experience in the field of oil management. During the Mandate most of the country's economic resources had been directed to agriculture, a small amount to industry and a mere fraction to the oil industry.[7] The reasons were obvious. The British had complete control of the energy field and there had been few opportunities for citizens of the newborn state to develop the necessary technical and theoretical skills required for the effective running of the refineries. Even if Israel wanted independence in oil refining and sales in 1948, its ability to do so was heavily circumscribed.

Therefore, Israeli diplomacy on the oil front in the immediate aftermath of the War of Independence underlined two key assumptions that became axioms for the national leadership. The first was that Israel could not stand alone in a power clash with the oil companies; the second was that even if it somehow succeeded in this confrontation in peacetime, its energy resources would be placed in jeopardy in times of war, rendering the state vulnerable. Therefore, every effort had to be made, in the short to medium term at least, to guarantee the continued operation of British oil companies in Israel. Moreover, there were broader political concerns that influenced Israel. Two American companies, Socony and Esso, were involved in the refining process at Haifa. From the perspective of Jerusalem they helped balance what would otherwise have been a near total British monopoly over the industry, thus providing Israel with a degree of manoeuvrability while at the same time being a practical expression of Israel's ties to the United States, a connection vital to Israel's longer-term strategy.

The possibility of purchasing oil with American assistance and the released sterling reserves were decisive factors in shaping Israel's oil strategy, which condoned the monopoly of foreign control over the refineries that dated from the Mandatory period. Two years later another monetary dimension entered the picture that further strengthened this tendency. Despite procuring sterling reserves in 1951, Israel still found itself in a situation where, for all practical purposes, it lacked sufficient foreign currency to buy oil.[8] Given the parlous state of Israel's finances, British companies decided not to sell oil to Israel, a decision that presaged economic paralysis across the Jewish state. Catastrophe was only averted by the reparations agreement with Germany, according to which the German government was committed to financing, in sterling, the purchase of Israel's oil from British companies for a period of half a decade. While these agreements greatly helped Israel in guaranteeing its energy sources, they nonetheless reduced its ability to sever ties with the British oil companies.

Secret Entry into Iran

In the search for a more secure supply of oil, Israel now turned increasingly towards Iran. Given the regional animus towards the Jewish state, how Israel brokered such a deal is an object lesson in clandestine diplomacy. The Israeli foreign minister, Moshe Sharett, had expressed concern at Israel's regional isolation during a closed meeting of the Mapai party in the Knesset at the end of July 1949 when he declared that 'We are living today in a state of pernicious isolation in the Middle East, we have no traffic with the neighbouring countries, we have no recognition of our existence from the neighbouring states. If we must, we can manage to survive in such a state; but even if we must, we cannot ignore the distress that isolation brings to our Nation.'[9]

It is little wonder therefore that, from the beginning, Israeli foreign policy unceasingly, although for the most part covertly, attempted to break the wall of political isolation across the region. Until the signing of the Camp David peace accords with Egypt in 1979, such activities—whose aim was to establish formal diplomatic ties with states across the Middle East—could claim only two outright achievements: Turkish recognition of Israel and the establishment of diplomatic relations at the end of 1949, and de facto Iranian recognition of Israel in 1950. It is perhaps no coincidence that such recognition was gained from the two main non-Arab Muslim states in Middle East, yet with few cards to play Israel's success in gaining this recognition should not be disparaged. As the architects of Israel's foreign policy at the time predicted, and as later historical developments proved, these ties bore significant political, intelligence and economic advantages for Israel across the region and beyond.

It is impossible to understand how Iranian recognition of Israel was achieved without touching on the special domestic conditions existing within Iran, not least the nepotism and corruption of a political system that prompted Israeli officials to coin the term 'Persian Bazaar' in describing how influence was exercised internally. Along with similar petitions to states throughout the world, the Israeli government formally applied to Iran for recognition and the creation of political ties in June 1948. A similar petition was made nine months later; neither was accepted. At that time the establishment of political ties with Iran was not at the forefront of Israel's concerns and therefore, although the issue of future ties to Iran was raised by officials in Jerusalem, more pressing needs in the midst of a war determined diplomatic priorities.

This situation soon changed. Beginning in October 1948 and during the course of the following nine months, the Mossad managed to create and ensure by various means—including bribery—an escape channel through Iran for Jews from what one Mossad leader dubbed 'the Iraqi hell'.[10] After two groups had been smuggled out—the first numbering just seven, the second comprising over 100 Jews—a pattern was established that was tacitly condoned by the Iranian prime minister, apparently in consultation and agreement with the Iranian royal court. This escape route now allowed for hundreds of Iraqi Jews to pass through Iran with the authorities' approval. The greatest threat to this exodus was in Iraqi pressure being exerted on the Iranian government to close its borders against such illegal migration. As early as the beginning of December 1948, the Iraqi legation in Tehran approached the authorities with the demand that they ban the entry of Iraqi Jews and prevent those that had crossed the border from emigrating to Israel. A second demand from Baghdad was that they be returned to Iraq on the pretext that they were communists. The true Iraqi motive was clear enough, however: to prevent the demographic strengthening of the State of Israel through Jewish immigration.[11]

This demand was rejected by Tehran at the end of 1948, but by the middle of the following year more direct pressure applied by the Iraqis did result in Iran—on several occasions at least—forcing Jewish refugees to return to Iraq. By September 1949 such actions were discontinued due in no small part to the actions of the Mossad and their ability to win over local politicians as well as to use personal ties with officials at the US embassy in Tehran. But the Israeli Foreign Ministry and even more so the Mossad cast doubt on whether their modus operandi would continue to bear fruit in the absence of Iranian recognition, particularly given the reports of an Iranian decision, allegedly taken in the autumn of 1949, to commence once more with the deportation of Jews in response to a massive upsurge in the numbers fleeing Iraq in the face of renewed persecution. The Foreign Ministry therefore decided to act on several fronts concurrently. To begin with, Iranians would be offered commercial opportunities in the Jewish state as an incentive towards recognition. In particular, Israel made it known that it wished to purchase manufactured products as well as raw materials, consumer goods and foodstuffs from Tehran that Israeli industry might need, such as fish, meat, preserves, agricultural produce, pelts, wool and carpets. Underpinning this idea was a belief that by developing business links with interested parties in Iran such commercial ties would result in pressure being brought to bear on the Iranian government to recognise

Israel, thereby allowing trade to develop still further to the mutual benefit of all concerned.

This proposal was initially passed on to and dealt with not by Mossad or the Jewish Agency personnel in Iran—the direct Israeli agents in situ—but rather by a US diplomat named Gideon Hadary who served as a State Department intelligence officer at the US embassy in Tehran.[12] Although born in Chicago, Hadary had spent much of his youth in pre-state Palestine before returning to the United States to study. During the war he had been recruited into the Office of Strategic Services, the forerunner of the Central Intelligence Agency, and he was thus well versed in the ways of secret service. Given this and his own political sympathies, Hadary was on good terms with several Mossad and Foreign Ministry officials in Israel, who gave him the codename 'Adam'. As such, he now came to play a major covert role in liaising at the highest level between Israel and the Iranian authorities. Due largely to his initiative and his secret activities—activities that were supported by Mossad officers inside Iran—Israeli pressure for recognition brought some success. The Foreign Ministry in Jerusalem was certainly swayed by the optimistic appraisal of Hadary that the economic inducements on offer would be accepted by the Iranians. First of all, the proposal that Israel purchase substantial quantities of Iranian goods involving the payment of millions of dollars in foreign currency was, in view of the economic realities prevailing in Tehran at the time, extremely tempting. To this end, he felt that the government there could be influenced—in other words, bribed. As he noted somewhat laconically, 'The present members of the [Iranian] government know their time is up and that in a few months [with the king's return from the United States] they will no longer have any influence. They all want to gain something before it is too late.'[13]

Knowing this, Hadary was able to manipulate both national aspirations and personal avarice through the contact he had made with a key local personality, a merchant by the name of Ahad Wahab Zadah, a friend and discreet business partner of Iran's prime minister, Muhammad Maraghal Said. The merchant had already proven the extent to which he could influence Iranian government policy; he had ensured Tehran's support, under difficult and unusual terms, for an opium deal with the United States and had conducted negotiations with the Soviet Union for the purchase of 100,000 tons of wheat for Iran. It was Hadary's opinion that, '[T]his man could equally put pressure on the government to grant recognition, if it were financially profitable.'[14] He was a very shrewd observer of Iranian politics and his assessment eventually proved right. After a long process of clandestine bargaining the Iranian prime minister made it clear that the price for recognition of the Jewish state would be the personal payment of a couple of million Iranian rials, the 'clinging inducement' as it came to be known by Mossad officials.

In the first week of 1950 the pros and cons of accepting the terms of recognition were debated at some length among officials in Jerusalem. The humanitarian advantages seemed especially significant: above all else, recognition was likely to mean the salvation of Iraqi Jewry. The Mossad exerted heavy pressure in favour of the transaction, arguing that it would also bring about far-reaching changes in its capabilities, not least in its ability to penetrate other Middle Eastern states. Ranged against these arguments were several weighty considerations. To begin with, the agreement involved payment of what was at the time, and in view of Israel's desperate economic situation, an enormous sum of money. Second, the discussions in Tehran had revealed several disturbing facts, one being that the transaction apparently depended on a personal bribe paid to a single politician and not on the possible benefits it might bring Iran nationally. A third concern was the opposition to recognition current among influential circles in Iran and the uncertainty of the shah's position. These collectively raised the question of the actual value of recognition, not only practically—whether it could in fact be achieved and what might the end results look like—but also as a fundamental question of the Israeli government's mode of operation.

After prolonged bickering the deal was finally concluded. On 6 March 1950 the Iranian Cabinet decided on de facto recognition of Israel, and significantly, agreed to open up its borders to refugees fleeing Iraq. But while the 'Persian connection' now greatly facilitated the flow of Iraqi Jews to the Jewish state, Jerusalem remained dissatisfied that de facto recognition was the most that Israel could extract from Iran at the time. From the end of November until July 1951, considerable effort, both within Iran and beyond, continued to be expended in the attempt to extract de jure Iranian decision. For example, Muhammad Maraghal Said, by now the Iranian ambassador to Turkey, was approached by Israeli officials in the hope that he could exercise his influence over the Iranian government to confer such recognition, the Israeli argument being that '[A]s the man who gave us recognition and was paid for that service, he must feel responsible for the unpleasantness caused us by the rejections [de jure recognition] and [must] do all he can to settle the issue in the desired manner as quickly as possible.' For the most part, however, Israel attempted to work from within Iran, using the tried and tested technique of bribery. Jerusalem now sought to gain the influence of a local politician willing to champion the cause of full bilateral political relations and the man eventually selected for the task to all intents and purposes chose himself. From early 1949 a prominent Iranian politician named Zia ad-Din Tabataba'i had engaged the Israeli government claiming reparations for damage done during the 1948 war to his farm near Gaza. In late November 1950 he openly declared his willingness to aid the Israeli cause in return for expediting his reparation claims. The Israelis feared that if he was appointed to the Cabinet before his claims were settled, Tabataba'i might bring harm to Iranian Jewry and efforts to promote aliyah (immigration) to Israel.[15] On 13 April 1951, following lengthy deliberations and with the assistance of a fund-raising campaign among the local Jewish population, a Mossad agent reported that the deal had been concluded to settle the claim: 'I paid Tuvia [Tabataba'i] 100,000 [rials] and got a receipt from him. I ended the affair on a positive and friendly note. He promised to conclude our matter [de jure recognition of Israel] as soon as he made contact with Abdullah Entezam, the new Iranian Foreign Minister.'[16]

But the outcome of this Israeli matter was not entirely to Israel's satisfaction. We have no precise information on the exact chain of events in the Tabataba'i affair but it became clear that he did not, or could not, keep his end of the bargain. Moreover, information that arrived from Iran later led Israeli Foreign Ministry officials to conclude by mid-June that not only did Iran have no intention of posting a special emissary to Jerusalem, but that it even intended to rescind its de facto recognition of Israel. The Foreign Ministry was well aware that propaganda within Iran advocating the cancellation of all ties with Israel had increased. It was a demand that had been raised several times in the Majlis (parliament) and which enjoyed the support of the governing National Front Party under Mossedegh, which was closely allied to opposition religious parties and interest groups. As the political power of the National Front grew, so the likelihood of the annulment of de facto recognition of Israel became a strong possibility.

Such a decision was not unexpected in light of Iran's growing tension over the scale of its oil concessions to the United Kingdom, which only served to exacerbate still further Arab pressure on Tehran to annul recognition. Accordingly, Jerusalem feared the worst when, in his reply to a parliamentary question on 7 July 1951, the Iranian foreign minister announced before the Majlis that the Iranian consulate general in Jerusalem had been closed and that 'for the time being' Iran would not receive an Israeli envoy. However, what immediately caught the attention of the Israeli Foreign Ministry was the formulation of the announcement which indicated that closure of the consulate general in Jerusalem was not linked to any annulment of Tehran's de facto recognition of Israel. Later reports that reached Jerusalem subsequently confirmed this interpretation.

Undoubtedly, the closure of the Iranian mission in Israel did forestall Israeli hopes for full diplomatic relations between the two states. It brought home to Israeli Foreign Ministry officials that as much as Israel may have wished to repeat the success of gaining recognition from Turkey in 1949, existing conditions across the region—not least pressure from Arab states—precluded such ties from being established with Tehran. Moreover, such limitations meant that little possibility existed in the immediate future for ties to go beyond de facto recognition. Yet given these limitations, the ties that were established with Iran did herald a series of political, military and economic agreements with Tehran in later years that would have been unthinkable to Israel's early diplomatic pioneers. Self-interest certainly explains why Iran did not abrogate de facto recognition, and indeed, despite the closure of its consulate in Jerusalem, Iran proved keen to maintain strong ties with Israel albeit through less obvious channels. Having no access to Iranian documentation, we cannot reach definitive conclusions as to Iranian motives, but it is reasonable to assume that this formative period in relations with Israel, and the contacts established with Israel's representatives, demonstrated to Tehran the potential significance of ties to Jerusalem. Certainly, for Israel, this period served as a 'diplomatic laboratory' in terms of assessing the risks involved in dealing with uncertain interlocutors where avarice as much as sound statecraft determined the patterns and modes of diplomatic exchange. To this extent, the immediate experience of dealing with the Iranians precipitated an attitude of caution in Israel's diplomatic overtures to other regional players. Even so, in its attempts to breach what appeared to be the unified wall of Arab enmity towards the Jewish state throughout the 1950s, Israel learnt useful lessons and continued to reap some reward from the Iranian experience.

To begin with, the overt and unhampered presence of Israeli (non-diplomatic) representation in Tehran even after closure of the Iranian consulate in Jerusalem was the clear outcome of the political efforts previously invested in Iran. And this presence went far in creating continuity in relations between the two countries, allowing Israeli representatives to feel the pulse of Iranian politics and take advantage of opportunities to promote Israeli interests when they arose. Maintenance of de facto recognition and the Israeli presence in Iran were, however, only two of the Israeli achievements in the Iranian arena. No less important in the context of this period was the impact of aliyah activities in Iran on the fate of Iraqi Jewry. A definitive study has not yet been written on the motives and circumstances that lay behind the February 1950 Iraqi decision to permit emigration of Jews from Iraq. Certainly the formal explanations given cannot be taken at face value. The evidence in Israeli Foreign Ministry files points to, inter alia, two factors in particular: the Iraqi failure to prevent the illegal flight of Jews from Iraq to Israel via Iran, and the practical cooperation that developed between Iran and Israel that facilitated such immigration. It is therefore difficult to exaggerate the importance of Israeli activities in Iran regarding the intertwined issues of diplomatic recognition and aliyah. Certainly, the mass evacuation of Iraqi Jews to Israel via Iran can be considered one of the most remarkable achievements of the Jewish state in its formative years.[17] Moreover, the successful overtures that were now made to Tehran regarding the purchase of oil could not have been made had Jerusalem lacked the diplomatic ability to enter and exit Iran freely from 1950 onwards, and with it the establishment of open commercial links.

Opening the Iranian Oil Gates

From the declaration of independence onwards and especially after the establishment of Delek, Israel's state-owned oil concern, a key Israeli objective was obtaining secure supplies of oil from Middle East sources. This oil had two key advantages. Its basic price was generally less than that of alternatives from the American continent. In addition, the cost of transportation of Middle East oil via the Iraqi pipeline or Suez Canal was obviously less than imports from Venezuela or Mexico. This meant that the price of Middle East oil in Haifa in the early 1950s was 30 per cent cheaper than that imported from the Americas. Moreover, from the start, the Haifa plants had been constructed for refining Middle East (Iranian) crude, a grade that was lighter than other oils. The refining of other types of crude oil was more costly and created serious wear and tear on the machinery involved, while overall production did not measure up to the required basket of refined products vital for the development of Israel's petrochemical industry. This explains why oil imported from the Persian Gulf had been the preferred option of the British oil companies and for these reasons the pre-1948 supply to Palestine had been based on this source (and on Iraqi crude). It is not surprising, therefore, that shortly after the resumption of Haifa's refineries, the Anglo-Iranian Oil Company (AIOC) made an undisguised attempt to renew this supply source by circumventing the Iraqi pipeline.[18]

Operationally, by early 1953, Anglo-Iranian had an unmistakable interest in turning Kuwait into Israel's main oil source. The reason for this lay in the massive development of the Kuwaiti oilfields and the possibility of channelling the oil to the developing Israeli market without upsetting the post-war global allocation determined by the international oil companies. The merging of interests between Delek and the AIOC was realised in agreements that allowed Delek to purchase Kuwaiti oil from British sources. All these plans went awry, however, at the beginning of 1953 due to the intervention of the British Foreign Office. Its officials had grown increasingly apprehensive over the impact this commercial alliance would have in the Arab world if it was discovered that Britain was supplying Arab oil to Israel. Thereafter, starting in early 1954, all the British companies in Israel had to revert to importing expensive oil from Venezuela.

During this period Anglo-Iranian and Delek were unable to rely on Iranian oil because of the nationalisation by Tehran of its oil industry in 1951. The crisis, which was to last three years, prevented the use of Iran as a major source of oil, leaving British oil companies across the Middle East effectively moribund until early 1955. Delek, for its part, tried to overcome this plight by courting a huge increase in Soviet oil exports. Despite the opposition of the British companies, Delek lowered the price of crude oil, especially that of light fuel oil, which was vital to industry across Israel and in the production of electricity. Since the Soviets were offering their oil at such attractive prices with no political strings attached, the timing could not have been better from Israel's perspective. The result was that from late 1955 until late 1956, when imports from the Soviet Union ceased following the 1956 Suez campaign, Soviet oil supplied one-third of the country's needs.[19]

Despite this, in the mid-1950s Israel did not envision the convenient, cheap Soviet oil as a long-term strategic solution to its oil problem. The solution was seen exclusively in the import of oil from Iran, even before the possibility presented itself as an attainable objective. The main reasons for this were qualitative, both in terms of Iran's potential as a supplier as well as the political influence that could accrue with the purchase of Iranian crude. These factors led to the decision in 1954–5 to cut back the purchase of Soviet oil to one-quarter of the total oil imports in order to guarantee a diversity of supply sources, strengthen Israel's bargaining chip in negotiations with British oil companies and lessen the price of imports. The remaining oil imports—roughly three-quarters—were now expected to come from Iran.

This goal was ambitious, yet it was far from simple to achieve. The gates seemed to nudge open when, in August 1954, an agreement was signed between Iran and Britain settling the bitter dispute that had broken out in 1951 over the issue of nationalisation.[20] According to the terms of the agreement an international consortium was to be established for administering Iran's oil industry. A relatively large number of companies would make up the consortium, in which the British would forfeit their monopolist position. In addition, an Iranian national oil company, named NIOC, would be established, and given a production share of 12.5 per cent of the total allocated to the consortium and given the choice between production and selling or receiving money in exchange. These terms resulted in the opening of two channels of activity for Israel to secure the supply of Iranian oil: the first through connections with international companies (especially small ones known as the IRICON group, and several others that had no commercial ties with the Arab world); and the second by establishing immediate contact with NIOC, which was eager to flex its newly won rights and develop into an independent national alternative to the foreign companies that still dominated the oil industry in Iran.

Nevertheless, Israel had to confront the concerns of the oil companies operating in Iran over selling Jerusalem oil because of their anxiety over adverse reactions across the Arab world. In late 1954 it met this challenge on three fronts. The first was the signing of an agreement for the direct supply of Iranian oil, a move that created an important precedent in the eyes of the British, IRICON and NIOC. Fortune now favoured Israel when an Italian company, 'SUPOR', was found whose own status in Iran had suffered following the establishment of the IRICON consortium. SUPOR was prepared to take a chance and sign a deal in November 1954 to sell Iranian crude directly to Delek.[21] The signing of this deal (which was to go into effect in early 1955) played an important part in the negotiations that opened that month between Israel and foreign oil companies operating in the country. Israel's greatest achievement in these negotiations was an agreement with Royal Dutch Shell for a trial delivery of Iranian oil to Israel, although it stipulated that the continued supply of this source depended on reactions around the region. Since BP was more dependent on the Arab world it refused to take part in this arrangement, but due to the political volatility that now engulfed the Shell and SUPOR agreements, Israel now tried to make direct contact with NIOC. The ensuing negotiations met with success, and an agreement was signed in June 1955 according to which Iran would sell Israel 75,000 tons of Iranian crude. The agreement further determined that the sale would begin in October 1955, terminate in September 1956 and that the oil would be sold to an Israeli-owned straw company with front offices established in Geneva. The Iranians avoided the transportation issue that was intended to take place along the 'Vasco da Gama' route. The foreign companies active in Israel subsequently overcame their reservations and began importing Iranian oil to Israel.

The new map of oil supply to Israel that took shape in mid-1955 and remained in operation until late 1956 is instructive in that, contrary to received wisdom, by 1955 Iran had already become Israel's main source of crude oil. This situation remained in force throughout 1956 despite the American companies' decision to cease their operations in Israel following the Suez Crisis. Even Shell continued to supply Iranian oil in 1956 under the same conditions that were agreed upon in 1955. The foreign companies guaranteed two-thirds of Israel's consumer market, and the vast majority of the oil was supplied by Iran. In the same period Delek was supposed to provide slightly more than one-third of the total imports for domestic consumption, consisting mainly of crude oil and light fuel oil imported from the Soviet Union. These supplies were transported in a number of small tankers, some of which were Israeli-owned and had been bought with reparation money from West Germany, while others arrived on tankers which were leased.

The Sinai campaign in 1956 completely altered the map of Israel's oil supply by hastening the Soviet decision to cease providing Israel with oil and accelerating the departure of foreign companies from Israel the following year. Israel's alternative was the Iranian oil market, and in 1957 it now became Israel's main source of energy.[22] Israel's political interest in Iran at this point was exclusively economic. Oil was the main goal. The intelligence and military cooperation that developed between the two sides from 1958 onwards turned into a means of sustaining this source. For the next twenty years Israeli diplomacy would invest enormous resources to protect its Iranian supply line. It was only to end with the fall of the shah in 1979.

Conclusion

Given its paucity of natural resources and facing the political might of the Arab world, Israel's ability to sustain its oil industry and maintain a secure supply of oil was be considered one of the main triumphs of its use of clandestine diplomacy. Undoubtedly, Jerusalem was helped by the endemic corruption that afflicted the Iranian political system, but even so, its ability to identify and manipulate such practices allowed Israeli officials, most notably from the Mossad, an entrée into Iranian politics and society from which it was to reap rich rewards, not least in smuggling Jews out of Iraq before making aliyah to the Jewish state. Israel has always viewed such migration not just as a foreign policy goal, but a foreign policy value in its own right that encapsulates the very essence of Zionism. Coming at a time when Israel remained politically, economically and militarily vulnerable and looked to lessen its dependence on Western oil companies, its use of clandestine diplomacy to secure its energy supplies served in no small part that most existential of Israel's needs: the very survival of the state itself.

5

BACK-DOOR DIPLOMACY

THE MISTRESS SYNDROME IN ISRAEL'S RELATIONS
WITH TURKEY, 1957–60

Noa Schonmann

Introduction

A love affair has long been the metaphor of choice for observers of Israeli–Turkish relations. It surfaces in academic and media discourses as often as it does in policy-making and policy-analysis circles.[1] In 2007, for instance, the American ambassador to Turkey set out to review the 'flirtatious history' of this interstate relationship, comparing it to 'a late-life love affair'.[2] WikiLeaked in 2011, his confidential cable echoes a dispatch composed back in 1959 by the head of Israel's legation in Ankara, who referred to the same relationship as one of 'love outside marriage'.[3] Six decades of use and abuse may have beaten the metaphor into a cliché but it remains apt, effectively evoking the secretive, intricate and volatile nature of the Israeli–Turkish relationship.

From the outset Israel proved a keen suitor for Turkey, a Western-oriented regional power, and a Muslim democracy at that. Israel's courtship met with success for the first time in 1957, when Turkey signalled its willingness to engage in intense collaboration. Over the next decade meetings were held between the two states' prime ministers, foreign ministers, chiefs of staff and secret service directors. Protocols of economic cooperation were signed, and plans drawn for collaborative ventures in the fields of oil and water supply, industrial development, finance and tourism. Turkish and Israeli diplomats in Western capitals advocated one another's interests, coordinated votes in UN fora and launched parallel public diplomacy campaigns. So intimate was the relationship that joint military action-plans were drawn, military-industry technologies shared and sensitive intelligence exchanged.[4]

What is remarkable about this extensive array of activities is that it was largely kept out of the public eye, receiving little publicity at the time and decades on. More striking still is the fact that throughout this decade of closeness, formal relations between the two states remained at a very low level, with mere chargés d'affaires heading their reciprocal diplomatic legations. Turkey's insistence that the relationship be kept a secret led Israel's Prime Minister David Ben-Gurion to remark that 'The Turks have always treated us as one treats a mistress, and not as a partner in an openly avowed marriage.'[5]

Secrecy is by no means a condition of rare occurrence in international relations. States regularly withhold publicity on matters pertaining to their national security. Sensitive processes of negotiations are often subject to strict secrecy, as are episodic exchanges with adversaries, or the management of crisis situations. It is far less common, however, for states to conceal formally sanctioned relations with friendly states, certainly as far as these pertain to long-term, routine collaborations in civilian spheres of activity. It is this rather exceptional phenomenon, displayed in Israel's relations with Turkey between 1957 and 1960, that is the focus of this chapter.

To capture this peculiar mode of secret diplomatic practice, the term 'back-door diplomacy' is put forward. Diplomacy is defined here broadly, as the conduct of international relations by means short of war. Secrecy has proven to be one of the most pervasive and enduring features of diplomatic practice throughout history. Indeed, very few diplomatic interactions are ever conducted entirely in the public eye. This recognition, that almost all diplomatic interactions are kept a secret—wholly or in part, at one stage or another—from one or more interested parties, leads to the conclusion that it is hardly meaningful to speak of 'secret diplomacy' as an analytical category distinct from 'open diplomacy'. Recognising that secrecy is a matter of aspect and degree, this chapter pursues a more discerning distinction.[6]

Instead of secret diplomacy, the concept of back-door diplomacy is advanced here to denote the conduct of officially sanctioned relations between friendly states under conditions of secrecy as a matter of course. Contrasted with the more conventional practice of 'front-door diplomacy', the concept of back-door diplomacy highlights the opening of a marked gap between the low level of formal diplomatic representation between two friendly states, and the high-level of intimacy that comes to characterise their substantive collaborations. Framing interstate relationships in terms of back-door diplomacy calls attention to this gap between the formal and substantive dimensions of interstate relations, and raises a fundamental question: why would states consent to straddle such an uneasy gap? What could induce them to occupy this precarious position, in which they stand highly exposed to public scandal, external manipulation and the constant turn of political tides?

The chapter takes a first step towards answering this general question by looking at the case of Israeli–Turkish relations in the 1950s. Its analysis builds on an outline of the principal rationales for front-door and back-door diplomacies. Front-door diplomacy operates on the understanding that formality is prerequisite to substance. It assumes that normalised diplomatic relations provide the most solid foundations for long-term substantive collaborations between states. The practice of back-door diplomacy, on the other hand, is employed when circumstances preclude normalised diplomatic relations. It operates principally on the understanding that when the only open door is the back door, informality is the price of substance. States turn to this option when both are equally loath to forge formal relations, or when one stipulates to another a precondition of informality for substantive collaboration. Recognising such constraints, states may settle for an informal framework in the understanding that although their capacity to sustain substantive collaborations is lesser, it enables them to satisfy certain immediate needs. Thus they opt to straddle the gap between formality and substance when they perceive the benefits of substantive collaboration to outweigh the risks inherent in informal relations.

At first glance, the rationale behind Israel's resort to back-door diplomacy in its early relations with Turkey appears straightforward. The ring of Arab hostility surrounding the nascent Jewish state put a high price tag on establishing normalised diplomatic relations with it. Israeli policy-makers perceived Arab animosity as a serious and imminent threat, and saw themselves compelled to conduct state affairs in flexible and unconventional ways. As Aharon Klieman put it, Israeli leaders often proved willing to 'set aside considerations of pride and diplomatic protocol, and make their peace with backdoor respectability'.[7] Indeed, the vulnerable and isolated Israel of the 1950s was in need of developing substantive collaborations with Turkey, and had little choice but to succumb to Turkey's preconditions of secrecy and informality if it was to fulfil this need.

Yet if it was the case that Israel understood and accepted the rules of back-door diplomacy, what could explain the growing sense of frustration and indignation that developed among its policy-makers and diplomats in the course of this decade of quiet collaboration with Turkey? Why was it that even though Israeli policy-makers seemed to work on the premise that informality was precondition to substance, their resentment towards the back-door situation swelled to the point of undermining collaboration with their Turkish counterparts? This chapter traces the narrative of Israel's resort to back-door diplomacy in the case of its early relations with Turkey. In so doing it seeks to explain the rationale behind Israel's concession to circumvent formal diplomatic procedures, and to question whether back-door diplomacy was a reasonable approach to fulfilling Israel's particular set of needs at the time.

Setting the Stage 1949–56

In March 1949, less than a year after Israel's proclamation of independence, Turkey became the first Muslim state formally to accord the Jewish state de facto recognition. The move signalled not a pro-Israeli stance, but rather Turkey's determination to align itself with the Western powers. Keen to mitigate Arab backlash, Turkey put off the exchange of diplomatic representatives with Israel. It was only in December that legation-level missions opened in Ankara and Tel Aviv. Quietly, Israel was informed that it should regard the legations' opening as Turkey's extension of de jure recognition.[8] Turkey's proclivity for concealing and downplaying its relations with Israel was thus evident from the start. Its initial manoeuvres clearly signalled the limits of its willingness to engage with Israel in the international arena.

Following its admittance into NATO in 1952, Turkey began courting Arab states to join Western-led regional defence schemes. In late 1954, Israel anxiously looked on as Turkey negotiated the Baghdad Pact agreement with Iraq. In the process, Turkey was censured for maintaining cordial relations with Israel, and in response tried to minimise them. Desperate to salvage what it could of the nascent relationship, Israel proposed quiet collaboration in the military field. In so doing, Israeli policy-makers were acknowledging the constraints under which relations with Turkey were to be forged, and already at this preliminary stage were signalling back their willingness to resort to back-door diplomacy.

Turkey's initial response was promising. The Israelis were told by the secretary general of the Turkish Ministry of Foreign Affairs (MFA) that Turkey was 'obviously interested in tightening the relationship between the militaries … but let's avoid delegations and publicity'. The Turkish official was also quick to recognise the pitfall of back-door diplomacy. He implored his Israeli interlocutors 'not to get offended by the whisper of Turkey's solid friendship for Israel', and assured them that Israel 'was not like a lover with whom the husband secretly cheats on his Arab wife, while openly denying any relationship with her'.[9] In any case, Israel's initiative proved inopportune. Delivered shortly thereafter, the Turkish prime minister's formal reply made it abundantly clear that he did not appreciate Israel's 'attempt to obstruct Turkey's Middle East foreign policy'.[10]

Turkey's efforts to draw the Arab states into the Western orbit dictated the slow pace and low profile that characterised the development of relations with Israel in the early 1950s. These fragile relations took a major hit in 1956. Following the Suez War, mounting anti-Israeli sentiment in the Arab world drove Turkey to downgrade diplomatic representation. It recalled its minister, leaving a chargé d'affaires ad interim to head the Turkish legation in Tel Aviv.[11] Despite the high points yet to come in Israeli–Turkish relations, diplomatic representation would not be raised beyond this level before 1992. From this point on the story is one of Israel's struggle, in vain, to restore its formal ties with Turkey.

A Foot in the Door 1957–9

Relief came in the summer of 1957 as the West grew anxious over Syria's apparent move into the Soviet orbit. Frustrated with Washington's inaction, Turkish Prime Minister Adnan Menderes decided to open a back-channel to Israel. He sent his confidant Burhan Belge to meet with Israel's head of legation in Ankara, Moshe Alon, in order to suggest that 'something could be done to curb this dangerous development immediately' by Israel and Turkey.[12]

The prospect of a possible thaw in relations with Ankara stimulated a series of high-level consultations at the Israeli MFA. Discussions seemed to reflect a clear understanding on Israel's part of the principles governing the practice of back-door diplomacy. Discussants agreed that Turkey was unlikely to risk moving openly towards Israel. In light of this constraint, MFA Director General Walter Eytan suggested that Israel attempt to expand contacts with the Turkish military, 'which could be done with less publicity'.[13]

The man assigned the task was Eliahu Sasson, Israel's ambassador to Italy who previously served as the first head of legation in Ankara, and in that capacity had developed warm personal relations with Menderes. Sasson was instructed to try and schedule a secret meeting with the Turkish prime minister. In accepting his mission, Sasson highlighted the need to get Menderes to overcome his inhibitions over dealing with Israel by promising him 'something concrete' in the military or economic fields. To ensure the meeting's secrecy, Sasson further counselled against making contact through the Turkish MFA, recommending instead a secret, informal line of communication—the Belge backchannel.[14]

In choosing to follow this course of action, Israeli policy-makers appeared to be signalling their willingness to engage with Turkey on its own back-door terms. They accepted that secrecy and informality were preconditions for the forging of substantive collaboration. But to what extent and for what purpose exactly? A cable from Sasson to his superiors elucidates. In considering his options, Sasson noted that if Israel was 'merely striving to tighten its relations with Turkey in secrecy' it could settle for backstage activities, such as initiating quiet talks between their ambassadors in Washington. Sasson anticipated that such endeavours would encounter no difficulties, as Turkey 'would welcome any exchange of information and cooperation with us … as long as it is done secretly, allowing it to continue to appear publically as supporting the Arabs'. However, if Israel 'was hoping to restore "past glory" and stop Turkey from continuing to support the Arabs', Sasson argued that far more strenuous efforts were required, specifically 'the storming of all decisive constituencies in the United States, and of all Nato member states, and at the same time rather than prior to it, establishing direct contact with Menderes'.[15]

The latter was the course of action taken. While awaiting Menderes's response, Israeli policy-makers began to increase pressure on Turkey to restore diplomatic representation. Israel's ambassadors were instructed to press Western governments to appeal to Turkey to cultivate its relations with Israel.[16] This correspondence shows that while Israel was interested in developing substantive ties with Turkey, it did not aspire to do so merely for the sake of attaining the concrete benefits of behind-the-scenes political and security collaboration. No less important to it was the issue of restoring formal diplomatic relations. Israel wanted to signal this intent to Menderes, but would only do so indirectly, for fear he would recoil from the entire initiative.

Israel's sustained efforts to draw closer to Turkey paid off when Menderes consented to a discreet meeting with Sasson in Paris in December 1957, marking a turning point in Israeli–Turkish relations.[17] Sasson reported back to the MFA about a shared willingness to explore ways to deepen cooperation between the two governments. Although secrecy and informality served as premise for this meeting, Menderes did recognise Israel's marked interest in formalising bilateral relations. He said that he had been looking for an opportunity to restore diplomatic representation, and intended to reinstate ministers of legation within eight months. In the meantime, however, he suggested that the governments settle for regular secret meetings between Sasson and Foreign Minister Fatin Rüştü Zorlu.[18] Eager to win Menderes's confidence, Sasson proposed to establish contact between the Israeli and Turkish secret services. His interlocutors requested time to consult and think the matter over.[19]

In January 1958, Foreign Minister Golda Meir charged Sasson with the 'delicate and difficult' task of scheduling a follow-up meeting with Menderes.[20] A memo prepared by MFA Political Advisor Reuven Shiloah set out the guidelines for further communications. Sasson was instructed 'to latch on to Menderes's word that he intended to reinstate ministers to the two capitals within eight months', and try to work out the specific steps involved in restoring diplomatic relations. However, if Sasson were to get the impression that such a plan was impractical and its implementation might drag out, he was instructed to settle for back-door relations. Sasson was told that Israel would agree to dispatch to

Ankara a high-ranking diplomat who would retain the title of chargé d'affaires if he were guaranteed access opportunities equivalent to those of a diplomatic minister. Furthermore, until such a time that full diplomatic relations were restored, Sasson was to strive to establish regular, if secret, contacts by instituting monthly meetings between himself and Menderes or Zorlu, and by asking them to facilitate Alon's access to high-level Turkish officials. Sasson was also instructed to try and establish concrete arrangements for regular consultations between the Israeli and Turkish general staffs, and propose cooperation between their diplomatic missions in Western capitals and in the UN.[21]

Sasson's letter to Menderes followed these guidelines. It added that Israel sought to preserve the regional status quo and would take action to prevent Lebanon and Jordan from joining Egypt and Syria in becoming Soviet satellites. He therefore proposed initiating 'tight and fundamental cooperation' in the form of military and political exchanges of information.[22] Sasson reported to the Israeli MFA that he decided to bring up such sensitive issues in his letter only to present Menderes with 'some proof of the importance of relations with Israel, and ensure that he fulfils the promises made in our Paris talk'.[23]

At the outset, it emerges, Israeli policy-makers prioritised the need to forge substantive collaboration with Turkey over the demand to formalise interstate relations. This priority was clearly articulated both in their internal discussions and in communicating their terms to Turkey. Yet the rationale for Israel's concession to circumvent formal diplomatic procedures and engage in back-door diplomacy was not a straightforward one of accepting informality as the price of substance. Israeli policy-makers were certainly interested in opening avenues of substantive collaboration for their own sake. But by no means were they ready to give up on the prospect of upgrading formal relations with Turkey. In fact, they sought to use these avenues of political, security and economic collaboration to induce Menderes to overcome his inhibitions and openly deal with Israel. Indeed, they persistently raised the issue and sought to concretise any encouraging Turkish statement to this effect. However, they were willing to pursue this aim only as far as it did not endanger the fragile rapprochement itself.

It took another regional crisis to jolt Turkey into full-fledged collaboration with Israel. On 1 February 1958 the establishment of the United Arab Republic (UAR), a union between Egypt and Syria, was announced.[24] Menderes first pressed London and Washington 'for immediate action inside Syria', but it soon transpired that neither could be persuaded to partake in a conspiracy to overthrow the Syrian regime.[25] Turkish officials again decided to take the matter up with Israel. Zorlu, who had postponed scheduling a follow-up meeting with Sasson since January, finally proposed to meet him in Paris in April.[26] In their meeting, he said the need of the hour 'was to demolish this union while there was still time, and that could only be achieved through a coup from within'. To that end he suggested arranging a secret conference of Turkish and Israeli security experts to explore possible courses of action.[27]

Ben-Gurion instructed Sasson to reply that 'Israel would not involve its military or arms in any internal Arab coup, but was willing to engage in political cooperation with Turkey and any other friendly state.'[28] When he reconvened with Zorlu two weeks later, Sasson sought a way around outright rejection of Turkey's conspiratorial proposition. He said he had not asked his superiors for a clear-cut response, and proposed to convene the secret conference of Israeli and Turkish experts to conduct a thorough assessment of the situation before discussing the operation itself any further.[29] Sasson later reported to Meir that had he executed his instructions faithfully, contact with Zorlu would have discontinued. He opted to push for the experts' conference so as to bring Turkey 'in an indirect way to sit at one table' with Israel. Zorlu agreed to Sasson's suggestion, but to ensure complete secrecy requested that the conference be held in a European capital, and that the experts would not to be notified in advance of their study's objective.[30]

The week-long security experts' conference took place in June 1958, in a villa on the outskirts of Rome.[31] Israel's delegation was instructed to try and get the Turks to recognise the danger Nasser posed to regional security, and develop a permanent framework for cooperation between the governments and secret services of Israel and Turkey, as well as between them and the region's other periphery states—namely Iran, Sudan and Ethiopia—for the purpose of initiating clandestine operations in the political arena. These objectives were achieved in full, and a meeting between Israel and Turkey's foreign ministers was scheduled for 2 August.[32] The technical nature of this experts' meeting dictated the narrow concrete objectives set for it. The issue of diplomatic representation was left for the higher level follow-up meeting.

In the meantime, the radical tide of Arab nationalism that swept through Lebanon and Jordan hit Iraq, where a bloody coup toppled the

Hashemite monarchy on 14 July. It gave fresh urgency to the foreign ministers' meeting that took place in Zurich two weeks later. Meir arrived under the pretence of a stay at a health resort. Zorlu travelled incognito, concealing his visit even from the Turkish ambassador in Bern. Having exchanged assessments of international and regional developments, the two foreign ministers agreed to institute effective working relations between their governments, their general staffs and heads of secret services.

The meeting took place nearly eight months after Menderes's meeting with Sasson, in which he announced his intention to restore diplomatic relations with Israel. It was Zorlu who broached the thorny issue. He told Meir that while diplomatic representation ought to be restored, he did not believe the time was right, for Nasser would undoubtedly exploit the move to pressure the pro-Western Arab states. Meir strongly objected to this line of reasoning. Shiloah and Sasson further pressed their Turkish interlocutors, saying that Meir considered cancelling the afternoon session as a result. It is impossible to establish whether Meir's threat to halt discussions was serious or empty, but evidently it sufficed to make the point that Israel was keen to have the matter satisfactorily resolved. Zorlu moved to suggest that a meeting be scheduled between the two prime ministers, at which point the question of diplomatic representation would reach a positive conclusion. Meir accepted.[33]

The historic meeting between Turkish and Israeli prime ministers took place in complete secrecy in Ankara on 29 August 1958. A concluding document, signed by the two prime ministers, indicates that they 'have now agreed to develop even closer military, economic, political, scientific and cultural cooperation between the two countries'. It was also decided that diplomatic representation would be upgraded to ambassadorial level within four months.[34]

Chronicle of Indignation Foretold 1959–60

With this document formalised, Israeli policy-makers believed their foot was firmly wedged in Turkey's door. The first year of substantive cooperation proved highly rewarding in many respects. Significant strides were made in terms of the volume and intensity of political and economic exchanges, as well as in military and intelligence collaborations. The one area that proved decidedly difficult to advance was that of formal relations. Menderes had promised Ben-Gurion that ambassadors would be exchanged by January 1959, and as soon as the United Nations General Assembly (UNGA) vote on Cyprus was out of the way in early December, Israel expected him to fulfil his promise.[35]

Shiloah took the opportunity of a work visit to Ankara in late December to put the matter to Zorlu. Having concluded their discussions on the regional situation, Shiloah said that Ben-Gurion had now authorised him to finalise arrangements for the imminent exchange of ambassadors. Zorlu promised they would resolve the matter before Shiloah's return to Israel. Yet, at the end of the week, it was again Shiloah who had to broach the topic. Zorlu asked him to inform Ben-Gurion that Menderes intended to keep his promise, but the right moment had to be found. He understood Israel's demand, but establishing embassies was ultimately just a formality and what mattered was that substantive relations of cooperation were well under way. For the time being, he advised, Israel should not attempt to precipitate matters.

Shiloah responded angrily, saying his superiors had regarded the matter as closed and expected him merely to finalise arrangements for opening embassies. Shiloah pointedly remarked that he hoped Turkey's evasion would not affect the tightening cooperation between the two states, but could not pretend that it did not damage the integrity of the understandings reached. He did not hesitate to evoke 'all the UN friends' that Israel had mobilised in support of Turkey, who were puzzled by the anomalous state of relations between the two states. Zorlu remained unmoved. Was the foundation of Israeli–Turkish cooperation so shaky, he wondered, that as superficial a matter as embassies could spoil it? Shiloah retorted that Israel did not consider the matter to be merely superficial. It would be impossible, he said, to continue this 'secret romance' for long. Upon departing, Shiloah said that on the occasion of an upcoming visit of Adnan Kural, who was informally designated as Turkey's ambassador to Israel, he would be expected to deliver clearer news regarding the restoration of diplomatic relations.[36] But Kural arrived in Israel 'armed with nothing but non-committal reassurances'.[37]

Disillusionment set in as repeated attempts to raise the issue met with a wall of Turkish evasiveness. By now it must have become painfully obvious, even to the most naive or optimistic of Israeli policy-makers, that their Turkish counterparts were leading them by the nose, with little intention of fulfilling the promise. Frustrated by the Turkish wavering, Israeli policy-makers sought ways of holding Menderes to his word.

Sasson advised that Shiloah entirely avoid Zorlu during their next meeting, and even go as far as conditioning Ben-Gurion's participation in the planned heads-of-government meeting on the restoration of diplomatic relations. He warned that by continuing to develop secret cooperation with Turkey, despite its refusal to normalise relations, Israel was creating the impression that it could be manipulated. Sasson suggested reminding Zorlu, rather bluntly, why Turkey needed to cooperate with Israel against Nasser. Zorlu may wish to take into account, he noted, that if the two did not work together to preserve Iraq's independence from Nasserist or Soviet takeover, Israel may well opt to support Iraq's inevitable partition into a Kurdish and an Arab state.[38]

Sasson's heated suggestions notwithstanding, the Israeli MFA seems to have decided to give Turkey the benefit of the doubt for a while longer, while continuing to develop substantive cooperation between the two states. The Turks for their part continued to obfuscate and Israel's patience was now wearing thin. In an internal MFA discussion, Meir described Zorlu's latest promise to upgrade relations soon after the next UNGA session, scheduled for September 1959, as 'unfair', and noted that she did not want him left with the impression that he had managed to pacify Israel. Israeli officials should not appear resentful towards Turkey, Meir instructed her subordinates, but they should no longer raise the topic of diplomatic representation. At the same time, Israel's newly established consulate in Cyprus was directed to strive to repair relations with Turkey's traditional adversary, Greece.[39]

When, in his next meeting with Alon, Zorlu failed to raise the issue of diplomatic relations, the Israelis grew wary and decided to step up the pressure. Alon was instructed to withhold Israel's reply to Zorlu's request for assistance in pressing Washington to join the Central Treaty Organisation (CENTO), and support for Turkey's candidacy for a non-permanent seat at the UN Security Council (UNSC). Instead, Alon told Zorlu that such matters required serious discussion, and he therefore proposed a high-level meeting with Meir on the sidelines of the upcoming UNGA session. When Zorlu accepted, Alon remarked that on that occasion Meir would be expecting to hear something concrete regarding the restoration of diplomatic relations.[40]

In the run up to the crucial meeting between Zorlu and Meir, Israel's representatives were instructed to refrain from raising the issue of diplomatic relations in conversations with Turkish interlocutors because 'expressing anger would only prove weakness, and arguing would only damage Israel's prestige'.[41] Several days before the meeting, Sasson was informed that Zorlu intended to speak to Meir about the designated date for restoring relations. Sasson wryly responded that if Zorlu was thinking of requesting another postponement, he best avoid raising the issue altogether. The Israelis should therefore have been less surprised when Zorlu opted to do just that. When the two foreign ministers met in New York in late September 1959, Meir consented to help Turkey convince US public opinion of CENTO's importance. Zorlu discussed ways of intensifying joint action in Western capitals. Neither addressed the proverbial elephant in the room.[42]

It was now clear to the Israelis that Zorlu had no intention of restoring diplomatic relations anytime soon.[43] Although Meir had determined in June 1959 that Israel's frustration with Zorlu's evasions ought not interfere with the substantive aspects of bilateral cooperation,[44] it seems that their futile UNGA meeting had stretched her patience to the limit. 'The fact that Turkey did not even deem it necessary to apologise in October 1959 is humiliating', an MFA official wrote in early November, capturing the Israeli state of mind. 'Of course the existing contacts are better than nothing, but the bitter taste of the unfulfilled promise taints the entire relationship.'[45] Over the next six months Israeli–Turkish relations grew markedly strained.

While the Israeli MFA resolved not to make the restoration of diplomatic relations a precondition to continued military, economic and political cooperation that was in Israel's interest, its dissatisfaction with this 'mistress relationship'[46] was clearly demonstrated by a far less forthcoming attitude towards requests for assistance that were beneficial essentially for the Turks. Thus, despite persistent Turkish approaches, Israeli officials would not commit to supporting Turkey's candidacy for a non-permanent UNSC seat in late 1959 and refrained from lobbying on its behalf, even though Turkey was indeed Israel's preferred candidate.[47] In consultation with Meir it was decided to cut back on the intelligence information and assessments transferred to the Turks, so that they 'would sense this, and start coming to Israel for it'.[48]

Despite the growing resentment and flagging willingness to support one another's political causes on the international arena, Israel and Turkey carried on cooperating throughout this period in so far as key common interests were concerned. Much of Israel's efforts in the first half of 1960 focused on trying to schedule a personal meeting between Sasson and Menderes, in a last-ditch attempt to get relations back on track.[49] This was not to be, however, as on 27 May 1960 a group of military officers overthrew the government. Menderes and Zorlu were arrested, and eventually hanged in September 1961.

The End of the Affair 1960–6

Many researchers point to the military coup of May 1960 as the termination point of the special relations forged between Israel and Turkey in August 1958.[50] Others conclude that relations were sustained, and in many ways even flourished, through the mid-1960s, and the documentary evidence in the Israeli State Archives bears out their assertion.[51] Relations progressed and diversified. For a brief period Turkey even agreed to 'appear together in broad daylight' with Israel, in the words of Moshe Sasson, Israel's new head of legation in Ankara (and Eliahu Sasson's son).[52] In one respect, however, nothing changed. Efforts to restore diplomatic relations yielded little results.

Sasson had been facing growing resistance from his colleagues in Jerusalem as he urged them to see the broader picture and show restraint and patience. While he agreed that Israel should not give Turkey the impression that 'it would put up with anything', he reminded them that restoring diplomatic relations was a means to a higher end. 'We must not let our "exasperation" [over Turkish deferrals of diplomatic normalisation] cloud the broader picture of excellent and diverse relations.' He cautioned that there was very little room left for manoeuvre and sternly warned against hot-headed suggestions.[53] His warnings were mostly, but not always, heeded.[54]

A second meeting between Israeli and Turkish prime ministers, which took place in Paris in July 1964, marked the zenith of Israeli–Turkish relations. In the meeting, İsmet İnönü told Levi Eshkol that Turkey would continue to perceive Israel's enemies as its own, strengthen bilateral relations and take the first opportunity to restore diplomatic relations. When Eshkol expressed disappointment that Turkey had not yet taken that initiative, İnönü turned to his foreign minister and asked: 'So when can we exchange ambassadors?' The matter was top-priority, came the response, and it would be resolved 'shortly',[55] in a matter of weeks.[56]

Whether İnönü had made another knowingly empty promise to Eshkol mattered little. Soon thereafter domestic and international developments came to shift Turkey's foreign policy course. The Cyprus crisis that erupted in December 1963 and the rise to power of Süleyman Demirel's Justice Party in October 1965 heralded the end of the Israeli–Turkish affair. Turkey's foreign policy was shifting from a line of quietly yet consistently developing relations with Israel, to one that fully prioritised rapid and ostentatious development of relations with the Arab states, at Israel's expense.[57] The substantive collaborations between Israel and Turkey had little to sustain them but tacit understandings and hollow assurances. The final blow came in May 1966, when Turkey's foreign minister informed his Israeli counterpart of Turkey's resolve to end all 'direct contacts' between their senior officials, military and civilian.[58]

Conclusion

In terms of the secrecy surrounding it, the case of Israel's early relations with Turkey may be remarkable, but it is not altogether extraordinary in the history of the country's foreign relations. The State of Israel is one actor on the world stage that, as Klieman put it, has turned secrecy 'into a diplomatic art form'.[59] Klieman's study, *Statecraft in the Dark*, distinguishes Israel as an exceptional actor on the world stage in terms of the broad scope and relative frequency of the state's resort to secret diplomatic activities. 'Open, formal ties are really only the tip of the diplomatic iceberg', he concluded.[60]

It is beyond the scope of this chapter to establish a firm claim as to the relative prevalence of the practice of back-door diplomacy in the context of Israeli statecraft, and indeed beyond, but even a cursory glance at its history turns up some potential case studies. First to come to mind are Israel's other periphery pact partners. In the mid-1950s Israel developed its relations with Turkey in parallel to relations with two other non-Arab states on the periphery of the Middle East: Iran and Ethiopia. All three channels of collaboration came under the framework of the periphery pact, an ambitious foreign policy initiative that sought to establish Israel at the apex of this tripod regional grouping. Israel's relations with the three periphery states developed along different trajectories and at different paces, reflecting the domestic and international circumstances particular to each partner-state. Nonetheless, a marked gap between the formal and substantive dimensions of routine interstate relations opened in all three cases.

Two altogether different examples suggest that Israel was just as capable of being the party that insists on the opening of this gap, as it was the party hoping to close it. First, the case of Israel's early relations with West Germany, which saw more than a decade of extensive reparation payments, infrastructure development projects and secret arms deals preceding the establishment of formal diplomatic relations in 1965. Second, the case of Israel's relations with apartheid South Africa, which saw the practice of back-door diplomacy extended beyond Israel's founding period. In this instance, both states had reason to refrain from normalising diplomatic relations. With only consul generals in place up to the mid-1970s, their defence industry and political exchanges quietly flourished in the aftermath of the June 1967 war.

This chapter sought an explanation for Israel's willingness to apply an extraordinarily high-level of secrecy to what essentially was a case of routine, long-term, officially sanctioned exchanges with a friendly government, Turkey. To this end, an examination of the operational logic underlying Israel's practice of back-door diplomacy was undertaken by constructing a historical narrative of the rise and demise of its early relationship with Turkey, based on a pool of newly declassified documents filed in the Israeli State Archives.

As suggested in the introduction, the basic rationale for front-door diplomacy assumes that form breeds substance. The practice of back-door diplomacy, on the other hand, operates principally on the rationale that when full diplomatic relations are not an option, states may settle for an informal framework that would enable them to satisfy certain immediate needs. This emerges as a reasonable course of action when they perceive the benefits of substantive collaboration as outweighing the risks inherent in informal relations—public scandal, external manipulation and systemic volatility. Israel, it appears, was not ready to prioritise substance over form. Wanting both, it practised back-door diplomacy believing it could turn conventional logic on its head—it worked on the assumption that over time substance would yield form.

The narrative suggests that while Israel engaged in back-door diplomacy, it never actually accepted the terms of the back-door game. The decision to straddle the precarious gap between substance and form did not follow on from the prioritisation of substance over form. Rather,

Israeli policy-makers sought to develop in parallel both dimensions of relations with Turkey. Only very begrudgingly did they end up paying for substance with the coin of form. Ultimately they may have deemed it a price worth paying, but it was not what they had in mind as they went along. It is argued here that, from the outset, Israel used back-door diplomacy as a foot-in-the-door tactic. The benefits of substantive collaborations with Turkey were no doubt of intrinsic value to Israel. But at the same time, and of equal importance, behind-the-scenes collaboration was meant to bring Turkey to recognise Israel's value as a partner, and put Israel in a position to press Turkey more effectively to close the precarious gap between substance and formality in their relations.

What appears to be a win–win strategy conceals an inherent tension. The beaten yet apt metaphor of an adulterous relationship goes a long way in helping us identify the source of tension underlying Israel's particular twist on the practice of back-door diplomacy. Throughout its engagement with Turkey, Israel aspired to achieve both substantive collaborations and diplomatic recognition. In pursuing both concurrently it gave its Turkish partner the substantive collaboration it wanted upfront, in exchange for a horizon of formal respectability, a course of action that inevitably bred frustration and indignation. It is this tension that triggered in Israel a pattern of behaviour characterised as the 'mistress syndrome'.[61]

Israel pictured a doomed-to-fail scenario, whereby Turkey would fall in love with its mistress. Hope that substance would yield form may be well placed when a clear sense of priority renders credible the threat to withhold substance if form is not forthcoming. Israel however tried to get Turkey to leave its Arab wife, but was not prepared to play hard-to-get by conditioning some or all of the substance of cooperation on the formalisation of relations. If the substantive benefits of a short-term relationship were clearly prioritised over form, and considered desirable enough in themselves, Israeli diplomats would have done well not to waste time and energy on half-hearted, empty threats to withhold substantive collaboration. Calls to take such a decision, and clearly prioritise form over substance or vice versa, were occasionally heard at the Israeli MFA but ultimately went unheeded.[62] Instead, Israel allowed resentment to build so far as to undermine substantive cooperation, while Turkey dangled the ring with promises of full diplomatic relations.

6

CONFRONTING CAIRO

ISRAELI PERCEPTIONS OF NASSER'S EGYPT, 1960–6

Yigal Sheffy

Introduction

The 2011 Arab Spring that swept across the Arab Middle East, and in particular the events in Cairo's Tahrir Square, brought to the fore in Israel questions that had practically disappeared from the public agenda for more than three decades. These questions revolved around the future of the 1979 Egyptian–Israeli peace treaty and the ability of the Israeli leadership and intelligence community to understand the conditions that led to mass unrest across the Middle East and North Africa, and more specifically the impact that the Arab Spring might have on bilateral ties with Egypt. In turn, this has also led to renewed interest in the pre-1979 period, with regard to previous Israeli views of Egypt and, in the light of new material being made available, the accuracy of these perceptions as they related to times of tension and conflict, most notably in the run up to the June 1967 and October 1973 Arab–Israeli wars.

Accordingly, this chapter examines Israel's perception of Egypt from the beginning of the 1960s through to the eve of the June 1967 war with a particular focus upon the assessments made by Israeli intelligence and defence officials of Egyptian strategy under the charismatic leadership of its president, Gamal Abd al-Nasser. Indeed, in the decade between the Sinai War of 1956—'Operation Kadesh' in Israeli terminology—and the outbreak of the June 1967 Six Day War the position of Egypt and its president as the self-declared leader of the Arab world dominated Israel's security horizons.[1] As such, this chapter begins by focusing on the deep impact that the so-called 'Rotem Affair' of February–March 1960 had upon Israel's conception of early warning. 'Rotem' was the Israeli codename for a surprise move by Nasser in which most of the Egyptian army—three divisions, about 500 tanks, 500 APCs and 330 guns—suddenly deployed along Israel's southern border in Sinai, ready to invade the Negev if Israel would attack Syria, at that time a part of the United Arab Republic (UAR), the union between Egypt and Syria. Israeli intelligence failed to detect the Egyptian build-up or issue sufficient warning. As a result, the Israel Defence Forces (IDF) were taken by complete surprise, waking to the danger on its border only after almost a week had passed and the Egyptian deployment completed. Throughout this time southern Israel was totally exposed to the real threat of attack. Only belatedly did the IDF raise its level of alert and deploy its regular forces and several mobilised reserve units to meet this looming threat. Although conflict was avoided, the trauma experienced by the IDF and AMAN (Israeli Directorate of Military Intelligence— DMI) continued to haunt Israeli decision-makers and intelligence officials for years to come and considerably influenced the political and military leadership in Israel over the extent to which it was willing to take strategic risks prior to the June 1967 war. Finally, the experience of the 'Rotem Affair' had a profound impact upon the Israeli intelligence community, most notably AMAN, and led directly to both a quantitative and qualitative investment in the provision of an early warning capability, something that has underpinned Israeli military doctrine ever since.[2]

Assessment of Egyptian National Security Policy Towards Israel

'Rotem' was indeed a milestone—perhaps even a turning point—in the development of Israeli intelligence, but as far as its impact on perceptions of Egypt were concerned, its main outcome was to reinforce existing assumptions held by the Israeli establishment vis-à-vis Egyptian national security policy towards Israel. Summarising the DMI and IDF annual and semi-annual reviews for the period (which will be referred to in detail below), it is apparent that these beliefs were governed by five basic assumptions:

1. Egypt was the major threat to Israel, due to its role as leader of the Arab world and as the only state bordering Israel possessing an army with sufficient offensive capability to threaten Israel.

2. The annihilation of Israel was an unchanging strategic goal of President Nasser. On the one hand, the 1956 war and the Anglo-French attack on Egypt impeded, at least temporarily, the ability of Nasser to achieve this goal, but on the other, his burning desire to avenge the defeat in Sinai at the hands of the Israeli aggressor served as a catalyst for taking all necessary steps to exact retribution. Hence an all-out war, led by Egypt, was unavoidable.

3. The Egyptian Army's expansion, modernisation and conversion to Soviet-bloc armament and military doctrine, which had begun in 1955 only to be interrupted by the 1956 war, resumed in earnest shortly afterwards. Even so, by the early 1960s Egypt—according to the prevailing Israeli view—was only too aware of its continuing inability to initiate a large-scale war against the Jewish state. This was due to the partial nature of its military build-up which had yet to reach maturity, as well as the growing splits within the Arab world which pitted republican regimes led by Cairo against their dynastic counterparts, most notably Saudi Arabia. This competition expressed itself most visibly in Yemen when a military coup in September 1962 overthrew the old imamate and ushered in an Egyptian-backed republican government. With Nasser anxious to ensure the survival of the new republican regime and anxious to bloody the nose of the House of Saud, Egypt committed increasing numbers of troops from 1963 onwards in its backing of the new regime. However, it soon became a war of attrition with the tribes in the north of Yemen choosing to remain loyal to the imam, backed by Saudi largesse in the form of money and weapons. Given his increasing difficulties in Yemen, AMAN remained concerned that Nasser might look to facilitate a crisis with Israel which, in the short run at least, could rally Arab opinion to Egypt's side, perhaps giving it a way out to extricate itself from the Yemeni morass. According to this view, therefore, Egypt was looking to regain the political initiative as well as its

operational freedom. Indeed, by also enhancing his air and missile strike capability with new Soviet and Egyptian-manufactured weapons systems, Nasser was looking to threaten the Israeli hinterland.

4. Nasser viewed Israel's developing nuclear capability in the form of the atomic reactor located just outside the small Negev town of Dimona as a strategic threat whose realisation would frustrate his military plan to destroy Israel and might even threaten his hegemony in the Arab world as well. He therefore saw no alternative but to act—either politically or militarily—in order to remove this looming threat before the Dimona reactor became operational.

5. Israel assumed that the region might equally slide into a wide-ranging war resulting from clashes elsewhere along its borders. This might be ignited on the Jordanian frontier because of Egyptian intrigue aimed at destabilising the Hashemite regime. With Syria, it was reckoned that conflict could be sparked by the 'war over the water'—the construction of the Israeli national water carrier and the Arab diversion of the headwaters of the Jordan River[3]—and from 1965 onwards, the sabotage activities of Palestinian Fatah guerrillas. Finally, there was also the probability that war might break out with Egypt should it attempt to attack Dimona or block the Straits of Tiran, thereby denying freedom of navigation to Israeli shipping and vessels bound for the Israeli port of Eilat at the end of the Red Sea.

As such, the Israeli political and military leadership shared the widely held perception that nothing less than the total annihilation of Israel dictated Egyptian policy toward the Jewish state. Looking through this Israeli prism, the prospects of reaching any sort of political or economic arrangement with Cairo was remote if not totally impossible. This perception was reinforced by experience, as several clandestine overtures made by Prime Minister David Ben-Gurion between 1961 and 1963 in an attempt to initiate talks with Nasser had come to naught.[4] This, apparently, left its mark on the new prime minister and minister of defence, Levi Eshkol, who assumed office in June 1963. A month later, reading an interview granted by Nasser to *Le Monde*, in which he had hinted at the possibility of peace, Eshkol asked the intelligence community to look into the matter and to make every effort to interview the reporter for *Le Monde* who broke the story in order to hear first hand what had actually been said. However, a discussion in his presence that followed this request, with the participation of deputy minister of defence,

Shimon Peres, the chief of the General Staff, *Rav-Aluf* (Lieutenant General)[5] Zvi Zur, the DMI and director of the Mossad, *Aluf* (Major General) Meir Amit[6] and others who were privy to Ben-Gurion's overtures, belittled the significance of such an interview and, as far as the available documentation suggests, the matter was dropped.[7]

Although most of the Israeli files regarding clandestine diplomacy during this period and the entire archives of the Mossad are still classified, one episode in particular, detailed in the memoirs of its former director, Meir Amit, sheds light on such episodes. Between 1964 and 1966 secret overtures were made to Cairo by the Mossad through an Egyptian intermediary, General Mahmud Khalil, who claimed he was operating on behalf of President Nasser and Minister of Defence Abd al-Hakim Amer. The talks centred on the possibility of Israeli financial loans being extended to Egypt and for Jerusalem to desist from exerting pressure in Washington to withhold economic aid to Cairo. In return, Israel looked for reciprocal gestures from Egypt, such as an easing of the Arab boycott against the Jewish state, the release of Jewish prisoners convicted in 1954 of spying for Israel—the so-called 'Bad Business' or *Esek Ha'bish*—and for Cairo to use its influence with Damascus to prevent the diversion of the headwaters of the Jordan River. The mood among the few Israelis involved was that 'we had indeed opened up a small crack in the wall that may make negotiations possible, and we should hold on to it for all it's worth and not let go'.[8] Yet, from a further reading of Amit's memoirs as well as records of discussions over this very issue that took place in the office of the minister of defence, one cannot escape the conclusion that most participants, including Eshkol, were captive to their own basic mindset, viewing Egyptian readiness to open talks as at best insincere, the mere purpose of which was at the very least to embarrass Israel or to gain influence in international forums such as the United Nations and other diplomatic arenas.[9]

This deeply rooted distrust of Egypt, a position not helped by an all out power struggle at the very apex of Israel's intelligence community that saw Amit pitted against Isser Harel, his predecessor at the Mossad and now Eshkol's advisor on intelligence, conspired finally to torpedo the continuation of the talks.[10] To be sure, the lack of Egyptian documentation regarding this episode makes it impossible to judge if the overtures had the potential to make any headway from the Egyptian perspective, or even whether the Egyptian leadership was truly involved in the process. It may have been another example of an alleged self-appointed envoy, whose interest was mainly prestige or financial gain. But what is absolutely clear is that it was the Israelis who backed off first from this diplomatic dialogue, however tentative it might have appeared. Viewed at the time through an Israeli prism, a dialogue with Cairo remained first and foremost a military one dictated by the perception of Egypt as an existential threat to the state.

The Timing of War

Such opportunities for dialogue, whether real or otherwise, were to remain rare until 1977. In reality, two conflicting basic assumptions—the Egyptian desire to obliterate Israel yet its inability to muster sufficient military strength to do so—now coloured the assessments of AMAN. An almost ritual but avowedly theoretical warning over Egypt's basic intent determined prevailing attitudes across the political and military elite up to 1967, but equally, AMAN also issued calming assessments to the effect that an Arab-initiated war was not to be expected in the near future. In December 1961, for example, AMAN asserted following the collapse of the UAR in October that 'Nasser realizes that he does not have the power nowadays to carry out his scheme against Israel for at least two years.'[11] Again in 1963, AMAN predicted that no major Arab offensive was to be expected before Egypt completed its military build-up plan sometime in 1965.[12]

Again, towards the end of that year, it maintained that 'Nasser will not put his might to test as long as he is uncertain of the outcome.'[13] Colonel Aharon Yariv, then the deputy DMI, told his colleagues at a General Staff meeting that economic aid given to Egypt by Washington might facilitate an Egyptian military build-up in the longer term, but that the conditions attached to such aid diluted the more immediate danger of war breaking out any time soon. AMAN therefore predicted with some confidence that the danger of an actual confrontation between the IDF and the Egyptian Army had been postponed to at least the end of the decade. A year later, in 1964, the intelligence assessment concluded that as long as the Yemenite conflict continued, and considering the international atmosphere, 'an Egyptian hostile initiative is not possible'.[14] It predicted that the civil war in Yemen would not end before 1966, and, therefore, that the threat of an Egyptian all-out offensive before 1968 was unlikely.

Nevertheless, towards the end of 1964 AMAN warned that the Egyptians had achieved a defensive capability which might tempt them to try and lure the IDF into making aggressive moves in Sinai, thus provoking an international outcry against premature Israeli aggression while concurrently providing Nasser with a legitimate pretext to act against Dimona.[15] By early 1965, Egypt's bellicose threats against Israel were certainly increasing, but Major General Yariv, Amit's successor as DMI, tried to assuage concerns that this might develop into a deeper crisis. He explained that Egyptian pressure for commencement of the diversion of the sources of the Jordan River—which might at first carry the risk of provoking a wider conflict—was mere rhetoric, as Nasser was certain that Washington would prevent Israel from committing any act of aggression.[16]

While intelligence assessments became increasingly alarmist in tone as far as limited action against Dimona was concerned, they did not revise their prediction regarding the likelihood of broader offensive moves by Egypt: this would not occur before 1968–9 and would most likely occur sometime around 1970–1. Nasser's speech at the second conference of the Palestine Liberation Organization (PLO) in May 1965 in which he stated that he would not go to war because of a single damaged Syrian tractor somewhere on the Jaulan (Golan Heights) while 50,000 Egyptian troops were still engaged in bitter fighting in Yemen appeared to suggest that supreme caution determined Cairo's view of Israel. When taken in conjunction with the evasive behaviour of Egyptian delegates during the second conference of Arab prime ministers, held in Cairo in May 1965, over a Syrian demand that an effective Arab military response was required following an attack by the IDF against the water diversion project on the Israeli–Syrian border, Israel's perception that Nasser remained determined to avoid involvement in a large-scale war with Israel was only reinforced.[17]

The last intelligence assessment prior to the June 1967 war presented early in March again predicted that no war was expected before 1970.[18] Furthermore, following the shooting down of six Syrian MiG fighters in April by the Israel Air Force—just two weeks before the Egyptian Army began its build-up in Sinai, the act that presaged the outbreak of the Six Day War—AMAN, perhaps still influenced by the fall-out from the 'Rotem Affair' issued an assessment that the Egyptian moves were of a piece with Nasser's preferred policy of brinkmanship.[19] When taken in conjunction with reliable intelligence reports that Nasser flatly rejected Syrian demands for retaliation, AMAN assessed that Egypt would act militarily 'only in case of a total Israeli offensive against Syria ... the current Egyptian cornerstone [of policy] is not to get involved in a war with Israel'.[20]

Collectively, such intelligence assessments led the military and political leadership to three operational conclusions. The first was that Israel's most important security interest was to delay the unavoidable war until the country possessed what was considered its ultimate means for deterrence. The intelligence annual assessment for 1966 stated that 'Israel's deterrence capability is the key and basis for its relations with our neighbours in the foreseeable future.'[21] However, if deterrence fails, Israel should be in a position to wage a large-scale war—either preventive or responsive—by conventional means. Israel was thus granted a period of grace to develop, enhance and increase, in a relatively calm environment, its military strength prior to the expected confrontation. Notwithstanding the need to be on constant alert and readiness against any eventuality deriving from deterioration along the northern or eastern borders, a larger part of the available resources could be allocated to a military build-up at the expense of immediate military readiness. This was the 'green light' which enabled the IDF to adopt in 1959 its first tri-annual build-up, the 'Bnei Yaakov' [Sons of Jacob] plan, followed by the 'Hashmonayyim' [Hasmoneans] and 'Bnei Or' [Sons of Light] plans in 1962 and 1965 respectively. All three greatly enhanced the army's capability on the eve of the war.[22] In addition, the major steps taken by Israeli intelligence in improving its early warning capability vis-à-vis Egypt (detailed below) contributed to increased Israeli self-assurance that they could put the emphasis on military build-up rather than on readiness.

The second operational conclusion was that Israel had been granted a golden opportunity to act freely against threats on other fronts, such as the water diversion project or Fatah activity whether in Syria or Jordan, with minimal risk of Egyptian interference. Even the mutual defence treaty concluded between Egypt and Syria in November 1966 was viewed by AMAN (although less so by the chief of the General Staff, Lieutenant General Yitzhak Rabin) as Cairo paying mere lip service rather than a pact that could trigger Egyptian military intervention so long as Israel restricted its actions in terms of both time and geographical space.[23] Ami Gluska, in a groundbreaking study on the events leading up to the Six Day War, demonstrated how these intelligence assessments contributed to the adoption of a hawkish line by the IDF General Staff towards Syria and their willingness to take risks.[24] Indeed, we now know that from early 1965 onwards several incidents that involved an exchange of fire between the IDF and Syrian forces over the continuation of the Arab water diversion project were actually initiated and even provoked by the IDF in the belief that an Egyptian military response was unlikely.[25]

The third operational conclusion, however, was that for Israel to complete its own military build-up it remained necessary to prevent the Egyptians from completing their own military preparations or, alternatively, from launching limited attacks against the Israeli rear areas and strategic infrastructure. To this end Israel now looked to support efforts that would keep a large portion of the Egyptian Army bogged down in the Yemen, while at the same time doing everything it could to neutralise the nascent Egyptian missile project and thwart any military attempt against Dimona.

The Bogs of Yemen

For the IDF, any opportunity to assist in keeping the Egyptians bogged down in Yemen far from Sinai and the Egyptian–Israeli border was one to be welcomed. The story of the Israeli involvement in the Yemen Civil War, until recently almost a state secret in Israel, has gradually come to be disclosed in recent years. Clive Jones was the first to point reliably to Israeli military assistance to the royalist forces loyal to the deposed imam through the covert supply of weapons and ammunition via parachute drops. Former *Sunday Telegraph* journalist Duff Hart-Davis revealed further details of these drops, and even in Israel, the case of 'Rotev' (sauce) and 'Durban' (porcupine), the codenames for the arms drops, have now been disclosed in the official journal of the Israeli Air Force.[26] For the purpose of this chapter—which is concerned with Israeli assessments of Egypt—it is sufficient to focus on only a few relevant points.

Extending military support to the Yemenite royalists was part of a broader Israeli policy of materially assisting internal forces opposing hostile Arab regimes, designed mainly to boost Israel's international and regional standing, while at the same time helping to impose costly campaigns of attrition on Arab armies in remote corners of the Middle East. Aside from Yemen, other examples of this practice include the well-known case of providing arms and military advisors to the Kurds in northern Iraq as well as the less well-known episode of the assistance given to the Anya Nya rebels in southern Sudan in the 1960s.[27] In the case of Yemen, there is no doubt that military considerations determined Israeli covert involvement. In total, some fourteen arms drops were carried out between 1964 and 1966 in which rifles, machine guns, anti-tank weapons, ammunition, mines, explosives and even two 20mm anti-aircraft guns were supplied (not to mention several cases of whiskey and beer dropped at the request of British mercenaries, mostly former members of the elite Special Air Service Regiment who were among those liaising between Israel and the royalist forces). Further drops were planned only to be postponed indefinitely because of technical or operational reasons, although at least one arms shipment was sent by other means after the June 1967 war.

But just as Israel assumed that military assistance to the Kurds in their struggle against Baghdad would never be enough on its own—and certainly not without the active participation of Iran—to keep Iraqi expeditionary forces away from Israel's eastern borders should war break out, so was there never any illusion on the part of the decision-makers in Jerusalem and Tel Aviv that Israel alone could impose a costly war of attrition on Egyptian forces in Yemen. The amounts of weapons and ammunition sent were simply not of a magnitude to tip a decision on the battlefield in favour of the royalists. Indeed, Israel's interest was to see war perpetuated for as long as possible and to avoid a clear-cut triumph for either side which could cause the Egyptian expeditionary forces to leave Yemen and return to Sinai. Accordingly, it was in the Israeli interest that this conflict, some 2200 kilometres from the Jewish state and which had imposed such a heavy toll on the Egyptian expeditionary force, should continue for as long as possible without a clear victor emerging.

To this end, Prime Minister Eshkol tried to reach a secret yet formal understanding with London over how direct aid to the royalists could best be provided, rather than relying on liaison through former British officers, who, however close their personal relations with key individuals in British intelligence, were effectively running a private operation that had been paid for by the Saudis. Indeed, Eshkol hoped a similar package of joint military assistance to the royalist forces could be arranged with the British government along similar lines to the agreement reached with the shah of Iran over military assistance given to Kurdish guerrillas in Iraq. Eshkol therefore proposed to raise the issue with Harold Wilson, the new British Labour prime minister, during their first meeting in London on 25 March 1965.

Official documents relating to the security aspects of their talks still remain classified. However, given the cautious conduct of Israel's future support for the royalists, coupled with a thinly veiled statement issued by a British Foreign Office spokesman in the immediate aftermath of the meeting that 'Britain opposed interference by any country in the region with the internal affairs of any other country and opposed encouragement of subversion in the Middle East area', then it is unlikely any agreement was reached.[28] Indeed, if Eshkol did actually raise the issue of Anglo-Israeli clandestine collaboration in support of the royalist forces—collaboration which from Israel's perspective would also help the British defend their military base in Aden—he was almost certainly rebuffed by a government decidedly uneasy over how best to deal with one of the last vestiges of the British Empire in the Middle East. This outcome certainly explains why Eshkol and even the usually combative chief of the IDF General Staff, Lieutenant General Yitzhak Rabin, now adopted a cautious approach towards future involvement in Yemen. Therefore, when it was suggested by some of the British mercenaries as well as serving IDF officers and members of the Mossad that Israel carry out the aerial bombing of Sana'a, this was rejected outright by both the prime minister and the chief of staff.[29]

While greater involvement in the Yemen Civil War was therefore deemed politically (as well as militarily) too risky, Israel still wanted to avoid acts that might precipitate a redeployment of Egyptian military forces from Yemen to the Sinai while at the same time wishing to maintain military pressure on Syria over its plans to divert the headwaters of the Jordan River. This need to calibrate carefully the use of military power for a defined political end certainly informed the discussions of the General Staff. That Rabin, as well as the more hawkish of his generals, were in favour of hitting Syria heavily—indeed, even increasing the tempo of active operations against Damascus—in the midst of the 'war over the water resources' and the subsequent escalation of fighting with Syrian-sponsored Fatah terrorists (especially after the rise of the Ba'ath regime to power in February 1966), is well known.[30] What has received far less attention in the extant literature is the extent to which perceptions of Egypt now determined Israeli actions. As noted, the IDF found itself on the horns of a dilemma: keeping the Egyptian Army pinned down in a costly war of attrition in Yemen was felt to give Israel considerable freedom of action against Syria. However, the General Staff was also of the opinion that the line should not be crossed by which intensified or prolonged Israeli actions against Syria might leave Nasser with no alternative but to act militarily if he wished to maintain his standing in the Arab world. Equally, the IDF was also concerned that tension in the north should not be used as diplomatic cover by Egypt to evacuate Yemen (an intention, AMAN believed, that was already uppermost in the Egyptian president's mind) even if this meant actually refraining from involvement in the Israeli–Syrian clashes.[31] As a result, proposals to widen operations against Syria during 1964–6 were considered, among other factors, with an eye upon their potential to provide Nasser with such an opportunity. In March 1965, for example, in the midst of the clashes along the northern border over the issue of water diversion, AMAN concluded that Nasser was attempting to pull his army out of the Yemeni morass, or, at least, to reduce substantially his military presence there. Therefore, plans for large-scale raids or for actual occupation of the high ground in Syrian territory on the Golan Heights, presented to the General Staff by the Operation Division of the IDF as one of the proposals for future military action, were rejected in favour of limited operations, involving artillery and air strikes on machinery associated with the diversion project rather than actual land-based operations that may have prompted Nasser to commit more fully to a withdrawal of his forces from Yemen.[32]

Perceptions of Egypt's Strategic Missile Capability

The subject of nuclear weapons in Israeli strategy and of the image of Israel as a nuclear threat in Arab eyes has been extensively discussed in the available literature.[33] What has received less exposure is the way Israel interpreted the effect of such an image on Egyptian determination to act and therefore the measures taken by Israel to confront this determination. The first public disclosure about the building of an Israeli nuclear reactor appeared towards the end of 1960.[34] Early in 1961

AMAN told its clients that Egypt could not ignore such information. According to the chief of AMAN, Colonel (later Major General) Chaim Herzog, the news had stunned Nasser, whose basic conviction—that time was on the side of the Arabs—was shaken.[35] The common view in the defence establishment was that Nasser would first try diplomatic means to frustrate Israel's nuclear ambitions, but, failing this, would consider applying military means, especially when the time for the reactor's activation drew near.

Israel's concern became more acute in 1962 when the first Badger (TU-16) long-range Soviet-built bombers arrived in Egypt, soon to be followed by the successful launch of four medium- and long-range surface-to-surface missiles which, according to Israeli intelligence, were to be armed with unconventional warheads.[36] Such weapons systems had the potential to alter dramatically the regional balance of power between Cairo and Jerusalem and increased the danger of a surprise attack on strategic targets, such as airfields, the Dimona complex itself or Israel's main urban areas, even if such an attack was designed to be limited in scope and scale. Issues such as the country's lack of strategic depth, a perception of decreased deterrence and with it a reduction in the early warning capability of the intelligence community were once again placed on the Israeli security establishment's agenda.

The 'Missiles' Scare', also known in Israel as 'the German scientists' affair', which evolved into a political crisis in June 1963 that finally ended Ben-Gurion's tenure as prime minister, is too well known to be repeated here. Suffice it to say that it was gradually realised that the Egyptian missile project had run into serious difficulties (mainly with regard to the small number of missiles produced and their deficient guidance systems), and by 1966 Israel's concern over the missile issue had largely abated.[37] Moreover, the rather upbeat assessment issued by AMAN that war with Egypt was not imminent, an assessment informed in no small part by Egypt's continued involvement in Yemen Civil War, served, at least temporarily, to lessen interest in Egypt's reaction to Israel's emerging atomic capability. It was revived again, however, in 1965, following a series of articles in the Arab and Egyptian press pointing out the danger of allowing Israel to develop its nuclear capabilities. Most outspoken were articles written by Muhammad Hassanyn Haykal, Nasser's close associate and published in *Al-Ahram* during October 1965, in which Haykal warned against the pending threat to the Egyptian nation by the near completion of the Dimona reactor. This new situation, he told his readers, would establish strategic parity between the Jewish and Arab states, preventing the latter from annihilating Israel.[38]

Late in February 1966, during the course of a press interview, Nasser now stated that Israeli nuclear efforts made an Egyptian preventive war unavoidable.[39] The articles left Eshkol and Rabin decidedly uneasy, while AMAN, although downplaying the declarations about preventive war, nevertheless, did amplify the increased danger of a limited strike on the Dimona reactor.

According to AMAN, it was only in late 1965 that the Arabs came to a clear realisation over the Israeli nuclear programme and that this might constitute an actual longer-term strategic threat.[40] The incumbent DMI, Major General Aaron Yariv, as well as Rabin, suspected that despite his military inferiority, Nasser might come to believe a strike against Dimona could remain an isolated event. Given the weight of international opinion that opposed the right of Israel to develop a nuclear capability in the Middle East, Israel would find it difficult under such circumstances to respond to such an attack with overwhelming force without suffering international isolation. Moreover, having won over the court of international opinion, Nasser's prestige would be enhanced further by the demolition of the Dimona reactor, an act that would nullify the Israeli quest for regional strategic hegemony. As the AMAN assessment of December 1965 noted: 'We are well acquainted with Nasser's mode of reaction towards Israel ... he is reluctant to take chances ... but the severity [in which he treats] the nuclear issue might force him to react. The abstract concept of destroying us turned this year into something more concrete.'[41]

AMAN presented several scenarios for such an Egyptian strike, including a limited ground attack, a commando raid or a sudden air-assault, the latter of which was considered the most likely. The General Staff and the Ministry of Defence adopted this view as well, agreeing that prevention of an attack on Dimona had become a vital interest. In his study, Gluska pointed to three layers of prevention: strategically—a conventional deterrence of Egypt from initiating military action; operationally—a preventive air strike on the Egyptian air force in case of an immediate and present danger to Dimona; and tactically—an enhanced early warning capability as well as strong air and ground defence around the reactor.[42] In February 1966, AMAN again pointed to Nasser's public declarations, assessing that 'Arabs' worries of Israel's nuclear capability accelerate their [Egyptian] military build up.'[43] In July 1966, Eshkol finally decided that 'securing Dimona becomes an ultimate policy'.[44]

Intelligence and Early Warning

The extensive efforts made by the intelligence community to penetrate Egyptian armed forces and decision-making circles in the 1960s and the valuable information they produced prior to the Six Day War is beyond the scope of the present chapter.[45] Nonetheless, one aspect of these efforts—the establishment of a dedicated early warning system against attempts to attack Dimona—is worth mentioning here, even if only in outline.

The portrayal of Nasser as Israel's arch-enemy committed to destroy the Jewish state combined with the lessons of the 'Rotem Affair' made Egypt the primary objective of intelligence coverage for the purpose of early warning. However, 'Rotem' also made it clear that the existing apparatus of early warning deployed against Egypt had been found wanting. AMAN and—for the first time—the Mossad were therefore tasked to give top priority to the urgent development of all necessary means to ensure that the IDF would receive adequate early warning on time that was informed qualitatively over Egypt's exact intent and capabilities.

The Egyptian involvement in the Yemen War made the task less pressing, as no war was predicted before the end of the decade. In fact, Yemen served as a first-rate intelligence laboratory to observe the Egyptian Army during its post-1956 phase of structural reorganisation based on the Soviet model. It is not often that intelligence services are provided the opportunity to study, uninvolved, the organisation, doctrine, armament, efficiency and quality of an enemy army in combat, and Yemen presented an opportunity not to be missed. AMAN, in its strategic early warning role, also looked for key indicators that would demonstrate an impending withdrawal of the Egyptian Army, using signal intelligence (SIGINT) to pay particular attention to the conduct of ground and air operations. This task was relatively simple for the Israelis as communication between the Egyptian forces in Yemen and Cairo was done mostly by radio messages that could be intercepted with ease. Special emphasis was also placed on keeping track of Egyptian chemical warfare and the Egyptian decision-making process in using gas, due to its operational impact on the IDF chemical defence.[46]

Although a general offensive against Israel was not predicted, nevertheless, by 1965 the increased threats against Dimona and the Israeli hinterland by Egyptian air and missile capabilities also increased the IDF's awareness of its need for an effective early warning, particularly in its operational and tactical modes. A new branch of Electronic Intelligence (ELINT) was created to monitor and locate transmissions emitted by air, ground and naval radars, and in early 1966 a special intelligence project for the enhancement of the early warning system, codenamed 'Senator', was announced and funds allocated. 'Senator' was based on three elements.

The first was improved SIGINT capability to cover the activity of the Egyptian air force continuously, in and around its main bomber bases, including deep inside Egypt. This actually presented AMAN with a considerable challenge as it had to find some innovative technical solutions to overcome the long distances and the lack of a 'line of sight' capability usually deployed to monitor such activity. The second was the establishment of a system of early warning indicators, aimed to sound the alarm even without explicit information, such as, for example, extraordinary activity by Egyptian and Jordanian air defence units, assumed to be on high alert against an Israeli response even before Egyptian bombers could get airborne. The third was the creation of a rapid dissemination and reporting process, from the interception sites to the operational units and squadrons.

For the first time, two early warning centres were established, one in the central SIGINT agency (under the unimaginative codename 'Shofar'—horn in Hebrew), the other in the Production-Assessment Department, manned twenty-four hours a day and connected to the Air Force and territorial commands. By late 1966, it was estimated that even in an extreme case, such as the collapse of the early warning system, air-interception squadrons and air defence units around Dimona would still be able to receive thirty minutes' warning.

Until 15 May 1967 the system, which operated under the undeclared motto of 'Rotem will not happen again', was put to the test several times following indications of Arab, mainly Egyptian, preparations for offensive actions. The most serious case took place in November 1966, after the Israeli retaliatory raid on the Jordanian village of Samoa. SIGINT-derived information, interpreted erroneously as possibly indicating an immediate general Arab attack on Israel, caused the IDF to go for several days into the highest state of alert, deploying its entire regular ground force along the Egyptian–Israeli border and activating all reservists' mobilisation centres. Although no actual meaningful incidents were registered during the entire period, examination of statements and actual responses clearly demonstrates that the threat to Dimona touched the raw nerves of the Israeli leadership.[47]

Conclusion

The dominant question in Israel in the period covered by this chapter was not 'if' but 'when'—'when would hostilities break out' with Egypt and the surrounding Arab states? Nobody in Israel had any doubt that the neighbouring Arab states, under Egyptian leadership, intended to initiate the 'Second Round' (the first being the Israeli War of Independence, or the 1948 war) and that it would materialise within a few years. However, the Israeli perception in the 1960s asserted that Egypt would do its utmost to avoid war as long as its military build-up was not completed and its army was involved elsewhere, and despite the rhetoric of Arab solidarity, certainly not in response to events along the other Arab borders.

The effect of the 'Rotem Affair' created a mental fixation among Israeli intelligence officers and decision-makers, according to which the Egyptian leadership had chosen a deterrence policy of brinkmanship. Prevailing opinion views the crisis of May/June 1967 as undeniable proof of the collapse of this erroneous perception.[48] However, the available evidence makes it impossible to eliminate the opposite conclusion: namely, that this perception was not entirely off the mark even in May. In fact, it is still unclear whether Nasser, in the first instance at least, actually intended to attack Israel or whether his aim was—as most historians conclude—only to deter it from attacking Syria in order to curry favour with the wider Arab world (an outcome similar to the 'Rotem Affair').[49] In other words: it is the irony of fate that what finally led to war was neither the actual intent of Egypt nor the major perceptions of threat which dominated Israel's strategic horizons, but a combination of misjudgement and the deterioration in the current state of security surrounding the activities of Syria, particularly in its increased support of Fatah guerrilla activities. The June 1967 war was perhaps a vindication of the second part of Israel's overall assessment: that the pace of these small-scale incidents led to a war that nobody actually wanted.

7

THE LIMITS OF PUBLIC DIPLOMACY

ABBA EBAN AND THE JUNE 1967 WAR

Asaf Siniver

Introduction

Since the early days of its existence, Israel's foreign policy was predicated on the assumption that Arab hostility was a permanent feature in the region and that the Arab states had no genuine interest in reaching a political settlement. In such an environment of continuous conflict, Israeli foreign policy was thus the product of a 'worst-case scenario' outlook whereby peace negotiations were subservient to security considerations. Fearing that a desire for peace would be interpreted as a sign of weakness by the Arabs, for many years—and to some extent to this day—the making of Israeli foreign policy was invariably subordinated to the defence and intelligence communities. On the international stage, this meant that foreign policy was primarily aimed at securing international legitimacy and establishing a positive image abroad through effective public diplomacy at a time when Israel's military operations caused much consternation internationally. But to some, public diplomacy (*hasbara*) was not as important as creating facts on the ground, echoing David Ben-Gurion's sentiment that 'it doesn't matter what the Gentiles say, what matters is what the Jews do'. Shimon Peres also pointed to the limits of public diplomacy, saying that 'good policy doesn't need *hasbara*, and bad policy cannot be helped by the best *hasbara* in the world'.[1]

From the outset secret diplomacy therefore became a cornerstone of Israel's foreign policy, either for the purpose of developing relations with countries which publicly did not recognise the Jewish state, or as a tool to secure Israel's national interests in the periphery. As a result the Foreign Ministry rarely played a central role in the shaping and executing of such clandestine practices. This reality was compounded by prevailing bureaucratic rivalries between the defence and intelligence establishment on the one hand, and the Foreign Ministry on the other. This competition was brought to a head in the period preceding the June 1967 Six Day War and immediately after it; the fact that the foreign minister in this period was Abba Eban, arguably Israel's greatest diplomat, makes this a particularly compelling episode in the country's history.

The war is widely viewed as a watershed in the contemporary history of the Middle East and an important junction in the superpower rivalry during the cold war. Israel's swift victory had quadrupled its territory at the expense of Egypt, Syria and Jordan, and made it a regional military superpower. The war also brought the conflict—and the region—to the fore of superpower competition and created clear strategic divisions between the US-backed 'moderate' regimes of Israel, Jordan and Saudi Arabia, and the Soviet-backed 'radical' regimes of Egypt, Syria and Iraq. Moreover, the war led directly to the launch of Israel's settlement project in the occupied territories, placed the plight of the Palestinian refugees on the international agenda and contributed to the strengthening of the nascent US–Israel special relationship. As a result of Israel's territorial expansion and the growing military and political commitment of the superpowers to their respective clients in the region, the price of Arab–Israeli peace had also changed irreversibly with the introduction of UN Security Council Resolution 242 in November 1967, which set the fuzzy yet accepted formula of 'land for peace'.

The origins and conduct of the Six Day War of June 1967 have been the subject of a rich and diverse scholarship from the immediate aftermath of the war.[2] Over the years the extant literature on the war has tackled this episode from a multitude of perspectives, ranging from civil–military relations in Israel before the war and the role of intelligence in shaping preparations for the war, to the regional balance of power and the global context of superpower confrontation by proxy. Despite their different orientations, the majority of these studies nevertheless converged around an agreed thesis that the war was inadvertent, or merely the result of miscalculations on the part of Israel and the Arabs alike. This view is shared by traditional as well as revisionist accounts, and was summed up aptly by Avi Shlaim, who noted that 'Of all the Arab–Israeli wars, the June 1967 war was the only one that neither side wanted.'[3] Still, some studies attempt to dispel the myth of Israel being 'poor little David' against the mighty Arab Goliath, or assign Israel a larger portion of the blame for the war, while others contend that Syrian and Egyptian provocations left Israel no choice but to launch a pre-emptive strike.[4] Most recently, however, and based largely on the partial declassification of records in the former Soviet national archives, several studies have challenged the 'accidental war' theory to suggest that the war was the result of a deliberate Soviet–Arab effort to draw Israel to launch a pre-emptive strike which would legitimise subsequent Soviet intervention, not least for the purpose of obviating Israel's nuclear programme in Dimona.[5]

An important aspect in the period leading to Israel's decision to launch a pre-emptive attack against the Arabs concerns the place of public diplomacy in Israel's orientation towards war. Here, secret diplomacy ran almost in parallel to public diplomacy, culminating in two visits of Israeli officials to Washington for the purpose of securing American support. On 26 May 1967 Abba Eban was dispatched to meet with President Lyndon Johnson in the White House, but returned to Israel empty-handed. Four days later Meir Amit, the head of Mossad, secretly met in the Pentagon with Secretary of Defense Robert McNamara and CIA Director Richard Helms. By all accounts his visit was more fruitful and proved decisive in convincing the Americans (and Israelis) that diplomacy had run its course. Ironically, Abba Eban's honed diplomatic skills and suave demeanour had made him one of the most eminent casualties of his government's dependence on back channelling, which was further compounded by a national atmosphere of perpetual anxiety.

Eban the Individual

Abba Eban is often described as the father of Israeli diplomacy and one of the most eloquent orators of the twentieth century. Eban was born in

Cape Town in 1915 and moved with his family to London two years later. He gained a rare triple first in classical and Oriental languages from Cambridge University and shortly after the outbreak of World War II joined the British Army where he rose to the rank of major, serving as a liaison officer between the British and the Yishuv in Palestine. After the war he joined the Jewish Agency's Information Department and was later appointed liaison officer to the UN Special Committee on Palestine, where he defended the case for partition. At the young age of thirty-three Eban was appointed Israel's first permanent representative to the United Nations, and in 1950 he was also appointed ambassador to the United States in Washington, holding both positions simultaneously until he entered Israeli politics in 1959. During his tenure in New York and Washington Eban was repeatedly noted for his brilliant oratory skills and his outstanding ability to defend Israel's case, leading Prime Minister David Ben-Gurion to dub him 'The Voice of Israel'. Ben-Gurion was particularly impressed with Eban's ability to defend policies which he personally disagreed with. Thus following a botched military raid on Syrian positions in 1955 (Operation Kinneret) which led to fifty Syrian and six Israeli deaths, Ben-Gurion asked Eban to defend the controversial action in front of the UN. Eban, who opposed the operation, was so successful in his task that Ben-Gurion wrote to him afterwards: 'I fully understand your concerns about the Kinneret operation. I must confess that I, too, began to have my doubts about the wisdom of it. But when I read the full text of your brilliant defense of our action in the Security Council, all my doubts were set at rest. You have convinced me that we were right, after all.'[6]

Beyond his brilliant rhetorical skills Eban had cemented his place as one of the most vocal proponents of peaceful relations with the Arab world, thus making him the ideological successor to Moshe Sharett, who stepped down as foreign minister in 1956. Eban identified and shaped what would gradually become the key pillars of Israel's foreign policy, albeit with varying degrees of effective implementation. The first of these was the need to match actions on the ground with effective public diplomacy. Even before Israel's independence Eban was aware that a future Jewish state would not exist in a political vacuum and therefore harnessing international recognition and support for the Jewish/Israeli cause was instrumental in expanding Israel's space for manoeuvre in the region. The second was the importance of strategic cooperation and the development of special relations with the United States, based on common security and ideological interests (and the formation of a strong pro-Israel lobby in Washington as a crucial vehicle to achieve this goal). Finally, Eban was a constant advocate for the normalisation of relations with the Arab world and the active pursuit of peaceful compromise before resorting to military means. Here was perhaps the widest gap between Eban's dovish outlook on the potential for peace and the prevailing political mindset displayed by most of his peers and his countrymen.

However, for all of his international accolades, Eban's global status was never matched by equal adulation at home. The reasons for this were both personal and political. First, Eban's elitist education, military career in the British Army and more than a decade abroad as Israel's chief diplomat had made him quintessentially international in his orientation and so far removed from the Israeli experience that he was often viewed as an alien in his own country. Unlike the political heavyweights of his time, such as Ben-Gurion, Golda, Dayan, Allon, Sapir and Eshkol, Eban was not a pioneer (*halutz*) who spent his youth working the land in a kibbutz, or joined the Haganah in the pre-state years. Since Eban was not a member of the Yishuv—he did not even settle in Israel until 1959—he invariably struggled to connect to the sabra mentality, and certainly had no appetite for the wheeling and dealing of Israeli politics. Eban struggled to realise that his rare oratory skills and passion for the art of diplomacy did not mean a great deal in the Israeli domestic scene. His urbane demeanour and proficiency in ten languages did not endear him to the average voter who cared more about social welfare, housing and jobs.[7] Eban was always perceived as too 'English', to the extent that even his Hebrew was too perfect for his listeners, free of grammatical errors in a melting pot of cultures and traditions. His accomplishments on the global stage were now his Achilles' heel in a society of immigrants, and he never managed to shake off the caricature-like image of a pompous, aloof aristocrat. Even abroad his demeanour was the subject of many jokes—Lyndon Johnson could not resist mimicking Eban's expressive intonation and called him 'a mini-Winston Churchill' after their fateful meeting at the White House in May 1967, while Henry Kissinger was alleged to have described Eban as 'a man who cannot get into an elevator without holding a press conference'.[8] Those who were closest to Eban, however, took pains to explain this perceived aloofness as nothing more than absent-mindedness and shyness.[9]

Michael Brecher's seminal study of the foreign policy system of Israel offers some striking observations about the links between personality traits and foreign policy orientation. Eban, according to Brecher, '[I]s more formal than his peers in bearing, dress, manner and speech. He is less quick to make decisions, more inclined to delay while the complex forces at work ... As a diplomat, with a donnish air, he has a basic mistrust of "the generals" and their *bitzuist* mentality, with the strong taint of chauvinism, total self-reliance, isolationism and disdain for "the world ..."'[10] As a man of words rather than deeds, Eban was more reactive than active; responding to international developments rather than initiating his own proposals.[11] Against this background Eban's ascendency to the position of foreign minister seems particularly remarkable, and his long tenure in office even more so given the limitations bureaucratic politics and interpersonal rivalries placed on his ability to drive Israel's foreign policy in his preferred direction.

Eban the Foreign Minister

Throughout his tenure, Eban's gradual exclusion from the decision-making process was compounded by a national state of perpetual anxiety over security matters, which in effect cemented the institutional subordination of the Foreign Ministry to the defence and intelligence bureaucracies. In the absence of strong personalities with wide political support to countenance the unchallenged hegemony of Defence Minister Moshe Dayan and against the exigencies of regional security, the Foreign Ministry gradually succumbed to the expansionism of the Defence Ministry. Over time, functions which were traditionally assumed by the Foreign Service, such as arms purchases and foreign military exports, overseas intelligence-gathering, policy assessment and planning, as well as negotiations with some Arab states, were now appropriated by the Defence Ministry.[12]

As foreign minister in the governments of Levi Eshkol (1966–9) and Golda Meir (1969–74), Eban's experience and intimate knowledge of diplomacy was unparalleled, though he was often excluded from the informal inner circle of decision-making. Eban's experience is not unique, however—Israeli foreign ministers rarely played a substantive part beyond that of public relations officers for the Ministry of Defence. In the late 1950s Prime Minister (and Defence Minister) Ben-Gurion tried to use Ambassador Eban as a secret backchannel to keep a check on the truculent foreign minister, Golda Meir (the failed attempt was described by Eban as 'an infallible prescription for antagonistic explosions'),[13] whereas a decade later, Prime Minister Meir herself bypassed Foreign Minister Eban by consulting secretly and directly with Yitzhak Rabin, her ambassador to Washington.

Eban's view of the art of diplomacy as a noble vocation was scorned by Golda Meir, his predecessor at the foreign office, who observed that, 'all a foreign minister does is talk and talk more'.[14] While Meir's disparaging view of diplomacy was legendary, her assessment was undoubtedly a more accurate depiction of the Israeli reality than Eban's romantic version. It is not surprising therefore that under Golda's premiership Eban increasingly found himself excluded from the inner circle of decision-making. She often went behind his back to talk directly with Ambassador Rabin in Washington, and excluded him from her famous 'kitchen cabinet'—an informal forum held in Golda's apartment which preceded Cabinet meetings and included Defence Minister Moshe Dayan, Deputy Prime Minister Yigal Allon and Israel Galili, one of the political heavyweights of the Mapai party. But even under the premiership of Eshkol, who was far more moderate than Golda both in temper and in political orientation, Eban's support base in the government was insignificant before, and certainly after, the June 1967 war.

Dubbing Eban 'the wise fool', Eshkol admired his foreign minister's eloquence but had little regard for his abilities as a statesman.[15] Indeed, compared to his peers Eban was decidedly positioned on the opposite side of the spectrum. In his analysis of the personality traits of the core decision-making group during Israel's first two decades, Brecher places Ben-Gurion and Golda at one end of the spectrum, which is defined by 'decisiveness', 'extremism' and 'men of deeds', while Sharett and Eban are placed on the opposite end of the spectrum, defined by 'hesitancy', 'compromise' and 'men of words'. Eshkol and Sapir are placed roughly in the middle, but with Dayan, Allon and Peres known for their hard-line attitudes, it is easy to see why Sharett and particularly Eban were often frustrated by the actions of their governments.[16]

Public and Secret Diplomacy in the Run-Up to the June 1967 War

Nowhere was this sentiment more accurate than during the fateful period leading up to the June 1967 war. This episode exemplified the limits of public diplomacy, particularly during times of crisis when information is incomplete, time to respond to unfolding events is limited and levels of anxiety amongst policy-makers is high. Under those circumstances Eban's diplomatic skills could not help his government choose between restraint and war; rather it was the secret and less subtle approach of the spymaster Meir Amit which proved decisive in pushing Israel to war.

In the decade following the 1956 Suez Crisis neither Israel nor her Arab neighbours were happy with the prevailing status quo of a suspended state of war. Still, even as late as April 1967 neither side believed that war was imminent. By the third week of May, however, a series of actions and counteractions by Egypt, Israel and Syria had made the prospect of a third Arab–Israeli war a real possibility. On 14 May Israeli intelligence reported that President Gamal Abd al-Nasser of Egypt had moved forces into the Sinai Peninsula. Two days later, Nasser ordered the United Nations Emergency Force (UNEF, established in the aftermath of the 1956 war) out of Sinai, in clear violation of the terms of the 1956 ceasefire. And when Nasser announced on 23 May that the Straits of Tiran would be closed to Israeli shipping, the crisis reached boiling point. In Israel, the effective blockade of passage to and from its southern port of Eilat was viewed as a *casus belli*; according to Foreign Minister Eban, Israel was now 'breathing with only a single lung'.[17]

During the ensuing two weeks Prime Minister Levi Eshkol was branded as indecisive by the media and the Israeli public, and had to withstand the mounting pressure of his generals who wanted to strike against Egypt. His lack of military experience also led parties across the political spectrum to call on the prime minister to establish a national unity government and even give the helm back to Ben-Gurion, but Eshkol refused: 'These two horses cannot be hitched to the same carriage.'[18] He initially refused IDF Chief of Staff Yitzhak Rabin's request to call up the reserve units and only agreed to raise the level of alertness for war, though he later succumbed to the pressure and agreed to call up more than 30,000 reservists. Still, throughout the period leading to the war (*hamtana*, 'waiting') he made every effort to prevent escalation by diplomatic means.

In Washington, President Lyndon Johnson urged Eshkol to demonstrate restraint, making it clear that he could 'not accept any responsibilities on behalf of the United States for situations which arise as the result of actions on which we are not consulted'.[19] Johnson's message was followed by a tentative pledge to act multilaterally to guarantee the safe passage of Israeli ships through the Straits of Tiran. With the Cabinet uncertain how to interpret Johnson's message and split over which course of action to take, Eban suggested that he leave at once for Washington to impress upon the American president the need to reopen the straits. However, Eshkol feared that Eban's moderate disposition would not make him a popular choice in the eyes of the Israeli public. Sensing that in this gravest of hours Israelis and American Jewry alike needed to be spurred and inspired and not coaxed by diplomatic subtleties, Eshkol turned instead to Golda Meir, hoping that her tough negotiating style would be more effective. When Eban heard of this he threatened to resign, and even produced a cable reporting that French President de Gaulle was more likely to meet with him than with Golda. Already under increasing pressure from the public, the media and the parties in opposition, Eshkol was in no mood for another political crisis. He grudgingly succumbed to Eban's pressure and sent his foreign minister on the fateful mission.[20] On 24 May Eban met with de Gaulle in Paris and then with British Prime Minister Harold Wilson in London, but neither leader was particularly forthcoming. De Gaulle warned Israel not to launch a pre-emptive strike against Egypt, whereas Wilson, while expressing his support for Israel, argued that only the United States could lead any international action to break the blockade.

Ironically, Eshkol was not the only one who did not want Eban despatched to Washington—President Johnson also preferred him not to come. The White House had to balance its previous commitments over ensuring the safe passage of Israeli shipping through the Straits of Tiran and the strategic need to deter Soviet meddling on the one hand, with the political and constitutional constraints of actively supporting the Israeli war effort on the other. In short, it would be best if Israel would go it alone, though Johnson did not want to push Israel to war. The task was therefore to get the 'message across without giving the impression what its real aim was. This could only be accomplished in a secretive, low-key manner.'[21] Eban's presence in Washington was therefore seen as detrimental to that approach, and Johnson made every effort to avoid meeting the foreign minister, preferring instead to meet with Ephraim Evron, the number two at the Israeli embassy in Washington.

Shortly after Eban's arrival in Washington on 25 May he received an alarming cable from Eshkol: the Egyptians had moved more forces across the Sinai and a surprise attack was imminent. He was asked to convey this intelligence assessment 'in the most urgent terms' to Washington and ask that an official statement be made by Washington that an attack on Israel was tantamount to an attack on the United States. The issue was no longer the need for multilateral action to reopen the Straits of Tiran, but a demand that the United States come to Israel's help if war broke out. Eban's dramatic message surprised his interlocutors, Secretary of State Dean Rusk and Undersecretary Eugene Rostow, and they asked their intelligence agencies to corroborate the information. Eban also informed them that he had to see the president that Friday, 26 May, as the Cabinet was scheduled to meet in Jerusalem on Sunday, and Johnson's message would likely determine Israel's next course of action—'perhaps the most crucial cabinet meeting in our history', warned Eban.

On the morning of 26 May Eban met in the Pentagon with Defense Secretary Robert McNamara, Chairman of the Joint Chiefs of Staff Earl Wheeler and CIA Director Richard Helms. He was told that American intelligence had concluded that the Israeli assessment was incorrect and that an Egyptian attack was not pending. And even if war did break out, the CIA estimated that Israel could 'defend successfully against simultaneous Arab attacks on all fronts ... or hold on any three fronts while mounting successfully a major offensive on the fourth'.[22] Sensing that Eban was trying to use the now discredited Israeli intelligence reports to compel him to make a quick public statement in support of Israel's right to strike, Johnson reportedly exploded, telling his aides 'I don't like anyone to put a pistol to my head. This Sunday cabinet meeting of his to decide on peace or war—it's an ultimatum, and I don't like it.'[23]

Later that evening Eban finally arrived at the Oval Office, accompanied by Ambassador Avraham Herman and Ephraim Evron, where they met Johnson, McNamara, Walt Rostow, Eugene Rostow and George Christian. Johnson reiterated his view of the blockade of the straits as illegal and reassured Eban that he was still considering a multilateral approach to lift the blockade. Eban thought he had the Americans cornered. Israel, he said, had the firm guarantees of the Western powers to ensure its freedom of navigation in the Gulf of Aqaba, and it was now time to draw on these guarantees—which served as the basis for the Israeli withdrawal from Sinai in 1957—either via a multilateral effort to reopen the straits (based on Harold Wilson's idea to send an international flotilla of the maritime powers through the straits), or failing that, by letting Israel open the straits by force.

Johnson, however, emphasised the political constraints he was operating under: 'All this is important, but I tell you that this is not worth five cents unless I have the people with me ... We have constitutional processes. I'm not a King. How to take Congress with me I've got my own views. I'm not an enemy or a coward.' Then he assured Eban twice that he would do everything in his power to open the straits to all shipping, but qualified this by stating that he could not accept Israel's demand that the United States consider an attack on Israel as equivalent to an attack on the United States. Johnson's mixed signals were further compounded by his enigmatic glib that 'Israel will not be alone unless it decides to go alone', which he repeated twice.[24]

The approach of Johnson at the meeting was largely based on the confident assessment of his intelligence people that Israel could easily win the war without American help. According to a report prepared by the Board of National Estimates, 'Israel could almost certainly attain air supremacy over the Sinai Peninsula in less than 24 hours after taking the initiative ... Armored striking forces could breach the UAR's double defense line in the Sinai in three to four days ... Israel could contain any attacks by Syria or Jordan during this period'; as one senior intelligence official later recalled, 'rarely has the Intelligence Community spoken as clearly, as rapidly, and with such unanimity'.[25] Johnson therefore dismissed the Israeli's gloomy assessment, telling Eban 'All of our intelligence people are unanimous that if the UAR attacks, you will whip the hell out of them.' Eban tried again to get an explicit commitment, asking 'Hasn't Barbour [the US ambassador to Israel] conveyed the mood in Israel?', but he was shot down by Walt Rostow: 'Mood isn't intelligence.'[26]

By the end of the meeting the Israelis felt they were still in the dark about the American position. Ambassador Harman conceded that '[it] was undoubtedly a disappointing conversation. The Israelis were hoping for more', and Eban was not persuaded by Johnson's reassurances either: 'Whether an international effort to run the blockade would be mounted was in mind a matter of doubt'; and summed up Johnson's attitude as 'the rhetoric of impotence ... [of] a paralyzed president'.[27] Johnson too felt that his efforts came up short: 'I've failed.'[28] 'They'll go', he said to his aides at the end of the meeting.[29] But the president was also satisfied that he had avoided falling into the trap Eban set him. 'They came loaded for a bear, but so was I! I let them talk for the first hour, and I just listened, and then I finished it up the last 15 minutes', he said. According to the president's daily diary, Secretary McNamara was so pleased with the outcome of the meeting that 'he just wanted to throw his cap up in the air, and George Christian said it was the best meeting of the kind he had ever sat on'.[30]

Eban's report on his meeting with Johnson was received in Jerusalem with some confusion. Did he fail to convey to Johnson the true gravity of the situation, or worse, did he misrepresent Johnson's message to suit his own dovish outlook? In particular, the Cabinet struggled to make sense of Johnson's message that Israel will not be alone unless it decides to go alone. Major General Ahron Yariv, chief of AMAN (military intelligence), informed Eshkol that Eban's report and assessment was 'catastrophically mistaken'—he had not interpreted correctly the American position; both Eban and Eshkol placed too much importance on what Washington was saying officially.[31] He therefore suggested to Eshkol that he send the head of Mossad, Meir Amit, to Washington to find out through intelligence channels exactly what the Americans would do if Israel was to strike first, and to assess how advanced the plans to reopen the straits using an international flotilla were. Amit flew incognito to Washington on 31 May, having no qualms about what Israel should do next. He was angered by the 'helplessness and inaction at the top', and despised the scores of Israelis who left the country in fear of the war. 'It's all right—if people want to run away, let them. Whatever we're left with at the end of the war will be healthier.'[32]

By 1 June Eban was persuaded that war was inevitable, and that the only question remaining was the timing. There were several reasons for Eban's change of heart. First came the news that Jordan had signed a defence pact with Egypt, which put Jordanian forces under Egyptian command and completed Israel's encirclement. The same day Eban also received a secret report on a meeting in Washington between Ephraim Evron and Justice Abe Fortas, Johnson's informal advisor on Arab–Israeli affairs. 'Israelis should not criticize Eshkol and Eban', Fortas reportedly said, 'If Israel had acted alone without exhausting political efforts it would have made a catastrophic error.' Eban interpreted this as evidence that further diplomatic manoeuvres were no longer necessary to protect Israel if it landed the first blow.[33] Later in the afternoon Eshkol finally succumbed to the public and political pressure and invited Moshe

Dayan, the hero of the 1956 Sinai campaign, to replace him as defence minister in the newly formed national unity government.

The last piece of the puzzle was the fateful report from Amit on his meetings in Washington. Unlike Eban, the chief spy did not come asking for cover, but to inform the Americans that he intended to recommend to his own government to go to war. And unlike Eban's frustrated efforts with Johnson, it seemed that the head of Mossad was more successful in relaying his government's intentions. First, it became evident to Amit that the plan to lead an international flotilla through the straits would not materialise.[34] In his meetings with McNamara and Helms, Amit made it clear that Israel now had no choice but to act alone, and he asked the Americans for three things: to continue to supply weapons already arranged for, to give diplomatic support at the United Nations and to keep the Soviets out of the fighting. Following the meeting, on 2 June, Helms reported to Johnson:

Amit thinks the Israeli decision will be to strike. Regarding the outcome of a war, Amit said he sees an Israeli victory in three to four weeks, with Israeli losses of about 4,000 military personnel. There would be damage to Israel from Egyptian air strikes and from the Egyptians' missile boats, but, Amit said, Israel had 'some surprises' of its own … Amit told one of our senior officers this morning that he felt this must mean the time of decision has come for the Israeli Government. He stated there would have to be a decision in a matter of days.

Then, referring to Eban's meeting with President Johnson a few days earlier, Helms explained that:

He [Amit] said that Eban's mission was seen by him and the Israeli nation as a failure. Here Amit almost certainly shares the views of General Dayan, Israel's new defense minister, since Amit and Dayan have been very close for many years. Both are Sabras—men born in Israel—and their past careers have been closely connected. It seems clear from Amit's remarks that the 'tough' Israelis, who have never forgotten that they are surrounded by hostile Arabs, are driving hard for a forceful solution, with us and with their own government. Dayan's appointment, combined with Amit's and Harman's recall, can be interpreted as an ominous portent, considering the Israelis' military capability to strike with little or no warning at a time of their choosing.

According to Helms, the substance and tone of Amit's message left no doubt in his mind about what Israel should do next: 'Israel's economy is suffering with each additional day of crisis. There are no workers in the fields, and the harvest is still standing, but so long as 82,000 Egyptian troops remain in the Sinai, Israel cannot demobilize its reserves … It is better to die fighting than from starving.'[35] Amit then told McNamara that he intended to recommend to the Cabinet in Jerusalem to launch a pre-emptive strike, and the secretary of defence replied, 'I read you loud and clear.'[36] Amit's tough message evidently achieved the desired result. In a preliminary report to the Cabinet in Jerusalem Amit concluded that 'There is a growing chance for American political backing if we act on our own.'[37] Amit was right. McNamara conveyed his message to Johnson, and the president, now under no illusion that Israel was going to strike, set up a task force headed by McGeorge Bundy to handle the situation. According to Harman, Amit's visit to Washington was the decisive factor which affected the change in Johnson's position.[38]

It was also the decisive factor which finally relieved Eshkol of his misgivings about going to war. Johnson had seemed to abandon his efforts to prevent the war via international channels. He did not communicate with Amit directly, though the following day, on 3 June, he wrote to Eshkol, saying again that Israel will not be alone unless it decides to go alone, adding that he received Amit's message. That night Amit arrived at Eshkol's private residence and reported on his meeting: 'The United States won't go into mourning if Israel attacks Egypt.' That night Eshkol, Dayan, Allon and Rabin decided on war, and the full Cabinet was summoned the following morning. The ministers were presented with two options. Eban recommended postponing military action by a few more days to allow Johnson to exhaust all diplomatic avenues, whereas Dayan pressed for immediate action.

The same day the Israelis were informed that Zakariya Mohieddin, the Egyptian vice president, would be leaving the UN for a secret meeting with Johnson in Washington on 7 June to discuss 'totality [sic] Palestine problem, resolution of which would permit regulation [sic] Tiran Straits issue'. Dean Rusk believed that 'The great value of Mohieddin's visit is opportunity for private discussions. The less said about it the better', while Eugene Rostow suggested that Washington inform the Israelis of the visit, although he added that 'my guess is that their intelligence will pick it up'.[39] That issue became irrelevant however, as in Jerusalem the government voted unanimously in favour of Dayan's proposal.[40] Mohieddin's secret visit never took place—by the time of his scheduled meeting the war was practically won, with Israeli forces in control of Sinai and the West Bank.

Even in the midst of the fighting Eban had no illusions that Israel would not and should not be able to hold on to the occupied territories. As he put it to his wife: 'What are we going to do with all those territories? We will have to give them back after some frontier adjustments which will be necessary for security.'[41] However, with the war over and the nation enveloped by nationalistic fanaticism, Eban could not count on the support of other doves in his party, such as Sapir or Aran, who placed their loyalty to the party before their loyalty to their political views. Even the parties on the left were split over the question of the territories, with Ahdut Haavoda vacillating between morality and sentimentality. The rift was profound and the debates within the national unity government continued to dominate the last two years of the Eshkol government. At the root of these internal debates stood a very real tension between the desire to hold on to the territories for security, religious and ideological reasons, against the unsavoury notion of becoming an occupying power. This dilemma was highlighted by Eshkol himself shortly after the war. Asked by Golda Meir, then general secretary of the Mapai party, 'what are we going to do with one million Arabs?' Eshkol replied: 'I get it. You want the dowry, but you don't like the bride!'[42]

Eban's woes were further compounded by the emergence of Moshe Dayan as the new centre of gravity in Israeli politics. Together with Chief of Staff Yitzhak Rabin and the other generals, Dayan was carried away by unprecedented waves of public adulation. Now he was personally involved in the daily administration of the occupied territories, and any attempts by a weakened Eshkol to clip his wings were met by a threat to resign. Dayan's overbearing control of the foreign and security policies of Israel between 1967 and 1974 was so profound that it became apparent that no diplomatic initiatives vis-à-vis the Arabs were ever going to succeed without his approval. According to Eli Zeira, former chief of military intelligence, Dayan's assessments were rarely challenged by other ministers, who lacked the necessary analytical skills and professional background.[43]

Conclusion

Against Dayan's imperiousness and the engulfing nationalistic zeal, Eban lost whatever shreds of influence and credibility he enjoyed before the war. On many occasions during the 1950s Eban was not afraid to criticise Ben-Gurion and challenge him, particularly with regards to Israel's retributions policy—a fact which won him the trust and respect of the prime minister. Now, however, it seemed that Eban gave up the fight. With the hardening of the public's views on territorial compromise and with no substantial support within his party, he was running out of options. By his own admission, he now 'lived in an isolated realm of anxiety while the noise of unconfined joy kept intruding through the window'.[44] And with inconclusive negotiations with the Arabs through Ambassador Jarring of the UN dominating much of the political framework until the 1973 Yom Kippur War, Israel's most skilful foreign minister had become the harbinger of a vacuous diplomacy.

Eban's experience is representative of a general pattern of the institutional decline of the Foreign Ministry which began in the early days of the state and did not recover (temporarily) until the early 1990s when, under the leadership of Shimon Peres, the ministry managed to achieve rough parity with the Ministry of Defence in terms of leverage and authority. One reason for this ascendance of the Foreign Ministry was the launch of the Oslo peace process and the start of a dialogue with the Arab world, though it still lagged behind the Ministry of Defence in terms of budget and manpower. Another reason for this resurgence was personal. As foreign minister between 1992 and 1995, Shimon Peres possessed the rare combination of a veteran politician with a wide support base, a relentless drive and strategic vision, and international adulation on the back of his 1993 Noble Peace Prize for masterminding the secret Oslo channel with the PLO. Abba Eban enjoyed none of the contextual or personal features which characterised the Peres years. Even his international reputation as a brilliant diplomat counted against him back home, and while he was an ardent supporter of compromise and peace, it is hard to point to an Eban-esque peace strategy, policy or plan of substance. Ironically, Eban's long tenure as foreign minister under two prime ministers who had more regard for his oratorical skills than his strategic vision only confirmed Golda's jibe that the task of the foreign minister is first and foremost to be the face of public diplomacy by defending the government's policies abroad, rather than being a source of policy in the first place.

8

ISRAEL IN SUB-SAHARAN AFRICA

THE CASE OF UGANDA, 1962–72

Zach Levey

Introduction

Israel established relations with Uganda upon its independence in October 1962, creating the basis for a relationship which endured until Idi Amin severed the connection in March 1972. Israel became heavily involved in Uganda, engaging in activities of both a 'normal' diplomatic and clandestine nature. Michael Michael, Israel's first ambassador, wrote that Israel and Uganda had 'no natural common interests'.[1] Nevertheless, the Israeli Foreign Ministry saw utility in ties with Uganda, such as the attainment of diplomatic objectives including support in the United Nations and an embassy in another black African country from which the Arab states would not be able to exclude Israel.

Israel also pursued four strategic objectives in Uganda. First, Israel sought access to the White Nile River, which contributes 16 per cent of the waters that reach Egypt. Second, Uganda was a 'hinterland' to Ethiopia, the security of which was of great concern to Israel. The third was a route to the Anya Nya movement in the southern Sudan, which Israel supported in order to destabilise the regime in Khartoum. Fourth,

Israel cultivated a security connection with Uganda, using arms and training to bolster ties. Yet military assistance brought about engagement in Uganda's volatile politics and fomented conflict between Israel's Foreign Ministry and Defence Ministry. The Foreign Ministry protested what it considered Israel's damaging association with the unstable Kampala regime and opposed arms sales to disreputable African leaders. Competition between these bureaucracies became a 'turf war' in Africa, and this chapter notes that rivalry.

The first period in this study covers the ties between the two countries under Milton Obote, prime minister from 1962 until 1966 and president from 1966 to 1971. A second period begins with Amin's January 1971 coup and ends with his turn against Israel in late February 1972. The third part of the chapter deals with the four weeks that preceded the sudden end, on 30 March 1972, of Israel's decade in Uganda.

Israel and Uganda Under Obote 1962–71

On 9 October 1962 Uganda gained independence, and Israel become one of the first countries to open an embassy in the capital Kampala.[2] Obote wished to use arms and training from Israel in order to reduce dependence upon Britain. In late 1962 the Israel Defence Forces (IDF) commenced courses for Uganda's army. Lt Colonel Ze'ev Shaham, East African representative of the IDF and Defence Ministry, described the absence (despite the British presence) of planning and purpose that marked Ugandan military affairs. Shaham asked Ugandan officials 'Why do you need to build an army? Who are your enemies? What is your security doctrine?' The answer was 'vigorous'. The Ugandans replied, 'For that we have invited you. You will tell us what we want and how to achieve it.'[3] The newly independent state felt the need for a larger army as a symbol of its sovereignty.[4]

By late 1962 Israel had begun to provide agricultural assistance and youth programmes similar to those of its Gadna and Nahal movements, which combined military service with intensive agrarian development. Moreover, Israel responded to Uganda's call to help achieve its most important national goals. Britain retained control of the armed forces. Yet the creation of local cadres was of great importance to Uganda. This was the process of Africanisation, through which the Ugandans sought to foster national norms and unity, and they turned to Israel for guidance.[5]

On 4 April 1963 Israel and Uganda signed a defence agreement, which stipulated that Israel would create a second battalion for the Ugandan army, equip and train its air force and establish a special forces unit. Uganda committed itself to purchase £1,000,000 worth of military hardware from Israel.[6] Obote wanted Israel's help in achieving both Africanisation and 'Israelisation'.[7]

In January 1964 the Ugandan army mutinied, the causes of discontent being British domination and the low level of pay. Obote appealed for British intervention to quell the revolt, and in that manner Britain maintained his government in power.[8] Yet Obote paid a price beyond resentment at having to turn to London. Major Idi Amin, hastily promoted to commissioned rank in 1961, played a prominent role in maintaining order, persuading the troops to return to their barracks.[9] Five months later Obote awarded Amin the rank of lieutenant-colonel, also appointing him commander of signals at army headquarters.[10]

The 1964 mutiny afforded Israel the opportunity to expand its role and exert greater influence on the government. According to the Foreign Office in London, the Israelis bribed Uganda's minister of defence, Felix Onama, with £25,000, handing out personal weapons and clothing to Ugandan officers and ministers.[11] In fact the British colonial authorities offered much greater inducements in their attempt to persuade the Ugandans to retain British tutelage of their army. Moreover, the Israelis did not have to use bribery. They were highly effective teachers, even if the liveliest account of their training is that of the IDF's top officer in Uganda. Thus Shaham describes the astonishment of British officers who, alongside Obote and tribal kings, watched an Israeli-trained Ugandan unit successfully execute a live-fire exercise.[12] In late July 1964 Uganda refused to extend Britain's contract, and the British terminated their military involvement almost completely.[13] Israel assumed the dominant role and in 1964 sold Uganda two Potez-IAI Magister training aircraft. Uganda also purchased ten Piaggio 149D training aircraft from the Federal Republic of Germany, but the planes that Israel provided were jets.[14]

By late 1964 Obote turned increasingly toward neutralism.[15] First, in July 1964 Obote met in Cairo with Gamal Abd al-Nasser, Egypt's president. Obote assured Nasser that Uganda would not be the tool of a foreign power, while the latter admitted Egypt had no right to dictate Ugandan policy.[16] That accord notwithstanding, wrote Michael, Obote had received 'a real brain-washing'.[17] Second, Uganda consistently acted against Israel in the United Nations, especially regarding the Palestinian refugee issue.[18] The best that Israel could hope for was Uganda's abstention.[19] Third, Israel and Uganda were on opposite sides of the volatile situation in the Congo.[20] Israel cooperated with the US Greene Plan and helped train the Armée Nationale Congolaise of the pro-Western Leopoldville government. In Ugandan eyes, the Congo struggle was an attempt by imperial powers to reassert control in Africa, and Israel actively supported the West.[21] Fourth, Britain's withdrawal removed the inhibition that had obviated involvement with Eastern Bloc countries. In 1964 the Soviet Union began to provide arms and training to the Ugandan armed forces.[22] Ideological, religious and tribal conflict in Uganda created a fifth element that undermined Israel's standing in that country. Thus many of Uganda's Muslims (5.6 per cent of the population in 1962) were hostile to Israel.

By 1965 Obote maintained an increasing political distance from Israel, although he would still 'listen intently as long as the subject was military'.[23] That notwithstanding, Colonel Ze'ev Bar-Sever, who in 1965 took over the IDF mission, spent several months waiting for a meeting with the minister of defence. Uri Lubrani, who in August 1965 replaced Michael as ambassador, wrote that Uganda might terminate Israel's role in its military. The ambassador attributed the uncertainty of Israel's circumstances to Obote's Eastern connection; in July 1965 Obote visited China, Yugoslavia and the Soviet Union.[24]

On 21 September 1965 Lubrani met with Obote, where he recited details of Israeli civilian aid programmes in Uganda and queried him regarding an extension of military assistance. Obote expressed real interest only when the ambassador mentioned a paratrooper unit for the Ugandan army.[25] Lubrani wrote that Uganda would almost certainly not oust Israeli instructors from its air force before the return of cadets from the Soviet Union in late 1967.[26] Moreover, he reported a modest improvement in relations with the Ugandan defence establishment.[27] At the end of November 1967 Onama urged Lubrani to expedite the departure to Israel of Ugandans to train as parachute instructors. Lubrani recommended preparation that would extend several years, thereby ensuring Israel's protracted military engagement in Uganda.[28]

In 1966 events in Uganda provided Israel with the opportunity to deepen both military and civilian involvement. In early 1966 the commander of the army, Brigadier Shaban Opolot, conducted a large-scale unauthorised movement of troops away from Kampala, lending weight to Obote's claim that his opponents were preparing his overthrow. Obote moved Opolot to a meaningless post, appointed Amin chief of staff, and having asserted control of the military, promoted Amin to brigadier.[29] Obote decreed a constitution combining the office of prime minister with that of president and assumed the latter title.[30] The Israelis provided Obote and Amin with valuable intelligence, while assistance to the Obote-dominated government afforded Israel legitimacy based on close ties with a 'progressive' African regime. Yet Moshe Leshem, head of the Africa Division, asked Lubrani, 'into what currency can we convert the good will we have earned with Obote, Amin and company? My impression is that this is a sly lot that knows how to exploit without giving much in return.'[31]

On 12 June 1966 Israel's Prime Minister, Levi Eshkol, arrived in Uganda for a visit, underscoring the extent of Israel's involvement. Israeli companies built agricultural stations, public buildings, roads and housing estates. The Foreign Ministry's Mashav (Division of International Cooperation) had spent $323,000 on projects in Uganda from 1962 to 1966, including agricultural development. The Mossad trained the Ugandan security services.[32] In early July 1966 senior officials of the Foreign Ministry, Mossad, the Prime Minister's Office and IDF officers representing the Defence Ministry conducted consultations regarding Africa. These officials were keenly aware of their country's financial constraints and the likelihood Eshkol would cut their budgets there. The meeting produced a consensus regarding the need to phase out costly programmes such as paramilitary training and most courses for Africans in Israel. Representatives of the Mossad pointed out that their principal operations were in Ethiopia, Uganda and Tanzania, all three of which were vulnerable to 'Arab subversion' but which were also fertile ground for collaboration against Arab interests. The Mossad expressed pride in its achievements in sub-Saharan Africa, noting that it had 'accomplished much' with a limited budget and only twenty-five agents and had aroused no inter-office controversy.

The same cannot be said of the demands that the two IDF lieutenant colonels representing the Defence Ministry raised. They called for a steep increase in military involvement in Uganda, which they claimed would create opportunities and future profits for the Israeli Military

Industries, Soltam Systems (arms manufacturers) and the Israel Aircraft Industries.[33] Foreign Ministry officials reacted indignantly. Military assistance to Uganda alone had already cost Israel millions of dollars. Would it not have been possible to secure influence principally through economic ventures? In the view of the Foreign Ministry, Israel had become overextended in all of Africa. Moreover, by 1966 Israel was in a deep recession. Consolidation rather than expansion had become Israel's 'watchword' in Africa.[34]

On 21 September 1966 Moshe Bitan, deputy director general of the Foreign Ministry, visited Uganda. Bitan was irked at what he considered both the Defence Ministry's waste of resources and its overzealousness in pursuit of military ties. Bitan reported to Abba Eban (who earlier that year succeeded Golda Meir as foreign minister), severely criticising the role of the Israeli Defence Ministry in Africa. He challenged what his office viewed as the Defence Ministry's desire to turn Africa into an Israeli arms bazaar. Israel's over-commitment, he observed, was in great measure the result of conflicting bureaucratic interests and the ambitions of the Defence Ministry. Bitan wrote to Eban that:

I've encountered a dangerous redundancy of operations. With no justification a security empire has been erected in Africa. This interferes with work, foments turmoil, and creates great political risk. We can overcome these encumbrances, but to do so we will have to prevail over vested interests while slaughtering a few holy cows.[35]

The manner in which the Defence Ministry 'handled' Amin also created inter-office tension. The Foreign Ministry wanted nothing to do with the bribery facilitating influence with Amin, the primary means of which was large sums of cash and the construction of ostentatious villas for the chief of staff and high-ranking officers. Lubrani reported the 'corruption' that attended Bar-Sever's activities. The ambassador was unwilling to confront the IDF delegation chief and unable to assure the Foreign Ministry that there would be no more of this 'mortification'.[36]

Foreign Ministry officials also subjected to increasing criticism their government's support of unstable regimes. They had become sceptical of both civilian aid and military assistance to African states, many of which rested on shaky foundations. Coups in early 1966 in Ghana, the Central African Republic and Nigeria heightened their wariness of 'personal' defence contracts with 'tottering' African leaders, identification with whom would leave Israel burdened after they fell.[37] Nevertheless, Israel helped ensure that Obote and Amin remained in power. In early October 1966 a British 'source' told the US ambassador in Kampala that Opolot had spoken to him of assassinating Obote. The US envoy passed this intelligence to Lubrani, and Israel decided to act upon it. Bar-Sever informed Amin. Haim Tsfati, Mossad head in Uganda, met with Obote. The Israelis were the first to alert Obote and Amin, thus eliciting the gratitude of Uganda's 'strong men'.[38]

In 1967 a series of promotions in the Ugandan army heightened Kampala's interest in Israeli assistance,[39] helping Israel to maintain its dominant role in the Ugandan army.[40] By September 1967 Uganda's military procurement from Israel had reached $12.5 million, and it had signed contracts worth an additional $7 million. Lubrani wrote that a principal task was urging restraint upon Brigadier Amin, convincing him to 'keep equipment simple and against shopping for more glamorous items'. In truth, few Israelis at that time ascribed to the chief of staff the appetite for power that he later displayed. In June 1967 Lubrani told the US ambassador that Amin was 'completely loyal to Obote, aware of his own intellectual limitations, and without political ambitions'.[41] Yet as Ingham writes, 'Obote had never doubted Amin's shrewdness.'[42]

In August that year, some 300 Ugandans attended a reception for Bar-Sever and Colonel Baruch ('Burka') Bar-Lev, his replacement. Yet Lubrani wrote of an ambivalence towards Israel, the source of which was Uganda's desire to be a 'revolutionary' state. The ambassador cautioned, 'we cannot disregard the possibility that relations will deteriorate'.[43] Circumspection notwithstanding, in mid-October 1967 Lubrani reported Uganda's request to buy £1.4 million worth of ammunition, six additional Fouga jet trainer aircraft and C-47 Dakota transport planes, five of which Israel delivered to that country in 1968 and 1969.[44] By mid-1969 the value of Uganda's arms purchases from Israel had reached $25 million, and Ugandan soldiers attended parachute school and tank-training courses in Israel.[45] In 1969 Israel also supplied Amin's army with twelve (obsolete but functional) M4 tanks, complete with Israeli-manufactured tank shells.[46] The IDF mission continued to cultivate ties with the Ugandan army and especially Amin. According to an Israeli account, Bar-Lev acted as Amin's 'personal advisor wherever he went'.[47] Yet at the beginning of January 1970 Aaron Ofri (who in June 1968 replaced Lubrani as ambassador) protested 'the extensive assistance provided with such a generous hand, yet so little thought to Israel's demands upon Uganda'.[48]

In late 1970 a growing struggle between Obote and Amin brought the Ugandan president to transfer his chief of staff to a non-operational post, creating the circumstances for the coup d'état that the latter carried out in January 1971. Thus in late September 1970 Obote took the opportunity of Nasser's death to send Amin to represent Uganda at the funeral, in his absence appointing as army chief of staff Brigadier Suleiman Hussein and demoting Amin to the position of chief of the defence staff.[49]

Amin and Israel: January 1971–March 1972

The Israel State Archive has only recently declassified files on Israeli involvement in the 25 January 1971 coup in Uganda. In the absence of such documents most scholars adopted a careful approach, citing the conjectural nature of the evidence of an Israeli role. Woodward notes that Amin was in close contact with the Israeli military delegation and especially Bar-Lev.[50] Avirgan and Honey remark on 'considerable circumstantial evidence' that Britain, Israel and the United States were involved.[51] According to Mazrui, 'circumstantial evidence supports Obote's claim that Amin's success ... was partly attributable to brilliant advice from some of his Israeli friends'. Yet Mittelman points out that 'no hard facts implicate the Israelis', and although they were 'initially pleased ... this does not mean that the Israelis had a hand in planning'.[52]

On the day following the coup Colonel Bar-Lev reported that Amin had months earlier told him of his plans to overthrow Obote.[53] Arye Oded of the Africa Division, writing in April 1972, noted that while the head of Israel's military delegation was not complicit in Amin's coup, he had guided the general during its critical first hours. 'Burka' ordered Israeli instructors not to arm Ugandan aircraft, lest Obote's supporters use them to thwart the chief of staff's scheme.[54] On 27 January Hanan Bar-On, head of the director general's office, cabled Foreign Ministry instructions to abstain from interference in Uganda's affairs. Bar-Lev ignored insistence that he refrain from meddling.[55] In fact Bar-Lev extended his influence to the fate of officials and army officers. He interceded on behalf of E.W. Oryema, the police chief with whom Israel had worked closely. 'Burka' convinced the chief of staff to spare Oryema's life because he was of the Acholi tribe, the support of which Amin would need. The Israeli colonel also urged Amin to accept Felix Onama's pledge of loyalty. Yet at the same time, wrote Oded, Bar-Lev told Amin whom he should eliminate.[56]

The Foreign Ministry regarded with circumspection Israel's future in Uganda. Thus, wrote Ofri, the 'intellectually challenged' Amin was loyal to friends, and this would stand Israel in good stead. But Amin had killed scores of officers, and the promotions to follow would leave Israel familiar with few of the army's commanders.[57] Oded predicted, 'this will be a dictatorship based on terror'.[58] The Foreign Ministry viewed with concern the impact that Israel's engagement in Uganda would have on both the future of relations with that country and its image in the rest of black Africa. Israel's envoys rejected completely Obote's accusations that Israel had been involved in Amin's coup.[59] Nevertheless, the IDF mission was a conspicuous presence, and Ofri wrote of his dismay at the manner in which these officers comported themselves during the weeks following the coup. Ofri cabled that IDF personnel took part in all of the events that Amin hosted, appearing on a daily basis in Ugandan television broadcasts. As for Amin's promises of a new chapter in his country's relations with Israel, wrote Ofri, 'time will tell'.[60]

In early March 1971 Ofri again voiced apprehension regarding Israel's 'complete identification' with Amin's coup, emphasising the peril of such a high profile.[61] In truth, Amin entertained hopes that Israel would fill a more significant role in building his arsenal. On 9 February he turned to Israel's defence minister, Moshe Dayan, writing 'I request that for the strengthening our forces [sic] … you make available to us a squadron of skyhawk and phantom fighter/bomber aircraft.'[62] In early April representatives of the Foreign Ministry and Defence Ministry met to study the request that Uganda had submitted to Israel. Israeli officials did not take under consideration Amin's appeal for Skyhawks and Phantoms. The Ugandans' list included seven additional tanks, 600 command cars, an infantry school and the creation of two additional paratrooper battalions. Israel and Uganda had since the January coup signed contracts for the construction of military installations worth nearly $20 million. The Foreign Ministry questioned the wisdom of meeting his ambitious demands. Uganda's plans would require an increase in Israeli personnel from forty-four to sixty-three officers and technicians. The Africa Division counselled caution regarding commitments that Israel would be unable to meet.[63]

On 22 April Ofri reported Amin's slaughter of hundreds of his opponents, observing, 'the general has neither changed nor become wiser'.[64] Misgivings notwithstanding, the Foreign Ministry in May agreed to the

Defence Ministry's call to draft a new agreement for military assistance.[65] Ofri observed that Amin was still imbued with 'touching faith' in Israel.[66] In June 1971 the Defence Ministry sold Amin an Israel Aircraft Industries (Westwind) Jet Commander for his personal use.[67] Yet Oded issued another word of caution. A 'honeymoon' had marked the beginning of relations with Obote, too, and 'as Amin finds alternatives to Israel, so will ties cool'.[68]

Amin came to Israel on 11 July, meeting with Meir, Dayan and Eban. His hosts were neither able nor willing to meet his expectations. Thus the Ugandan leader asked for a loan of £10 million on easy terms, which Israel refused.[69] Meir writes in her autobiography that their meeting convinced her that the dictator was 'quite mad'. Amin told her 'I want Phantoms.' Meir exclaimed, 'We don't manufacture Phantoms; we buy them from the United States, when we can … why do you need Phantoms?' Amin responded, 'to use against Tanzania'.[70] By that time the Foreign Ministry and Defence Ministry had closed ranks regarding arms, in July 1971 reaching agreement that Israel would defer as long as possible any response to Amin's demand for military hardware.[71]

In late September Bar-On wrote to Daniel Laor, who had replaced Ofri on 26 July, that 'we are all partner to the view that we must dismount the tiger called Amin'.[72] In truth, Laor gained Amin's confidence and became closely involved in Ugandan affairs. Laor also defended Amin. 'He is a friend', he noted, 'and Israel must make certain he not act foolishly'. Israel's new envoy insisted the president was neither 'mad nor stupid', pointing out that he 'believed blindly' in Israel, and in their frequent meetings 'poured his heart out'. At the same time, the ambassador complained, 'we are trying to lower our profile', because, in the Foreign Ministry's view, 'in the 1970s it is not seemly to be entangled in assistance to a military *junta*'.[73]

Bar-On responded that Israel was reducing its role in Ugandan security affairs in order both to shift the focus from that dimension and to avoid involvement in Uganda's growing conflicts with its neighbours. In August and October 1971 skirmishes erupted near Lake Victoria on the Tanzania–Uganda border. President Julius Nyerere permitted Ugandan opponents of the Amin regime to train in Tanzania, and from there these dissidents shelled Ugandan units. The number of casualties was limited to several dozen. Nevertheless, this marked the 'internationalisation of Uganda's political violence'.[74] Moreover, the Mossad reported a development that other sources do not mention; during the clashes, the Ugandan Air Force entered combat for the first time. Its commander, Major Wilson Toko, flew one of the planes.[75] Israel refused Amin's repeated requests that its own pilots fly such missions, eschewing involvement in Uganda's border skirmishes.[76]

Laor continued to meet with Amin frequently and on 15 November 1971 assured the Foreign Ministry, 'I can promise you that dreams of conquering Tanzania have been laid aside.'[77] Yet Israel had its own concerns, including support in the United Nations. The Ugandan delegation had voted against Israel on five occasions from 1968 to 1971, and on four others it abstained on resolutions dealing with the occupied territories and rights of the Palestinians. In no instance did Uganda support Israel.[78] On 24 November Laor cabled that Amin promised an immediate change in Israel's favour.[79] On 13 December the General Assembly was to vote on a resolution calling for Israel's compliance with UN Security Resolution 242 of November 1967. On 9 December Laor reported on his recent conversation with Amin: 'one thing is clear; Uganda will not, repeat not, vote against Israel'.[80] Four days later the UN General Assembly passed Resolution 2799, and Uganda voted against Israel. On 22 December Shalev instructed Laor to tell the president of his shock at the results of this 'first test of the new Uganda'.[81] By that time Amin was in Mecca, to which he flew on 20 December as a haji (Muslim pilgrim).[82] Bar-Lev protested 'I never dreamt that what happened, could happen ... while the Israeli Military Mission supports the Ugandan Army.'[83]

Uganda's retreat from engagement with Israel now proceeded apace. The Israeli presence had become a source of discomfort for a leadership seeking support from Eastern, communist and Arab countries. Regional developments lent further impetus to this process, principally the November 1971 Addis Ababa negotiations that ended the Anya Nya rebellion and Amin's desire for the approval of Africa's radical states.[84]

Laor next met with Amin on 2 February 1972, their discussion highlighting the growing tension between the two countries. The president candidly told the Israeli envoy of his intention to visit Cairo, where he would refute claims that Uganda had granted Israel bases for operations in Sudan.[85] Amin met with that country's president, Anwar Sadat, pledging to forge closer ties with the Arab world.[86] Laor warned of the effect on relations of the large-scale projects for which Amin's government had contracted with Israel. Amin had not consulted with Israel about the economic feasibility of the airfields he wanted, and the Defence Ministry had found him an Israeli company to carry out the work. Yet officials in Kampala claimed that Israel had saddled their country with unmanageable financial obligations. Now, wrote the ambassador, Israel had 'placed its head in Uganda's economic sickbed', becoming partner to its unrealistic undertakings. He urged that any future commitment regarding military assistance to Uganda be scrutinised carefully.[87]

On 13 February 1972 Amin landed in Tripoli. Amin and Libya's president, Muammar Gaddafi, issued a joint communiqué, affirming support for 'the Arab people's just struggle against Zionism and Imperialism'. Amin also agreed to turn Uganda into a black Muslim state and received as a grant from Libya the £10 million he had earlier requested of Israel.[88] On 17 February Oded wrote that Israel could assist Uganda even while that country worked against it in the international arena or initiate its own exit, completing only those projects in Uganda that appeared profitable.[89] The next day the Foreign Ministry decided that Israel would not 'slam the door' in Kampala.[90]

On 21 February a Libyan delegation began talks at Entebbe with Ugandan ministers; the result was assistance for the Ugandan army and building of mosques and schools for Islam in Uganda.[91] Three days later Amin boasted to Laor that he would dictate matters to the Arabs and said that he wanted to talk about intelligence on the Arab world. Laor urged scaling back before Amin served Israel with 'unpleasant surprises'.[92] Oded notes that some Israelis thought it still possible to ignore Amin's behaviour. Yet *The Jerusalem Post* wrote that it behooved Israel to 'conduct itself with a minimum of self-respect' and sever ties before Kampala so decided. Amin himself drove home that point, on 29 February summoning Laor in order to accuse Israel of subversion in Uganda.[93]

At the beginning of March Bar-Lev convinced his superiors that the crisis in relations was a passing phase. In truth, neither the Defence Ministry nor the Foreign Ministry viewed matters in that light but agreed that Israel initiate no break in ties.[94] In mid-March Amin cancelled a trip to Cairo and Khartoum in order to deal with tribal unrest, lashing out at Israel when the newspaper *Davar* reported the reason for his deferred plans. The Israelis, he said, had written of Ugandan domestic troubles they themselves were fomenting.[95] On 22 March he used the

Davar article as pretext for notice that Uganda would extend no contracts for IDF assistance. The next day Amin ordered Laor to divest the embassy of its first secretary and staff, remove the IDF mission and 'intelligence operatives' and leave in Uganda only the Israeli Air Force training staff. On the following day Amin told the heads of several Israeli companies to halt work on most major projects.[96]

'Operation Afikoman': Exit from Uganda

On 24 March 1972 the Ministry of Defence commenced 'Operation Afikoman', the purpose of which was to remove IDF personnel and families from Uganda as quickly as possible.[97] The operation was aptly named. The search for the Afikoman brings nearly to its conclusion the Passover Seder, the date of which in 1972 was 30 March. Amin's eviction of the IDF delegation shocked the Israeli public; members of Knesset called upon the government to close the embassy in Kampala immediately.[98] Archival sources provide only part of the explanation for the government's irresolution. Thus on 26 March Laor cabled, 'we need a few days in order to deal with interpretations [of Uganda's intentions] and [the Foreign Ministry's] instructions'.[99]

Later that day Idi Amin ordered all Israelis to depart. The foreign minister, Wanume Kibedi, told Laor 'no one can stand up to the general' and apologised repeatedly.[100] That night Laor reported that Amin, who accused the Israelis of engaging in 'subversive activities' backed by a 700-man 'secret army' in his country, had placed the Ugandan army on alert.[101] On 28 March Abba Eban convened officials of the Foreign Ministry. They anticipated that Amin's next step would be to instruct the Israeli embassy to shut its doors, noting 'better that we initiate such a move ourselves'.[102] Yet the Israeli government issued no such order.

On 30 March Amin directed Israel to close its embassy within ten days.[103] Absent Ugandan notice regarding termination of relations, Israel refrained from a step it feared would jeopardise their remaining assets there. Yet on 2 April Amin froze all Israeli accounts in Uganda and demanded to know of companies in his country employing Jews.[104] On 8 April Laor departed Uganda. The Israeli press devoted much attention to the 'Exodus' from Uganda but noted that this was not a break in ties. The next day the government in Kampala announced that it had in fact severed diplomatic relations with Israel.[105]

Conclusion

The analysis of what had gone wrong began even before Israel closed its embassy. Oded listed the factors that had contributed to Israel's ouster. First, Amin discovered that his debt to Israel was an 'asset' and exploited it to make a 'deal' with the Arab states. Second, Amin believed that distancing himself from Israel would relieve his isolation, bringing him into a fold that included the radical African governments, Arab states, the Soviet Union and China. Third, once Amin had openly announced his hostility toward Israel, he feared the Israelis, foremost the head of the IDF mission and the Mossad chief in Uganda, would move against him. For that reason, he ordered that they be the first to exit the country. A fourth component was the Arabs' view that airfields Israel had built in Uganda threatened them, heightening their determination to end the Israeli presence there. Fifth was the supply of inferior equipment and the inordinately high prices that Israeli companies on occasion charged Uganda for services, which also affected relations. Finally, wrote Oded, the Israelis had behaved like a 'power' in Uganda, convincing themselves Amin was under their sway, when in fact Israel could neither contain his ambition nor solve Uganda's problems.[106] On 9 April Alouph Hareven, director of the Information Division of the Foreign Ministry, wrote that ultimately Israel could have controlled neither Amin's personality nor Gaddafi's initiatives. Moreover, had all Israelis assigned to Uganda comported themselves with propriety, the outcome would not have been different.[107] Meir promised that when the last Israeli had left Uganda, 'everything would be told'. Yet the prime minister intended 'all that Israel had achieved there', and not 'everything that Amin had done'.[108]

Within a fortnight of Amin's first eviction notice Israel evacuated all but a few of its 470 citizens from Uganda. Seventy of these were military personnel, eighty were technical experts and employees of Israeli companies and the rest women and children.[109] By the beginning of 1972 these advisors had trained thirty Ugandan pilots and hundreds of air force technicians. In 1971 several hundred Ugandan ground troops had passed through courses in Israel.[110] That year Israel's exports to Uganda had reached $7.9 million, the volume of those sales increasing by $2.3 million in each of the two years since 1969. The Israeli companies Solel Boneh and Vered had carried out building projects valued at $34 million, and Israeli firms such as Hiram Ze'evi had under contract work worth an additional $30 million.[111] Israel later recovered only half of this sum.[112]

The Foreign Ministry viewed the break with Uganda as an opportunity to reassess Israel's strategy in Africa. Israeli diplomats urged Mordechai Gazit, the director general, to exploit the failure in Uganda to restore to that office greater control of activities on the continent and forestall a further deterioration of Israel's position there.[113] In fact there were divergent views of the effect of the 'exodus' from Uganda. Some of Israel's diplomats attributed Amin's break to the caprice of a disturbed dictator but of limited impact upon Israel's position on the continent. Oded wrote that 'damage to Israel's reputation from the Uganda expulsion is limited; the Africans know Amin'.[114] Yet Israeli ambassadors in African capitals reported on the deleterious effect of Israel's 'flight' from Kampala. At the beginning of April, Reuven Dafni, ambassador in Nairobi, wrote that even if the views of Kenya's President Jomo Kenyatta and his closest advisors were to remain unchanged, 'it would be foolish to think that at lower levels [of government] and in public opinion no damage has been done [to] Israel's standing'.[115] The Mossad noted that the general view among officials in Nairobi was that Amin's move was 'strange', but most thought 'he must surely have had a reason'.[116] On 19 April Tamar Golan, the Israeli journalist and Africa expert, wrote to Ya'acov Shimoni, deputy director general of the Foreign Ministry, that Israel's image in Africa had suffered a severe setback. 'The effect ... is mainly on the psychological plane ... [but augurs] ... a difficult time in the future'. Golan expressed her regret that the Foreign Ministry had to bear the brunt of a 'fiasco' for which Israel's defence establishment had been primarily responsible.[117]

In mid-1972 senior officials of the Foreign Ministry visited fourteen African countries and on 14 June they met in Jerusalem to share their impressions. Hanan Bar-On, whose itinerary included five countries, reported that his African interlocutors were well aware that Israel had done much more in Uganda than in other countries on the continent. They asked, 'what were 700 Israelis doing there?' A minister in Swaziland told Bar-On that while his colleagues in the government knew of Amin's true character, the people and even the intellectuals did not. Israel's 'fall' in Uganda, he warned, would yet influence Israel's standing in Africa. Gazit noted that 'the situation is worrisome ... our image has been hurt and sullied'.[118]

Epilogue

During the months following Amin's abrupt severing of relations, Israel sought to contain the damage that the 'Uganda affair' had done to its reputation and ensure that no more African governments follow suit. Israel watched closely Uganda's burgeoning relations with the Arab states and the Palestine Liberation Organization. Thus in November 1972 an extensive Foreign Ministry report noted that Amin had in June visited nine Arab countries, signing defence agreements with Egypt, Libya and Sudan. In July 1972 a PLO delegation visited Kampala, and Amin announced his gift to the Palestinians of the Israeli embassy for their use as an office.[119] Between late November 1972 and from January to May 1973 Chad, Congo (Brazzaville), Mali, Niger and Burundi severed relations with Israel, and in October and November 1973 twenty-one more black African states broke off ties. Yet most of those governments terminated relations with Israel for reasons very different than those of Amin. Moreover, during the four years that followed the rupture, three elements set apart Israel's experience with Uganda from relations with all other black African states.

First, in September 1972 Amin wrote to UN Secretary General Kurt Waldheim, justifying Nazi Germany's extermination of the Jews. African governments were among those that expressed indignation at Amin's crude rantings. Second, Uganda's neighbours turned to Israel for assistance in the face of the threat from Kampala. In October 1975 Munyua Waiyaki, Kenya's foreign minister, asked Israeli Foreign Minister Yigal Allon to convince the United States to sell Nairobi combat jets in order to deter Amin.[120] Waiyaki turned to Allon even though his government had two years earlier severed diplomatic relations with Israel. Finally, Israel made a brief 're-entry' to Uganda, when on 4 July 1976 it successfully executed Operation Thunderbolt. In that operation, IDF commandos rescued Israeli nationals and Jewish passengers that Palestinian hijackers had held hostage at Uganda's Entebbe Airport. Kenya was among the African states that publicly condemned but privately lauded the Israeli mission.[121]

9

ISRAEL'S CLANDESTINE DIPLOMACY
WITH SUDAN

TWO ROUNDS OF EXTRAORDINARY COLLABORATION

Yehudit Ronen

Introduction

Israel's geostrategic interest in Sudan and its Arab and African neighbours gathered momentum throughout the mid-1950s, particularly in the aftermath of the establishment of the Sudanese state on 1 January 1956—nearly eight years after Israel had gained its independence. Israel's increased attentiveness to the political situation in Khartoum at that juncture was clearly discernable by its prompt message of congratulations to the new Sudanese state on the 'memorable occasion of the proclamation of the Sudanese Republic' and in the subsequent wishes for the 'prosperous future and peaceful consolidation of the Sudanese nation'.[1] In fact, Israel had already identified the value of Sudan's geostrategic potential for its own essential security interests on the eve of its independence, holding its first diplomatic contacts with Khartoum's leading political-religious Umma Party under the leadership of Abdallah al-Khalil in 1954.[2]

During the 1950s, Israel's foreign policy-makers considered Sudan, as well as Ethiopia—with which Israel established diplomatic relations in 1956[3]—as two major pillars in its broader strategy, the so-called 'periphery doctrine'. This strategy was designed to minimise what Israel perceived as the danger inherent in the two overlapping Arab circles of threat: the 'first circle of confrontation' comprised frontline Arab countries hostile to Israel with an aggressive Egypt very much to the fore, while the 'second circle of confrontation' was made up of other Arab and non-Arab states located on the geopolitical periphery of the first, with Sudan being notable among them.[4] Following the rationale of this strategy, Israel was interested in urging Sudan to concentrate its political and military energies on Sudanese internal affairs rather than focusing its attention on the Arab–Israeli conflict. In particular, Israel was concerned about a potential Sudanese–Egyptian alliance. Sudan borders Egypt to the south and is also strategically positioned along the Red Sea—a vital maritime link for Israel. Thus it was not surprising that the Israeli government considered Sudan a pivotal asset in Jerusalem's periphery doctrine.

The high priority given by Jerusalem to eroding Cairo's political and military capabilities, thereby reducing the Egyptian threat toward Israel, converged with a key objective of Sudan's ruling Umma Party: to deter Egypt's militant interventionist policy toward Sudan. This convergence of interests resulted in a short-lived clandestine diplomatic collaboration between Jerusalem and Khartoum. This bilateral chapter in relations was finally closed with the ascent to power of Sudan's first military regime in November 1958.

During the 1960s and most of the 1970s, Sudan and its geostrategic environment underwent a series of dramatic upheavals. Both Khartoum's domestic and foreign arenas had changed, beginning with the rise to power of Jafar Muhammad al-Numayri in 1969 in Sudan's second military coup since independence. Other events affected Sudan's domestic and foreign affairs, such as the escalation of the Sudanese Civil War, the intensifying international environment of the cold war and Egypt's peace agreement with Israel.

Amid these developments, the civil war, which first erupted in 1955 between Sudan's two largest, non-monolithic ethnic-religious human blocks—the hegemonic Arab Muslim governing elite in Khartoum (the North) on the one hand, and the minority Christian, Animist and African society living in the south on the other (the South)—affected relations between Jerusalem and Khartoum. Inasmuch as the war continues to fester, it had turned from an intrastate conflict into an interstate conflict, drawing into the conflict a series of regional and international players.[5] Needing urgent financial, military and political injections in order to survive politically, the Sudanese regime fully turned to the Arab orbit, with Khartoum positioning itself in the anti-Western and anti-Israeli Arab camp. This new turn, perceived by the Israeli government as threatening the state's strategic position, spurred Israel to extend assistance to the southern rebel party in the Sudanese armed conflict, thereby undermining the political, ideological and military engagement of the Arab Muslim Sudanese government in the inter-Arab arena.

Yet in the late 1970s and the first half of the 1980s, the wheel had turned as the essential interests of Israel and Sudan converged again, paving the way for a new strategic opportunity. Israel and Sudan opened a second chapter of clandestine diplomatic contacts, this time basing their collaboration on an entirely different agenda. Moreover, in stark contrast to the earlier round of strategic cooperation, this time Egypt was not a focus of common animosity but rather a strategic partner for both Jerusalem and Khartoum, demonstrating the dynamic twists prevalent in Middle Eastern politics. This episode of clandestine diplomacy was conducted under the sponsorship of Washington and with the participation not only of Israel and Sudan, but of Ethiopia and Egypt as well.

This secret cooperation proved highly successful from Israel's perspective, culminating in the massive transfer of the Ethiopian Jews through Sudan's territory to Israel. This diplomatic round also proved beneficial to Sudan, at least for a period of time, providing its regime with desperately needed political and military aid during a time of acute domestic turmoil. Yet despair and eventually popular rage against the chronic incompetence of Khartoum eventually doomed its political survival. On 5 April 1985, senior commanders of the Sudanese military deposed the regime in the third military coup in Sudan's history. The ousting of Numayri from power brought to an end the second period of clandestine diplomatic ties between the governments in Jerusalem and Khartoum.

This chapter focuses its discussion on the two major junctions of Israeli–Sudanese clandestine diplomatic relations, providing new observations by encompassing both the regional and international players and by using new documentary materials, notwithstanding the official limitations on accessing many relevant documents.⁶ It is important to note, however, that the chapter makes no effort to map and systematically analyse the historical and political dimensions of the complex contact points between Jerusalem and Khartoum, either of collaboration or of conflict. Rather, the chapter concentrates on two periods. The first occurred in the mid-1950s and the second in the mid-1980s. Notwithstanding this collaboration, these periods mark not only a commonality of interests but also major points of divergence and competition between Israel and Sudan.

Israel's Clandestine Diplomatic Contacts with Independent Sudan: 1954–8

The objection of the Umma Party, the leading force in Sudan's political system in the mid-1950s, to Egypt's demanding aspirations for establishing a unity framework with Sudan, known as the 'Unity of the Nile Valley',⁷ and for achieving a greater political and economic foothold in Khartoum, spurred Sudan's first pro-Western coalition governments into remaining ideologically and politically aloof from Cairo and from the Arab–Israeli conflict. The Egyptian fear was shared by Israel and Sudan, who observed the growing Soviet influence in Cairo and the growing Egyptian drive for Arab unity under President Gamal Abd al-Nasser's leadership.

In the fall of 1956, one unnamed Sudanese official affiliated with the governing Umma Party stated in clear terms that 'Sudan perceives the Egyptian military empowerment [as] a direct danger for its independence, fearing that Egypt will attack Sudan rather than attacking Israel.' He continued that the government in Khartoum '[H]as an interest to weaken the regime in Egypt and tighten cooperation with Nasser's opponents.' Yet the Sudanese official remained circumspect over ties with Israel, emphasising that concurrent factors, primarily 'Sudan's dependence on the Suez Canal, the [Nile] allocation water problem [between the two countries and Sudan's distressing] financial difficulties', obliged the Khartoum government 'to be nice to Egypt'.⁸ Being acquainted with Sudan's politics, the Israeli official, who reported this Sudanese message from Addis Ababa,⁹ evaluated the ability of Khartoum's government to block the Egyptian endeavour to gain an influential foothold in Sudan as one yielding 'encouraging prospects'. The Israeli official noted, however, that the success of the Sudanese endeavour to fend off Egypt's pressure '[D]epends on the extent of [foreign] political and economic aid' which Khartoum will get. The Israeli official implied that Israel alone cannot meet this challenge, and that it should establish triangular cooperation with France,[10] an idea, he further argued, which was acceptable to the Sudanese government. The Israeli message ended with a clue on an imminent secret meeting to be held with the participation of the Sudanese representative 'at the end of the week in Paris' to advance this matter.[11]

Israel's appeal to France was influenced by Khartoum's repeated exertions of pressure on Jerusalem, urging it to gird up its loins and make 'greater efforts' to reinforce Sudan's resilience against Egypt's militancy. This was exemplified by the message delivered by Prime Minister Abdallah Khalil to Jerusalem in May 1956, intertwining it with a hinted threat that if the Sudanese call for greater help would not be met, Sudan might be forced to resort to moves detrimental to Israel. 'Does Israel not understand that if Sudan would be compelled to join the Arab League,[12] then Israel would pay a much higher price as Sudan might be compelled to send a military brigade to Israel's border [with Egypt]?'[13]

Although the contacts, which were maintained between the representatives of Israel and Sudan's leading Umma Party, remained mostly undisclosed by Israel, there were reports claiming that the two sides held talks in various European capital cities. In one of these rounds, which was held in London between top Sudanese politicians from the Umma leadership and Mordechai Gazit, the first secretary of the Israeli embassy in London who had served earlier in Israel's diplomatic mission in Addis Ababa, the two sides hatched 'various schemes for anti-Nasser cooperation'.[14] These contacts were established with the help of British Intelligence (MI6), which advised a delegation from the pro-Western Sudanese Umma Party to go to London in mid-1954 to seek Israeli assistance in their efforts to ward off interventionist pressure from pro-Soviet Egypt. In September 1955, Israel's Prime Minister Moshe Sharett supported the idea of establishing 'commercial ties' with Sudan, depicting this option as 'an interesting initiative which deserves to be developed'.[15] In late August 1956, a senior Sudanese official made a secret visit to Israel to discuss the economic assistance that was to be delivered to the Umma Party.[16]

The motivation of the Umma Party to find a counterweight to Egyptian pressure was reinforced by the fear of the growing power in

Khartoum of the political-religious Khatmiyya sect—a pro-Egyptian movement and the sworn political rival of the Umma Party. Sudan also feared the imminent building of the Aswan Dam (as decided by Cairo already in 1952) and the consequent damaging effect on the agreed allocation of Nile waters to Sudan. Khartoum was also concerned that Egypt would not pay compensation in return for the dam's adverse consequences in the region of Wadi Halfa, an area which was expected to be partially flooded by the Nile waters after the completion of the dam. Sudan was also concerned about the Egyptian exploitation of the Cairo-based and headed Arab League, which might impose on Sudan Egypt's pan-Arab unity policy along with other problematic moves which the Khartoum government considered as being to the detriment of Sudan.[17]

The Umma Party also hoped to benefit politically and economically from what it perceived as Israel's powerful military position and close diplomatic ties with the United States and Britain. This Sudanese perception was further strengthened following the raid on 28 February 1955 by the Israel Defence Forces (IDF) on Egyptian bases in Gaza, which inflicted a heavy blow on Cairo. Furthermore, Israel's participation alongside Britain and France in the Suez War of October 1956, a campaign in which the IDF inflicted heavy losses on the Egyptian Army in the Sinai Peninsula, enhanced the image of Israel as a powerful state aligned with the West. The ongoing cold war, which affected Middle Eastern politics, not least in the growing ties between Moscow and Cairo in the second half of the 1950s, further pushed the Western-oriented Umma Party to keep the diplomatic road with Israel open.[18]

Israel for its part had strong enough motives to prevent any crystallisation of political and strategic-military collaboration developing between Sudan and Egypt. Moreover, Nasser's vehement promise to mobilise the Arab world to fight the 'Zionist state' until its annihilation, and Egypt's perception of Sudan as a most valuable strategic and military rear base, injected further momentum to Jerusalem's efforts to maintain an effective influence upon Khartoum's inter-Arab policy. This was further exemplified by the clandestine meeting held in Paris in August 1957 between Israel's Foreign Minister Golda Meir and Sudan's prime minister and leader of the Umma Party, Abdallah Khalil.[19]

The conduct of these clandestine diplomatic contacts fully dovetailed with Israel's periphery doctrine. Accordingly, in July 1958, Israel's Prime Minister David Ben-Gurion requested that US President Dwight D.

Eisenhower extend 'political, financial and moral support' to the Umma government in Khartoum.[20] Ben-Gurion argued that such support would not only serve Israeli strategic interests, but would also serve the American national interest since Nasser was in effect acting as the Soviet spearhead in the Arab Middle East and the Horn of Africa.[21]

The ascent to power by General Ibrahim Abbud in a November 1958 military coup led to the cutting of clandestine diplomatic ties between Jerusalem and Khartoum. Not only did Abbud call for solidarity with Egypt's pan-Arab president Nasser, but the new Sudanese head of state also acted to sever contacts with the West and to avoid any association with Israel. The dramatic changes in Khartoum coincided with the growing wave of Nasserism and the directly linked rise of pan-Arab nationalism, as exemplified in the establishment of the United Arab Republic in early 1958 between Egypt and Syria. This new zealous pan-Arab framework, accompanied by Nasser's declaration for 'other Arab countries to join',[22] led Israel to search for alternative strategic routes. Israel hastened to strengthen its strategic position in the Middle East, a process concluding with a series of 'secret pacts' with Turkey, Iran and Ethiopia during the latter part of 1958.[23] Indeed, in their study of Israel's intelligence community, Dan Raviv and Yossi Melman claim that the United States and Great Britain 'supported and valued Israel's strategic contributions in establishing peripheral alliances', presumably referring among others to the case of Sudan.[24]

Abbud's ouster in late 1964 was followed by the installation of a civilian coalition government under the premiership of Muhammad Ahmad Mahjoub of the Umma Party. Tragically for Sudan, the new regime failed to offer solutions which might have alleviated the internal schisms. Instead, repeated political crises, economic downturns, social unrest and growing bloodshed in the civil war between the South and the government in the north now defined Sudan as a fractured polity. It was primarily the chronic civil war that dragged the Sudanese multiethnic state deeper into militancy across various domestic and foreign fronts, including the Arab–Israeli conflict. This ideological, political and strategic polarisation between Sudan and Israel carried a dangerous military risk in Israel's eyes and spurred Jerusalem to find a counterbalance against an increasingly pro-Egypt Sudan. This inevitably led Israel to offer direct support to the southern, mainly Christian rebels fighting Khartoum. Yet this chapter of starkly conflicting interests between

Jerusalem and Khartoum, which began in the 1960s and ended in 1972 with the signing by the warring Sudanese parties of the Addis Ababa peace agreement, remains beyond the scope of this chapter.[25]

The Second Round of Clandestine Collaboration

Once a year as winter approaches, massive flights of white storks from Europe, passing over Israel, head for Ethiopia where they eventually settle in the vicinity of Lake Tana, where most of the Jewish community live. Casting their eyes upon the big birds with excitement and recalling their folklore, the Jews ask the storks with yearning, 'Storks, storks, tell us how is our country Yerusalem?'[26] This annual ritual, one of the many unique customs of Jews in Ethiopia, demonstrates the deeply rooted religious and emotional longing of the Ethiopian Jews for their historic home. Identifying themselves as Beta Israel, broader circles in Christian and Muslim Ethiopia refer to them as 'Falashas', meaning strangers or invaders, the Ethiopian Jews have always dreamed of reaching Zion.

In 1973, a groundbreaking ruling by the rabbinical establishment in Israel formally recognised their Jewish status, perceiving them as the descendants of the lost Dan Tribe from among the tribes of the Kingdom of Israel.[27] Another version, prevalent in non-Jewish circles, claimed that the Ethiopian Jews were the descendents of the Cushitic group of the Agau, who adopted Judaism as a religion when they arrived in Ethiopia in the fifth century BC.[28] Additional theories about their Jewish origin stipulate that they may be descendants of Menelik I, son of King Solomon and Queen Sheba, or the descendants of Jews who fled Israel for Egypt after the destruction of the first temple in 586 BC and eventually settled in Ethiopia.[29]

From 1977 until 1991, most of the Beta Israel community was airlifted from Sudan's territory through interim destinations in Western Europe to Israel.[30] About 200 Jews left Ethiopia directly for Israel aboard Israeli military transport aircrafts that had emptied their military cargo and were returning to Israel.[31] This specific operation, being the result of clandestine diplomatic contacts between Jerusalem and Addis Ababa, may have been the precursor of the mass exodus of Ethiopian Jews in the mid-1980s—Operation Moses—and the successful product of clandestine diplomacy. For while in 1977 less than 100 Ethiopian Jews lived in Israel, their numbers steadily increased, reaching around 125,000 people in 2011.[32]

The massive departure of the Ethiopian Jews to Israel was portrayed by the Israeli media in flowery language, being branded as 'The Exodus from Ethiopia', thus drawing direct parallels with the biblical story of the exodus of Jews from Egypt. The biblical spirit was further mirrored in the names attached by Israel to the two major phases of the airlift operation—'Operation Moses' between 1984 and 1985, and 'Operation Solomon' in 1991, while the regime of Haile Mariam Mengistu was on the verge of downfall.[33] Indeed, it is difficult to find an example in modern history where a state mobilised its military, intelligence and diplomatic resources and initiated intricate clandestine operations in hostile territory in order to reclaim a segment of its people from exile in distant regions.[34] One may also note in the same breath that there is no precedent in modern history where a minority community of such a size, with such a deep cultural legacy dating back 2,500 years in a specific Diaspora, had devotedly mobilised itself to leave its country of residence in a clandestine way in order to fulfil its dream of reaching 'Jerusalem'—a sacred destination in the community's historical collective memory.[35]

A wide gallery of 'players' took part in this human and political drama, shedding light on the multi-party, clandestine diplomatic role in this complex engagement. Unequivocally, the Sudanese regime under the leadership of President Numayri (1969–85) was pivotal among them, providing the territorial base for launching the mission. The Israeli cooperation with Numayri had been developed from the late 1970s onwards, with the significant help of the Saudi businessman Adnan Khashoggi.[36] The dominant influence of the United States convinced Numayri to allow the airlift operations to take place, while also serving as a mediatory platform for clandestine diplomacy and as a facilitator for overseeing various practical aspects of the whole affair. The American role was indispensable, also solving financial and logistical problems and smoothing over difficulties, primarily though not solely between Israel and Sudan, as during the ongoing clandestine collaboration each continued to perceive the other as an enemy.

At the same time, the terrible famines which caused such human tragedy and wreaked havoc on the economy of Ethiopia in the mid-1980s motivated the hitherto Marxist and pro-Soviet regime under Mengistu in Addis Ababa to try and obtain any help it could irrespective of ideological concerns. To this end, Ethiopia initiated clandestine diplomatic contacts with both the United States and Israel.[37] These contacts resulted in Ethiopian approval for Jews to immigrate to Israel in an exchange for famine relief, military assistance and other aid deemed necessary to ensure the survival of the regime.[38] Israel reportedly supplied the Ethiopians, who were still fighting rebels in Eritrea, with '$20 million (US) worth of Soviet military hardware and spare parts' while by 1985, if not earlier, Israeli military advisors were active in Ethiopia.[39] One may speculate that these actions were linked to what was revealed later as the transfer operations of the Ethiopian Jews to Israel. Clearly, the intelligence apparatus of Ethiopia, Sudan, the United States and Israel were clandestinely involved in these operations.[40] Moreover, before his assassination in October 1981, Egypt's President Anwar al-Sadat played his part, appealing to his close ally Numayri on behalf of Washington and Israel's Prime Minister Menachem Begin to turn a blind eye to the migration of Ethiopian Jews as they transited through Sudanese territory.[41] Between 1981 and 1982, the Israeli Mossad and the Israeli navy—with the knowledge of the United States and Sudan—rented a deserted tourist village via a Swiss front company. The Arous village as it was known was located to the north of Port Sudan on the coast of the Red Sea, and became the point from which thousands of Jews were transported to Israel.[42]

The Closure of the Clandestine Diplomatic Relationship

The secrecy with which the whole operation had been shrouded for more than half a decade was shattered on 5 January 1985, following disclosure in a hostile Ethiopian press (and other international media), which claimed that the Numayri regime was directly complicit in the airlift operation of the Ethiopian Jews to Israel via Sudan.[43] A political storm now took hold in Sudan and across the wider Arab world with Khartoum fearing the dire consequences that exposure of its collaboration with Israel would have on the regime's stability. Numayri therefore rushed to issue full public denials of any Sudanese involvement while in fact halting the operation two days later.[44] In fact, the Ethiopian press reports on the airlift operation were not the first. A number of Jewish newspapers and magazines in the United States had published the information on the airlift operation in late 1984.[45] In response, the Israeli government officially acknowledged the airlift operation for the first time on 31 December 1984.[46]

On 4 January 1985, the Ethiopian Foreign Ministry released a strongly worded statement directing Addis Ababa's rage upon Khartoum's role in the '[S]inister [airlift] operation' and accusing Sudan and other foreign powers of 'gross interference' in Ethiopia's internal affairs.[47] Fearful of the dangerous ramifications of the whole affair on its already heavily eroded position at home and in the Arab world, the politically weak regime of Numayri hurried to categorically deny any involvement in the airlift operation.[48] At the same time, Sudan's Foreign Ministry rushed to release an official explanatory statement denying what it termed the 'Ethiopian allegations' regarding Sudan's role in 'transporting Ethiopian Jews to Israel'. The Sudanese official statement termed these 'allegations' as 'unfounded' and classified them as 'malicious conspiracies' aimed against 'Arab solidarity and against every sincere … effort to confront the Israeli enemy'.[49] Yet Sudan grew alarmed as various Arab commentators began to allege that the airlift operation was 'a part of Israel's expansionist policy' designed to 'boost the Jewish population of the occupied West Bank', an accusation that made Sudan complicit in empowering the 'Zionist state'.[50]

Stung by such criticism, Sudan tried to turn the blame back on Ethiopia. Relations between Sudan and Ethiopia reached their lowest ebb in the middle of the 1980s with both states accusing the other of supporting their respective rebel movements. Khartoum accused Addis Ababa of providing asylum, training and arms to the southern Sudanese rebels while Ethiopia claimed that Sudan was supporting the Eritrean secessionists.[51] Sudan was particularly troubled by Ethiopia's aid to the rebels in southern Sudan, where the civil war had flared up again with renewed vigour in 1983.[52]

Desperately fighting for its political survival, the regime in Khartoum emphasised four points in its official statement in the wake of the airlift exposure:

First: Ethiopia has always been using Ethiopian Jews as a bargaining chip with Israel for obtaining arms and money. Second: Sudan has always served as a haven for Ethiopian and other refugees … irrespective of their race, colour or religion … As the Sudan is not a prison for those refugees, thousands of them have left Sudan for some European countries and elsewhere with the knowledge of the UNHCR [United Nations High Commissioner for Refugees]. Large numbers of them have also left for some Arab countries where they found job opportunities. Third: Ethiopia is the only one responsible for its subjects and if any one of them has found his way to Israel, that has undoubtedly been [done] in collusion [with] Ethiopia and Israel … Fourth: The Sudan need not [declare] its unswerving positions and policies toward the Israeli enemy which is still occupying Palestine and other Arab territories.[53]

Sudan was insistent in placing all the blame on Ethiopia while simultaneously maintaining its denial of any involvement with aiding and abetting the airlift or onwards transportation of Ethiopian Jews to Israel. This tactic seemed to be working as the tumult over the airlift appeared to abate. Yet it soon proved to be very much the calm before the storm. On 23 March 1985, the airlift affair made media headlines again when information came out that a new evacuation of 800 Ethiopian Jews from their temporary camps in Sudan had been completed, this time on American planes.[54] This was a CIA-sponsored follow-up mission to Operation Moses, named 'Operation Joshua' by the United States, but known in Israel as the 'Sheba operation'.[55] Even now, however, Khartoum claimed total ignorance of this operation, stating that it 'had not been and never [would] be a party' to such an action.[56]

Sudan's Motives for Cooperating with Israel Diplomatically

While Israel's motivation to collaborate with Sudan was clear, many in Sudan and in the Arab world and even beyond wondered what had motivated Numayri to take the risk of collaborating with the 'Israeli enemy'. The sudden collapse of the screen of secrecy over Sudan's role in serving Israel's interests in early 1985 provides an opportunity to analyse the motives behind Numayri's conduct in this regard.

During this period, frightened and unsure, Numayri's regime was making its utmost effort to secure its political hold on the country during a terribly difficult period in its domestic and foreign affairs. While the closely linked economic crisis and the civil war in South Sudan were intensifying at an alarming rate, Numayri was preoccupied with eliminating the urgent political dangers threatening his grip on power. Although he managed to remove potential challengers from top positions—most notably those associated with the militant Muslim Brothers—he failed to fill the ensuing vacuum with his own political presence and loyalists.[57] By the first half of the 1980s, an increasingly desperate Sudanese president invested all of his energies in the struggle for his political survival, to the detriment of the ethnic, religious, social and economic turmoil that now wracked the Sudanese state. The well-known scholar John O.

Voll correctly concluded that this crisis of governance remained inseparable from the ethnically and religiously fragmented society, noting that 'neither civilian party politics nor military revolutionary programs have been able to overcome the basic factors of instability in the country'.[58]

As if domestic affairs were not distressful enough, Sudan's mounting foreign pressures significantly exacerbated Numayri's problems. He sought the maximum amount of immediate support—politically, financially and militarily—particularly from the United States and from Sudan's pro-American Arab neighbours with Egypt, Saudi Arabia and the Gulf States in the lead. The American pressure on Numayri to let the operation begin from Sudanese territory placed the Sudanese leader in a difficult situation. He was caught between Sudan's pro-American Arab supporters Egypt and Saudi Arabia on the one hand and the militant, pro-Soviet Arab and African states Ethiopia and Libya on the other. Given the difficult political circumstances, Sudan's dependence on the American-backed camp was crucial for Numayri's political survival.

Another political and ideological battle that cast a long shadow over Sudan in the first half of the 1980s was the division of the Arab world into two major opposing camps over Cairo's rapprochement with Jerusalem under the 1978 Camp David Accords. Sharing a common border with pro-Western Egypt and perceiving it as a major pillar of Sudan's security, Numayri's regime hurried to support the Egyptian peace policy. Yet Numayri had to navigate his way through the turbulent waters of inter-Arab politics carefully. While staunchly supporting the trip of Egypt's President Anwar al-Sadat to Jerusalem in November 1977 and praising it as 'the bravest mission … in our modern history',[59] it was not long before Numayri understood that this position threatened his own political survival. This soon resulted in repeated zigzagging and even regressions in Khartoum's position toward the peace process during the first half of the 1980s, as the Sudanese leader sought to minimise the damage in relations with so-called rejectionist states in the Arab world. These 'rejectionist' and largely pro-Soviet Arab states—Libya, Syria and Iraq foremost among them—vehemently objected to any political settlement of the Arab–Israeli conflict and in fact rejected the right of the State of Israel to exist.[60] Numayri was aware of Moscow's antagonism toward his Western-oriented regime. Since the abortive communist coup against Numayri in July 1971, Sudan had distanced itself from the Soviet Union and moved closer to the West. Relations between Khartoum and Moscow steadily deteriorated, reaching their lowest point in the summer of 1976 with Numayri accusing the Soviet Union of being 'the merchant of death' and 'the major force' behind a serious coup attempt on 2 July 1976.[61] The Sudanese president repeatedly claimed that this coup attempt was 'planned in the Kremlin, implemented by [pro-Soviet] Havana, financed by Libya and [the coup leaders] trained in Ethiopia'.[62]

Against this disturbing constellation of adversaries, both domestic and foreign, it was obvious that the power-striving Numayri could not afford to reject American pressure to allow the airlift operation to take place on and above Sudanese territory. Moreover, the offer of immediate economic, military and political support quickly overcame any objections. This explains the Sudanese involvement in the airlift operations in return for immediate help by Israel. The meeting held between Numayri, First Vice President Umar Muhammad al-Tayyib and Israel's Defence Minister Ariel Sharon in Kenya on 13 May 1982,[63] attested to Numayri's preparedness to go to great lengths in order to attain immediate assistance. Numayri himself paid repeated visits to Washington during the first half of the 1980s (November 1981, November 1983 and March 1985), further discussing various issues connected with the airlift operations and the possibility of receiving more aid. Moreover, the three-day visit by US Vice President George Bush, which began on 4 March 1985, and which included trips to 'refugee camps in East Sudan' in geographic proximity to Ethiopia, may have further indicated the centrality of the airlift operation on the Sudanese–American agenda. This assumption gained further support by a later claim that it was during this visit that an American plan was hatched to fly additional Ethiopian Jews via Sudan to Israel.[64]

Facing violent unrest in Khartoum, triggered primarily by socio-economic despair and political grievances, the Sudanese president left for a working as well as medical visit to Washington on 27 March 1985, hoping to receive prompt economic and military assistance in order to assuage the mounting pressures at home. However, he was forced to cut his visit short after the massive riots threatened to remove him from power. By the time Numayri got to Cairo on his return trip, he learned that he had been overthrown in Sudan's third successful military coup on the morning of 6 April 1985—two months after the exposure of his role in helping to expedite the flight of Ethiopian Jews to Israel.

General 'Abd al-Rahman Muhammad Hasan Siwar al-Dahab assumed the reins of power, becoming Sudan's new president. One of his first steps was to arrest Tayyib, hitherto Numayri's first vice president and the head of the State Security Organisation, which played the central role in the airlift of the Ethiopian Jews to Israel. In addition, the new regime demanded the extradition of Numayri from Egypt in order to investigate his involvement in the airlift of the Ethiopian Jews via Sudan to Israel. This was one charge among others, but the new regime gave it a prominent status. This issue dominated the attention of both the government and the population during Dahab's one-year transitional period in power, helping the new military regime gain political legitimisation and stabilise Sudan's internal situation leading up to the election of a democratic government in Khartoum in the spring of 1986.[65]

Conclusion

Israel and Sudan, which were created around the same time, experienced two significant rounds of clandestine diplomatic collaboration, with about three decades separating one from the other. Each round was characterised by starkly different characteristics and circumstances, reflecting to a large extent the diversity and contrasts between the two countries in a variety of areas, among them geography, ethnicity, religion, ideology, cultural and political systems. Although Israel and Sudan had regarded one another as enemies since the late 1950s, on two occasions they were able to build tactical bridges in order to promote their respective essential interests. In each of these two rounds of clandestine diplomatic collaboration during the 1950s and 1980s, the convergence of the two states' vital national interests served as the spans which bridged the gulf that had hitherto separated them. These episodes, and particularly the airlift of Ethiopian Jews in the 1980s, witnessed not only Israeli and Sudanese active clandestine collaboration but also came to involve other regional powers (Arab and non-Arab) and international 'passengers', trying to take advantage of the situation for their own respective interests. Yet while being engaged in the clandestine diplomatic process, these 'players' helped to promote the aims of both Jerusalem and Khartoum, shedding light on the realities of secret diplomacy.

While the first round took place during each country's 'infancy period', just after they gained independence from British colonial rule, the second round took place when both countries were experienced politically. Both periods of clandestine diplomatic cooperation between

Jerusalem and Khartoum were of a short-lived character and of a different nature in objectives, scope and essence.

Both rounds of these clandestine diplomatic interactions were regarded positively by each side at the time, being well aware of the inherent threats and the challenges. In the 1950s, Israel referred to Africa in general and to the Sudanese state in particular as a means of 'leaping over the Arab wall',[66] and as an important element in the Israeli periphery security belt encircling the belligerent Arab core. Sudan's Umma-led governments harnessed this collaboration to thwart Egypt's interventionist policy in Sudan and to consolidate the threatened position of the Umma Party in Khartoum's politics. Later in the 1980s, Israel referred to Sudan primarily as a launching pad for the massive transfer of the Ethiopian Jews to Israel. Israel used this mission as an emergency operation and was willing to go to great lengths to achieve this end. This context of urgency also dominated the Sudanese agenda, with Khartoum being desperate to get immediate as well as maximum economic and military aid, whether directly from Israel or from a third party. This was essential for providing the tottering regime with the urgently needed breathing space so that it could politically cross the turbulent waters and reach safe land, until the just discovered oil could be leveraged for empowering Numayri's political position.

The Sudanese president was determined to attain what he perceived to be 'a bridgeable relief' and was even willing to collaborate with what the Arab world perceived as the 'devil', that is, Israel. This reality set the stage for what turned out to be two fascinating chapters of clandestine diplomatic collaboration between Jerusalem and Khartoum. Certainly, clandestine diplomacy, as outlined in these two episodes of secret diplomatic relations between Israel and Sudan, proves that 'secrecy and confidentiality' allow the parties involved to negotiate on the basis of reciprocity without being subjected to domestic pressures. Secret negotiations, indeed the clandestine meetings that became such a hallmark of Henry Kissinger's diplomacy, also enable the negotiators. As Kissinger said himself, such diplomacy frees the parties involved 'from the necessity of living up to criteria set beforehand by the media and critics'.[67] This ensured, to a large extent, the success of the extraordinary collaboration between Israel and Sudan.

10

SHADOWY INTERESTS

WEST GERMAN–ISRAELI INTELLIGENCE AND MILITARY COOPERATION, 1957–82

Shlomo Shpiro

Introduction

From the late 1950s onwards, West German–Israeli relations developed in two parallel tracks. On the one hand were the open bilateral relations, encompassing political, economic, cultural and, after 1965, also diplomatic relations. These relations were influenced by the historical legacy of the Second World War and the Holocaust, generally characterised by periods of closeness but also fraught with difficulties and crises. Parallel to the open bilateral relations, extensive covert relations developed between the intelligence services and armed forces of both countries. These relations, which were kept secret, remained stable even during times of crisis in the open relations. As such, they were used not only to advance tangible security interests but also to stabilise the wider bilateral relations. The intelligence services of both countries became important foreign policy actors in the shadowy diplomacy which connected West Germany and Israel by providing each side with practical, tangible security benefits through their cooperation. Not only Israel but also Germany benefited greatly from this bilateral security cooperation, which extended across the fields of intelligence collection and analysis, the development of military systems and analysis of enemy military capabilities.

A complex network of contacts and cooperation developed between the West German and Israeli intelligence services, ministries of defence and armed forces from 1957 onwards. These relations have exercised considerable influence on the overall security posture and military capabilities of both countries. The clandestine relations were motivated mainly by national security interests and were less influenced by the historical legacy of the Holocaust. These relations involved considerable cooperation and joint operations across a wide spectrum of intelligence and military issues. Exploring these relations clearly shows that the West German side committed substantial resources and undertook considerable political risks not only because of its historically motivated commitment to support the State of Israel but also due to the strong and tangible benefits this cooperation offered to Germany's security and defence.[1]

This chapter examines and analyses the covert West German–Israeli relations and cooperation in the fields of intelligence and security, and the interests which motivated the two countries to develop such intricate and politically risk-laden cooperation in the years 1957 to 1982. It begins with the first Bundesnachrichtendienst (BND)–Mossad contacts, which came in the aftermath of the 1956 Suez War, and ends with Israel's 1982 invasion of Lebanon, in which military technologies developed together by Israel and West Germany played an important role.

West German–Israeli security relations were based on two distinctly separate pillars: military cooperation, one the one hand, and intelligence cooperation efforts on the other. These pillars often converged but did not always run parallel. Military cooperation consisted of a wide range of covert activities affecting national security policies and armed forces. These include the sale, purchase, joint design and production of major weapon systems, the financing of arms purchases from third countries, the procurement of enemy weapons for testing and evaluation, the training of officers and military personnel and the development of military strategies and tactics. The scale of this cooperation was often very considerable and it influenced major weapons systems design and the battlefield capabilities of both the IDF and the Bundeswehr. The largest arms development programmes over which both countries cooperated were the Tornado fighter-bomber aircraft, the Leopard II and Merkava main battle tanks, the Marder armoured personnel carrier, the Sidewinder air-to-air missile and the Dolphin and Type 212 attack submarines. The Tornado cooperation, in the form of Operation CERBERUS, is examined in detail later in the chapter as a case study illustrating the depth and military importance of the covert relations.

Intelligence cooperation was conducted principally between the Mossad, on the Israeli side, and the BND on the German side, and was aimed at obtaining information and enhancing intelligence capabilities. This cooperation was conducted not only in Europe and the Middle East but also in Africa and Asia. The division between the intelligence and military pillars was not necessarily one of different institutions or services. On the contrary, often the lines between the responsibilities of the military and the intelligence services were blurred, or even intentionally transgressed. During other times, however, the distinction was more clearly maintained. The reasons for this can be traced to three elements: the personal authority and control of the heads of the respective intelligence services; the institutional and legal restrictions on the activities of the military in Germany; and the development of long-term personal contacts between mid-level intelligence executives responsible for particular operational issues.

Initiating Intelligence Cooperation

Until 1955, West Germany's unofficial but effective foreign intelligence service was known as the Organisation Gehlen (OG), after its commanding officer General Reinhard Gehlen, and was run in a semi-private way. It was funded largely by the Americans and tied only in a loose and informal way to the government of the Federal Republic. In 1955 the OG was made into a fully accountable, official government service called the Federal Intelligence Service (BND) responsible for civilian and military intelligence collection and analysis. Many of the OG officers were former Nazis, some of whom barely bothered to disguise their Nazi past.[2] Until 1955 the OG was considered by the Mossad to be a private information service peddling its wares for profit. Many Mossad officers at that time were Holocaust survivors, or had lost members of their families in the Holocaust, and found the idea of cooperating with the OG abhorrent. Only in 1955, when the BND was officially created and given a

171

legal mandate of collecting and evaluating information for the West German government, and began to recruit a new, younger generation of officers who had not served in the Second World War, could attempts be made at establishing official contact with Israeli intelligence.[3]

In 1957, BND President General Reinhard Gehlen sought to make first contact with the Mossad. His reasons were threefold: first, he was deeply impressed by Israel's military victory in the 1956 Suez campaign, which was achieved through extensive and accurate intelligence work.[4] In Gehlen's eyes, this triumph of arms turned Israel into a regional 'intelligence power' in the Middle East. The second reason was Gehlen's need to diversify his sources of information on which he depended for the continued political support of the West German government for his organisation. In its first decade of operations, the OG/BND relied on old networks of agents in Eastern Europe, left over from the Second World War. But by 1957 many of these agents behind the Iron Curtain were aging or had been captured, and the intelligence produced from these old networks was in marked decline. The problem of lack of sources was exacerbated by the 'economic miracle' in West Germany, which turned German political attention to countries and potential markets beyond Europe. Gehlen's organisation was thus forced to gather information on other parts of the world, for which he had neither the experienced personnel nor the contacts. The third reason for cooperation with Israel was Gehlen's wish to distance himself and his organisation from the CIA and to carve out his own intelligence niche within the Western alliance. For these reasons Gehlen wanted to be able to draw upon the Mossad's global sources, and was willing to go a long way, both morally and materially, to make this cooperation work.

In 1957, Gehlen dispatched a trusted associate to meet with Mossad officials in Paris and request cooperation in fields of interest to both services. The Mossad leadership had misgivings about working with West Germany in general and especially with Gehlen, who served the Nazi regime as intelligence chief on Hitler's Eastern Front. But the promise of operational freedom in Germany and the German-speaking origins of many Mossad officers won the day. Another element in the BND's appeal for the Mossad was its developing relations with Arab countries, especially Egypt. BND representatives, many of whom were former Nazis, proved to be welcome guests in Arab capitals. Their activities provided the BND with much information needed by Israel. In return, the BND needed information on Eastern Europe, which the Mossad, through its collection efforts in communist countries and the questioning of new immigrants to Israel, could provide.

The head of Mossad, Isser Harel, trusted, at first, neither Gehlen's approach to the Mossad nor the real capabilities of his service. Though not a Holocaust survivor himself, Harel had lost much of his family in Nazi concentration camps.[5] He strongly disliked everything German but realised the potential for cooperation with the BND. He therefore initiated a series of 'tests' for the BND to prove its worth for the Mossad. These activities, undertaken by the BND for the Mossad, involved the smuggling of Mossad personnel into and out of Eastern European countries. It also involved assisting the Mossad in organising the immigration of Jews from these countries to Israel by illegal means. The BND carried out these tasks as required, and Harel then authorised the expansion of the relations and the stationing of the first Mossad liaison officer in Germany, who worked under cover at the Israeli mission in Cologne.[6]

On the German side, Gehlen entrusted one of his close confidants, General Wolfgang Langkau, also known under the cover names 'Langendorf' or 'Holten', to be the liaison officer with the Mossad.[7] Langkau was an experienced intelligence officer who headed the 'Strategic Service', a small semi-independent group within the BND which was answerable directly to the BND president.[8] The Strategic Service was running its own agent networks but it was also used to maintain contacts with foreign intelligence services.[9] Langkau came to respect the Mossad's professionalism and its constant flow of reliable information, and became one of the Mossad's strongest supporters in Pullach. He developed good working relations with the head of Mossad, Meir Amit, who took over from Harel in 1962, and with the Mossad liaison officers to the BND. Under Langkau's influence the cooperation continued to develop and entered new fields of operations.

The BND's need to ensure the Mossad's goodwill became even more paramount after the arrest, in November 1961, of Heinz Felfe, a senior BND official who for many years had been a mole working for the Soviet KGB.[10] Felfe was responsible for counter-intelligence work at the BND and enjoyed access to information on the BND's agents behind the Iron Curtain. It is hard to overestimate the damage Felfe's treachery inflicted on the BND and its operations in Eastern Europe. Felfe betrayed to the Soviets almost every BND network or intelligence asset behind the Iron Curtain, carefully built and nurtured over fifteen years. He passed on to his KGB controllers tens of thousands of secretly copied documents detailing BND plans, structure, personnel, agents and communications. After his arrest, the Soviet security services rounded up dozens of Western agents, many of whom were tried and executed. It is estimated that as a result of Felfe's work for the Soviets at least sixty agents lost their lives, and he betrayed virtually every ongoing BND operation in Eastern Europe. Almost overnight the BND had lost most of its important sources of information and its institutional survival was at stake.[11]

BND President Gehlen, who was personally shocked by the disastrous treachery of such a close friend and colleague, entrusted the rebuilding of the BND collection efforts behind the Iron Curtain to General Langkau. Gehlen and Langkau realised that for keeping even some semblance of effective collection in Eastern Europe the BND had to rely on extensive cooperation with other intelligence services, which could provide up-to-date information which, in turn, the BND could present to German politicians as its own. This needed to be done at least as a temporary measure, until new agent networks could be recruited over a period of several years. Gehlen and Langkau could not rely on the British or French intelligence, both of which were struggling at the time with the throes of decolonialisation, the French preoccupied with the violent conflict in Algeria and the British pulling back from their former colonies and not enthusiastic about sharing information with Gehlen, whom they considered to be 'as leaky as a sieve'.

Another reason which made Gehlen reluctant to count on the British or French intelligence was their wish to keep exclusive control of the intelligence relations with newly independent African states, an area in which Gehlen, and German politicians, wanted to expand their activities and which was fast becoming another arena in the cold war conflict. Neither did Gehlen want to return to a dependency on the CIA. The BND was, therefore, pushing for even more cooperation with Israel. Gehlen was so desperate to secure Israeli goodwill that he offered to provide the Mossad with confidential German information, including an offer to regularly supply the Mossad with a copy of one of Germany's most secret documents—the BND daily report to the Kanzler (Chancellor).[12] The year 1961 marked a major increase in West German–Israeli intelligence cooperation, which incrementally spread in the ensuing decades to cover not only Eastern Europe and the Arab countries but also parts of Africa and Asia as well.

Two Stages of Cooperation

Two distinct stages in the West German–Israeli military and intelligence relations can be discerned. During the first stage, from 1957 until the late 1960s, these relations ran on parallel but separate tracks. The first track consisted of Mossad–BND intelligence cooperation, which involved the collection and analysis of information as well as operations in third countries. The second track was direct cooperation between the Israeli Ministry of Defence (IMoD), on the Israeli side, and the German Ministry of Defence (BMVg) and German army—the Bundeswehr—on the German side. This state of affairs meant that both the Mossad and the Israeli Ministry of Defence had permanent representatives in Germany, who often knew little about the activities of one another. This situation of parallel, competitive interests reached a somewhat absurd climax in the very late 1950s when the Israeli MoD tried to conceal its arms deals with Germany from the Mossad, fearing that Mossad head Isser Harel might use this information as a political tool against Prime Minister David Ben-Gurion and his policy of reconciliation with West Germany.[13]

The second stage began in the late 1960s after a short lull in military relations following the events that led to the establishment of diplomatic relations between Israel and West Germany in 1965. Media reports, in 1964, of covert arms sales from Germany to Israel caused a public sensation and forced the German government to issue an official statement that it would not in the future supply Israel with weapons. As compensation to Israel, and following protracted negotiations conducted through a German intermediary, Kurt Birrenbach, the West German government offered full diplomatic relations with Israel, despite its fear of an Arab recognition of East Germany. The second stage was characterised by the foreign intelligence services on both sides acting as 'service providers' for their respective defence establishments in order to better maintain secrecy. The Mossad and BND were now handling various aspects of the secret military relations, which by their operational nature required the use of intelligence methods for camouflage, the secret transfer of funds and the provision of secure civilian services. Thus the foreign intelligence services became, in reality if not in policy, an integral part of the military relations. This integration had two effects: firstly, the internal competition in Israel between the Mossad and the military establishment over reaping the benefits of the German–Israeli cooperation was all but eliminated. Secondly, closer personal relations between Mossad and BND officials opened the way for deeper cooperation in other fields as well.

The German–Israeli military cooperation produced tangible military and economic results. The BND was especially interested in Soviet arms captured by Israel in the various Middle East wars. These weapons, including tanks, aircraft, rockets and missiles, were closely analysed and evaluated to discover their strengths and weaknesses and to enable the development of effective countermeasures. Such capabilities significantly enhanced the military potential of both Israel and West Germany, as well as providing them with a larger degree of independence in the design and manufacture of weapon systems, with the concomitant economic and trade benefits to be had in terms of competing on the global arms market.

On the Israeli side, cooperation with West Germany gave it technical means which made a considerable contribution to the military victories of 1967, 1973 and 1982. It also contributed significantly to the development of Israel's military high-tech industries and thus to the country's economic growth. On the West German side, cooperation with Israel significantly enhanced the Bundeswehr's main land and air weapon systems in the 1970s and 1980s, including the Leopard II tank and the Tornado aircraft. It enabled Germany to produce and procure systems especially designed with the Bundeswehr's requirements in mind, as well as diversify its weapon supply and become less dependent on the United States as weapons supplier.

One example of the benefits of the West German–Israeli security relations resulted in one of the most important inventions in armour warfare since the Second World War—Reactive Armour. This armour, which today provides the basic protection for all modern tanks, was first developed by West German scientist Professor Manfred Held after participating in tests on Soviet tanks captured by Israel following the June 1967 Six Day War. These tests involved firing different projectiles at a large number of captured armoured vehicles and tank wrecks in order to assess the effectiveness of the armour against different munitions and projectiles. In several of the tanks tested, even strong shaped charge projectiles failed to penetrate. Held noticed that these tanks still contained some old ammunition which exploded upon the external impact of an incoming shell.

He concluded that an internal explosion, within an armour plate, can negate the effects of an external explosion, such as an incoming enemy shell.[14] This discovery paved the way for the development of reactive armour, which is made up of numerous 'boxes' attached on the top and sides of every modern tank. These boxes contain explosives which detonate when the tank is hit by an enemy shell, negating the explosion and saving the tank and its crew. This technology was incorporated into Israeli and German tank design and first used in combat by the IDF during the 1982 Lebanon war with impressive results. Today reactive armour is considered an absolute prerequisite for any modern tank and more recently was used extensively by the US, British, Canadian and Danish armed forces in Iraq and Afghanistan.

Operation CERBERUS

Radar plays a crucial role in military capabilities since it can accurately detect moving objects, such as ships or aircraft, at great distances. Radar is also used to guide missiles on to a target, such as anti-aircraft missiles fired from the ground. The ability to disrupt an enemy's radar is paramount for achieving and maintaining aerial superiority or being able to penetrate enemy airspace. As radar systems became ever more sophisticated, so did their importance for intelligence services. Technical details and capabilities of enemy radars became prime targets for intelligence collection and analysis efforts. These details were critical not only for wartime planning but also for aerial intelligence operations. For example, in 1960 the CIA underestimated Soviet radar capabilities to detect and guide missiles to its top secret U-2 reconnaissance plane, leading to the shooting down of Gary Powers' aircraft over the Soviet Union. Accurate radar intelligence ('Radint') became a core function of military intelligence during and well after the cold war.

The West German Ministry of Defence and the BND launched a decade-long operation in the early 1970s to uncover the secrets of Soviet radars and develop electronic countermeasures to defeat them. This operation, codenamed first CALIGULA and later CERBERUS, was aimed at providing West Germany's new fighter-bomber aircraft, the

Tornado, with the best possible electronic warfare capabilities to enable it to penetrate East European airspace and deploy tactical nuclear weapons in the event of war in Europe. The BND 'Radint' operation was conducted with Israeli assistance and involved worldwide collection efforts, ranging from Northern Europe to China, as well as cooperation with other Western intelligence agencies.[15] Since Israel was also facing, at the time, similar Soviet radars and missiles supplied to the neighbouring Arab states, its intelligence community was determined to assist the West Germans in cracking Soviet radar secrets and thwarting the threat they presented.

In early 1965 Israeli intelligence received information indicating that the Egyptian Army was being provided with Soviet-made SAM-2 anti-aircraft missiles. These missiles were transported to Egypt under great secrecy and reportedly deployed in the Helwan area, where they could shoot down Israeli fighters penetrating Egyptian airspace. These warnings caused great consternation for the Israeli military, and air force Commander General Ezer Weizman requested the permission of Prime Minister Levi Eshkol to send Israeli aircraft on a perilous reconnaissance mission over Egypt in order to photograph the new missiles and their emplacements. After being briefed on the threat posed by these missiles, Eshkol authorised the flight.[16] While the reconnaissance flight was conducted by two Israeli jets, Eshkol himself stayed at the air force command post to enable split-second decisions to be taken during such a critical operation. The Israeli pilots returned safely and the aerial imagery they made confirmed that the Egyptians could now mount a serious threat to Israeli air superiority over the Suez Canal area.[17]

Detailed information on the SAM-2 missiles was obtained in the West for the first time by the British Secret Intelligence Service (SIS) from a high-ranking agent in the Soviet Union codenamed 'HERO'. 'HERO' was Oleg Vladimirovich Penkovsky, a colonel in the Soviet military intelligence (GRU). Born in 1919, Penkovsky enjoyed a brilliant career in the GRU, reaching the rank of full colonel at the young age of thirty-one. He graduated from the Soviet Military Diplomatic Academy and was decorated for distinguished service. However, further promotions were blocked by the KGB because his father had been a White Russian officer during the revolution. Bitter and disappointed, Penkovsky turned to the CIA and SIS offering his services as an agent.[18] Penkovsky proved to be an incredibly wealthy source of secret information, especially on

Soviet military technology and developments. The material he provided revealed to the West the complex capabilities of a new Soviet anti-aircraft missile, designated as the SAM-2 'GUIDELINE'.[19] Unfortunately, having successfully passed to the West much secret information on Soviet military capabilities, Penkovsky was arrested by the KGB in October 1962 and later executed.

Both the West German and the Israeli intelligence services became interested in the SAM-2 and its smaller counterpart SAM-3 in the late 1960s, as the Soviets began to equip large units of their Warsaw Pact and Arab allies with the new missiles. NATO and its air forces urgently required a way of overcoming the SAM missile threat in order to continue presenting a credible nuclear deterrent against the Soviet Union. During the June 1967 war, the Israeli air force achieved almost total air superiority by destroying in a surprise dawn attack most of the Egyptian, Syrian and Jordanian air forces. The SAM missiles, although used on several occasions, did not play a major role in that conflict. But on the few times they were used, they proved their superior capabilities.[20]

In February 1972, Egyptian Defence Minister General Ahmed Ismail Ali visited Moscow as part of the Egyptian preparation for a major military thrust against Israel, planned for late 1973. Ali explained to his Soviet hosts that Israel's aerial superiority presented his forces with the biggest problem in crossing the Suez Canal. In return, the Soviets promised to beef up Egyptian anti-aircraft defences and construct the world's most formidable formation against the Israeli air force—a virtual curtain of SAM-2 and SAM-3 missiles across its borders with Israel, which would prevent a repetition of the Egyptian air defeat of 1967.[21] Israeli strategic planners began to view the problem of Soviet anti-aircraft missiles and radars as a growing strategic threat.

Nascent work on the development of electronic warfare and radar countermeasures had already begun in 1964 when the Israeli navy began a small development programme to provide its vessels with some form of protection from Soviet ship-launched 'STYX' missiles. This programme, codenamed 'Avshalom', was based on a revolutionary idea: not only would the system jam the enemy's missile radar, but it would also create a fake artificial target for the missile to home in on. Such an 'active' system would provide double protection by first jamming the homing enemy radars and then creating a non-existing 'phony' target on which the radar-guided missile would expend itself harmlessly into the sea.[22] The practicality of the active countermeasures concept had, at that time, never been proven in battle. Many experts doubted the possibility of projecting a realistic image of a false target that was convincing enough to fool a missile's accurate radar.[23] Work on 'Avshalom' continued at a slow pace, and it was not until the October 1973 war that its operating principles were proven to work.[24] Once the 'Avshalom' system demonstrated success, it was decided to try and expand the concept to provide a solution also to the Soviet SAM anti-aircraft missiles. However, the requirements for an aerial system were far different from those of ships, where space and power were not a problem. A radar countermeasure system for combat aircraft had to be very compact and at the same time powerful in order to be effective over many kilometres. Since Israel could not finance such a costly and lengthy development programme alone, a decision was made to seek a joint project together with West Germany.

In the early 1970s, West Germany embarked, together with the United Kingdom and Italy, on a new programme for building the Tornado, the world's most advanced fighter-bomber aircraft. The Tornado project, described by West German Kanzler Helmut Schmidt as 'the biggest armaments program since the birth of Christ', needed an electronic countermeasures system to foil Soviet missiles and be able to deliver nuclear weapons over Soviet territory in case of war. In secret negotiations, the West German and Israeli ministries of defence agreed that Israeli governmental defence contractors would covertly develop the Tornado's electronic warfare systems for Germany, but that the new systems would be presented as having been entirely made in West Germany to prevent any political trouble between West Germany and the Arab states. The BND and the Mossad were entrusted with keeping this highly sensitive project secret.

In October 1972, therefore, German Defence Minister Georg Leber authorised the joint development of a radar deception jammer with Israel. To prevent any possible leak of the sensitive project, Leber ordered strict secrecy precautions. The project was to be handled only by a small circle of trustworthy officials at the German Ministry of Defence and BND, who were instructed to exercise the strictest secrecy.[25] The word 'Israel' was to not to be used anywhere in writing, but would instead be replaced by the code 'I-20'. The German Ministry of Defence gave its part of the project the codename 'CALIGULA'. All CALIGULA documents were delivered under special security arrangements and a special registry was set up for the CALIGULA documents, separate from the ministry's central registry.[26] The multiple codes and circuitous ways of communications were meant to confuse and prevent all but the selected few from gaining an overview of the entire project. In later years the codename for the project was changed to 'CERBERUS'. The German Ministry of Defence allocated large amounts of money from its overall Tornado budget to the CERBERUS programme. These amounts were paid over to the BND, and from there passed on to Israel via special means. In the years 1972–88, the cost of the CERBERUS project amounted to over DM 415 million.[27]

Monitoring Soviet Radars

The crucial question facing the Israeli CERBERUS designers was to try and discover which radar frequencies would be used by the Soviets in wartime. Soviet radar crews, and Arab radar crews trained by the Soviets, used one frequency for everyday training but a completely different frequency at wartime. Since Soviet radar systems controlling the SAM missiles were capable of operating over a broad range of frequencies, the CERBERUS system had to be designed to have the capability of instantly recognising the specific frequency used and adapting its systems to jam them accordingly. In theory, this capability would assure maximum effectiveness of CERBERUS over the different frequencies, but scientists were aware of the fact that different frequencies 'reacted' differently to the jamming and wanted to know more precisely which frequencies the Soviets would use against hostile aircraft penetrating their airspace.[28]

The Israeli intelligence services were already aware of the importance of analysing enemy radar frequencies. On 26 December 1969, under the codename 'Operation Rooster', an Israeli special forces unit was dispatched on a hazardous mission deep inside Egyptian territory to capture a new Soviet P-12 radar station in Ras Arab, which was directing Egyptian fighter activities against the Israeli air force.[29] Under the cover of darkness, Israeli special forces arrived at the station and quickly overpowered its Egyptian garrison. Special intelligence teams went into action, dismantling the radar unit, which weighed over 4 tons, and collecting all relevant operating manuals and secret documents. The radar was slung underneath a helicopter, which took off immediately and flew towards Israel. During the hazardous flight, one of the cables holding the radar broke loose and the pilots were ordered to release the load over the Red Sea to prevent their helicopter from crashing. The crew, however, realising the crucial importance of their mission, kept on flying with the radar hanging by only one cable until they could land within Israeli territory.[30] This capture enabled Israeli scientists to discover some of the latest advances in Soviet radar technology, but more information on frequencies was still needed.

The main problem in ascertaining which radar frequencies would be used by the Soviets against NATO aircraft in wartime was that these radar systems stationed in East Germany were kept switched off. Soviet crews would only operate them in real emergencies, thus preserving tactical surprise. The BND was anxious to obtain accurate frequency readings of the Soviet radars for the CERBERUS project. Thus a decision was made to try and 'provoke' Soviet radars stationed along East Germany's borders in to switching their radars on against Luftwaffe aircraft, a risky manoeuvre since 'accidental' penetrations could have been interpreted by the East Germans as an attack. The BND arranged with the Luftwaffe to have military aircraft 'mistakenly' penetrate East German airspace during manoeuvres, hoping that Soviet units stationed on the internal German border would switch their equipment on against the incoming aircraft, thereby enabling the BND's electronic monitoring stations inside West Germany to take accurate readings of the frequencies used by the Soviet radars. Several such 'accidental' penetrations of East German airspace took place but the Soviets did not respond to the bait and their radars remained off.

Determined to obtain accurate radar readings, in the mid-1970s the BND created a chain of three electronic monitoring stations surrounding the Soviet Union through cooperation with other intelligence services. These stations were equipped with state-of-the-art electronic receivers and were designed to record Soviet radar frequencies over long periods of time. The first station was constructed near the town of Husum in north Germany. Codenamed 'KASTAGNETTE', it was constructed to monitor radar transmissions from the Warsaw Pact countries.[31] A second station was constructed in cooperation with the Italian intelligence service SISMI near the Italian airbase in Lecce, in southern Italy near Brindisi, to monitor radar transmissions from

South-East European countries. A third station was built together with the Iranian intelligence service, Savak, close to Tehran, to monitor radars on the Soviet Union's southern borders. This chain of three electronic monitoring stations recorded Soviet anti-aircraft radars whenever these were operated, during training sessions, manoeuvres or emergencies. The monitoring stations provided BND analysts with an accurate long-term picture of the Soviet use of different frequencies against different threats and enabled the BND, together with the Luftwaffe's strategic planners, to construct operating scenarios against Soviet aggression in NATO's central front in Germany. The information on the Soviet frequencies was provided to the Mossad and incorporated in the design and modifications of CERBERUS. The monitoring stations were also used to track down the movements of Soviet mobile headquarters, especially those of nuclear forces, providing intelligence warning against a possible Soviet attack.[32]

Following the 1979 Revolution in Iran, the BND was forced to close its Tehran monitoring station. In an effort to find a substitute station, since complete coverage of the USSR was essential for the success of the radar monitoring operation, in 1980 the BND signed, together with the CIA, an agreement with the Chinese intelligence service over the construction and maintenance of an electronic monitoring station in the Pamir Mountains, adjacent to China's Xinxiang border with the USSR.[33] Under codename 'LANZE', the BND provided over DM 26 million for the construction of the Pamir station, which was manned by twelve German, American and Chinese intelligence specialists. A further DM 20 million for the establishment of the Pamir station came directly from the Tornado budget.[34] This base was also used by the Americans to monitor the movements of Soviet mobile nuclear headquarters deep inside Russia. After the Soviet invasion of Afghanistan, the Pamir station was used to follow troop movements inside Afghanistan. In a similar ploy to earlier efforts over East Germany, the BND arranged with the Chinese to have their aircraft 'mistakenly' penetrate Soviet airspace, in the hope that the lesser-trained Soviet radar crews on this dormant border would panic into switching on their equipment and thus revealing their emergency frequencies. This ploy was successful and the Pamir station was able to report the precise frequencies used, information that was incorporated without delay into CERBERUS. By the early 1980s the CERBERUS project provided the West German Luftwaffe and the

Israeli air force with the world's best electronic countermeasures system able to defeat a wide range of Soviet radar threats.[35]

The security significance of CERBERUS for West Germany can only be fully understood when examined within the context of NATO's overall strategy for a major conflict in Europe against the Warsaw Pact powers. CERBERUS technology became a lynchpin within the Luftwaffe's overall conflict strategy and had a strong impact on Germany's military capabilities in the event of an all-out European war.[36] In the late 1960s, NATO's move from a strategy based on massive retaliation to that of 'flexible response'[37] depended on having the capabilities to deliver accurately tactical and strategic nuclear weapons over targets in Eastern Europe and the Soviet Union.[38] This ability, in which the Tornado aircraft armed with tactical nuclear weapons were assigned a key role, was crucial if a strong NATO military posture was to be maintained and Moscow deterred from undertaking military action.[39]

Against the strategic threat of a massive Warsaw Pact attack, the Bundeswehr, as a central part of NATO's defences in Europe, relied on response with theatre nuclear weapons. Unlike France and Britain, Germany did not have long-range strategic nuclear missiles and therefore had to rely on air-delivered tactical nuclear warheads. As Germany was not allowed to have its own nuclear weapons, these warheads were held and commanded jointly together with the US forces in Europe.[40] The capability to deliver these weapons effectively despite heavy Soviet air defences was perceived by German military strategic planners as a major contribution to NATO's overall nuclear strategy. This contribution depended on the success of CERBERUS to allow nuclear-armed Tornados to penetrate Soviet airspace with minimal losses and deliver the nuclear weapons accurately over their targets.

Israeli superiority in the development of electronic countermeasures was dramatically proven during the June 1982 Lebanon war. Within the space of a few hours, Israeli aircraft attacked and destroyed all of Syria's most modern Soviet-made anti-aircraft missile batteries in Lebanon's Baka'a Valley. The Syrian air force sent up its best pilots to fend off the Israeli attack. In the ensuing dogfights over a hundred of the most modern Soviet-made Syrian fighter aircraft were shot down without a single Israeli casualty, an unprecedented defeat for Soviet air capabilities, one which had strong reverberations not only for the Arab states but also within the Soviet military.

The element of secrecy played a crucial role in West German–Israeli security relations. Not only did the military superiority of systems developed jointly depend on the enemy being kept ignorant of their capabilities, and therefore being unable to develop appropriate countermeasures, but the political risks of exposure were severe. The political risks to Germany of military cooperation with Israel became even higher after the 1973 Arab oil embargo. However, the risks were not always one-sided: earlier Israeli governments faced internal political risks in military cooperation with Germany at a time when Israeli public opinion was strongly against any form of relations with the Federal Republic, let alone supplying it with weapons. However, throughout decades of close and expanding cooperation, both the Israeli and German governments perceived the benefits of this cooperation to be greater than the risks of their exposure. Both sides went to great lengths to hide or camouflage their cooperation.

But even in the few instances when these relations were discovered they were not abandoned, only disguised, and like a military chameleon resurfaced quickly in parallel fields. This is clear testimony to the importance attached by both sides to this cooperation and to the success of the military and intelligence communities in developing resilient interpersonal relations between key officials. It was often this personal element, rather than firm policies dictated from above, which made the difference between success and failure and contributed to the attainment of many of the common goals of this cooperation.

Regional and Cold War Threats and Interests

There are three main prerequisites for effective intelligence and military cooperation: common interests; common threats; and unique knowledge or technologies wanted by the other side. Common interests enable joint work towards achieving targets which would provide benefits or advance these interests. Common threats do not only mean being faced with the same, or similar, enemies, but also include facing similar military, technical or ideological threats. Specialist knowledge or technologies are the 'coin' which is being exchanged by the intelligence services, including secret information, arms sales, joint developments of military hardware, training, funds, access to facilities or capabilities or the intervention with third parties.

Throughout the cold war, Israel and West Germany had strong common interests, spanning reconciliation with the past, foreign policies, economics and social issues. There were also strong common military interests: although both countries did not face the same military enemy in the field (East German assistance to Syria during the 1973 war notwithstanding), they did face, on their immediate borders, similar Soviet-made weapon systems, ranging from the simplest infantry weapons to sophisticated missiles, radars, tanks and aircraft. Both countries possessed, or acquired over time, specific knowledge or technologies that the other desired. These were the basic motives for the West German–Israeli intelligence and military cooperation presented above.

Beyond immediate security interests, the wider framework for Israeli–West German security relations was provided by the cold war. Many West German decision-makers perceived Israel as an integral part of the Western alliance in the cold war and considered its defence not only a moral obligation but also a realistic prospect for blocking Soviet advances in the Middle East. At a lecture in Cologne University in June 1967, the influential German politician and architect of German–Israeli diplomatic relations, Kurt Birrenbach, explained the reasoning to help Israel as '*Hier die Araber—dort Nord Vietnam!*' (Here the Arabs, there North Vietnam!). In return, the military assistance Israel provided to West Germany enhanced the Bundeswehr's military capabilities and thus contributed to NATO's military position on its central front in Europe.

The main security interests for West German–Israeli military cooperation were fourfold: improving military capabilities; saving time and money through the joint research and development of military projects; enhancing indigenous military industries and manufacturing capacities, as well as arms exports; and maintaining the relations for their own sake (relational dynamics). Many of the joint initiatives and projects were aimed at improving the military capabilities of both countries. The acquisition of Soviet military technologies and the development of electronic countermeasures, ships, submarines, tanks and ammunition all influenced significantly the military capabilities of the Bundeswehr and the IDF. The acquisition of Soviet military technologies enabled a significant reduction in the time needed for research and development of major weapon systems. The element of time is crucial in arms manufacturing—a system that takes too long to research, develop and manufacture will only be effective against older designed weaponry and equipment. Military technology advances at a rapid pace and any advantage in product development times can improve not only its military value but also its export marketability.

Last but not least, the military and intelligence cooperation developed its own momentum. As one former head of the Mossad noted, 'you know who your friends are today, but you can't know who you will need as friends tomorrow'. Cooperation was also enhanced by the development of a multitude of personal relations among day-to-day decision-makers, often mid-level defence or intelligence executives, and by long-term institutional interests. Even on issues where there seemed to be no apparent immediate benefit, the German and Israeli intelligence services and defence establishments seemed ready to assist their counterparts because of existing patterns of cooperation. The West German government's willingness to undertake political risks in their covert cooperation with Israel well illustrated the perceived value of these military relations on the German side.

Conclusions

German–Israeli security relations have moved a tremendous distance in the three decades between the mid-1950s and mid-1980s. The covert relations flourished in the shadows, even while public sentiments in Israel were strongly anti-German. Until 1965, Israeli passports were regularly stamped 'valid for all countries except Germany', reflecting public animosity and recoil from Germany and its responsibility for the Holocaust. During the early years of their cooperation with the BND, Mossad officers who travelled to West Germany on duty were forbidden to sleep at hotels in Munich and were warned against socialising too closely with their BND counterparts. In contrast, today the Israeli army's chief of staff's official car is a German-made BMW and this does not raise any eyebrows in Israel, while more Israelis travel to Germany than to any other European country.

When examining not only the open German–Israeli relations but also the covert intelligence and military relations, German interests must be defined as twofold, a combination of cold war realpolitik security needs and of long-term historical perception. It is undeniable that the historical need to come to terms with its Nazi past, not only within German internal politics but also as part of Germany's international acceptance, led to some degree of West German political support of Israel in the 1950s and 1960s. As shown in this chapter, some of this support was motivated by cold war security and intelligence needs. As West Germany established itself again as a leading economic and military power in Europe, it could allow itself to decrease the intensity of its relations with Israel.

But what actually happened was not a decrease but indeed an increase on both the open and covert levels. German historical commitment to Israel was augmented to a large degree by the increasingly important security needs of the Bundeswehr as an integral and crucial part of NATO. The relations between both countries, while paying lip service to their common historical heritage, fulfilled current security needs and came to be considered indispensable for the security postures of both countries. Secrecy was the prime consideration in preventing a crisis between West Germany and its Arab oil suppliers. But the value of the covert relations to both sides was so high that political risks were undertaken by consecutive West German governments in order to maintain its security cooperation with Israel. The ways or means changed, but the interests and cooperation targets remained the same throughout the cold war and even beyond.

11

PUBLIC TENSIONS, PRIVATE TIES

IRELAND, ISRAEL AND THE POLITICS OF MUTUAL MISUNDERSTANDING

Rory Miller

Introduction

Since the 1920s the Palestine conflict has occupied a place in the Irish consciousness far greater than its geographic, economic or political position appears to merit. This chapter examines how Ireland, motivated by its identification with the experiences of both Arabs and Jews, has attempted to involve itself in the covert as well as overt diplomacy of the Arab–Israeli—and after 1967, the Israeli–Palestinian—conflict on a bilateral level, at the United Nations and inside the EEC/EU. It also examines how in turn Israel looked to capitalise on the shared experience of anti-British struggle with Irish nationalists in the pre-state era in an attempt to influence bilateral relations with Ireland and the Irish attitude towards the Arab–Israeli conflict. It concludes by examining why, despite this shared historical experience, ties between Dublin and Jerusalem, while formally correct, never developed beyond the purely functional, much to the frustration and regret of the Israelis.

The Early Years

On 28 May 1948 Moshe Sharett, Israel's first foreign minister, formally expressed his desire to 'establish a relationship of sympathy and friend-ship between [the] people of Eire and the Jewish people in Palestine to [the] mutual advantage of both'.[1] On 2 June, two days before the deci-sion on whether to recognise Israel was discussed at Cabinet and one day before a second formal telegram arrived in Dublin from Jerusalem requesting recognition, a number of Irish–American leaders (James J Comerford, Sean Keating, Paul O'Dwyer and Joseph McLaughlin) sent their own telegram to the Irish government demanding that it be 'among the first…to recognise officially the establishment of the new state of Israel' and warned that it would be a 'sad commentary on the sacrifices made by Ireland's sons and on the memory of her patriots who fought so valiantly to establish nationhood if the present Irish govern-ment awaits guidance from the British Foreign Office before welcoming the New Hebrew nation…we therefore urge in the interests of world freedom that immediate action be taken not only to recognize the new nation but to aid them officially in preserving their hard won liberty'.[2]

The co-opting of the pro-Zionist Irish–American leadership by the nascent Israeli state as evidenced in these stirring words marked the first attempt by Jerusalem to use secret diplomacy to influence Irish policy towards Israel. Over subsequent decades there would be numerous other attempts by Israel to use Irish Jews who had emigrated to Israel and held senior roles in the Israeli state apparatus to open up secret diplomatic channels between the two nations as part of the attempt to win Irish support on a bilateral and multilateral level. This strategy was in part driven by the fact that Ireland was held in high esteem by officials in Jerusalem in the first twenty-five years of Israel's existence. In terms of individuals who occupied the post of head of an operational department or higher within the Israeli Ministry for Foreign Affairs, or in related civil or military branches ranked better than many nations with far larger Jewish communities such as Hungary, Italy and Egypt. Indeed, the contribution of Irish Jews was only equalled by those of Austria and Iraq and was only surpassed by eight nations including Germany, Russia, Poland and the United Kingdom.[3]

This strategy was also driven by a historical memory on behalf of the Israeli post-independence elite who believed that the past experience of the Jews and their struggle for self-determination against British rule made them natural partners of the Irish. At least until the late 1930s when the issue of the forced partition of Palestine came to the fore and increasingly alienated Irish nationalist leaders from the Zionist movement, there was significant Irish sympathy for Zionist aspirations. Part of this sympathy was sentimental. There were obvious parallels between the suffering of the Irish under the Penal Laws and the restrictions of the Jews of Russia under the tsarist regime and the shared and traumatic experience of large-scale migration in the nineteenth century, which would fundamentally alter the demographic and cultural maps of both peoples.

But Irish sympathy with Zionism was also due to the fact that it was viewed as a national movement fighting for self-determination. That was how Irish republican leader Arthur Griffith described it,[4] and it explains why the 1917 Balfour Declaration was almost universally welcomed across Irish society. As an editorial in *The Irish Times* put it, the decision of the British foreign secretary to support the establishment of a Jewish national home in Palestine 'is from every point desirable', concluding with the stirring words, 'The faith with which Jewry has never surrendered in an ultimate return to the historic seat of its national existence is at last to be redeemed.'[5]

This positive attitude towards Zionism across Irish society in the pre-1948 period made it a lot easier for Irish Jews to be openly critical of what was viewed to be British anti-Zionist actions in Palestine than it was for their co-religionists in Britain, who had to be careful to ensure that when they publicly opposed policies introduced by the British in Palestine that they were not seen to be displaying dual loyalties in attacking their own government and criticising their own troops. For Irish Jews, openly condemning British policies in Palestine was not only a way of promoting their Zionist beliefs but of declaring their anti-British and Irish nationalist credentials.

Certainly by the time of the establishment of the Irish Free State in the early 1920s Ireland's Jews were very involved in Irish nationalist politics. The Irish-born Chaim Herzog, subsequently a two-term president of Israel, remembered how his father, Ireland's chief rabbi until 1936 when he became chief rabbi of Palestine and later the first chief rabbi of Israel, had been an 'open partisan of the Irish cause'.[6] Indeed, on taking up his post as chief rabbi of Palestine in 1936, British officials serving there were deeply suspicious of Herzog because of his sympathy for, and close ties with, the Irish republican movement.[7]

In turn this led Zionist leaders in London, New York and Palestine to hope that Ireland would draw on what David Vital, the distinguished Israeli historian, would later describe as 'an Irishman's intuitive understanding of the Jewish–Israeli predicament'[8] and support it in its struggle for survival and security following its establishment in 1948. In these terms it is important to note that unlike other nations examined in this volume, Ireland was never viewed by Israel as important in terms of providing military or intelligence cooperation. Nor was it viewed as a major hub of Jewish Diaspora activity or, at least until the late 1990s, an important trade or economic partner.

As such, Israel's attempts to use covert as well as overt diplomacy in the Irish case was purely motivated by a desire to gain diplomatic legitimacy from a neutral country that: (a) could claim good relations with both the non-aligned movement and the anti-Soviet Western alliance, notably the United States; (b) had a very active involvement in peacekeeping and conflict resolution at the United Nations; and (c) from 1973, exercised an equal vote on all foreign policy matters inside the European Economic Community (EEC).

Despite past sympathies for the Zionist cause and its own struggle for independence from Britain, Irish policy-makers had a deep hostility towards partition as a solution to territorial conflict which was born out of experience with the partition of Ireland in the 1920s. This infused the Irish with a deep identification with the Arab nationalist struggle, which ultimately, as will be seen, evolved into consistent support for the PLO and the Palestinian cause in the contemporary era both in public forums and more covertly.

However the most significant explanation for the evolving Irish attitude towards Israel did not relate to Irish antipathy towards partition. Though successive Irish governments never shed their dislike of partition as a solution to territorial conflict they were not averse to recognising the diplomatic legitimacy of other newly partitioned states (Ireland established diplomatic relations with India in January 1949, for example). Rather, the primary factor in Ireland's reluctance to upgrade ties with Israel in these years relates to what Conor Cruise O'Brien has neatly termed the 'Vatican Factor'[9] and, more specifically, the evolving status of Jerusalem after Israel's birth and the cessation of hostilities in early 1949 (which was followed between February and July of that year by the conclusion of armistice agreements between Israel and Egypt, Jordan, Lebanon and Syria).

In October 1948 Pope Pius XII issued an encyclical on Jerusalem (*In multiplicibus*) that endorsed an 'international character to Jerusalem and its vicinity' and this was followed by another encyclical in April 1949 (*In redemptoris*) that called on the nations of the world to 'accord to Jerusalem and its surrounding states a juridicial status'.[10] The Vatican's position greatly influenced Ireland's official approach. During his time as Taoiseach (prime minister) John A. Costello believed that 'a Christian policy was in Ireland's best interests'.[11] His successor, Eamon de Valera, held much the same belief, and indeed in 1958 he met with Cardinal Tisserant to discuss the matter of the holy places because he was 'rather anxious to have a correct impression' of the Vatican's position (Tisserant explained that the Vatican favoured the establishment of Jerusalem as a sovereign state governed by a council representative of those with interests in the holy places).[12]

Lobbying for Bilateral Diplomatic Ties

Given the hopes that Israeli leaders placed in support from Ireland following the establishment of the Jewish state, senior officials in Jerusalem were surprised over the Irish reluctance to grant anything more than de facto recognition in 1949. By 1958 Israel had fifteen ministers accredited to twenty-nine countries, one diplomatic representative, three charge d'affaires and thirty-seven consul generals and consuls, including honorary consuls, abroad. But not in Ireland, and by this time Israeli surprise had turned into puzzlement and anger.

For example, in 1958, Walter Eytan, the first director general of Israel's Foreign Ministry, noted that 'Ireland, for some Irish reason, to this day does not recognise Israel de jure.'[13] At the same time, a small number of Irish politicians, most notably, Dr Noel Browne (a National Progressive Democrat TD from Dublin and minister for health in the first inter-party government) began to question Minister for Foreign Affairs Frank Aiken in the Dáil (the Irish parliament) as to whether the minister would 'consider establishing diplomatic relations with Israel' given the 'considerable scope for the development of cultural, trade and other associations'. In response, and without directly referring to Israel, Aiken would only state that at that time the 'additional cost involved' did not justify opening further diplomatic missions.[14]

From an Israeli perspective Irish intransigence on this issue had become increasingly significant following Ireland's entry into the United

Nations in 1955. In a September 1960 meeting with his Irish counterpart, Arthur Lourie, Israel's ambassador in London, argued that the 'time had come for normalising the position' over recognition. In doing so he not only noted the potential economic benefits of improved ties but also raised the matter of Israeli support for Irish diplomat Frederick Boland's possible candidacy for the presidency of the United Nations General Assembly (UNGA) in 1960. Lourie explained that though Israel was 'disposed' to support Boland's nomination for the post there was an 'incongruity in the situation' if the country of the president of the General Assembly did not fully recognise Israel.[15] He also explained the practical nature of relations that Israel envisaged. This would begin by accrediting the Israeli ambassador in London or, if Ireland preferred, the ambassador in Paris, to Ireland with the simultaneous opening of an office in Dublin with a resident charge d'affaires.[16]

In May of the following year Lourie travelled to Dublin to discuss the matter with Aiken. Foreign Ministry official Cornelius Cremin, a future Irish ambassador at the UN, attended the talks. Soon afterwards Cremin recalled that Lourie had 'laid it on the line about de jure recognition' and had argued that the Irish refusal to upgrade relations was 'discrimination against Israel'. He also offered Aiken three alternative ways of moving diplomatic relations forward. The first, Israel's preferred solution, was the exchange of diplomatic missions; the second was the establishment of an Israeli mission in Dublin (either directly or by way of dual accreditation) and the last was a simple public announcement by Ireland of its de jure recognition of the Jewish state.[17]

Aiken was unmoved by Lourie's arguments and indeed Cremin was of the view that the minister had been somewhat irked by the exchange.[18] But in January 1962 Aiken had to repeat the exercise when Max Nurock of the Israeli Foreign Ministry secretly travelled to Dublin with the express purpose of asking why Ireland had not as yet accorded de jure recognition to the Jewish state so that he could make an official report back to the Israeli authorities.

Nurock had been born in Dublin and educated at Trinity College. Prior to World War Two he had been a member of the British administration in Palestine and he had then worked in the British administration of post-war Austria. After the birth of Israel he joined the Israeli Ministry of Finance and then spent five years as Israel's ambassador to Australia.[19] During his meeting with Aiken, Nurock asked whether

Ireland viewed a possible future trade agreement with Israel as equivalent to implicit de jure recognition and, if so, whether he would allow Israel to establish a diplomatic mission in Dublin 'unobtrusively' in the wake of a trade agreement. He also noted that Ireland did not need to 'reciprocate' by opening up its own mission in Tel Aviv.

Aiken's response was that Ireland did recognise the existence of the State of Israel and that he was prepared to favour a trade agreement 'in due course' from which de jure recognition might well be implied. He felt, however, that it would be embarrassing for Ireland to establish diplomatic relations without reciprocity and Ireland could not afford this financially. He added that even if the funds existed he himself had no authority to sanction the establishment of an Israeli diplomatic mission, as it was a matter for the entire government. All he could do was give the Cabinet his opinion and he was unable to 'assent' to such a move at this time. He did however suggest that the issue could be further discussed by the Irish and Israeli delegations at the United Nations in New York.[20]

Nurock's failure to return to Israel with any substantive concessions from Aiken was a personal disappointment for an individual who truly believed that the country of his birth—Ireland—and his new home, Israel, had much to gain from close relations. But sentimental attachments aside, Israeli efforts in these years must be viewed in the context of Ireland's prospective election to the United Nations Security Council (UNSC) as a one-year half-term temporary member for 1962. This provided a first, and indeed rare, opportunity for Ireland to exert diplomatic influence at the highest forum of international diplomacy (Ireland would serve a two-year term on the UNSC during 1981–2 and then again in 2001–2). As such, despite the recent failure of Lourie and Nurock to influence the Irish position on the upgrading of relations, Israel continued to apply what the Ministry of Foreign Affairs in Dublin termed, 'considerable pressure' on Ireland on the matter throughout 1962.[21] In the meantime, the Israeli preference for secret diplomacy was driven solely by the need to observe the external sensitivities of successive Irish governments who were not willing to engage openly with their Israeli counterparts in the diplomatic sphere.

The Irish decision to grant Israel de jure recognition in May 1963 was not a significant departure from Ireland's cautious stance up to this point. Nor was it due to the relentless attempts at covert diplomacy on Israel's behalf in the previous few years. Indeed, it was a bare minimum and was granted only on the basis that it was clear that it in no way endorsed acceptance of Israeli sovereignty over Jerusalem. This underlines the fact that Ireland consistently viewed bilateral relations with Israel in terms of broader regional considerations. By 1965 the Foreign Ministry officials in Dublin were of the opinion that the decision to grant de jure recognition to Israel two years previously 'did not give rise to any significant unfavourable reaction in Arab countries'.[22] The relatively muted Arab response to the decision of the Federal Republic of Germany (West Germany) to establish full diplomatic relations with Israel in 1965 also reassured the Irish. Indeed, as Ireland's senior diplomat in Bonn reported back to Dublin, though all but three (Tunisia, Morocco and Libya) of the twelve Arab ambassadors in Germany had been withdrawn following the 'courageous' decision to extend diplomatic ties with Israel, the 'crucial point' was that junior diplomatic personnel had remained and their superiors were expected to return shortly.[23]

Nevertheless, there can be no doubt that the Irish hesitancy to extend diplomatic relations with Israel was in part influenced by a concern over the reaction within the increasingly important oil-producing Arab world. As an editorial in the *Irish Press* noted in mid-1963 'if it comes to a matter of competition for the friendship of Israel or of the Arab League, nobody can doubt what the outcome will be: the oil-rich Arab states possess an attraction denied to Israel'.[24]

As part of their policy of isolating the Zionist movement, the Arab states had initiated an economic boycott of Jewish Palestine in December 1945, and after the birth of Israel this had developed into a three-pronged policy with a primary boycott prohibiting direct trade between Israel and the Arab nations; a secondary boycott directed against companies doing business with Israel; and a tertiary boycott that involved the blacklisting of firms that traded with companies that did business with Israel.

Thus Irish firms, potentially at least, faced the economic wrath of the Arab world for developing trade with Israel at a time when the Arab states were exerting considerable diplomatic pressure and warning the Community of the 'danger' and 'discrimination' of rising economic relations between Europe and the Jewish state.[25] Indeed, by 1966, as Israel prepared to apply for association status with the EEC, *The Financial Times* was of the view that the 'main difficulty' for Israel in achieving association was that several of the EEC states 'were afraid of offending

Israel's Arab neighbours'.[26] And Sergio Minerbi, Israel's ambassador in Brussels at this time, admitted to his Irish counterpart that his government was under 'no illusions' about the 'faint embarrassment' and 'political difficulties that their request [for association] will create for the community ... the Arab countries ... will not welcome this move'.[27]

This Irish reluctance to build on de jure recognition and establish further diplomatic relations with Israel at this time left Israeli officials involved in discussions 'crestfallen' and 'disappointed'.[28] But the Irish attitude did not translate at any point before 1967 into Irish support for Arab and Muslim efforts to isolate Israel politically in the international arena. For example, in 1965, the Department of External Affairs (DEA) instructed the Irish delegation at the Conference of the Commonwealth Agricultural Bureaux to abstain in the vote on a draft resolution proposed by Pakistan, calling for the Commonwealth to withhold technical facilities to Israel. The DEA also noted that if Ireland had been a full member of the organisation (it only had associate status since the Republic of Ireland Act came into force in 1949) it would have voted against such a boycott.[29]

Ireland joined the EEC in 1973, and as Gideon Rafael, Israel's ambassador to London in the wake of the first EEC enlargement, recounted in his memoirs, this made it a 'major objective' of Israeli foreign policy in the early 1970s to improve diplomatic relations with Ireland, a country that still only recognised Israel on a de jure basis.[30] In 1974 the Irish government decided to formalise diplomatic relations with Israel on a non-residential ambassadorial basis. Gideon Rafael's presentation of his credentials to President Cearbhall O'Dalaigh the following March was an important milestone in bilateral Israeli–Irish relations.[31] Indeed, Israel's failure to achieve this earlier had been both frustrating and puzzling, with Rafael's successor, Shlomo Argov, recalling in 1981 that the delay in a normalisation of relations between the two countries until 1975 was for 'reasons best known to Ireland'.[32]

But the exchange of non-residential ambassadors also had a wider significance in the context of Israel's increasingly important relationship with the EEC. Indeed, as Rafael later explained, the agreement 'closed the ring' and meant that for the first time the Jewish state had diplomatic ties with all members of the 'Nine'.[33] However, despite further lobbying, there was an ongoing Irish refusal to allow Israel to open a resident diplomatic mission in Dublin following the 1974 decision to upgrade diplomatic relations to the ambassadorial level. Thus, from 1975 until December 1993, bilateral diplomatic ties between the two states were maintained through the Irish embassy in Athens and the Israeli embassy in London, making Ireland the last EU member state to allow Israel to open a resident mission.

Overt and Covert Diplomacy at the UN 1956–67

Due to its exclusion from the United Nations (UN) until 1955, Ireland did not participate in any way in the UN's debate over the Arab–Israeli conflict during its first decade. Indeed, it was only with the Suez Crisis of 1956 that Ireland had its first opportunity to involve itself in Middle East diplomacy. Following this crisis Ireland's foreign minister, Liam Cosgrave, addressed the matter during a speech at the UNGA at the end of November 1956. In this speech he 'deplored and condemned' the Anglo–French attack on Egypt and recalled that Ireland had 'applauded' Egypt's 'struggle for freedom' from colonial rule and that there had always been 'friendly feelings' between the two countries. But he also expressed regret that Cairo had failed to use its independence with more 'moderation and realism' both in regard to its decision to nationalise the Suez Canal unilaterally and its effort to 'encompass the destruction of Israel', adding that Israel's neighbours 'must be ready to accept as a fact the existence of Israel and must renounce their projects for the destruction of that country'.[34]

Cosgrave's criticism of Egypt for its anti-Israeli stance is notable, as was his call for the wider Arab world to 'accept as a fact the existence of Israel'.[35] Two years later, in August 1958, Cosgrave's successor as foreign minister, Frank Aiken, also spoke at length on the Arab–Israeli crisis during a speech before the UNGA. In his speech he addressed directly the problem of the Palestinian refugees, which he described as the 'greatest single obstacle' to a lasting peace in the Middle East. He called on the UN to 'guarantee full compensation' for the refugees for both the property lost and the damage suffered as a 'result of their exile'. Though he accepted that Israel was not exclusively responsible for the tragedy, he did call on it to state how many refugees it was prepared to accept and argued that the UN should 'arrange for repatriation for the maximum possible number of those who would rather return than receive full compensation'.

In subsequent years, Aiken—who was foreign minister until 1969—and other Irish representatives at the UN would become some of the leading international advocates of the need for the UN to find a solution to the Palestinian refugee crisis. Irish officials invested significant time in both overt and covert diplomacy aimed at influencing international policies towards the refugee issue. Indeed, during a 1962 meeting with an Israeli diplomat, Aiken noted that as far as the Middle East was concerned Ireland's 'main preoccupation' was the Arab refugees.[36]

This commitment to, and sympathy for, the plight of the Palestinian refugees was due to a sincerely held belief that while Ireland lacked any real political and diplomatic influence over the parties to the conflict, it did have an important, if not unique, moral position in the international arena born out of its anti-colonial credentials, its military neutrality and its much-admired struggle against British occupation. This provided Irish officials with significant credibility when dealing with the Arab world, and the great powers, including the United States and the USSR, both of whom Ireland lobbied on numerous occasions to (in the words of Aiken in December 1967) make 'a really extraordinary effort to break the deadlock by guaranteeing full compensation to the refugees' and to ensure that 'all refugees not repatriated should get full compensation for the property they had lost and the damage they had suffered'.[37]

Overt and Covert diplomacy and the 1967 Arab–Israeli War

Ireland's first really significant diplomatic contribution to Arab–Israeli conflict resolution came during the intense five-week UN debate following the Six Day War of June 1967. On 27 June, Aiken made a speech on the crisis to the fifth emergency special session of the UNGA. This comprehensive statement was recognised as a major contribution to the UN's debate on the conflict. For example, Arthur Lall, India's former ambassador to the UN and the author of a 1968 scholarly analysis of the UN's role in the Six Day War (to this day one of the most fluid and authoritative works on the subject), highlighted for special attention Aiken's 'distinctive and important statement', which he viewed as 'perhaps the most far reaching of all those made in the Assembly's debate'.[38]

Aiken also made a significant contribution to the deliberations among the Western European states as to whether they should introduce their own draft resolution on the crisis to be considered by the fifth emergency special session and, if so, which country would sponsor it. At various times the Norwegian and Italian representatives suggested that if the Western countries agreed to support a Latin American draft of the resolution that was also being negotiated then Ireland should be one of the co-sponsors representing the West.

At one point, Denmark's representative and president of the Security Council, Hans Tabor, and Britain's ambassador, Lord Caradon, suggested that if negotiations with the Latin American states broke down, then Ireland 'should go it alone' and be the sole sponsor of a Western draft resolution. Caradon's suggestion was welcomed by both the Canadian and Dutch representatives. Although flattered by this acknowledgement of Ireland's centrality to the negotiations, Aiken favoured the idea of a Latin American draft resolution that would be supported by the Western nations.[39] In the end, Aiken was responsible for suggesting the wording ultimately adopted as the basis for operative paragraph 1 (a) of the Latin American draft resolution submitted to the special session, calling for Israel to withdraw its forces from 'all the territories occupied by it as a result of the recent conflict'.

Causes of Tension in the Bilateral Relationship 1970s–1982

Following its entry into the EEC in 1973 commentators increasingly viewed Ireland, in the company of Greece, France, and to a lesser extent Italy, as making up the 'pro-Arab bloc' within the Community.[40] This was due to a number of reasons. The first was its increasingly pro-Palestinian diplomacy at the UN. Most notably, on 14 October 1974, along with France and Italy, Ireland voted in favour of a Syrian-sponsored draft resolution calling for PLO participation in UNGA plenary meetings on the Palestine problem, which was adopted by a vote of 105 to four (with twenty abstaining). Israel dismissed this vote as 'Illegal and not binding … in any way' and an Israeli Foreign Ministry statement expressed 'astonishment' that these three EEC member states had 'sided with the approach of the most extremist Arab states'. It also noted that the Irish vote had 'greatly disappointed' Israel, as it had been 'hoped' that Ireland would 'not lend … support to an organization of murderers, but would have preferred progress towards peace over the encouragement of Arab extremism'.[41]

Ireland justified its vote on the Syrian draft resolution on the grounds that the Palestinian case deserved to be heard and because the PLO had the support of most of the Arab world. However, Ireland did not endorse the PLO at every turn. For example, it refused to support any UN draft resolutions that would have given the PLO 'legal recognition' on the same basis as a sovereign state.[42] But this cut little ice with Jerusalem.

This apparent Irish willingness to support the PLO diplomatically at the UN led Yigal Allon, the Israeli foreign minister, to engage his Irish counterpart Garret Fitzgerald in what a senior colleague described as 'some straight talking' when the pair met in New York in the autumn of 1974.[43] And it was also a topic of discussion during Fitzgerald's two meetings with Allon during the first official visit to Israel by an Irish foreign minister in June 1975.

In the same year, Fitzgerald, in his role as president of the European Council, faced several attacks in Arab capitals during a tour of the region over perceived EC support for developing trade ties with Israel. In an attempt to dilute this criticism the Irish foreign minister entered into a number of unauthorised discussions with Arab leaders. In one such meeting in Cairo with the Arab League's Mahmud Riad, Fitzgerald gave an assurance that the EEC–Israel trade agreement did not apply to territories occupied by Israel. However, he was clear that he was speaking on behalf of Ireland rather than the Community. As this would not satisfy his Arab League hosts he agreed to put in writing his conviction that the new agreement did not cover any of the territories occupied since 1967.[44]

On his return to Europe he informed a meeting of EEC foreign ministers in Dublin of the 'clarifications' he had given to the Arab states on the matter and argued that he had acted as he did in order to get Europe 'out of a fix' and to clear up 'serious misunderstandings'.[45] He went further by arguing that he now felt that there was 'scope for Europe to take a political initiative in the Middle East' and that if the Europeans did nothing, there was a risk that events would pass them by.[46] This was well received by the French government but infuriated the British and Dutch governments as an example of Ireland overstepping its mandate. It also increased tensions with Israel.

So did the role of Irish troops on UN duty in Lebanon from 1978. The Irish contingent was comprised of an infantry battalion, a communications section, an administrative company and staff officers, which joined the newly established United Nations Interim Force in Lebanon (UNIFIL), which was created by the UNSC in March 1978 in response to Operation Litani, the first Israeli invasion of Lebanon. Over the next twenty-three years almost 40,000 Irish troops served with the UN in Lebanon, making it the largest ever Irish overseas military commitment. The Irish UNIFIL contingent was deployed in the southern central sector of Lebanon—a highly sensitive area of southern Lebanon that was parallel to the main base of Israel's pro-Christian allies under the command of former Lebanese army officer, Major Saad Haddad, whose anti-Palestinian views were well known.

Following Israel's invasion of Lebanon in 1982, Irish troops clashed frequently with both Haddad's forces and the Israeli army in the course of operating patrols and manning checkpoints. This caused significant tensions in the bilateral political relationship between Israel and Ireland. One Irish politician evoked the general feeling on the matter when, in 1990, he admitted that he had lost much of his previous sympathy for the Jewish state when Israel 'commenced to use our UNIFIL volunteer soldiers as target practice'.[47]

Indeed, it has been argued that it was Irish anger over Israeli actions in Lebanon that, in part, influenced the third factor that impacted negatively on Israeli–Irish ties in the period—Ireland's growing support for the PLO. Most notably, in February 1980 the Irish government issued a communiqué, known as the Bahrain Declaration, which stated that the 'Palestinian people had the right to self-determination and the establishment of an independent State' and called on 'all parties including the PLO [to] play a full role in the negotiation of a comprehensive peace'.[48] By issuing the Bahrain Declaration, Ireland became the first EEC country to use the word 'state' in relation to Palestinian rights. As such it was heralded in the Arab world as 'Ireland's definitive commitment to an independent Palestine.'[49] In Israel the publication of the statement gained wide coverage in the media.[50] Shlomo Argov, Israel's ambassador to Great Britain and Ireland, told the *London Times* that the declaration was proof that 'Ireland is not being very friendly', and Israeli Prime Minister Menachem Begin went on Irish radio to argue that the decision to recognise the PLO at Bahrain was tantamount to Irish acceptance of the PLO's 'right to destroy the Jewish state'.[51]

Consolidating Chairman Arafat and the PA Position During the Oslo Era

During the early Oslo years Israel viewed Ireland's potential contribution to the peace process solely in terms of its role as a member of the

Community. Israeli Foreign Minister Shimon Peres, for example, called on Ireland to give '[A]ssistance [to the peace process] within the European Union', a view repeated by other leading Israeli figures such as Oded Eran, an Israeli ambassador to Jordan and a senior peace negotiator.[52]

However, the Palestinians envisaged a more ambitious role for Ireland— one that was covert as well as public. On his visit to Dublin in 1993, Yasser Arafat thanked his hosts by saying that '[D]uring our long march we have had real friends in Ireland who have given us unlimited support in difficult days when many others would not even listen to us ... they have supported us on many occasions and on many levels.' Arafat then asked the Dublin government to use its close ties with the US adminis- tration to promote Palestinian interests. This was reiterated by other Palestinian figures who throughout the 1990s repeatedly called on Ire- land to use its special relationship with the United States, strengthened by the role of President Clinton in the Northern Ireland peace process, to promote the Palestinian case in Washington.[53]

In response there were a number of symbolic moves by Ireland that were intended to highlight political support for the Palestinian position. During his landmark June 1995 visit to Israel, Ireland's foreign minister, Dick Spring, accepted an invitation from the PA to visit Orient House, the unofficial Palestinian headquarters in Jerusalem. Spring's decision caused controversy in Israel because at that time the highly sensitive matter of the final status of Jerusalem was outside the scope of Israeli– Palestinian negotiations. In an article entitled 'Dis-Orient House' a col- umnist for the leading Israeli daily *Yedioth Ahronoth* described Spring's visit to Orient House as a 'blatantly political' decision that 'cocked a snook at his host [Israel]'.[54] Again, in January 1999, Bertie Ahern, the Irish prime minister, became the first European leader to fly into Gaza directly via Tel Aviv (previously, European leaders including Britain's Tony Blair had to go by road as Israel was very sensitive to allowing the PA the trappings of statehood prior to a final agreement).[55]

In early May 1999 the Ramallah-based newspaper *Al-Ayam* quoted Nabil Shaath, the PA's minister for planning and international coopera- tion, as saying that Ireland would be 'the first European country' to upgrade its PA office to full embassy status. This claim was widely reported but was immediately rejected by the Irish embassy in Tel Aviv, which stated that Ireland would only change the status of the Palestinian office in Dublin as part of a 'common decision' with its EU partners.[56]

With the onset of Oslo deadlock, Arafat repeated earlier calls for Ireland to use covert diplomacy with the US administration during Clinton's visit to Ireland in May 1998.[57] In September 1999 and October 2001, Ahern and Arafat met again and on both occasions the Palestinian leader again urged the Irish premier to raise the matter of Palestinian rights in his upcoming meeting with US presidents Clinton and George W. Bush on his subsequent trips to Washington.[58] On this 2001 visit, Arafat noted that Ireland had always been a 'good friend' of the Palestinians and told a press conference that the Palestinians and the Irish had a 'historical and very important relationship together, more than friends, and we are proud of it and we are in need of it'.[59]

In December of 2001 Ahern was widely reported to have 'strongly backed'[60] Arafat at an EU summit in Brussels, and the following March he made a personal phone call of solidarity to the besieged Palestinian leader, during which time Arafat once more called on him to express his concerns to the new Bush administration and the EU presidency.[61] In mid-April, at the height of the intifada, Foreign Minister Brian Cowen did just that when he called on US Secretary of State Colin Powell to meet Arafat during an upcoming trip to the Middle East.[62]

In May 2002 Ireland offered sanctuary to two of the thirteen Palestinian militants who had left for European exile following thirty-nine days under siege in the Church of the Nativity in Bethlehem. The two men received 'leave to remain' for an initial period of twelve months, during which time they had to remain in the state. After twelve months they were to be eligible, with their families, for political asylum. In June 2003, in an incident that caused much controversy, Ireland's foreign minister chose to meet Arafat during his visit to the region even though Israel, at that time, refused to meet foreign representatives who met Arafat on the same visit. This made Cowen the first high-ranking international diplomat to choose to meet with Arafat over Israeli officials since Mahmoud Abbas (Abu Mazen) became Palestinian prime minister earlier in the year. Prior to his trip, the Spanish foreign minister made two official visits to the region in a five-day period to avoid the Israeli boycott, while Italian Prime Minister Silvio Berlusconi simply refused to meet Arafat at all.

This whole affair underlined clearly the behind the scenes Irish commitment to the Palestinian cause, but it especially highlighted the extent to which Irish policy-makers continued to view Arafat as the embodiment of Palestinian hopes until his death in November 2004. Indeed, during his visit to Arafat in June 2003, at a time when the optimism of the Oslo era was long-gone, terror was at an all-time high and a majority of Israelis, the American administration and significant sectors of the Palestinian population had lost faith in Arafat's capacity or desire to lead the Palestinians to their inevitable state, Cowen described Arafat as 'the symbol of the hope of self-determination of the Palestinian people', praising him for his 'outstanding work … tenacity and persistence'.[63]

Ireland's UNSC Membership 2000–2

Membership of the UNSC between 2000 and 2002, and especially its presidency of the Council during October 2001, placed Ireland at the centre of the Middle East crisis at a highly sensitive time. As Foreign Minister Cowen noted in a speech before the Irish parliament, Ireland's place on the UNSC 'complements the increased role the EU is playing in the Middle East'.[64] Or as one Irish media organ put it, the presidency was 'a role that may place our diplomats at the centre of efforts to end the current cycle of killing'.[65] Prior to taking over the presidency of the UNSC Cowen had expressed the hope that Ireland would make a 'constructive and effective contribution' to the Middle East crisis during its presidency.[66] While following his private meeting with Arafat in Dublin Ahern acknowledged that the Irish UNSC presidency gave it a 'special responsibility' and promised that Ireland would 'assist and support to the extent of our capacity any initiative by the parties to achieve resolution of the dispute'.[67]

Ahern's reaffirmation of Ireland's commitment to involve itself in the crisis at the UNSC during (and following) its presidency took on even more significance in the wake of the assassination of Rehavam Ze'evi, Israel's minister for tourism, in a Jerusalem hotel on 17 October 2001, the day after Arafat's visit to Dublin. In response the Israeli army encircled most of the major Palestinian-controlled cities in the West Bank and the Palestinians called on the UNSC (presided over by Ireland's Richard Ryan) to ensure 'the full and immediate withdrawal of Israeli forces from areas it occupied recently'.

The government had issued a statement condemning the assassination of Ze'evi,[68] but at the same time it gave full support to the UNSC's call for the 'withdrawal of all Israeli forces' from Palestinian-ruled areas occupied since the minister's assassination.[69] The government also continued its outspoken stance at the UNSC on this matter following the end of the Irish presidency. In late February 2002 Ambassador Ryan told the UNSC that 'the violence between Israelis and Palestinians does not exist in a political vacuum. It exists primarily because Palestinian national aspirations—legitimate aspirations—have been frustrated.'[70] The following month he explained that 'President Arafat is and will remain the only possible interlocutor for Israel in any process of dialogue.'[71]

Ireland used its membership of the UNSC to play what Cowen termed a 'full and active'[72] role in the ongoing debate over the crisis.[73] In March 2002 the Irish government fully endorsed (and Cowen hailed as a 'landmark resolution') the first UNSC draft resolution to refer to the idea of Palestinian statehood, which was adopted as UNSC Resolution 1397,[74] while in September 2002 Ireland co-sponsored UNSC Resolution 1435, which called on the PA to deal with terrorists and for Israel to end its re-occupation of Arafat's headquarters. It also demanded that Israel halt the destruction of the Palestinian civilian and security infrastructure and withdraw its forces from Palestinian cities back to positions held prior to September 2000.

Exporting the 'Irish Model for Peace'

Irish participation in the Northern Ireland peace process, the close relationship with American policy-makers (which had been fostered, in part, by cooperation over Northern Ireland) and a long tradition of supporting the Palestinian cause also contributed to a notable involvement in the ongoing crisis in Israeli–Palestinian relations. The Irish role in bringing about the ceasefire agreements of Northern Irish paramilitary organisations in the autumn of 1994, the publication of *A New Framework For Agreement* (known as the Framework Document) in cooperation with the British government in February 1995 and the comprehensive Good Friday Agreement of April 1998 gave Irish officials increased moral and political stature in dealing with the Israel–Palestine conflict.[75]

For example, in his meeting with Shimon Peres in early September 2001 Cowen drew on the Irish case as part of his attempt to convince the Israeli foreign minister to meet Arafat.[76] Or as the *Irish Times* put it, Cowen's message to Peres that 'political dialogue is an indispensable ingredient of peacemaking carries greater conviction by virtue of his own experience in the Northern Ireland peace process'.[77]

This point was reiterated by Ahern at the height of the second intifada in April 2002 when he told an audience at the annual Easter Rising commemorations in Dublin that 'the protagonists in the Middle East should study more closely the Irish experience',[78] and by Cowen the following month when he emphasised that: 'Ireland's own experience of conflict resolution has shown clearly that progress can be achieved only when those parties committed to peace refuse to allow the peace process to be made hostage to the latest atrocity carried out by men of violence.'[79]

The Irish government's experience of facilitating peace in Northern Ireland was acknowledged by various Middle Eastern figures from Benjamin Netanyahu and Ehud Barak[80] to Yasser Arafat and Egypt's then foreign minister, Ahmed Maher, who explained that though 'a small country … as a country that has itself been engaged in a peace process, I think they have a deep knowledge of how to handle these difficult moments'.[81]

But Israeli suspicion of Irish support for Arafat and the PA neutralised any lessons that the Irish government might offer from its own experience of conflict resolution. As Yoav Biran, of the Israeli Foreign Ministry, explained during a visit to Dublin in 2003, his government believed that 'some positions' adopted by Ireland on the Israeli–Palestinian conflict over an extended period could be construed as 'lacking the kind of balance and understanding of the terrible human difficulties of Israel that one would expect'.[82] Cowen used the opportunity of a well-received speech at Tel Aviv University in late January 2004 to dispel the view that Ireland was less friendly to Israel than other EU members and promised that Israel could rest assured that the Irish presidency would be 'constructive, open and even handed'.[83] But Ireland continued to oppose key Israeli policies. In particular, it was staunchly opposed to Israel's construction of its security barrier/fence. During the first weeks of its presidency, Ireland's written submission to the International Court of Justice at The Hague, which was considering the legality of the fence, was tougher on Israel than the collective written submission of the EU. Since that time, even as bilateral trade ties (which saw seventeen Israeli economic delegations visit Ireland between 2000 and 2008) have prospered, the Irish–Israeli diplomatic relationship has been strained, leading

Israeli officials to claim that at times Ireland had taken the most anti-Israeli position inside the EU.[84]

Conclusion

Motivated by a sincere belief (in the words of Zvi Gabay, Israel's first resident ambassador in Dublin) that 'as a small democracy, Israel is guided by the same school of thought that built Ireland', for almost its entire existence Israel has looked to transform its unofficial and secret diplomatic ties with successive Irish governments into a formal and public relationship.[85] While it may have been common for Israel in its dealings with other nations to use secret diplomacy as a short-term tactic rather than a long-term strategy or as a way of overcoming internal bureaucratic issues, in the Irish case the Israeli objective all along has been to turn secret diplomacy into public cooperation. However, the Irish preference for focusing on engagement with Israel through bilateral trade and multilateral diplomacy at the UN and inside the EU, as well as its championing of the Palestinian cause, has meant that Israel has consistently failed to achieve the level of relations it hoped to develop with a country it has long believed to be a natural ally. In so doing, it has also highlighted the limits of secret diplomacy in establishing closer diplomatic ties where common values, as much as common interests, shape bilateral relations.

12

ISRAELI TRACK II DIPLOMACY

THE BEILIN–ABU MAZEN UNDERSTANDINGS

Jacob Eriksson

Introduction

On 22 February 1996, Ze'ev Schiff published an article in *Ha'aretz* which disclosed a secret set of talks between Israeli and Palestinian academics. Held predominantly in Sweden—under the initial sponsorship of the Swedish Foreign Ministry and later the Olof Palme International Center (OPIC), a non-governmental organisation focusing on international politics and development—the talks were designed to create a basis for permanent status negotiations between the two parties. As such, the substance of these discussions revolved around the most complicated, divisive and emotionally charged issues which lay at the heart of the Israeli–Palestinian conflict: borders, settlements, refugees and, perhaps the most significant of all, Jerusalem. The results of these talks have commonly become known as 'the Beilin–Abu Mazen Understandings' (hereafter 'the Understandings'), and have since their dissemination into the public sphere become a very important yardstick in any discussion of permanent status.[1]

The talks are a textbook example of 'Track II diplomacy', a term based on a distinction between two levels of interaction; one formal and public known as Track I, and another informal and clandestine known as Track II. Track II talks are discussions held by non-officials of conflicting parties who attempt to clarify outstanding disputes and to explore the options for resolving them under circumstances that are less sensitive than those associated with official negotiations.[2] In such unofficial and more informal settings, concerns, limits, priorities and possible solutions can be creatively and honestly explored without commitment from either party, thereby preparing the ground for official negotiations.[3]

Though Track II talks are unofficial, the participants must have relations to officials in decision-making circles in order to communicate their impressions and conclusions, thereby making the task potentially politically significant. These 'mentors', or the high-level political leaders who supervise the talks, must consider it a useful exercise and devote time and energy to its organisation or monitoring.[4] Using non-officials as the primary interlocutors helps ensure that secrecy is maintained, as their movements are subject to less scrutiny than government officials, and it additionally provides an important cloak of deniability should the talks be exposed.

In this case, the Israeli negotiators were Yair Hirschfeld and Ron Pundak, the two original Israeli participants behind the Oslo Agreement. Their Palestinian counterparts were Hussein Agha and Ahmad Khalidi, two academics at Oxford University also affiliated with Chatham House in London. The eponymous mentors of the Understandings developed were Israeli Deputy Foreign Minister Yossi Beilin and Yasser Arafat's deputy and PLO member Mahmoud Abbas, also known as Abu Mazen. Their positions within their respective corridors of power and friendships with the academics made their delicate roles as mentors possible. Together, they tried to bridge the gulf between their two sides and articulate a realistic and equitable compromise. Schiff's revelation caused a whirlwind of controversy, due not only to the substance of the talks in Stockholm and what they were seen to represent, but also the manner in which the Understandings were reached. Israeli journalist Ari Shavit has claimed that Beilin acted:

[S]o as to establish irreversible political *faits accompli* in close cooperation with Yasser Arafat. In doing so, this deputy minister carried out what can be accurately defined as a 'diplomatic putsch' unprecedented in Israel's political history.

He forced his own world-view upon a government that had never adopted it and on a public that had never voted on it.[5]

This is an egregious misrepresentation of the motives, process and consequences of the initiative which this chapter aims to correct. This chapter will investigate the origins of the secret channel in Stockholm and examine the multitude of factors which prompted the use of Track II diplomacy. In his analysis of backchannel negotiation strategies, Klieman posits that 'domestic political incentives, ranging from the personal to the institutional and procedural, must be given separate attention and equal weight alongside backchanneling's external, diplomatic motives'.[6] As this chapter will show, this view certainly holds true in the case of the Stockholm talks, where backchannel strategy was preferred not only due to external factors, but also to Israeli domestic policy-making considerations. It will also consider the goals of the talks as seen by the participants and sponsors, and whether the chosen strategy was appropriate to achieve these ends. Furthermore, it will analyse the short-term and long-term effects of the channel and the ideas which it produced.

Towards Track II

The Oslo Agreement of 13 September 1993 produced euphoria among those who had been striving for peace between Israel and the Palestinians. It seemed to herald a new spirit of mutual coexistence between the two peoples and aimed to recalibrate the zero-sum attitudes which had long been the norm. Oslo was based on gradualism, a theory which espoused a step-by-step process of interim agreements moving towards a complete conflict-ending final status agreement. Gradually intensifying cooperation and the implementation of interim agreements at each stage would build trust between the two parties. This air of partnership rather than antagonism and the emergence of tangible positive results for both sides would make compromises on the hard final status issues more forthcoming.

What emerged, however, was a situation that Israeli head negotiator Uri Savir has described as 'a kind of purgatory between conflict and cooperation'.[7] The open-endedness of Oslo exacerbated the sense of uncertainty on both sides, and meant that each looked to keep its options open and improve their negotiating position ahead of any permanent status talks. Due to the zero-sum nature of the conflict, any

211

move by either side to strengthen their hand would automatically be perceived as a weakening of the other.[8]

While Savir believed in the interim process, Hirschfeld and Pundak did not. Hirschfeld thought that 'there was no need for an interim agreement. There was a need for a Declaration of Principles (DoP), and then go directly to permanent status, because we thought that major issues that were kept open—Jerusalem, refugees, security, settlements, territory—they were open wounds, and if you don't deal with them, they will come back at you, and unfortunately we were right.'[9] Pundak shared these fears, and additionally saw the need for a clarification of the basic principles that would inform a final status agreement. He believed that 'gradualism was the right thing to do', but 'only if you know where you're heading. You cannot move gradually to a non-existent target. ... An interim agreement with no final principles is very, very difficult to be implemented in a positive and honest way. ... Without an endgame, gradualism is doomed to fail. It was very clear unfortunately, very obvious, very fast.'[10]

Beilin, who had acted as the first official mentor of the Oslo channel, agreed with these assessments. Acutely aware that extremists on both sides would do their utmost to kill the process, he knew they could not afford to drag their heels for years before beginning work on final status.[11] Although it provided for an interim period, the terms of the Oslo Agreement also enabled immediate discussion of final status issues, stipulating that final status talks were to begin no later than 4 May 1996. In order to prepare for these negotiations, they sought to reach an agreement with the Palestinians on the principles of final status, to be used as a basis for future formal negotiations.

After the Oslo Agreement had been concluded, Beilin travelled to Tunis in October 1993 to speak with Arafat. Hirschfeld and Pundak did the same, though separately from Beilin. The message they brought, however, was the same. They wanted to start work on permanent status through a secret channel similar to the one that had been so effective in Norway, and were looking for Palestinian partners to engage with. Arafat agreed with the idea. At a conference in the UK in May 1994, Pundak met Khalidi, and the two met again later that summer in London, joined by Hirschfeld and Agha. Together, they developed a joint proposal for a secret channel. In June, while at an academic conference in Stockholm, Agha put their proposal to members of the Swedish

Ministry of Foreign Affairs, and Foreign Minister Margareta af Ugglas quickly agreed to sponsor the initiative.

Having found their host, Khalidi went to Gaza later that summer to inform Arafat about the project, whereupon Arafat assigned Abu Mazen to act as the PLO liaison. The teams agreed to keep their respective sponsors abreast of developments. Should any understandings be successfully produced, Beilin and Abu Mazen would present these to their leaders and seek official endorsement of them for use in the formal final status negotiations.

This channel was envisioned as an adaptation of the successful Oslo model, although it differed from the latter in a few critical ways. Initially, there was no clear unified vision as to what they were in Norway to achieve. Stockholm was very different. As Pundak explains, 'When we entered Oslo we didn't know where we were going—with Stockholm, it was very clear what we were aiming at.'[12] The academics agreed to try and reach an understanding on the basic principles of the core final status issues which could serve as the basis for official Track I negotiations on permanent status. It was to be a preparatory document, a 'pre-framework agreement'. Just as Hirschfeld's original text had been used as the basis for the Oslo Agreement and modified by Savir and legal advisor Joel Singer, he envisioned a similar use of a future Stockholm document.[13] The team's targets later had to be adjusted somewhat to suit the circumstances. As it became increasingly clear in early 1995 that Rabin was facing domestic political problems, 'the concept became more one of giving Rabin some tool with which he could go to the elections and say to his electorate, "Listen, I have the means of coming to a final status agreement with the Palestinians."'[14]

Thus whereas the origins of Oslo may be described as academic, the same cannot be said of Stockholm, despite the fact that it was being conducted by academics. Both channels benefited from the guise of academia, but although it was non-officials speaking to non-officials, Stockholm had an overt, strictly political purpose from the beginning. Hirschfeld suggests that 'it was something between Track I ½ and Track II, but it was more Track II than Track I'.[15]

They began at a level of parity, two academics speaking with two academics. Pundak remembers that the atmosphere in Oslo was 'a bit more rigid because we had to report to the two officials', while 'Stockholm was much more relaxed because of the composition of people.'[16]

At the level of sponsorship or political anchoring, however, there was more of an imbalance. 'On the Israeli side it was Track II because with all due respect to Yossi Beilin, he wasn't seen as a decision maker.'[17] Abu Mazen, on the other hand, was more of a political heavyweight, widely considered the second highest in the PLO hierarchy after Arafat. However loosely Arafat and Abu Mazen followed it, it was still anchored in the highest echelons.

On the Israeli side, however, Prime Minister Yitzhak Rabin and President Shimon Peres were unaware of the initiative. Beilin decided not to inform them for a number of reasons. First, he was convinced that if he briefed Peres on the matter, Peres would then inevitably be obliged to inform Rabin.[18] He feared that the prime minister might then demand that the channel be terminated on the grounds that it was too early to consider permanent status, and that the interim negotiations should not be prejudiced. He did not want the project to be vetoed before it had been given the chance to bear some kind of fruit. Again, this was precisely the model established in Oslo. There, Beilin had let the initial talks progress for around two months before informing Peres and Rabin, by which time a draft document containing a statement of principles had been produced and could be placed in front of them.[19]

Second, Beilin was keen to remain in control of the initiative and retain a certain amount of operational flexibility, which can be crucial to the early stages of effective Track II diplomacy. Reflecting on the changes which resulted from informing Peres and Rabin about Oslo, he noted:

From now on this was no longer a process of which I was in effective charge, capable of terminating it or joining it as I saw fit. I had become part of the team steering the process and this was a very complex feeling. I had no doubt that more gridlocks were to be expected—some of them perhaps capable of halting the entire enterprise—and that decision-making would be a much slower and more cumbersome process.[20]

Third, and related to the second, there was undoubtedly an element of personal political ambition at work. Klieman highlights personal ambition as particularly relevant in modern politics and a prominent reason for backchannelling, given the presence of 'highly competitive "political diplomatists"—those civil servants, foreign ministry experts, and political appointees to policymaking posts who are directly engaged at home in foreign affairs. Behind the back door is a calculated attempt at gaining policy primacy. Playing hegemonic or exclusionary politics aims at neutralising one's organisational rivals by, in effect, bypassing them.'[21]

This ambition was confirmed by Beilin's eventual campaign for the leadership of the Labour Party. Savir believes that 'Yossi felt the need to distance himself from his formidable mentor [Peres] and strike out on his own.' This was particularly true after Oslo when, according to Savir, Israel's peace policy was decided only by Rabin and Peres, with Beilin largely kept out of the loop. He had irritated the duo by portraying himself, Hirschfeld and Pundak as the pioneers and heroes of Oslo, rather than as supporters of the government's security and policy structure.[22] The success of an initiative he mentored would be a great triumph demonstrating his political vision, and truly bolster his standing and future career.

Beilin's commitment to his personal goals and national vision was clear. In addition to being highly involved in the Stockholm talks between the four academics, he also actively explored other options in parallel to see if he could get a better deal from other Palestinians. Beilin met twice with senior Palestinian official Nabil Shaath and General Abd al-Razzak Yihya, the PLO's chief military advisor, once in Stockholm in mid-February 1995 and once in Jerusalem in mid-April. Here, conversation also centred around the final status issues.[23]

As Beilin explained to the Swedish minister for international development cooperation, Pierre Schori, at a meeting 'between four eyes' in Jerusalem on 11 April, these meetings were not viewed as a priority. Shaath was an 'effective and knowledgeable' Palestinian spokesperson, an important figure to include in any deepening and political anchoring of the Stockholm document, but he would be sidelined for the time being if necessary. Furthermore, Beilin argued that these meetings provided useful cover for the academics, the avenue which he deemed most important. If questions were asked about any activity in Stockholm, they could refer to those meetings with Shaath and allay any further suspicion.[24]

On 28 September 1995 Rabin and Arafat signed the Interim Agreement, also known as Oslo II. Just over a month later, on 31 October, a lengthy final session of drafting was held in Beilin's office to finalise a draft document to present to both leaders. In addition to the two mentors and the four academics, Oslo veteran and member of the Palestinian Legislative Council (PLC) Hassan Asfour and Beilin's long-time associate and fellow 'dove' Nimrod Novik were also present. This last draft of the document bore the date 1 November 1995. Beilin was disappointed that they had not managed to finish earlier, acknowledging that 'the fact that we achieved our agreement only on the 31st of October was our failure. In my view, had it been possible to bring it to the parties before the Interim Agreement, which was very cumbersome and in many ways mistaken, it could have solved many problems.'[25]

At a meeting in Gaza shortly afterwards, the Palestinian team—Abu Mazen, Agha, Asfour and Khalidi—and the Swedes presented the document to Arafat and Abu Ala, the Palestinian negotiator in Oslo. When asked if he was willing to accept it as a basis for negotiations, Arafat replied, pointing to his colleagues, 'If these spies want to continue, then it's fine with me, you can continue.'[26] With the Israeli leadership, the plan was to present the working paper to Peres on 8 November, since Beilin believed that Rabin would ask him to obtain a reaction to it from Peres first before reading it himself. Moreover, he thought going straight to Rabin would offend Peres, given their political rivalry at the head of the Labour Party, and make him feel that he was being circumvented.[27] Still, given his position as prime minister, the Understandings were tailored towards Rabin and his thinking. Beilin remembers, 'We took the speeches of Rabin, the interviews of Rabin, the discussions that we had with Rabin, and we tried to see what he could accept.'[28]

Publicly, he had expressed his position on a number of final status issues which reflected the contents of the document. The academics and their Swedish hosts believed this was a sign which in part vindicated Arafat's and Abu Mazen's belief that Rabin was secretly aware of their work through Mossad or other intelligence sources, and was waiting to see what they would produce.[29] If this was indeed the case, Rabin was influenced by the discussions in Stockholm and simultaneously affected them.[30] At the time, Peres 'was not so enthusiastic about withdrawal from all territories and two states', and so the expectation was that he would react negatively towards the Understandings, whereas Rabin would then endorse them.[31]

This idea, however, was never put to the test; Rabin never read the document. On 5 November, just days before the Understandings were due to be presented to Peres, Yigal Amir, a Jewish religious fundamentalist, assassinated Rabin at a peace rally in Tel Aviv. Although Pundak believes that Rabin would have adopted the Understandings and used them as the basis for final status negotiations, we will never know for certain.[32] When Beilin eventually briefed Peres on 11 November, 'he was too overwhelmed by the assassination, and he said this was not the time, so we did not proceed with it'. To this day, Beilin truly laments this decision: 'I was not in a position to put my foot down and insist upon it, maybe it was my mistake not to fight for it enough, but the whole atmosphere then was so crazy that I felt that I could not push Peres more in this situation. He was broken.'[33]

Though Peres did have strong concerns about the substance of the Understandings, the contextual environment was also a primary reason for failing to act on them. As the new prime minister he had recently been briefed on the progress of secret negotiations with the Syrians which Rabin had not made him privy to. He was interested in exploring this dialogue further to try and establish the principles of a peace treaty with Syria. As for the Palestinians, Peres wanted to adhere to the principles of gradualism and focus attention on implementing the recent Interim Agreement, rather than moving to permanent status. He feared that such major moves on the Palestinian track would irreparably split an already deeply divided society at a time of great national trauma, and thought it important to reach out in a dialogue with the right and the religious rather than take actions which might appear to be a vengeful settling of scores. Additionally, the Labour Party would soon be trying to put together a coalition supported by the religious parties, and did not wish to alienate them.[34]

Beilin and the four academics had reasoned that the document would be a useful tool for Rabin to be included in the Labour Party platform and wielded in the future Israeli elections. With opinion polls suggesting that Rabin and Likud leader Benjamin Netanyahu were neck and neck, they believed that a political bombshell would be required to break the deadlock. It was hoped that the parameters of a framework agreement on permanent status would serve this purpose. Such a document 'would make it impossible for Likud to raise questions about the future' and help assuage a powerful sense of uncertainty among the electorate. Peres, however, was unconvinced by this argument, and doubted whether adoption of the document would improve his stance in the upcoming elections.

[H]e [Peres] said that he preferred to get through the elections and then negotiate with a mandate from the Israeli people rather than present an initialled agreement to the public and then turn the elections into a national referendum on an agreement that contained certain clauses that might be unacceptable to some people.[35]

Beilin believes that 'It was a huge mistake on Peres' side, a huge mistake. He could have used it. ... After the assassination—when he had an advantage of 25 per cent [in Israeli opinion polls]—at that moment he could have done anything. But he was shocked ... all of us were shocked. So the energies were not exactly there. But there is no question that he missed a huge opportunity to take it and to say, "I'm going for it."'[36]

With a 'no' from Peres, Beilin informed the Palestinians that the document would have to be shelved. He could not put Peres in a situation whereby Arafat said yes and he said no, so they could not go ahead with it.[37] Both sides thus agreed to keep it confidential. The status of the document was as follows: 'a consultative paper, to which neither side was committed and which neither side rejected out of hand, which could resurface at some time in the future as a first draft and a basis for negotiation, if and when such negotiation should begin'.[38]

Dissemination and Effects

As is so often the case with leaks in the context of the Israeli–Palestinian conflict, the source of the Beilin–Abu Mazen Understandings is disputed. Schiff, the Israeli journalist who broke the story, was on close terms with the Palestinian team, and according to Beilin, Schiff told him the Palestinians were the source. Khalidi strenuously denies the accusation. 'All the leaks are from the Israeli side. Every single leak. Neither Hussein, myself, nor Abu Mazen has ever leaked anything on any of the things that we did.' Beilin says he begged Schiff not to publish it before the elections scheduled for May 1996, but that Schiff could not oblige; apparently another Israeli journalist had also gotten hold of the scoop, and so he had to publish first.[39]

In his book entitled *The Difficult Road to Peace*, Neill Lochery offers a different perspective. He suggests that the Labour Party leaked it in order to rebuff accusations from the Likud-led right-wing bloc that, if elected, they would compromise on and divide Jerusalem: 'Interestingly, a decision was taken by the leadership to respond to the Likud's attacks by leaking details of the so-called Beilin–Abu Mazen plan at the start of the campaign to bring the issue to a head at an early stage ...'[40]

If they did indeed leak it, it proved a grave miscalculation. However, the timing of the leak suggests that this is doubtful. In campaign speeches in mid-February, Peres denied the right-wing allegations, pledging to keep Jerusalem united under Israeli sovereignty, and also denied charges from Rafael Eitan, leader of the right-wing Tsomet party, that secret negotiations were being held on the issue. When news of the Understandings surfaced a few days later, this denial appeared false and was damaging to Peres' credibility. Eitan had argued that such use of a secret channel 'shows a lack of honesty and demonstrates deceit', and it seems unlikely that Labour would have played directly into the hands of the right in such a manner.[41]

Eitan's indictment no doubt resonated with portions of the Israeli electorate, and it has since been repeated. Shavit, for example, suggests that 'from the democratic standpoint, it was highly unethical', and describes the Understandings as having been 'born in sin'.[42] Klieman observes that 'there is no way of getting around the fact that back-channel statecraft involves a strong element of deception; and that deception, no matter how warranted for the sake of expediency and in the name of peaceful relations, nevertheless remains deception'. This can result in public mistrust and policy confusion, two consequences which were significant in this case.[43]

Schiff's article did acknowledge that Peres had not authorised the talks and refused to adopt the Understandings—'The bottom line is that the document of understanding was prepared by official elements on both sides, but it cannot become an agreement as long as the Prime Minister opposes its main points.'[44] Despite this, Peres and the Labour Party were identified with the concessions it contained. Their denials notwithstanding, the document gave credibility to the Likud's most popular slogan 'Peres will divide Jerusalem', which proved extremely effective and gave them virtual possession of this vital national symbol.[45] Ambiguity about the precise terms of the Understandings generated a wave of rumour and speculation about the ultimate intentions of the Labour Party with regard to the final status issues, and relations with Arafat and the Palestinians. These were significant sources of public concern, used by Netanyahu and the Likud to devastating effect, throwing doubt on Labour's leadership credentials and their handling of the peace process.

Though Jerusalem was a critical issue central to Jewish identity, security rapidly became the primary concern. Four separate Palestinian suicide bombings between 25 February and 4 March 1996 in Jerusalem, Tel Aviv and Ashkelon killed a total of fifty-nine Israelis.[46] This was the most important turning point in determining the outcome of the election, widely seen as a referendum on attitudes towards the peace process.[47] The hopeful vision of Oslo was now placed in stark contrast to brutal reality.

Peres and Labour argued that this was the work of radical forces like Hamas who wanted to destroy the process and a change of course would be tantamount to handing them victory. The opposition meanwhile challenged Arafat's credibility as a partner for a secure and stable peace, suggesting that he was at best unable or unwilling to constrain radical Islamist forces, and at worst directly supportive of and complicit in their actions. By tying Peres to Arafat they effectively discredited the incumbent prime minister, notably in a television advert which showed the two walking hand-in-hand interposed with pictures of smouldering wreckage from terrorist attacks.[48] In such an atmosphere, the Understandings were portrayed by the right wing as a 'sell out' of Israel, a further step in a misguided Oslo process that had brought Israel nothing but bloodshed, and actively threatened its security and even existence.

Following that spate of terror attacks, Peres almost immediately lost his 10–15 per cent lead over Netanyahu and was all of a sudden narrowly trailing in the polls. While a majority of Israelis had previously felt that the peace process had enhanced personal security, that figure dropped to 16.5 per cent, with over 51 per cent feeling less secure.[49] In addition to the inability to prevent suicide bombings, the rumoured readiness to cede the Golan Heights to Syria and the Jordan Valley to the Palestinians further hurt Peres' and Labour's security credibility.[50] After all, Peres did not have the level of military credentials that had been so important to his predecessor. As it happens, the latter two points were quite unfair to Peres. First, concessions on the Golan, known as the 'deposit', had been mooted by Rabin and left for Peres to inherit. Second, though the Understandings proposed to relinquish the Jordan Valley to the Palestinians, this was actually one of Peres' main reservations against the document. He refused to abandon the long-standing Israeli idea of a security border with Jordan.[51]

Although the impact of the Understandings on the election is difficult to measure, it was certainly not positive. While in opposition, Labour Party leader Ehud Barak expressed his belief that the Understandings lost them the election, though his differences with Beilin make this view less than surprising.[52] Still, given that the margin of Netanyahu's victory was less than 1 per cent—less than 30,000 votes—any issue could conceivably have been crucial.[53] The Likud campaign was designed to discredit Peres on Jerusalem, the Golan Heights and the threat of a Palestinian state, and the Understandings thus played into their hands. As Likud Knesset Minister Limor Livnat explained, allegations on these issues would 'arouse a general suspicion of Peres' credibility. The Likud will not accuse Peres of lying, but we will instill doubts in people's minds.'[54] The Understandings certainly helped them accomplish that goal.

Beilin recalls that the situation was 'a disaster' for him. He had promised Abu Mazen not to say anything about the Understandings, and told Peres, 'I cannot breach my promise to Abu Mazen.' He could not even dismiss them as 'nonsense' and was therefore 'put in a very difficult situation'.[55] In an interview with Arye Golan from *Kol Yisrael* in July after the elections, Beilin said, 'Ultimately, all we did during the election campaign was issue denials without proving that it is possible—although there was no agreement—to reach a totally different kind of arrangement with the Palestinians.'[56]

While most of the right wing fiercely objected to the Understandings, Likud MK Michael Eitan came to Beilin shortly after Schiff's publication and was interested in exploring them in more depth. After the elections, Beilin and Eitan headed groups of Labour and Likud MKs respectively who sought to create cross-party consensus on Israeli final status positions. Based on the Understandings—though 'less forthcoming' to the Palestinians, particularly on settlements and Jerusalem—the resulting 'Beilin–Eitan document' was published in January 1997.[57] One can argue that the Understandings therefore 'left a lasting imprint on the Israeli internal ideological debate about the future of the territories and became a major factor in helping to create a new bipartisan Israeli consensus on partition'.[58]

In his efforts to reach out across the left–right divide, Beilin highlighted some of the significant concessions the Palestinians were willing to make under the terms of the Understandings. However, Abu Mazen and the Palestinians were concerned by the way he seemed to be appropriating the talks for his own political purposes, particularly Beilin's implication that they were prepared to accept Abu Dis and outlying municipal areas as a capital instead of East Jerusalem.[59] This notion did a lot of damage to Abu Mazen and to the document itself, since it robbed it of any credibility on the Palestinian side. Beilin's handling of the situation 'left a bad taste in Abu Mazen's mouth'. He was not happy about being identified with such purported concessions, and—without completely disassociating himself from the document—distanced himself from it.[60]

The effects of the Understandings are open to debate. Hirschfeld suggests that 'the effect of whatever you agree is irrelevant as long as the senior leadership doesn't endorse it', and that public knowledge of any such agreement may harm it: 'you create expectations that you do not fulfil, and you raise those people who don't like it. You give them enough substance to work against it, and you may de-legitimise some of the ideas that you're working on.'[61] Although this is undoubtedly a very real risk and was true of initial reactions to the Understandings, conversely, one should not overlook their long-term impact.

The Stockholm talks were the first real effort to establish principles of final status on a firm basis, and a number of the ideas that originated there remain part of the foundation of any equitable future two-state solution. First, what is Arab in Jerusalem goes to the Palestinians, and what is Jewish goes to Israel. Second, the idea of land swaps. Third, the distinction between the right of return and the actual physical exercising of that right. Fourth, the idea that the Jordan River can be the security border of Israel but not the sovereign border of Israel. These ideas were all expressed there for the first time. Agha observes that:

All the fundamentals of any future deal, until new fundamentals come up, have their genesis in the most comprehensive way in that document. So still, I think that document is the most revolutionary document between the two parties on the issue of final status. And if you look at [the] Geneva [Accord], it takes it to more detail, but it does not have any principles of its own away from the principles that we put together in that document. So it is very, very important.[62]

The Understandings have been a constant point of reference in any subsequent set of negotiations. Prior to the Camp David summit in 2000, White House officials put the Understandings on President Clinton's desk, who said, 'This is it. This is simply the whole framework agreement. It is exactly this paper that has to be signed.'[63] However, Barak did not accept them as the basis for the summit and threatened to leave if they were put on the table.

Nonetheless, they still informed discussion. Beilin remembers that US Secretary of State Madeleine Albright 'told me after Camp David that I was not in Camp David, but my spirit was there because everybody spoke all the time about Beilin–Abu Mazen. … Beilin-Abu Mazen was always there … in the negotiations. From time to time … they said, "Yes, but this doesn't appear in the map of Beilin–Abu Mazen." So they did not refer to it officially, but unofficially they referred to it all the time. Why? Because this was the only paper on the agenda.'[64] When Clinton later decided to issue what have become known as the 'Clinton parameters' in late December 2000, these bore the clear fingerprints of the Understandings.

Conclusion

The case of the Beilin–Abu Mazen Understandings illustrates a number of important features of Israeli backchannel diplomacy, both positive and negative. The Track II strategy is extremely useful in 'cutting the red tape' and its use by people like Beilin and Abu Mazen 'reflects the frustrations of domestic "policy activists" and "peace processors," those who strive for the "grand bargain"'.[65] This is particularly true when dealing with such contentious and sensitive existential identity issues.

Still, backchannels have their limitations. They are not always conducive to generating the public support necessary for landmark policy changes, as verbal and violent reactions to the Oslo Agreement also showed. As Henry Kissinger said, 'no foreign policy—no matter how ingenious—has any chance of success if it is born in the minds of a few and carried in the hearts of none'. An overreliance on backchannels:

no matter how warranted in foreign policy terms, tends over time to breed public cynicism toward leadership, principled policy, candor, and the like. In democracies, to fail to take the public into greater confidence and prepare it in advance for a fundamental policy departure is to risk the emergence of significant resistance at home, including conservative bureaucratic opponents of change, in general or on a specific policy.[66]

Had Peres adopted the Understandings and entered the election campaign using them as the Labour Party platform, this would have been less of an issue. The public would have had time to debate the merits of such a policy and the election would in large part have been a referendum on the matter. Over a year after the elections, Agha briefed Dore Gold, Netanyahu's advisor and later Israeli ambassador to the UN, on the contents of the Understandings. 'His reaction was, very clearly, that if Peres had adopted this document and went to the elections with it, he would have won.'[67] However, the way the Understandings came to light undoubtedly affected public perceptions of the activity, as did the context of terrorism.

Crucially, the discussions did not commit anyone to anything. The document was not signed and had no official imprint of any kind. Such is the nature of Track II diplomacy. It was intended to affect policy and though backchannel strategy was logically sound and based on successful precedent, Beilin and the academics ultimately fell short of their immediate goals. While personal ambition was certainly a factor, these were also informed by much larger issues concerning the future trajectory of the State of Israel.

Though the short-term effects of the Understandings were negative in the sense of adversely affecting Peres' election campaign, the long-term effects are less clear. Much like Zhou Enlai's assessment of the French Revolution, it is still too early to tell. The leak meant that the Understandings reached other key constituencies and stimulated public debate on the final status issues. Changing attitudes and perceptions in such an intractable identity-based conflict takes time. The peace process is precisely that: a process. It remains to be seen whether this episode will be remembered as a missed opportunity or the seeds of permanent peace. Whatever the case, secret diplomacy will undoubtedly continue to be a prominent part of the search for peace.

13

THE DEAL THAT NEVER WAS

ISRAEL'S CLANDESTINE NEGOTIATIONS WITH SYRIA, 1991–2000

Ahron Bregman

Introduction

Despite the initial optimism, the Israeli–Syrian peace negotiations in Washington that followed the 1991 Madrid Conference failed to produce any tangible results. Israel's right-wing Prime Minister Yitzhak Shamir was reluctant to make any concessions over the Golan Heights and did not want to negotiate their future, while the Syrians insisted that Israel should first agree to withdraw fully from the Golan Heights down to the 'June 4, 1967 lines'—namely the area under Syrian control before the 1967 war—as a precondition for further talks to continue at all.[1] The two sides were thus unable to overcome even the first hurdle. This stalemate, however, came to an end when Yitzhak Rabin's Labour Party defeated Yitzhak Shamir's Likud party in Israel's June 1992 general elections.

With unique access to transcripts of conversations and documents which have never previously been disclosed, this chapter traces the fascinating history of Syrian–Israeli peace negotiations, much of it clandestine, over a period of nearly a decade. Yet some of the sources for the information discussed must remain under wraps and as such specific references to some of this material is not made. However, what follows is a unique insight into how these negotiations were conducted, who were the key players, and when it mattered most how the lack of conviction and courage among key actors to move from the covert to the overt ultimately doomed the negotiations to fail.

The Rabin Period

Prime Minister Rabin put making peace with Arabs and Palestinians on the top of his agenda. He was a strong believer in the 'Syria first' option, the idea that Israel should first try to sort out her conflict with Syria before doing so with the Palestinians. This is partly because, domestically, no Israeli prime minister could pay the price for peace on these two fronts simultaneously, or to use Rabin's own words: '[We in Israel] can't raise more than one flag at a time'.[2]

There were three main reasons why Rabin preferred the Syria first option: first, he thought that the dispute with Syria, being mainly about territory, would be easier to solve than the complex and deep-rooted Israeli–Palestinian dispute. Second, Syria posed a greater threat to Israel's security than the Palestinians as, unlike the Palestinians, Syria had a proper army and long-range missiles and therefore it was more urgent to neutralise the Syrian threat first. Lastly, Rabin believed that a strong leader such as President Hafez al-Assad could be trusted to deliver on any deal he signed with Israel.

In the summer of 1993, when secret peace talks with the Palestinians were still underway in Oslo, Rabin tried to tempt Assad to come to the negotiating table by making him a startling offer. He proposed to US Secretary of State Warren Christopher that, in his forthcoming visit to Damascus, he should find out whether President Assad was ready to conclude a peace treaty with Israel on the basis of something that had never before been offered to him, namely a full Israeli withdrawal from the occupied Golan Heights.[3]

Rabin emphasised that Christopher should keep this offer secret and pose it to Assad as an entirely hypothetical American idea. Requesting this sort of deniability is standard diplomatic practice, done in order to ensure that the offer is not simply pocketed by Assad with nothing in return; in other words, Rabin's commitment to withdraw fully from the Golan was made to the United States. Rabin also explained to Christopher that the Israeli withdrawal, if things got that far, would have to be spread out over five years, so that Israel had time to ensure an orderly evacuation of her thirty-two Golan settlements and also—though this was not spelled out by Rabin—have enough time to monitor Syria and see whether it was sticking to its peace commitments. It is worth recalling here that the evacuation of the Sinai, following the signing of peace with Egypt in March 1979, took three years to complete, a period that enabled Israel to monitor Egyptian behaviour.

Furthermore, Rabin informed Christopher that in any future peace agreement Israel's water security must be safeguarded, as much of it originates in Syria and the snows of the Golan Heights; the Sea of Galilee, whose north-eastern portion was controlled by the Syrians until the 1967 war, provides Israel with more than 35 per cent of her fresh water needs. Assad also had to know, Rabin told Christopher, that any Israeli–Syrian peace agreement would have to be presented to the Israeli public to vote on in a referendum, as a withdrawal from the Golan had not been part of Rabin's Labour Party election manifesto. Finally, Rabin wanted Christopher to enquire whether Assad was ready, in return for the Golan, to rein in Hezbollah in Lebanon, expel from Damascus the ten Palestinian organisations that opposed the peace process and sever Syria's strategic ties with Iran. Rabin's bottom line, to quote from the original transcript of the Rabin–Christopher conversation, was, '[A]ssuming their demands are met [namely that Israel will fully withdraw from the Golan], are they ready for a real peace?'[4]

In his meeting in Damascus on 4 August 1993, Christopher tried Rabin's offer on Assad, telling him that Israel might be ready for a 'full withdrawal' from the Golan if Syria made some concessions; Christopher then listed Rabin's requirements on security, water, period of withdrawal and so on. For Assad, it is worth mentioning here, the most important element in any peace deal with Israel was the depth of the Israeli withdrawal. He insisted on full withdrawal from all the land which had been under Syrian control before the Israelis invaded in 1967, from the mountains of the Golan all the way down to what he called 'the June 4, 1967 line', which runs alongside, and indeed touches, the Sea of Galilee in its north-eastern sector.

Now, suspecting that what Prime Minister Rabin was offering via the US Secretary of State was less than what he regarded as a 'full withdrawal',

Assad asked Christopher two questions: first, 'When Rabin says "full withdrawal" does he mean a withdrawal to the posts Israel held on June 4, 1967?' to which Christopher replied: 'I have a commitment to a "full withdrawal" without a specific determination.'[5] Assad's second question was: 'Does Israel have further claims to any lands it occupied on the Syrian front in June 1967?' to which Christopher replied: 'not as far as I know'.[6]

In his report to the prime minister, upon his return from Damascus to Jerusalem on 5 August, Christopher confirmed that while Assad was ready for the normalisation of relations with Israel he still 'has a problem with the terms'. For instance, five years for the Israeli evacuation of the Golan as requested by Rabin was too long: Assad, Christopher now reported to the prime minister, would prefer 'something like half a year'.[7]

Assad's response to other points raised in the Rabin offer disappointed the prime minister, as he had expected boldness to be matched by boldness, and here he felt—rightly or wrongly—that Assad was staying rigid. Suspecting, therefore, that peace talks with Assad would be protracted, Rabin abandoned his Syria first strategy, and turned his attention to the Palestinian front, signing the Oslo Agreements with Yasser Arafat on 13 September 1993.[8]

But Rabin's secret offer through the Americans was not forgotten by either side, and Israel and Syria continued discreetly to exchange ideas. In April–May 1994, for instance, Rabin delivered more or less the same offer to Assad via Christopher and Assad tried again to find out what exactly the prime minister meant by 'a full' Israeli withdrawal from the Golan. Secretary of State Warren Christopher admitted that he was still unsure, but added this time that he thought Rabin meant a withdrawal to the 1923 international border, the line agreed between Britain and France in the aftermath of the First World War and which runs east from areas the Syrians controlled on the eve of the 1967 war and, most crucially, away from the water of the Sea of Galilee. This was not what President Assad had in mind and he rejected this position out of hand, stating that, as far as he is concerned, the 1923 border is no more than a line drawn by imperialism on the Arab map and that as an independent Syria did not participate in its drawing he would not accept it. Assad told Christopher that there would be no peace with Israel before it fully withdrew from the Golan Heights down to the 4 June 1967 border.[9]

On 18 July 1994, Christopher discussed the Syria issue with Prime Minister Rabin once again, telling him that it was essential to give Assad 'the one sentence of clarity', as Christopher put it, that Assad expects on the 4 June 1967 line, assuming the parties reach agreement on all other matters. Rabin replied, 'You can say that you have every reason to believe this is the result [namely, that the Israeli withdrawal would be to the 4 June 1967 lines], but Israel will not spell this out before knowing that our needs will be fulfilled.'[10] Christopher said, 'That's all I need', whereupon Rabin added, 'You can tell him you understand this, and that he will not get the commitment without fulfilling our needs.' Christopher replied, 'It is not on the table, it is in my pocket.' Rabin called this pledge to withdraw to the 4 June 1967 lines a 'deposit'; elsewhere this oral promise came to be known as 'the pocket'.

Rabin's thinking was that by letting President Assad know, indirectly and secretly, through the United States, that in the context of peace Syria could get from Israel the entire Golan Heights down to the 4 June 1967 line, this would enable Assad to open up and show what he could do to meet Israel's needs. In Damascus a suspicious Assad again asked: 'Does Rabin mean the withdrawal will include all the land that was under Syrian sovereignty in June 4, 1967?' Christopher now answered: 'Yes.'[11] A follow up visit by President Bill Clinton to Damascus was instrumental in persuading President Assad to send his most senior military officer to meet his Israeli counterpart, army Chief of Staff Ehud Barak, for discussions. Assad insisted, though, that this should be preceded by a meeting between his ambassador in Washington, Walid Moualem, and Barak, so that Moualem could check the matter before Assad allowed such a senior figure like his chief of staff to meet the Israelis.

The pair met at Blair House, the US president's guest house across the street from the White House. After a formal meeting, the Israeli chief of staff was able to entice Ambassador Moualem out of the room and into the garden, where he wished to talk to him off the record to assess how flexible Syria could be in meeting Israel's needs, often difficult to do around a formal negotiating table where notes are taken.[12] It later emerged that when Moualem discussed the Blair House meeting with his president in Damascus, he was a touch too positive. He led Assad to believe that future talks would be smooth and easy and the Golan would fully return to Syria. Perhaps he had failed to distinguish between what was said around the official table (very little) and what Chief of Staff Barak said in private in the garden (much more). But as a result, when Assad dispatched his Chief of Staff Hikmat Shihabi to Blair House again to talk with Barak, a month or so later, as Assad had promised Clinton he would do, expectations on the Syrian side were sky high.

They met secretly on 21 December 1994, and while Barak laid out a comprehensive plan of Israel's needs, Shihabi attempted to push the discussion towards the details of the future border between the two countries, which he hoped the chief of staff would confirm to be the 4 June 1967 line.[13] Shihabi, however, was deeply upset when Barak would not discuss the route of the future border at all. Barak, for his part, tried to take Shihabi aside, as he had Moualem, to tell him off the record that Israel understood Syria's needs, and that Barak expected him to show— even off the record—that Syria too understands Israel's needs. But Shihabi would not play ball and, throughout the two days they spent negotiating, Barak was never able to get the Syrian alone in the garden for a talk without notes being taken. The pair returned home disappointed and this, in fact, was the last major discussion between Israel and Syria during the Rabin period.

Nonetheless, it is safe to say that during Rabin's tenure as Israel's prime minister from 1992 to 1995, there was good progress in Israeli–Syrian peace negotiations—Rabin's 'deposit', for instance, would become a major element in future peace talks between the parties. This progress was down to two main reasons: first, secrecy, which enabled the parties to open up, even if only partially, and offer some concessions without being criticised by their publics back home; and, second, American diplomacy and willingness to act as the go-between, keeping the Rabin promise as a 'deposit' in their pocket.

The Netanyahu Period

Prime Minister Rabin was assassinated on 4 November 1995 and replaced by Shimon Peres, whose tenure as prime minister was short; during this time there was very little progress in Israeli–Syrian peace talks.[14] Then, in 1996, the Likud party won the general elections and Benjamin Netanyahu became Israel's premier. Publicly, Netanyahu insisted that the Golan Heights were not up for negotiation and would never be returned to Syria, but secretly he maintained an indirect channel with Syria's President Assad through one Ron Lauder, scion of the Estee Lauder cosmetics conglomerate. Secret, indirect negotiations between Netanyahu and Assad focused on a ten-point document entitled

'Treaty of Peace between Israel and Syria' which Lauder carried with him—shuttling between Jerusalem and Damascus.[15]

The document dealt with various matters related to bringing peace between Israel and Syria, not least the route of the future border between the two countries. Not trusting Netanyahu to give him the 4 June 1967 line, Assad, at one point, had asked to see a map signed by the prime minister depicting the proposed Israeli line of withdrawal. However, in Israel, two of Netanyahu's colleagues—ministers Yitzhak Mordechai and Ariel Sharon—objected to providing Assad with such a map as this would be a firm Israeli pledge, which they felt was premature. As a result, when Lauder returned to Damascus empty handed Assad ended the secret talks. Assad would later refer to this episode in these words:

Mr Lauder came to see me and … told me that Netanyahu … agreed to a full withdrawal to the June 4 lines, but that he could not announce it publicly because his platform during the election campaign had been against withdrawal … We did not discuss the June 4 lines because that was taken as agreed. But [later] we began to have doubts about whether we were on the same wavelength … it became apparent that there was a need for a map … indicating the line of [Israeli] withdrawal to the June 4 1967, but nothing was forthcoming. As it turned out we could not come to any conclusion because he could not provide the map. The 10 points in his paper do not at all reflect what we discussed and what was agreed upon. All this is now in the past. We should dismiss it completely.[16]

Although the Lauder channel eventually failed to produce a full peace agreement between Israel and Syria, it did demonstrate that even right-wing leaders such as Netanyahu were willing to negotiate the return of the Golan Heights, and even put things down in writing so long as it was kept secret.

The Barak Period

Perhaps the most significant progress in Israeli–Syrian peace talks took place during Ehud Barak's tenure as Israel's prime minister. He came to power in the general elections of 17 May 1999, and like his murdered mentor Yitzhak Rabin, he put making peace with Arabs and Palestinians at the top of his agenda.

In his first official meeting as prime minister with US President Bill Clinton on 15 July 1999, Barak presented his peace strategy. He told Clinton he would put peace talks with the Palestinians on ice in favour of negotiations with Syria; like Rabin, he felt that no Israeli prime minister could survive long in office while attempting to make peace on these two fronts simultaneously, and that, of the two, the Syrian threat was both more grave and yet potentially easier to neutralise than the Palestinian. Additionally, by now it was clear that Assad was gravely ill and unlikely to live for much longer; back in February 1999, Assad visited Jordan for the funeral of King Hussein where Israeli secret agents managed to attach a specimen canister to his hotel toilet and collected a urine sample which demonstrated just how ill he was. There was a chance, Barak thought, that Assad would therefore wish to make peace and regain the Golan Heights for his country before his time was up and he was replaced by a new leader, for whom it would likely be more difficult to contemplate a peace deal for some time, until securely ensconced in office.

Clinton agreed with the plan and, following his meeting with Barak, started putting pressure on Assad to agree to renew secret peace negotiations with Israel. On 26 August 1999 Clinton phoned Assad to suggest that they should start secret peace talks at once in Switzerland. Assad agreed, and direct talks between Barak's man, former IDF general and Director of Military Intelligence Uri Saguie, and the Syrian Foreign Ministry legal advisor Riad Daoudi followed at the residence of the US ambassador to Switzerland in Berne, on 27 August. But their talks did not go well as Barak would not allow Saguie to discuss the future route of the border, and the Syrian representative, Riad Doudi, would not engage in serious discussions before the Syrian precondition was met: Israel should reaffirm the Rabin deposit of a full withdrawal to the 4 June 1967 line.

Barak, however, was not deterred by the lack of progress and he went on to suggest a bold diplomatic move, namely that President Clinton travel to Damascus in person to 'stun' Assad, as he put it, into making the necessary concessions before the opportunity for peace was lost. Should Clinton agree to this idea, at some risk to his personal prestige, Barak then pledged that he might be able to go the extra mile and reaffirm Rabin's secret deposit, the promise made by the late prime minister back in 1994 to withdraw fully to the 4 June 1967 line.

Clinton who, like Barak, was by nature inclined towards taking such chances, was attracted by the idea, but his aides objected, labelling Barak's suggestion 'a high-risk endeavour'. They would not expose their president before the world on a high-profile mission that might fail, and suggested, instead, that Secretary of State Madeleine Albright should take on the task.

Barak was sceptical, but Albright's visit to Damascus was a success as President Assad agreed to resume peace talks at a high-level by sending his foreign minister, Farouk Shara, to the United States to lead a Syrian delegation at peace talks.[17] The move to foreign minister level was significant as for years Assad had rejected meetings of officials at a political level, as if that represented a level of recognition that he was not prepared to grant Israel. It was out of character for the rigid Syrian leader to move in such leaps, and Barak, sensing some change in Assad, decided to personally lead the Israeli delegation at the coming talks with Shara, which would take place in Washington. It was a remarkable breakthrough.

Blair House, Washington, 15 December 1999

Yet what was apparent from the outset of this widely covered summit was that the prime minister, who had pushed so hard to have it in the first place, was now backtracking and attempting to slow the process down. Barak, it is worth noting here, perhaps more than any Israeli prime minister before him, was an obsessive reader of opinion polls, and what these now indicated was that there was little enthusiasm among Israelis for any major concession on the Golan Heights. This is why, from the moment he landed in the United States for the summit, Barak was looking for an opportunity to stall in order to show his people back home that negotiations were tough and he was not giving up easily on Israel's interests. And there was yet another reason why Barak sought to stall, namely his conviction that no major progress could be made at such a public meeting with the press all around and both Israeli and Syrian negotiators playing to the gallery rather than seriously looking for compromise. Secrecy and clandestine diplomacy, as Barak saw it, was the key to success.

The opportunity to stall the talks was given to Barak on a silver platter by the Syrian foreign minister. On the first day of the summit Shara delivered quite a bold speech in which he criticised Israel, at some length, for the Golan occupation and other wrongdoings: his hard words flew in the face of a private request from President Clinton that his and Barak's speeches remain 'brief and positive'. Jumping at the chance, the prime minister said to Clinton, straight after Shara's speech, that given the Syrian's criticism the president could not possibly expect Barak to move fast or make public concessions. Clinton, who himself was quite upset and cross with Shara, agreed and was sympathetic to Barak's situation. And thus during the two days of talks at Blair House, Barak would not give up much and the most Shara was able to squeeze from the prime minister was a vague promise that the Rabin deposit of a full withdrawal would not be withdrawn, though Barak himself would not confirm it. In Barak's words: 'We don't erase the past ... not the negotiations [Syria held] with Rabin, nor with Peres not even with Netanyahu ...'[18] Overall, with the prime minister's backtracking and stalling, this high-level Israeli–Syrian meeting failed to lead to any significant breakthrough, though the parties did agree to resume their talks in the new year.

Shepherdstown, January 2000

Now, Prime Minister Barak pressed Clinton hard to find an isolated place for the negotiations where secrecy could be maintained in order to minimise leaks that could expose him—and indeed the Syrians—politically, and also to enable the Syrians to open up and compromise. Barak said to Clinton: 'I can't believe that the only remaining superpower can't find an isolated place ... take an island ... a cruiser ... have the talks there ...'[19] The place which was eventually settled on for the peace negotiations was the Clarion Hotel and Conference Center, just outside Shepherdstown in West Virginia, reasonably isolated but hardly a desert island. There, on 3 January 2000, peace talks resumed with Prime Minister Barak and Syria's Foreign Minister Shara again leading their teams of experts and advisors: President Clinton was also there himself to launch the talks.

On Friday, 7 January in a meeting between Clinton, Shara, Barak and five members of each delegation, Clinton presented an eight-page American draft for an Israeli–Syrian peace treaty. It was a distillation of his judgement of what was already agreed between Syria and Israel, and what remained to be resolved. However, it soon emerged that the American document was closer to Israeli than to Syrian positions, no great surprise given that Clinton had coordinated positions so closely with the Israeli prime minister. Thus while the critical issue of the future border was bracketed to show a gap in positions (an 'I' representing the Israeli position alongside an 'S' for the Syrian), the principles of peace had no brackets at all, giving the impression that Syria had offered Israel major concessions.

Sure enough, the prime minister was willing to negotiate on the basis of the American document, but no word came from the Syrians, positive or negative. With no response from the Syrian delegation on the document, President Clinton decided that there was no point in waiting any longer, and reconvened the group meetings where various practical matters were discussed orally. Barak dispatched Shlomo Yanai, IDF chief of planning, and Uri Saguie (who had represented him in earlier talks with the Syrians) to the border and security groups respectively. They both later reported Syrian flexibility, but the Syrians pegged their concessions on Israel's acceptance of the 4 June 1967 line as the future border demarcation, which the prime minister still would not confirm. In fact, Barak kept reminding his negotiators that they were not authorised to talk at all about the final location of the future border between the two countries. This, the prime minister felt, should be reserved for the end-game, a summit of leaders, where he could play his most important cards in person with President Assad himself. Barak instructed his negotiators that rather than discussing the route of the future border, whether 4 June 1967 line or otherwise, they should divert the entire discussion with the Syrians into what he called a 'philosophical' and technical debate of the future border: should it be an open border? What customs arrangements will be used? Barak's negotiators also reported that the Syrians had demonstrated flexibility in the meetings on water, and on the sort of peace they would agree to, the so-called 'normalisation' of relations. But again they conditioned any concessions on Israel accepting their demands regarding the future border, namely that the Israelis should withdraw from the Golan down to the 4 June 1967 line, enabling the Syrians access to the water of the Sea of Galilee. As with the previous events at Blair House in December 1999, the prime minister was slowing down the pace of talks by refusing to even touch the one main issue for the Syrians—the route of the future border—thus deeply upsetting them.

For Syria's President Assad, however, the supreme insult came on 13 January 2000 when the entire secret draft Clinton had presented to the parties at the conference was leaked and published first in the Israeli newspaper *Haaretz* and, on the next day, in the *Washington Post* with the headline 'Syria Offers Israel Major Concessions'. Martin Indyk, the US ambassador to Israel who was present at the Shepherdstown talks, commented that, 'the draft treaty's publication had the effect of sabotaging the Israeli–Syrian negotiations at a critical moment'.[20] Indeed, humiliated by the leak of the secret document, President Assad refused to send his negotiators to further talks with the Israelis.

Nevertheless, it is safe to say that the talks at Shepherdstown narrowed—quite significantly—the gaps between the parties, and many issues, particularly regarding the future relations between the two countries, were sorted out. Again, what enabled this progress was the maintaining of secrecy and the fact that the negotiators, Israelis and Syrians alike, could open up, safe in the knowledge that the substance of the discussions would not leak out; however, the moment this happened the talks were in deep crisis.

The Not-Quite Endgame

In spite of the crisis, Prime Minister Barak remained convinced that a final face-to-face meeting with Assad was all that was needed to secure a deal. He now proposed that President Clinton should invite Assad to an American cruiser in the Mediterranean, where Clinton would present Israel's final peace proposal and play out the endgame with Assad on Israel's behalf. Barak even proposed that he could parachute in from the sky and join the endgame meeting whenever Clinton felt it was appropriate.

On 26 and 27 February, Clinton's envoy Dennis Ross led a small team of Americans in discussions with Barak to establish exactly what the president could offer Assad in such an endgame meeting. It would be, they agreed, an American rather than Israeli offer, where the Israeli premier would deposit his pledge with Clinton rather than give it directly to Syria, thus enabling Barak to retain deniability should Assad fail to deliver. It was also agreed, upon Barak's insistence, that, as accuracy was paramount, President Clinton should read from a pre-prepared presentation of the Israeli proposals; Barak's aide, the former director of Mossad, Danny Yatom, and US ambassador to Israel Martin Indyk would work on the text together. But even at this advanced stage the prime minister still kept his real redlines close to his chest, citing concerns that they might be leaked ahead of the summit, as had happened at Shepherdstown. Barak promised that he would phone President Clinton on the very day of the summit to reveal these redlines.

By 10 March 2000, the Israelis, working closely with American officials, had produced a draft of the text Clinton would read to President Assad in their forthcoming summit. The main points mentioned in this draft included the following:[21]

1. **The Future Border:** Israel will fully withdraw to 'a commonly agreed border based on the June 4 1967 line', keeping along the northern-eastern side of the Sea of Galilee a strip of some 500 metres. Israel will also keep some 80 metres from the east bank of the upper Jordan River. Israel will compensate Syria for the lost land by giving her land in the southern-eastern sector of the lake (for that to be achieved the line would be drawn to the west of the 4 June line). The essence of this agreement was that Assad would be able to describe the line as the 4 June 1967 border and Barak would be able to say that the line provided Israel with full control and sovereignty over the Sea of Galilee.

2. **Early Warning:** There would be a ground station for early warning on Mt Hermon to warn Israel of any imminent Syrian military attack on her and it would be under the total control of the United States with nine Israelis at that site for a maximum period of seven years from the time of the agreement. Respecting the principle of equality and mutuality the US would run a similar early warning ground station in Israel with the presence of the same number of Syrians for the same period of time.

3. **Security Arrangements:** A monitoring force would be established under US auspices that would operate on both sides of the border. It would monitor with technical means an agreed list of military locations, equal in number on both sides.

4. **Time Frame and Phases:** Implementation would take place in three phases over thirty-nine months. Embassies would be opened in the first phase and ambassadors exchanged. Borders would be opened to people and vehicles. After nine to twelve months, Israel would make a second withdrawal that would include a few settlements. After thirty-six months, Israel would begin its withdrawal to the new border and evacuate all the settlers. The US would purchase the Israeli settlements and then give them to the Syrians.

5. **Signs of Peaceful Intentions:** Barak would visit Syria to meet Assad and the Syrians would make some humanitarian gestures towards Israel. For example, to boost the supporters of peace, selected Israelis could visit Syria even before an agreement was signed, perhaps some Rabbis accompanied by journalists.

The scene was now set for a historic summit, albeit at the Intercontinental Hotel in Geneva rather than the more dramatic settings proposed by Barak, and at 13:10 on 26 March 2000 on the day of the summit, the prime minister, as promised, phoned Clinton at the hotel and, over the secure line, relayed his final offer. Barak urged Clinton that his meeting with Assad should be with just the two leaders and a translator because, as he put it, 'a leader like Assad would not be able to listen in the presence of strangers and this will reduce, quite dramatically, his willingness [to compromise]'.[22] Clinton said that his plan is 'to start with a photo op with the two delegations, then one on one and then Dennis [Ross] will enter [the room] and present maps and then I'll finish with the rest [of the presentation] and then I'll hear Assad and then I'll phone you ...' The prime minister said that it would be sufficient if President Assad agreed to the deal in principle, 'without the knowledge of his people'. It is interesting to see that even in the endgame at least the Israeli premier still believed that secrecy could guarantee success.

Barak then proceeded to give Clinton Israel's bottom lines: on early warning stations, Barak said he would accept seven Israeli personnel instead of the nine mentioned in the original script and for five years instead of seven, and that Syria could have the same within Israel. On the length of Israeli withdrawal, Barak dropped his demand from thirty-nine months to complete the pull-out from the Golan to twenty, 'or another month or two'. Regarding the critical depth of the Israeli withdrawal and the width of the strip Israel would keep along the northern-eastern shore of the Sea of Galilee, Barak explained that his pollster, Stanley Greenberg, was telling him that there was still little support in Israel for a deal with Syria, particularly any that gave the Syrians access to the water of the Sea of Galilee, and therefore the strip, as Barak put it, 'could go down from 500 to 400 metres ... This is a make or break ... if he fails to agree to 500 metres or a minimum of 400 ...' Hearing these words, Clinton knew he now faced very little chance of success with Assad, who was still expecting a future border on the exact line of

4 June 1967, which would mean Syria sat physically on the water of the lake, not 400 or 500 metres off it. Clinton pleaded with Barak, but the prime minister would not budge.

Clinton met Assad later that afternoon in Geneva. But the moment President Assad heard that the Israeli withdrawal would not be to the 4 June 1967 line and, instead, that the border would be 'commonly agreed' and 'based' on the June 1967 line—which had become Israeli code for away from the water line—he simply shut off, not letting Clinton even finish reading his pre-prepared text. It was a disastrous failure. At 20:45, Clinton phoned Barak. 'I have done my best', he said, adding, 'He is not willing to give up on the water … He can't explain to the Syrians why he failed to bring them the land …' The prime minister replied, stating the obvious: 'if he isn't willing to be flexible on the strip then a deal is not possible'.[23]

The Lessons to be Learned?

Perhaps the most important lesson is that only clandestine diplomacy and off-the-record secret negotiations are effective in enabling the parties to open up, reveal their cards and even compromise. But it is also clear that, at least in as far as Israeli–Syrian talks are concerned, too much secrecy and deniability allowed Prime Minister Barak to backtrack and upset the talks. If there had been some mechanism (available to Washington for example which was deeply involved in the secret talks) to make the prime minister stick to earlier secret pledges, notably the promises made by the slain prime minister Rabin to withdraw fully from the Golan Heights to the 4 June 1967 lines, talks at Shepherdstown and Geneva might have been more successful. As it was Barak was free to walk away from making compromises.

A further problem is that, while secrecy in peace negotiations can enable the parties to bridge the gaps between their respective positions, it often opens new gaps between the negotiators and their own publics back home, the latter often being unaware of the compromises being made by their representatives. Moving from clandestine diplomacy to open disclosure is a tricky and delicate matter but it is critical, at a certain stage in the negotiations, to find a way to close the gaps between what is done behind closed doors and what the public actually know. Without closing these gaps, it is unlikely that the Israeli public would ever have supported a proposal that promised so much, but ultimately failed to deliver a treaty for both Israelis and Syrians alike: the deal that never was.

CONCLUSION

Tore T. Petersen

In the early spring of 2012, reports began to surface detailing the extent of Israel's secret ties to Azerbaijan, ties that were alleged to include agreements over the use by the Israelis of airbases conveniently situated close to the border with Iran. Given the obvious tensions that exist between Tehran and Jerusalem over Iran's seemingly inexorable drive towards acquiring a nuclear capability, such ties would seem to be of a piece with the themes discussed in this volume. Indeed, one US diplomat stationed in Baku, the Azeri capital, reported back on comments made by President Ilham Aliyev over the secretive nature of ties with the Jewish state which he compared to an iceberg: 'nine-tenths of it is below the surface'.[1]

It is this 'diplomatic fraction' below the surface that has been the subject of this volume, for clandestine diplomacy has long been part and parcel of Israel's arsenal that has helped Jerusalem 'not only surmount its regional isolation but help frame security agendas that pose equally complex, and often damaging dilemmas among erstwhile foes'. Israel remains the strongest military power in the Middle East and will no doubt continue to best its opponents on the battlefield. But whatever picture emerges by looking at Israel's past wars and military triumphs, we should also remind ourselves that this perception of overwhelming military prowess was not shared by Israeli political leaders during the nation's formative years as they struggled to secure Israel's existence amid a hostile environment but with a limited population base and resources to do so.

241

This had clear implications for how the Israeli leadership met, perceived and sometimes countered lesser threats to its existence. All too often, as Amnon Aran argues, the use of disproportionate force against its Arab neighbours—be they state or substate actors—'often came at the expense of exploring diplomatic initiatives'. The cost, longer term, may have been paid in terms of the absence of formal diplomatic ties, and in turn, increased reliance upon clandestine ties as Israel looked to secure its place in a predominantly Arab and Muslim Middle East. If indeed this was the case, then Israel already had a substantial reservoir of expertise and experience to draw upon. For as both Yoav Alon and Clive Jones demonstrate in their contributions to this volume, recourse to secret diplomacy by the leadership of the Jewish community in Palestine certainly predated the founding of the state as they struggled for independence.

Indeed, a constant theme in this book has been the immense resourcefulness displayed by Israeli diplomats and intelligence officers, not just in creating opportunities for Israel to move beyond the animus of the Middle East, but also in playing upon and benefitting from disagreements among the Arabs themselves. To be sure, as Malcolm Kerr argued in his seminal book *The Arab Cold War*, there was much to play on.[2] The rivalry between conservative and radical Arab regimes certainly overshadowed the Arab–Israeli conflict before 1967. The devastating defeat in the Six Day War prompted a seemingly united Arab front against Israel, but this was more apparent than real. Soon cracks opened in the façade, cracks Israel skilfully exploited for its own ends.

Not all was plain sailing however. One sore point for Israel, which Uri Bialer and Noa Schonmann highlight in Israel's early relations with Iran and Turkey respectively, was the issue of de facto as opposed to de jure recognition of the Jewish state. Both these countries—predominantly Muslim but non-Arab—were key to Israel's periphery doctrine. Both willingly worked with Israel, not least because it suited their own interests, but refused to establish formal diplomatic ties on the highest levels, that is, the formal exchange of ambassadors and the like. For anyone who blindly adheres to the thought that Israel has always been a regional superpower, such episodes act as a sobering reminder that for all its military might, Israel was effectively reduced to being a supplicant in its relations with Tehran and Ankara. Still, as Bialer notes, '[B]y 1955 Iran had already become Israel's main source of crude oil.' The Iranian–Israeli connection was further strengthened by intelligence and military cooperation from 1958 through to the fall of the shah in 1979. With his oil income booming after 1973, the shah sought to make Iran both the industrial and military hegemon across the region with the intention of projecting his influence way beyond the Persian Gulf. For what he considered to be his primitive and squabbling Arab neighbours he had nothing but disdain. Evidence regarding the closeness of the ties between Tehran and Jerusalem before the revolution is to be found in the recently declassified records held by the Jimmy Carter Library in Atlanta, Georgia. During a briefing held on 10 November 1977, the president was informed by his secretary of state, Cyrus Vance, that:

Iran quietly provides Israel most of its imported oil, and access to a secure source of oil is a critical factor in Israeli security. Iran also maintains excellent, but unpublished relations with Israel. [Israeli Foreign Minister Moshe] Dayan has secretly visited Tehran several times this year, and there is an active intelligence collaboration. At the same time, the Shah is bluntly outspoken about the need for Israeli moderation and flexibility in moving toward a Middle East peace, and he is willing to use his influence with both the Arabs and the Israelis as necessary to further the peace process—On this issue, the Shah is cooperative, and we rely on him very heavily to maintain the oil flow to Israel. It is not an issue we can use for bargaining.[3]

Certainly, Israel's strategy of establishing relations with states on the periphery was, as Noa Schonmann argues in relation to Turkey, entirely sensible given 'the ring of Arab hostility surrounding the nascent Jewish state'. Israeli policy-makers perceived Arab animosity as a serious and imminent threat, and saw themselves 'compelled to conduct state affairs in flexible and unconventional ways'. But ultimately, Israel was denied the diplomatic recognition it craved, with Turkey refusing to leave its Arab wife in favour of the Israeli mistress. A similar picture emerges in the contributions by Zach Levey and Yehudit Ronen to this volume, which examined Israeli relations with Uganda and Sudan respectively. For all its efforts Israel was again largely reduced to the role of a supplicant in its relations with these two countries. Why then meddle in Africa, particularly when the results were so limited? Again, the answer lies in the drive by the Jewish state to overcome its regional isolation, for as Ronen reflects in her chapter, throughout the 1950s 'Israel referred to Africa in general and to the Sudanese state in particular as means of "leaping over the Arab wall", and as an important element in the Israeli periphery security belt encircling the belligerent Arab core.' Zach Levey points out that despite there being 'no natural common interests' between Israel and Uganda, Israel pursued its connections for similar reasons, but also in the hope that it could accrue the support of Kampala 'in the United Nations and an embassy in another black African country from which the Arab states would not be able to exclude Israel'. But to pursue a policy on the periphery successfully and 'leap the Arab wall' Israel often had to forego formal recognition from its interlocutors, and yet again accept the less than satisfying role of being a supplicant, which denied the diplomatic legitimacy it so obviously craved.

Such frustrations were not just restricted to secret ties with the developing world. Israeli diplomacy can hardly be accused of lacking in sophistication and guile, but as Rory Miller shows in his thoughtful deliberation on Israeli–Irish relations, any hopes that Israel entertained of using the shared experience of struggling against British imperialism as an entrée into a new, close relationship took some time to be realised. Indeed, as he notes, 'despite this shared experience [of struggle against the British] ties between Dublin and Jerusalem while formally correct, never developed beyond the purely functional, much to the frustration and regret of the Israelis', who had longed believed Ireland 'be a natural ally'. Miller's conclusion to his chapter is particularly relevant for a book dealing with clandestine diplomacy for, as he notes, the saga of Israeli–Irish ties highlights 'the limits of secret diplomacy in establishing closer diplomatic ties where common values, as much as common interests, shape bilateral relations'. Despite the considerable efforts made by Israel, however, its efforts to use secret diplomacy as a precursor for more durable, public relations with Dublin were to prove only partially successful.

But more fruitful ties, not least in the field of intelligence and technology transfer, certainly marked ties with West Germany. In his authoritative contribution, Shlomo Shpiro shows how the relationship between Bonn and Jerusalem, a relationship initially conditioned by the legacy of the Holocaust, came to flourish by the late 1960s and 1970s into Israel's most important military and intelligence partnership next to that with the United States. While these ties had a functional purpose, they were underpinned by close personal relations between those involved that went beyond mere state-based interests. But while this relationship certainly enhanced Israel's qualitative military advantage over its Arab neighbours, clandestine diplomacy was also used to try and circumvent resistance within Israel itself towards advancing a peace process with the Palestinians. While much has been written over the backchannel negotiations that led to the Oslo Accords of 1993, relatively little attention has been paid to how, in 1995, the deputy Israeli foreign minister, Yossi Beilin, tried to circumvent his own ministry by using Israeli academics, Swedish diplomats and interlocutors in an attempt to break through the diplomatic logjam that had come to define the increasingly acrimonious talks with the Palestinians. Jacob Eriksson admirably fills this particular gap in our knowledge, highlighting in the process that the conduct of clandestine diplomacy was often piecemeal, the result of the often byzantine personality clashes that have long shaped bureaucratic and party politics across the Jewish state.

But if such 'maverick' examples highlight how the conduct of clandestine diplomacy can become so personalised, Israel's rather vexed relations with Egypt also demonstrate the importance of signalling as an important facet of such statecraft, not least in the run up to the June 1967 war. We now know that Egyptian military prowess was much exaggerated, perhaps matched only by President Nasser's rhetorical hubris. For while Israel would demonstrate its overwhelming military superiority in this war, the fragile nature of Egypt's martial prowess was not readily appreciated among the Israeli leadership. As Yigal Sheffy demonstrates, Egypt prior to 1967 was 'the major threat to Israel, due to its role as leader of the Arab world and as the only state bordering Israel possessing an army with sufficient offensive credibility to threaten Israel'. Furthermore, the 'annihilation of Israel was the unchanging strategic goal of [Egyptian President Gamal] Nasser'. When combined with a substantial military build-up courtesy of the Soviet Union, the potential consequences for Israel appeared bleak, although tempered somewhat by the growing rift between conservative and radical regimes in the Arab world. Yet even when increasingly bogged down militarily and politically in Yemen's civil war, which at its height saw Nasser commit some 60,000 Egyptian troops, Sheffy observes that 'the Israeli political and military leadership shared the widely held perception that nothing less than the total annihilation of Israel dictated Egyptian policy toward the Jewish state'.

It is easy to see how perceptions might drive policy, but it was also to Israel's advantage to maximise the Egyptian threat in Washington and across the capitals of Western Europe. Israel, as we know, reaped a great victory and tremendous strategic benefits from the Six Day War, but we should not forget that consensus over how to deal with a seemingly belligerent Cairo hardly marked Israeli diplomacy prior to the outbreak of conflict. Again, the role of the individual is paramount, for, in his perceptive study of the role played by Abba Eban, Asaf Siniver details how, despite his undoubted eloquence and respect on the international stage and his personal belief in a peaceful solution to the crisis, the Israeli foreign minister ultimately succumbed to a critical mass within the Cabinet which determined towards a military confrontation that changed the map of the Middle East.

Again, in echoing a major theme of this volume, Siniver notes that '[F]rom the outset secret diplomacy became a cornerstone of Israel's foreign policy, either for the purpose of developing relations with countries which publicly did not recognise the Jewish state or a tool to secure Israel's national interest in the periphery.' But as the final contribution in this volume shows, even as the dominant regional power, Israel has continued to use clandestine diplomacy to great effect in order to preserve and strengthen its position while equally driving a hard bargain over the scope and limits of its own concessions. Ahron Bregman shows how the Israeli Prime Minister, Ehud Barak, was able to string Syrian President Hafez al-Assad along in drawn out negotiations over the future of the Golan Heights. These eventually came to naught because of Barak's intransigence over allowing Syrian toes to be dipped in Lake Kinneret. Bregman's most interesting and effective use of confidential sources causes one to reflect on the sometimes parallel Israel–Palestine negotiations under the auspices of President Bill Clinton. Clinton would later blame Palestinian leader Yasser Arafat for the breakdown of the negotiations.[4]

Yet coming on the heels of the Oslo accords, the assassination of Yitzhak Rabin, and the fairly strong if ultimately short-lived wave of popular support for territorial compromise across Israel, Barak might have felt politically impelled to continue on the peace track against his better judgement. Therefore, one rather negative explanation for his actions towards Syria and the Palestinians was that he sought ways to impede the scope and pace of the peace talks without actually being held responsible if they were to break down. After all, did he not offer Syria the return of the vast majority of the Golan Heights? In any case, Israel was hardly less insecure after Barak's tenure in office and indeed, given the turmoil that came to engulf Syria in 2011, many Israelis saw the failure of the Geneva talks as a blessing whose longer-term benefits were only later realised.

But one should not, perhaps, exaggerate the extent of the difficulties facing the Jewish state. In the Persian Gulf, for instance, the storms coming from the Arab–Israeli conflict usually subsided into a mild breeze. Many Arab leaders publicly condemned Israel, but as has been argued elsewhere, they were perfectly willingly in private to let the Jewish state live and let live. It is important therefore not to confuse rhetoric with reality. The US embassy in Bahrain reported to the State Department on 8 March 1978 that 'Bahrain is far from the Arab–Israel confrontation arena and has few Palestinians living there. These factors combine with its own interest in orderly development to make Bahrain moderate on Arab–Israeli issues.'[5] Or take for example this missive to the Foreign and Commonwealth Office reporting a conversation between British officials and Sultan Qabus of Oman in October 1980 where his foreign minister, Zawawi, had given his opinion on the situation regarding Israel, 'Commenting on [the] recognition that the various problems facing the region are interconnected and that progress on the Palestine issue is essential, Zawawi said that the Arabs should realize that the U.S. support of Israel was nothing new, that it was probably less now than it had ever been and that co-operation with the Americans made more sense than the reverse.'[6] And as we have seen, even Saudi Arabia has, for all its bluster, survived the existence of Israel without undue difficulty for the ruling family and its wider regional legitimacy.

To be sure, our understanding of Israel's clandestine diplomacy remains partial and therefore passing judgement on its effectiveness, achievements and indeed drawbacks over seven decades must be subject to the obvious health warnings. But if the chapters in this volume indicate anything—based as they are on primary source material and revealed here in some cases for the very first time—they do suggest that Israel's use (and indeed abuse) of clandestine diplomacy has for the most part been an outstanding success for the Jewish state in bolstering its security, but its popularity probably less so. There is no question that Israel's leaders have operated in an often hostile environment, with six major wars and numerous other conflicts providing ample testament. Moreover, in a region of the world where states have traditionally sought security from one another, rather than with each other, the use of clandestine diplomacy has been crucial to ameliorating power differentials that would otherwise have threatened to overwhelm the Jewish state in its early years. But in an age of WikiLeaks and where Israel is now the regional power, secret diplomacy of the types discussed in this volume might be seen by some observers of diminishing utility in an era of globalisation. Perhaps. But unless or until a regional framework for peace across the Middle East emerges, clandestine diplomacy will remain integral to Israel's immediate security and longer term well-being.

NOTES

INTRODUCTION: THEMES AND ISSUES

1. Barak David, 'Wikileaks Blows Cover of Israel's Covert Ties', *Ha'aretz* [in English], 29 Nov. 2010.
2. See Clive Jones, *Britain and the Yemen Civil War: Among Ministers, Mercenaries and Mandarins—Foreign Policy and the Limits of Covert Action*, Brighton: Sussex Academic Press, 2010, pp. 146–51; Dana Harman, 'Leaving Bitterness Behind', *Ha'aretz* [in English], 28 Jan. 2011; Laurie Zittrain Eisenberg, 'From Benign to Malign: Israeli–Lebanese Relations', in Clive Jones and Sergio Catignani (eds), *Israel and Hezbollah: An Asymmetric Conflict in Historical and Comparative Perspective*, London: Routledge, 2010, pp. 48–78.
3. Ahron Kleiman, *Statecraft in the Dark: Israel's Practice of Quiet Diplomacy*, Boulder: Westview Press, 1988, p. 42.
4. Len Scott, 'Secret Intelligence, Covert Action and Clandestine Diplomacy', in L.V Scott and Peter Jackson (eds), *Understanding Intelligence in the Twenty-First Century: Journeys in the Shadows*, London: Routledge, 2004, p. 169.
5. Yossi Melman, 'Get Ready for Some Mossad Resignations', *Ha'aretz* [in Hebrew], 21 Apr. 2011.
6. Scott, 'Secret Intelligence, Covert Action and Clandestine Diplomacy', p. 170.
7. Ahron Bregman and Jihan el-Tahri, *The Fifty Years War: Israel and the Arabs*, London: BBC/Penguin Books, 1998, pp. 70–5, 84–5.
8. Exactly what was offered by Barak and rejected by Arafat remains the subject of heated debate. While much has been written on the failure of the summit, the most revealing interviews appeared in a series of articles in the *New York Review of Books* (NYRB). See Benny Morris, 'Camp David and After: An Exchange. 1. An Interview with Ehud Barak', *NYRB*, XLIX, 10 (13 June 2002), pp. 42–5; Robert Malley and Hussein Agha, '2. A Reply to Ehud Barak', *NYRB*, XLIX, 10

(13 June 2002), pp. 46–8. The belief that Israel's version of events at Camp David had benefited from a news blackout imposed during the conference itself is made by Aluf Ben, 'The Selling of the Summit', *Ha'aretz* [in Hebrew], 27 July 2001.

9. Michael Brecher, *The Foreign Policy System of Israel: Setting, Images, Process*, Oxford: Oxford University Press, 1972, p. 229.

10. See for example Bernard Avishai, 'Saving Israel from Itself: A Secular Future for the Jewish State', *Harper's Magazine*, 310/1856 (2005), pp. 33–43.

11. Amir Oren, 'Spilled out into the open', *Ha'aretz* [in English], 26 Nov. 2010.

12. Avi Shlaim, *Collusion Across the Jordan: King Abdullah, the Zionist Movement and the Partition of Palestine*, Oxford: Oxford University Press, 1988; Uri Bar-Joseph, *The Best of Enemies: Israel and the Transjordan in the War of 1948*, London: Macmillan, 1987.

13. Danna Harman, 'Leaving Bitterness Behind', *Ha'aretz* [in English], 28 Jan. 2011.

14. See for example Kirsten Schulze, *Israel's Covert Diplomacy in Lebanon*, London: Macmillan/St Anthony's College Oxford, 1998.

1. ISRAELI FOREIGN POLICY IN HISTORICAL PERSPECTIVE: STATE, ETHNO-NATIONALISM, GLOBALISATION

1. Stephen D. Krasner, 'Approaches to the State: Alternative Conceptions and Historical Dynamics', *Comparative Politics*, 16, 2 (1984), pp. 223–46.

2. Efraim Inbar, 'Arab–Israeli Coexistence: The Causes, Achievements and Limitations', in Efraim Karsh (ed.), *Israel: The First Hundred Years*, London: Frank Cass, 2000, pp. 256–71.

3. Benny Morris, *Righteous Victims: A History of the Zionist–Arab Conflict, 1881–2001*, New York: Vintage Books, 2001.

4. See Efraim Inbar, *War and Peace in Israeli Politics: Labour Party Positions on National Security*, London: Lynne Rienner, 1991; Ilan Peleg, *Begin's Foreign Policy, 1977–1983: Israel's Move to the Right*, New York: Greenwood Press, 1987.

5. Ian S. Lustik, *For Land and the Lord*, New York: Council on Foreign Relations Press, 1994; Akiva Eldar and Idit Zartal, *The Lords of the Land: The Settlers and the State of Israel 1967–2004*, Or Yehuda: Kineret/Zmora-Bitan, 2005.

6. Yoram Peri, *Between Battles and Ballots: Israeli Military in Politics*, Cambridge: Cambridge University Press, 1983; Yagil Levy, *The Other Army of Israel: Materialist Militarism in Israel*, Tel Aviv: Yediot Achronot, 2003 [in Hebrew]; Oren Barak and Gabriel Sheffer, 'Israel's Security Network: An Exploration of a New Approach', *International Journal of Middle East Studies*, 38, 2 (2006), pp. 235–61.

7. Avi Shlaim, *The Iron Wall: Israel and the Arab World*, London: Penguin, 2000.

8. Shlaim, *The Iron Wall*, pp. xvi, 14.

9. Theda Skocpol, *States and Social Revolutions: A Comparative Analysis of France, Russia and China*, Cambridge: Cambridge University Press, 1979, p. 29.

10. Fred Halliday, *The Middle East in International Relations*, Cambridge: Cambridge University Press, 2006, p. 46.

11. On *Mamlachtiyut* see Shmuel Sandler, *The State of Israel, the Land of Israel: The Statist and Ethnonational Dimensions of Foreign Policy*, London: Greenwood Press, 1993, pp. 97–8; Charles S. Liebman and Eliezer Don Yiyheh, *Civil Religion in Israel*, Berkeley, CA: University of California Press, 1983, pp. 81–131.

12. Yoav Peled and Gershon Shafir, 'The Roots of Peacemaking: The Dynamics of Citizenship in Israel, 1948–1993', *International Journal of Middle East Studies*, 28 (1996), p. 398.

13. Michael Shalev, 'Liberalization and the Transformation of the Political Economy', in Gershon Shafir and Yoav Peled (eds), *The New Israel: Peacemaking and Liberalization*, Boulder, CO: Westview Press, 2000, p. 130.

14. Lissak Moshe, 'The Ethos of Security and the Myth of Israel as a Militarised Society', in *Democratic Culture* [in Hebrew], 4, 5 (2001), p. 189.

15. On the ability to portray military service as the ultimate voluntary act, and its roots, see Levy, *The Other Army of Israel*, p. 65.

16. For a theoretical angle on the impact of societal actors on foreign policy see David Skidmore and Valerie Hudson (eds), *The Limits of State Autonomy: Society Groups and Foreign Policy Formulation*, Boulder, CO: Westview, 1993.

17. Baruch Kimmerling, *The End of Ashkenazi Hegemony*, Jerusalem: Keter, 2001.

18. Avi Shlaim 'Conflicting Approaches to Israel's Relations with the Arabs, Ben-Gurion and Sharett, 1953–1956', *Middle East Journal*, 37, 2 (1983), pp. 180–5.

19. Avner Yaniv, *Deterrence Without the Bomb: The Politics of Israeli Strategy*, Washington, DC: Lexington Books, 1987, pp. 164–6.

20. See Michael Karpin, *The Bomb in the Basement: How Israel went Nuclear and What That Means for the World*, London: Simon and Schuster, 2006, pp. 57–95.

21. For an overview of ethno-nationalism against other expressions of nationalism see Anthony D. Smith, *Nationalism and Modernism: A Critical Survey of Recent Theories of Nations and Nationalism*, London: Routledge, 1998, 170–96; for the application of this concept to the Israeli case see Gershon Shafir and Yoav Peled, *Being Israeli: The Dynamics of Multiple Citizenship*, Cambridge: Cambridge University Press, p. 6.

22. Morris, *Righteous Victims*, p. 311.

23. On this aspect of the war see Morris, *Righteous Victims*, pp. 415–17.

24. For a detailed account of this process see Eldar and Zertal, *Lords of the Land*, pp. 83–161.

25. Tamar S. Hermann, *The Israeli Peace Movement: A Shattered Dream*, Cambridge: Cambridge University Press, pp. 79–108.

26. On the bombing of the Iraqi reactor see Shlomo Nakdimon, *First Strike: The Exclusive Story of How Israel Foiled Iraq's Attempt to get the Bomb*, New York: Summit Books, 1987.

27. On the invasion of Lebanon and its aftermath see Zeev Schiff and Ehud Ya'ari, *Israel's Lebanon War*, New York: Simon and Shuster, 1984.

28. Yaniv, *Deterrence Without the Bomb: The Politics of Israel's Strategy*, p. 214.

29. William B. Quandt, *Peace Process: American Diplomacy and the Arab–Israeli Conflict Since 1967*, Washington, DC: Brookings Institution Press, 2001, p. 246.

30. The 1975 memorandum; see the Israeli Ministry of Foreign Affairs website http://www.mfa.gov.il/MFA/Foreign%20Relations/Israels%20Foreign%20Relations%20since%201947/1974-1977/112%20Israel-United%20States%20Memorandum%20of%20Understanding (accessed 13 Aug. 2007). For the full text of the 1979 memorandum see http://www.mfa.gov.il/MFA/Peace%20Process/Guide%20to%20the%20Peace%20Process/US-Israel%20Memorandum%20of%20Agreement (accessed 13 Aug. 2007).

31. On Israel's secondary and tertiary alliances see Yaniv, *Deterrence Without the Bomb*, pp. 71–2, 123–5 and 183–4.

32. On this latter point see Shlaim, *The Iron Wall*, p. 392.

33. Baruch Kimmerling, *Zionism and Territory*, Berkeley, CA: University of California Press, 1983, pp. 154–5.

34. Avi Shilon, *Begin 1913–1992*, Tel Aviv: Am Oved Publishers, 2007, pp. 295–315.

35. On this aspect of Israeli foreign policy see Kirsten E. Schulze, *Israel's Covert Diplomacy in Lebanon*, London: Palgrave Macmillan, 1997.

36. For the hyper-globalist, transformationalist and global sceptics classification see David Held et al., *Global Transformations: Politics, Economics, and Culture*, Cambridge: Polity Press, 1999, pp. 1–29.

37. The proposed critique is derived from, inter alia, Amnon Aran, *Israel's Foreign Policy towards the PLO: The Impact of Globalization*, Sussex: Sussex Academic Press, 2009, pp. 2–7; Tarek Barkawi, *Globalization and War*, Lanham: Rowman & Littlefield, 2006, pp. 1–59; Ian Clark, *Globalization and Fragmentation: International Relations in the Twentieth Century*, Oxford: Oxford University Press, 1997; Ian Clark, *Globalization and International Relations Theory*, Oxford: Oxford University Press, 1999; Martin Shaw, 'The State of Globalization: Towards a Theory of State Transformation', *Review of International Political Economy*, 4, 3(1997), pp. 497–513; Martin Shaw, *Theory of the Global State: Globalization as an Unfinished Revolution*, Cambridge: Cambridge University Press, 2001; Michael Mann, 'Has Globalization Ended the Rise and Rise of the Nation-State?' *Review of International Political Economy*, 4, 3(1997), pp. 472–96.

38. Chris Hill, *The Changing Politics of Foreign Policy*, London: Palgrave, 2003, pp. 193–4.

39. See Aran, *Israel's Foreign Policy towards the PLO*, p. 7.

40. Shaw, 'The State of Globalization', p. 498.

41. For data and an account of the economic role military exports played in the context of the economic crisis see Stewart Reiser, *The Israeli Arms Industry*, London: Holmes and Meier, 1989, pp. 121, 123.

42. For a critical evaluation of the magnitude of the crisis from a historical perspective see Michael Shalev, 'Liberalization and the Transformation of the Political Economy', in Gershon Shafir and Yoav Peled (eds), *The New Israel*, Boulder, CO: Westview Press, 2000, pp. 132–4.

43. Shalev, 'Liberalization and the Transformation of the Political Economy', p. 148; Emma Murphy, 'Structural Inhibitions to Economic Liberalization in Israel', *Middle East Journal*, 48, 1 (1994), pp. 70–1.

44. Shafir and Peled, 'Introduction', in Gershon Shafir and Yoav Peled (eds), *The New Israel*, Boulder, CO: Westview Press, 2000, p. 8.

45. Gershon Shafir and Yoav Peled, 'The Globalization of Israeli Business and the Peace Process', in Gershon Shafir and Yoav peled (eds), *The New Israel*, Boulder, CO: Westview Press, 2000, pp. 255–6.

46. Gershon Shafir, 'Business in Politics: Globalization and the Search for Peace in South Africa and Israel/Palestine', *Israel Affairs*, 5, 2 (1999), p. 114.

47. Shafir and Peled, *The New Israel*, pp. 255–6. Guy Ben-Porat, *Global liberalism, Local Populism: Peace and Conflict in Israel/Palestine and Northern Ireland*, Syracuse: Syracuse University Press, 2006; Uri Ram, *The Globalization of Israeli*, New York: Routledge, 2008.

48. Sharon's close decision-making circle included his son and a group of advisors from the business sector: Dov Wesglass, Lior Horev and Reuven Adler. Olmert's close circle included former businessmen including Dr Yoram Tubovich.

49. On the impact of business on the peace process see Pen-Porat, *Global Liberalism, Local Populism*, pp. 152–201; on India see Efraim Inbar, 'The Israel–India Entente', BESA, http://www.biu.ac.il/Besa/Inbar.pdf (accessed 3 May 2011).

50. Yoram Peri, 'The Changes in the Security Discourse in the Media and the Transformations in the Notion of Citizenship in Israel', *Democratic Culture*, 4, 5 (2001), pp. 247–9.

51. Ehud Olmert, 'Testimony before the Winograd Commission', pp. 36–8.

52. Peri, 'Changes in the Security Discourse', *The Other Army of Israel*, p. 210.

53. Shimon Peres with Aryeh Noar, *The New Middle East*, Henry Holt & Co., 1993, p. 53.

54. On Shas see Yoav Peled (ed.), *Shas: The Challenge of Being Israeli*, Tel Aviv: Yediot Achronot, 2001; On the immigrants from the former USSR see Moshe Lissak and Elazar Leshem (eds), *From Russia to Israel: Culture and Identity in Transition*, Tel Aviv: Ha-Kibutz Ha Meuchad, 2001 [in Hebrew].

55. See Shlomo Ben-Ami, *A Place For All*, Tel Aviv: Ha-Kibutz Ha-Meuchad, 1998, pp. 336–8.

56. On this see Oren Barak and Gabriel Sheffer, 'Israel's "Security Network" and its Impact: An Exploration of a New Approach', *International Journal of Middle East Studies* 38/2 (2006), pp. 235–261; Yoram Peri, *Generals in the Cabinet Room: How the Military Shapes Policy in Israel*, Washington, DC: United States Institute for Peace, 2006.

57. The most cogent empirical account of this remains Peri, *Generals in the Cabinet Room.*

58. For the global impulse in Rabin's and Peres' thinking see Peres, *The New Middle East*; Efraim Inbar, *Rabin and Israel's National Security*, Washington, DC: Woodrow Wilson Center Press, 1999, pp. 8–23, 84–113, 119–24, 137–9 and 159–63. For the impact of globalisation on the Sharon government see Aran, *Israel's Foreign Policy towards the PLO.*

59. For Sharon's speech see http://www.mfa.gov.il/MFA/Peace+Process/Guide+to+the+Peace+Process/Israeli+Disengagement+Plan+20-Jan-2005.htm#39 (accessed 16 Sep. 2008). Sharon made a similar argument in meetings he had with the Israeli export forum and Israel's manufacturers association. See, respectively, http://www.mfa.gov.il/MFA/Government/Speeches+by+Israeli+leaders/2004/PM+Sharon+speech+to+Conference+for+Advancement+of+Export+11-Nov-2004.htm (accessed 16 Sep. 2008); http://www.mfa.gov.il/MFA/Peace+Process/Guide+to+the+Peace+Process/Israeli+Disengagement+Plan+20-Jan-2005.htm#doc15 (accessed 16 Sep. 2008).

60. Benjamin Netanyahu, *A Place Among the Nations: Israel and the World*, London: Bantam Press, 1993.

61. Quoted in Shlaim, *The Iron Wall*, p. 574.

62. For a good account of the first Netanyahu government see Neil Lochery, *The Difficult Road to Peace*, Reading: Ithaca Press, 1999. The decision not to continue the settlement freeze in return for a very generous US offer epitomises the effect of ethno-nationalism in Netanyahu's second term.

63. See for example Mark Perry, 'Israel's Secret Staging Ground', *Foreign Policy*, 28 Mar. 2012 at www.foreignpolicy.com/articles/2012/03/28israel_s_secret_staging_ground? (accessed 29 Mar. 2012).

2. FRIENDS INDEED OR ACCOMPLICES IN NEED?
THE JEWISH AGENCY, EMIR ABDULLAH AND
THE SHAYKHS OF TRANSJORDAN, 1922–39

1. See Avi Shlaim, *Collusion Across the Jordan*, Oxford: Oxford University Press, 1988, p. 1; Yoav Gelber, *Jewish–Transjordanian Relations, 1921–1948*, London: Frank Cass, 1997, p. 5; D.K. Fieldhouse, *Western Imperialism in the Middle East, 1914–1958*, Oxford: Oxford University Press, 2006, p. 221.

2. Avi Shlaim, *The Politics of Partition*, London: Oxford University Press, 1990,

p. 42; Joseph Nevo, *King Abdallah and Palestine: A Territorial Ambition*, London: Macmillan, 1996, p. 17; Gelber, *Jewish–Transjordanian Relations*, p. 17.

3. Shlaim, *The Politics of Partition*, p. 42.
4. Ibid. For a different view see Nevo, *King Abdullah and Palestine*, p. 14.
5. For the latter see Yoav Alon, *The Making of Jordan: Tribes, Colonialism and the Modern State*, London: I.B. Tauris, 2007, pp. 42–3.
6. Weizmann's speech at a public rally, Tel Aviv, 22 Apr. 1926, in B. Litvinoff (ed.), *The Letters and Papers of Chaim Weizmann*, series B, Papers II, New Brunswick, NJ: Transaction Books, 1983, p. 471, cited in Gelber, *Jewish–Transjordanian Relations*, p. 19.
7. Mary C. Wilson, *King Abdullah, Britain and the Making of Jordan*, Cambridge: Cambridge University Press, 1987, p. 105.
8. Alon, *The Making of Jordan*, pp. 92–5.
9. *Davar*, 22 and 23 Feb. 1931, 2 Mar. 1931 (quoting from *al-Karmal*), 1 Mar. 1931 (quoting from *al-Ahram*) and 25 Feb. 1931 (quoting from *Filastin*).
10. Alon, *The Making of Jordan*, p. 64.
11. Gelber, *Jewish–Transjordanian Relations*, p. 37.
12. Ibid.
13. Ibid.
14. CZA S25/3491: Meeting between Mithqal Pasha al-Fayiz and the president of the Jewish Agency, 2 Jan. 1933.
15. *Filastin*, 18 June, 23 July, 6 and 13 Aug. 1929.
16. *Filastin*, 27 Sep. 1931.
17. CZA, S25/3492: Arlozoroff to members of the Jewish Agency Executive, 6 Dec. 1932; Gelber, *Jewish–Transjordanian Relations*, pp. 42–3; Wilson, *King Abdullah, Britain and the Making of Jordan*, p. 7; Suleiman Bashir, *Judhur al-Wisaya al-Urduniyya*, Jerusalem, 1980, pp. 11–18, 22–4.
18. Gelber, *Jewish–Transjordanian Relations*, p. 40; *Filastin*, 19 Mar. 1932; *Davar*, 11 Oct. 1932 (reporting from *Filastin*).
19. CZA, S25/3509: Pfefer to Kisch, 16 Mar. 1931.
20. CZA, S25/3492: Arlozoroff to members of the Jewish Agency Executive, 6 Dec. 1932; S25/3505: Cohen, 'Report from the visit at the Emir's Palace', 3 Dec. 1934; S25/3507: Shertok, 16 Mar. 1933; S25/6313: Cohen, 'Report from the visit to Amman', 10 Mar. 1933.
21. Weizmann's address to the Jewish Agency's administrative committee, 8 Aug. 1932, in Litvinoff, III, p. 17, cited in Gelber, *Jewish–Transjordanian Relations*, p. 41.
22. *Al-Ahram*, 16 Mar. 1932; Gelber, *Jewish–Transjordanian Relations*, p. 40.
23. *Al-Ahram*, 18 Jan. 1933; *Filastin*, 20 Jan. 1933.
24. Shlaim, *The Politics of Partition*, p. 50.
25. Yoav Alon, 'The Last Grand Shaykh: Mithqal al-Fayiz, the State of Trans-Jordan and the Jewish Agency', MA thesis: Tel Aviv University, 1999.

26. *Filastin*, 5 Feb. 1933.
27. CZA, S25/6313: Cohen, 'Report from the visit to Amman', 20 Jan. and 15 Feb. 1933; S25/3491: Mithqal to Arlozoroff, 3 Feb. 1933.
28. Gelber, *Jewish–Transjordanian Relations*, pp. 48–9.
29. *Filastin*, 1 July 1934.
30. *Filastin*, 26 May 1933.
31. CZA, S25/3491: Mithqal to Mrs Arlosoroff, 21 June 1933; 'Sa'id al-Mufti Yatadhakkaru', *al-Dustur*, 8 May 1976.
32. Gelber, *Jewish–Transjordanian Relations*, p. 51.
33. Ibid., p. 70.
34. Alon, 'The Last Grand Shaykh'.
35. Shlaim, *Collusion across the Jordan*, p. 54; Gelber, *Jewish–Transjordanian Relations*, p. 86.
36. Gelber, *Jewish–Transjordanian Relations*, pp. 86–7.
37. Ibid., p. 88.
38. Ibid., pp. 90–2.
39. Wilson, *King Abdullah, Britain and the Making of Jordan*, p. 85.
40. Alon, *The Making of Jordan*, pp. 115, 121–2.
41. Shlaim, *Collusion across the Jordan*, pp. 59–60.
42. Alon, *The Making of Jordan*, pp. 137–8; Ma'an Abu Nowar, *The History of the Hashemite Kingdom of Jordan: Vol. II: The Development of Trans-Jordan, 1929–1939*, Amman: Al-Ra'y, 1997, pp. 53–5.
43. Shlaim, *Collusion across the Jordan*; Gelber, *Jewish–Transjordanian Relations*, p. 283. Fieldhouse seems to fully accept this line of argumentation (see *Western Imperialism in the Middle East*, pp. 235–7).
44. Nevo, *King Abdullah and Palestine*; Avraham Sela, 'Transjordan, Israel and the 1948 War: Myth, Historiography and Reality', *Middle Eastern Studies*, 28, 4 (1992), pp. 623–88; Tancred Bradshaw, 'History Invented: The British–Transjordanian "Collusion" Revisited', *Middle Eastern Studies*, 43, 1 (2007), pp. 21–43.

3. INFLUENCE WITHOUT POWER? BRITAIN, THE JEWISH AGENCY AND INTELLIGENCE COLLABORATION, 1939–45

1. See Shlomo Aronson, *Hitler, the Allies and the Jews*, Cambridge: Cambridge University Press, 2007, pp. 84–5; Yehuda Bauer, *From Diplomacy to Resistance: A History of Jewish Palestine 1939–1945*, Philadelphia: Jewish Publication Society of America, 1970, pp. 51–67; Haggai Eshed, *Reuven Shiloah: The Man Behind the Mossad*, London: Frank Cass, 2005, pp. 76–80; Eldad Harouvi, 'Reuven Zaslany (Shiloah) and the Covert Cooperation with British Intelligence During the Second World War', in Hesi Carmel (ed.), *Intelligence for Peace: The Role of Intelligence in Times of Peace*, London: Frank Cass, 1999, pp. 45–6.

2. CZA S25/7902: Reuven Zaslany's Report on his activities, Jerusalem, 27 Nov. 1944. Zaslany was later to change his name to Shiloah.
3. TNA HS 3/209 242575: Memorandum: Manpower in Palestine, 23 Oct. 1939.
4. Ibid. See also Ashley Jackson, *The British Empire in the Second World War*, London: Hambledon/Continuum, 2006, pp. 139–43.
5. TNA HS 3/209: Strictly Confidential: Notes of conversation between David Ben-Gurion and the Right Hon. Malcolm MacDonald, P.C, M.P, Colonial Office, Wednesday, 15 Nov. 1939.
6. Ronald Zweig, 'The Political Uses of Military Intelligence: Evaluating the Threat of a Jewish Revolt Against Britain During the Second World War', in Richard Langhorne (ed.), *Diplomacy and Intelligence during the Second World War*, Cambridge: Cambridge University Press, 2003, p. 110.
7. See, for example, Judith Tydor Baumel-Schwartz, *Perfect Heroes: The World War II Parachutists and the Making of Israeli Collective Memory*, Madison: University of Wisconsin Press, 2010.
8. Ian Black, 'The Stern Solution', *The Guardian Weekend*, 15–16 Feb. 1992, pp. 4–6.
9. See for example, Yitzhak Gil-Har, 'British Intelligence and the role of Jewish informers in Palestine', *Middle Eastern Studies*, 39, 1(2003), pp. 117–49.
10. Harouvi, 'Reuven Zaslany (Shiloah) and the Covert Cooperation with British Intelligence', p. 35.
11. See Keith Jeffrey, *MI6: The History of the Secret Intelligence Service 1909–1949*, London: Bloomsbury, 2010, p. 421.
12. Jeffrey, *MI6*, pp. 421–3; CZA S25/7902: Reuven Zaslany's Report on his activities. In his report Zaslany stated that the initial contact with British intelligence (SIS) was 'due to the efforts that had begun in London and not *Eretz Yisrael*'.
13. TNA HS3/20: Letter from Hahitachdut Sel Hacijonim Halkalim, Andrassyut 67 II Budapest VI to The Confederation of General Zionists, L. Bakstansky Esq., 75 Gt Russell Street, London WC1, Subject: Zionists in Hungary, 28 Feb. 1940.
14. TNA HS3/201: Subject—Zionists, 22 Apr. 1940.
15. TNA HS3/201: Untitled Memorandum, 21 Mar. 1940.
16. Ibid.
17. TNA HS3/201: Subject—Palestine, Liaison with the Jewish Agency, 17 Apr. 1940.
18. See Jeffrey, *MI6*, p. 414.
19. TNA HS 3/201: Unmarked memorandum on notes of conversation with Zionist Leaders, 29 May 1940.
20. See, for example, Saul Kelly, 'A Succession of Crises: SOE in the Middle East, 1940–45', *Intelligence and National Security*, 20, 1 (2005), pp. 121–46.

21. TNA HS 3/201: Unmarked memorandum on notes of conversation with Zionist Leaders, 29 May 1940.

22. IWM Accession No. 66/297/1: Papers of A.C. Simonds. G.H.Q. Middle East, June 1941 to Sep. 1941.

23. CZA S25/8883: Report: Operations in States and in the Diaspora under Nazi control.

24. CZA S25/8908: ISLD 1939–45. Report from Damascus 12 March 1941.

25. CZA S25/8908: ISLD 1939–45. From Zaslany to Brigadier Clayton, Jerusalem, 23 May 1941.

26. Eshed, *Reuven Shiloah*, p. 50. The most detailed account of the likely fate of the 'Sea Lion' mission is to be found in the Haganah Archives in Tel Aviv. See Haganah Archive (HA), Accession No. 029/0006 (1/1/39–31/12/45): Correspondence: Operation Sea Lion—SOE.

27. Eldad Harouvi, 'British Intelligence Co-operation with the Jewish Agency during the Second World War', MA Thesis (Unpublished): Faculty of Humanities, University of Haifa, Dec. 1992, pp. 130–9.

28. HA-Accession No. 029/0006 (1/1/39–31/12/45): 'Correspondence: Operation Sea Lion—SOE'. See the letter marked 'Most Secret: From Lord Glenconner to M. Shertok', 19 Oct. 1942. Where perhaps MO4 was at fault however was in the delay of seventeen months in informing the next of kin of the likely fate of the *Sea Lion* crew long after the need to maintain operational security had lapsed. Even then, the Jewish Agency was only allowed to disclose to the relatives that their likely deaths had occurred during operations connected to the Syrian campaign, rather than the suspected circumstances of their demise.

29. The young SOE officer concerned was Julian Amery, later to be decorated for his bravery as an SOE officer in Albania and who went on to enjoy a colourful if ultimately frustrating career as a Conservative politician. See Julian Amery, *Approach March: A Venture in Autobiography*, London: Hutchinson, 1973, p. 280.

30. See C.M. Woodhouse, *Something Ventured*, London: Granada, 1982, pp. 17–19.

31. CZA S25/8883: Operations in States in the Diaspora under Nazi control; TNA HS 3/206: Memorandum: Palestine, Syria and Transjordan, 6 Apr. 1942. Although most of the documents relating to post-occupational planning across the Middle East, including Palestine, have been released, some remain heavily redacted. Even seven decades after the event, it would seem that discussing those individuals and organisations willing to collaborate with the British still remains sensitive.

32. TNA HS3/209: The Relations between SOE and the Jews: Memorandum by the Controller, 22 June 1942.

33. TNA HS3/209: To Sir A.N. Rucker KCMG, Most Secret; TNA HS3/209 214/93: The Relations between SOE and the Jews: Memorandum by the Con-

troller, 22 June 1942; TNA AIR 40/2606: Most Secret—SOE Sub-Committee of the Defence Committee. Reports of SOE Activities, 12th Report by the Controller (Terence Maxwell) for four weeks ending 20 July 1942.

34. TNA HS 3/209: Visit to Palestine and Syria, 6 Oct. 1942.

35. Interview with Colonel David Smiley, London, 18 Feb. 2005. Smiley was an SOE trainee at the time and recalled that all the guards at the camp were Jewish as was the main intelligence officer who held the rank of captain. Following the raid, they all disappeared.

36. David Stafford, *Britain and European Resistance 1940–1945: A Survey of the Special Operations Executive with Documents*, Toronto: University of Toronto Press, 1983, pp. 180–1.

37. Liddell Hart Centre for Military Archives (Kings College London), Papers of Julian Dobriski, File 21/7: From Julian Dobriski to Brigadier Barker Benfield, Subject: Post-War SOE Organisation, 23 Mar. 1944.

38. CZA S25/8883: Report: Operations in States and in the Diaspora under Nazi control (3A). The Office of Investigations in Haifa; Harouvi, 'Reuven Zaslany (Shiloah) and the Covert Cooperation with British Intelligence', p. 35.

39. CZA S25/8908, ISLD 1939–45: Letter from ISLD (Istanbul) 23 May 1941—Received 26 May 1941.

40. Sebastian Ritchie, *Our Man in Yugoslavia: The Story of a Secret Service Operative*, London: Frank Cass, 2004, pp. 63–5.

41. CZA S25/8908, ISLD 1939–45: Most Secret—From Zaslany to Squadron Leader Ross-Smith ISLD Cairo, 25 Feb. 1943.

42. See for example CZA S25/8908, ISLD 1939–45: 623/536 Letter to R. Zaslani [*sic*] Jewish Agency 8 May 1943; CZA S25 623/530: Letter to R. Zaslani [*sic*] Jewish Agency, 6 May 1943.

43. CZA S25/8908, ISLD 1939–45: Letter from Reuven Zaslany to Squadron Leader G. Reed, Jerusalem 12 Nov. 1943.

44. F.W.D. Deakin, *The Embattled Mountain*, London: Oxford University Press, 1971, p. 50; Franklin Lindsay, *Beacons in the Night: With the OSS and Tito's Partisans in Wartime Yugoslavia*, Stanford, CA: Stanford University Press, 1993, p. 361.

45. For a full history of MI9 see M.R.D. Foot and J.M. Langley, *MI9: Escape and Evasion 1939–1945*, London: Bodley Head, 1979, p. 364.

46. TNA WO208/325: Top Secret: Summary of MI9 Activities in the Eastern Mediterranean 1941–5: Section E, Middle East. Brief History of IS9(ME) Balkan Operations; IWM Accession No. 66/297/1: Papers of A.C. Simonds. G.H.Q. Middle East, Jewish Aid to Allied Escape and Rescue Work.

47. TNA WO208/325: Top Secret: Summary of MI9 Activities in the Eastern Mediterranean 1941–5: Section E, Middle East. Brief History of IS9(ME) Balkan Operations.

48. TNA WO208/325: Top Secret: Summary of MI9 Activities in the Eastern Mediterranean 1941–5: Section E, Middle East. Brief History of IS9(ME) Balkan Operations (B).

49. CZA S25/8883: Operations in States in the Diaspora under Nazi control (Evaluation of the collaborative endeavour).

50. CZA S25/7902: Reuven Zaslany's Report on his Activities, Jerusalem, 27 Nov. 1944.

4. THE POWER OF THE WEAK: ISRAEL'S SECRET OIL DIPLOMACY, 1948–57

1. The Anglo-Iranian Company (AIOC), which changed its name in 1954 to British Petroleum or BP, signed a convention with the government of Palestine in 1931 granting it the rights to refine oil in Palestine and to dispose of that right to other companies. Early in 1938 it transferred that right to the Consolidated Refineries Ltd, 50 per cent of whose stock was owned by the Anglo-Iranian Company and the remainder by Royal Dutch Shell.

2. See Uri Bialer, *Oil and the Arab–Israeli Conflict 1948–1963*, Macmillan/St Antony's Oxford Series: London 1999, pp. 7–38.

3. See Ze'ev Levkovitch, 'Oil Supply during the War of Independence: The Problem, Constraints and Solutions', *Ma'arachot* [in Hebrew], 304 (June 1986), pp. 16–23.

4. Daniel Silverfarb, 'The Revision of Iraq's Oil Concessions 1949–1952', *Middle Eastern Studies*, 32, 1 (1996), pp. 69–95.

5. D. Horowitz, *In the Heart of Events*, Tel Aviv: 1975, pp. 68–72 [in Hebrew]; Bialer, *Oil and the Arab–Israeli Conflict*, pp. 84–91.

6. Uri Bialer, 'Top Hat Tuxedo and Cannons: Israeli Foreign Policy from 1948 to 1956 as a Field of Study', *Israel Studies*, 7, 1 (2002), pp. 48–54.

7. See the authoritative analysis of Jacob Metzer, *The Divided Economy of Palestine*, Cambridge: Cambridge University Press, 1998.

8. See Uri Bialer, 'Sterling Balances and Claims Negotiations: Britain and Israel 1947–1952', *Middle Eastern Studies*, 28, 1 (1992), pp. 157–77.

9. Israel Labour Party Archive (Tel Aviv), file 11/2/1: Speech of Foreign Minister Moshe Sharett, 28 July 1949.

10. Uri Bialer, 'The Iranian Connection in Israel's Foreign Policy 1948–1951', *Middle East Journal*, 39, 2 (1985), pp. 292–315.

11. HA (Tel Aviv) File 14/39/A: notes of Moshe Chervinsky's notes (undated). On the topic which involved other intensive secret diplomacy by Israel see Moshe Gat, *The Jewish Exodus from Iraq 1948–1951*, London: Frank Cass, 1997.

12. See Uri Bialer, 'Between Rehovot and Tehran—Gideon Hadary's Secret Diplomacy', *Israel Studies*, 17, 1 (2012), pp. 1–23.

13. Ibid., p. 17.
14. Ibid.
15. ISA 2515/12: Pines' memorandum, 14 June 1951.
16. Bialer, 'Between Rehovot and Tehran', p. 17.
17. ISA 2563/6: Report titled 'On Aliyah from Iraq', 5 Jan. 1951.
18. Bialer, *Oil and the Arab Israeli Conflict*, pp. 130–5.
19. See Bialer, 'Top Hat Tuxedo and Cannons', pp. 53–4. It should be noted that Israeli Foreign Minister Moshe Sharett reluctantly agreed to approve the Soviet connection but warned his officials against dependence on Russian oil, which would imply 'putting our head into a noose'; Moshe Sharett's Diary, entry for 13 Oct. 1953, in *A Personal Diary*, Tel Aviv, 1978, p. 272 [in Hebrew].
20. On this topic see M. Elm, *Oil Power and Principle: Iran's Oil Nationalization and its Aftermath*, Syracuse: University of Syracuse, 1992, and James Bill and Wm. Roger Louis (eds), *Musaddiq, Iranian Nationalism and Oil*, London: I.B. Tauris, 1988. For the Israeli perspective see Uri Bialer, 'Oil from Iran: Zvi Doriel's Mission in Tehran 1956–1963', *Iyunim Bitkumat Israel*, Part 1 (1998), pp. 150–80, and Part 2 (1999), pp. 128–66 [in Hebrew].
21. Bialer, *Oil and the Arab–Israeli Conflict*, pp. 178–80.
22. For later developments see Uri Bialer, 'Fuel Bridge across the Middle East: Israel, Iran and the Eilat—Ashkelon Oil Pipeline', *Israel Studies*, 12, 3 (2007), pp. 29–67.

5. BACK-DOOR DIPLOMACY: THE MISTRESS SYNDROME IN ISRAEL'S RELATIONS WITH TURKEY, 1957–60

1. For a flavour: in the 1990s 'the old courtship game has been reversed'. Quote from Henri Barkey, *Reluctant Neighbor: Turkey's Role in the Middle East*, Washington, DC: United States Institute of Peace Press, 1996, p. 38; '[T]he two sides embarked upon a fast and furious diplomatic love affair', in Philip Robins, *Turkish–Israeli Relations: From the Periphery to the Center*, Abu Dhabi: Emirates Center for Strategic Studies and Research, 2001, p. 9; Israeli–Turkish relations resemble 'a late-life love affair' that has cooled off. 'Will they get back together or become "just friends"?' in Paul Scham, 'Israeli–Turkish Relations: New Directions', *MEI (Middle East Institute) Commentaries*, 16 Aug. 2004; Israel's 'Love Affair with Turkey', in Amikam Nachmani, 'A Triangular Relationship: Turkish–Israeli Cooperation and its Implications for Greece', *Cahiers d'Études sur la Méditerranée Orientale et le monde Turco-Iranien (CEMOTI)*, 28 (1999), p. 13; Raphael Israeli, 'The Turkish–Israeli Odd Couple', *Orbis*, 45, 1 (2001). Gabriel Mitchell, 'Breaking Up is Hard to Do: Israel and Turkey, A Love Affair Gone Bad', *The Jerusalem Post*, 9 July 2011.

2. 'Turkish–Israeli Relations: Volatile But Resilient', US Embassy in Ankara, 2 Feb. 2007, at http://wikileaks.org/cable/2007/02/07ANKARA222.html

3. ISA/RG130.23/3125/4: Alon to Moshe Sasson, 9 June 1959.

4. Noa Schonmann, 'The Phantom Pact: Israel's Periphery Policy in the Middle East', D.Phil. Thesis: University of Oxford, 2009.

5. Personal communications to George Gruen, who continues to cite: 'I heard Turkish diplomats and academics make the same analogy in private conversations about Turkey's relations with Israel and the Arab states: "A man may love his mistress more than his wife, and we admire Israel and share common interests, but Muslim Arabs are our family, we must keep up appearances in public." They also noted that the Arab wife brought with her a large dowry—the oil resources upon which Turkey depends.' George Gruen, 'Turkey and the Middle East after Oslo I', in Robert O Freedman, *The Middle East and the Peace Process: The Impact of the Oslo Accords*, Gainesville: University Press of Florida, 1998, p. 173.

6. The need for a distinction was inspired by observations made by Aaron Klieman, who suggested the term 'quiet diplomacy' to mark the halfway zone 'on the continuum between open diplomacy and secret diplomacy—the one unattainable, the other intolerable'. Klieman's conceptual framework, in contrast with the one offered here, builds on a normative debate. Aaron Klieman, *Statecraft in the Dark: Israel's Practice of Quiet Diplomacy*, Boulder: Westview Press, 1988, pp. 4, 7–10, 24–9, 75. For more on the narrower term 'backchannel diplomacy', denoting an informal mode of peace negotiations among adversarial states, see Aaron Klieman, 'Israeli Diplomacy in the Back Channel', *Leonard Davis Institute for International Relations Paper*, 80 (2000), pp. 10–11.

7. Klieman, *Statecraft in the Dark*, p. 42.

8. ISA/RG93.08/413/8: Gefen to Shimoni, 4 Oct. 1954; ISA/RG93.08/413/8: Eliahu Sasson to Eytan, 10 Jan. 1952; ISA/RG93.8/412/15: Gilead to Meroz, 9 Jan. 1958. See also Mahmut Bali Aykan, 'The Palestinian Question in Turkish Foreign Policy from the 1950s to the 1990s', *International Journal of Middle East Studies*, 25, 1 (1993), p. 92; George Gruen, 'Turkey, Israel and the Palestine Question, 1948–1960: A Study in the Diplomacy of Ambivalence', PhD Thesis: Columbia University, 1970; George Gruen, 'Dynamic Progress in Turkish–Israeli Relations', *Israel Affairs*, 1, 4 (1995), p. 42; Amikam Nachmani, *Israel, Turkey and Greece: Uneasy Relations in the East Mediterranean*, London: Frank Cass, 1987, pp. 44–5.

9. ISA/RG93.08/413/8: Ben-Horin to Najar, 14 Nov. 1954

10. ISA/RG130.23/3125/6: Alon to Eytan, 23 Sep. 1957.

11. ISA/RG130.23/3125/5: Fischer to Eytan, 29 Nov., 3 and 6 Dec. 1956; ISA/RG130.23/3125/6: Alon to Eytan, 23 Sep. 1957.

12. ISA/RG130.23/3125/6: Eliahu Sasson to Eytan, 8 Sep. 1957; ISA/RG130.23/3125/6: Alon to Eytan, 23 Sep. 1957.

13. ISA/RG130.23/3105/12: Shiloah to Eytan, 15 Sep. 1957.

14. ISA/RG130.23/3125/4: Shiloah to Eytan, 18 Sep. 1957; ISA/RG130.23/3125/6: Shiloah to Eliahu Sasson, 16 Oct. 1957; ISA/RG130.23/3125/6: Eliahu Sasson to Shiloah, 21 Oct. 1957; ISA/RG130.23/3125/6: Eytan to Eliahu Sasson, 7 Nov. 1957; ISA/RG130.23/3125/4: Eytan to Eliahu Sasson, 17 Nov. 1957.

15. ISA/RG93.8/409/4: Eliahu Sasson to MFA, 4 Nov. 1957.

16. ISA/RG130.23/3125/6l: Ilsar to Levavi, 3 Nov. 1957; ISA/RG130.23/3125/11: Levavi to Eliahu Sasson, 10 Nov. 1957; ISA/RG130.23/3125/6: Levavi to Shinar, 10 Nov. 1957; ISA/RG130.23/3125/5: Levavi to Lourie, 13 Nov. 1957.

17. ISA/RG130.19/4488/7: Shiloah to Meir, 1 Jan. 1958; ISA/RG130.23/3105/13: Shiloah to Meir, 7 Jan. 1958.

18. ISA/RG130.19/4488/8: Shiloah to Ben-Gurion, 14 July 1958; ISA/RG130.19/4488/7: Shiloah to Meir, 1 Jan. 1958; ISA/RG130.15/3750/3: Alon to Fischer, 9 Mar. 1958.

19. Yaacov Caroz, *The Man with Two Hats* [in Hebrew], Tel Aviv: Ministry of Defence, 2002, p. 123.

20. ISA/RG130.09/2358/2: Meir to Eliahu Sasson, Telegram R497, 6 Jan. 1958, ISA/RG130.09/2358/2, in Baruch Gilead (ed.), *Documents on the Foreign Policy of Israel (DFPI) 1958–1959* [in Hebrew], vol. 13, Jerusalem: Israel State Archives, 2001, pp. 769–71 (Document 408).

21. ISA/RG130.19/4488/7: Shiloah to Meir, 1 Jan. 1958; ISA/RG130.23/3105/12: 'Senior Staff Meeting', 5 Jan. 1958; ISA/RG130.19/4488/8: Shiloah to Ben-Gurion, 14 July 1958.

22. ISA/RG130.15/3752/14: Eliahu Sasson to Meir, 8 Jan. 1958, in Baruch Gilead (ed.), *Documents on the Foreign Policy of Israel (DFPI) 1958–1959*, vol. 13, Jerusalem: Israel State Archives, 2001, pp. 771–3 (Document 409).

23. ISA/RG130.23/3125/5: Eliahu Sasson to Shiloah, 19 Jan. 1958.

24. ISA/RG130.19/4488/7: Shiloah to Meir, 1 Jan. 1958; ISA/RG130.23/3105/12: 'Senior Staff Meeting', 5 Jan. 1958; ISA/RG130.19/4488/8: Shiloah to Ben-Gurion, 14 July 1958.

25. ISA/RG130.19/4488/3: Pragai to Elath, 31 Jan. 1958.

26. ISA/RG130.15/3750/3: Alon to Fischer, 9 Mar. 1958; ISA/RG130.23/3125/5: Alon to Eytan, 23 Feb. 1958; ISA/RG130.23/3105/13: Fischer to Eytan, 23 Mar. 1958.

27. ISA/RG130.15/3750/3: Eliahu Sasson to Meir, 1 Apr. 1958; ISA/RG130.19/4488/8: Shiloah to Ben-Gurion, 14 July 1958.

28. ISA/RG130.19/4488/8: BGD, 15 Apr. 1958, BGA; Shiloah to Ben-Gurion, 14 July 1958.

29. ISA/RG130.15/3750/3: Eliahu Sasson to Meir, 18 Apr. 1958; ISA/RG130.19/4488/8: Shiloah to Ben-Gurion, 14 July 1958.

30. ISA/RG130.15/3750/3: Eliahu Sasson to Meir, 18 Apr. 1958; ISA/RG130.19/4488/8: Shiloah to Ben-Gurion, 14 July 1958.

31. Caroz, *The Man with Two Hats*, p. 151.
32. ISA/RG130.2/4316/17 'Special Staff Meeting', 21 Apr. 1958; ISA/RG130.19/ 4488/8: Shiloah to Ben-Gurion, 14 July 1958; ISA/RG130.19/4488/9: Shiloah to Comay, 17 July 1958; ISA/RG130.19/4488/8: Shiloah to Ben-Gurion, 11 Aug. 1958.
33. ISA/RG130.19/4488/8: Shiloah to Ben-Gurion, 11 Aug. 1958.
34. ISA/RG130.02/2450/9: 'Conclusions of the Meeting of the Prime Ministers of Turkey and Israel in Ankara', 29 Aug. 1958, and Ben-Gurion to Eban, 8 Sep. 1958. This file remains classified, but several documents from it were released to me by the ISA archivist, while others were published, in partially classified form, in *Documents on the Foreign Policy of Israel (DFPI) 1958–1959*, vol. 13, pp. 819–22 (Documents 429 and 30). BGD entries of 28–30 Aug. 1958 remain mostly classified in BGA, but are nonetheless partially cited by his biographer, who enjoyed access to an uncensored version of the diary. See Michael Bar-Zohar, *Ben-Gurion: A Political Biography* [in Hebrew], vol. 3, Tel-Aviv: Am Oved, 1977, pp. 1316, 1329–30.
35. ISA/RG130.23/4315/2: 'Senior Staff Meeting', 14 Nov. 1958.
36. ISA/RG130.15/3752/4: Shiloah to Sasson, 5 Jan. 1959 in Baruch Gilead (ed.), *Documents on the Foreign Policy of Israel (DFPI) 1958–1959*, vol. 13, Jerusalem: Israel State Archives, 2001, pp. 837–41 (Document 440). ISA/RG130.15/3750/3: Memorandum by Shiloah, n.d. [1959?], ISA/RG130.15/3750/3: Shiloah to Alon, 24 Dec. 1958.
37. ISA/RG130.09/2358/6: Eliahu Sasson to Shiloah, Telegram MPR108, 9 Jan. 1959, in Baruch Gilead (ed.), *Documents on the Foreign Policy of Israel (DFPI) 1958–1959*, vol. 13, Jerusalem: Israel State Archives, 2001, pp. 842–3 (Document 441).
38. Ibid.
39. ISA/RG130.19/4488/14 'Senior Staff Meeting', 25 Mar. 1959.
40. ISA/RG130.15/3750/2: Alon to Moshe Sasson, 27 Aug. 1959; ISA/ RG130.15/3750/2: Moshe Sasson to Alon, 31 Aug. 1959; ISA/RG130.15/3750/2: Alon to Eytan, 8 Sep. 1959.
41. ISA/RG130.23/3125/4: Eliahu Sasson to Moshe Sasson, 26 Aug. 1959.
42. ISA/RG130.15/3750/2: Eliahu Sasson to Moshe Sasson, 13 Sep. 1959; ISA/ RG130.15/3750/2: Moshe Sasson to Eliahu Sasson, 7 Oct. 1959.
43. ISA/RG130.15/3750/2: Eliahu Sasson to Moshe Sasson, 7 Oct. 1959; ISA/ RG130.15/3750/2: Arbel to Herzog, 13 Oct. 1959.
44. ISA/RG93.8/412/15: Herzog to Moshe Sasson, 7 June 1959.
45. ISA/RG130.15/3750/2: Moshe Sasson to Eliahu Sasson, 6 Nov. 1959.
46. ISA/RG130.15/3753/4: Herzog to Moshe Sasson, 23 July 1959.
47. ISA/RG130.23/3125/4: MFA to Alon, 30 Sep. 1959; ISA/RG130.23/3125/4: Eytan to Alon, 9 Oct. 1959; ISA/RG130.23/3125/4: Fischer to Yahil, 26 Nov. 1959.

48. ISA/RG130.15/3757/2: Alon to Moshe Sasson, 2 Feb. 1960; ISA/RG130.15/
    3750/2: Moshe Sasson to Eliahu Sasson, 24 Nov. 1959.

49. ISA/RG130.23/3125/4: Alon to Moshe Sasson, 9 June 1959; ISA/RG130.15/
    3750/2: Alon to Moshe Sasson, 27 Aug. 1959; ISA/RG130.15/3757/2: ISA/
    RG130.15/3757/2: Eliahu Sasson to Fischer, 26 Jan. 1960; ISA/RG130.15/
    3757/2: Moshe Sasson to Alon, 6 May 1960; ISA/RG130.15/3757/2: Alon to
    Moshe Sasson, 24 May 1960.

50. Gruen, 'Dynamic Progress', p. 67, n.7; Benjamin Beit-Hallahmi, *The Israeli
    Connection: Who Israel Arms and Why*, New York: Pantheon Books, 1987, p. 16;
    Çağrı Erhan, *Turkish–Israeli Relations in a Historical Perspective*, London: Frank
    Cass, 2003, p. 30; William Hale, *Turkish Foreign Policy, 1774–2000*, London:
    Frank Cass, 2000, p. 129; Jacob Abadi, *Israel's Quest for Recognition and Accep-
    tance in Asia: Garrison State Diplomacy*, London: Frank Cass, 2004, p. 15; Philip
    Robins, *Turkey and the Middle East*, London: Royal Institute of International
    Affairs, 1991, p. 77.

51. Bar-Zohar, *Ben-Gurion: A Political Biography*, vol. 3, p. 1332; Ofra Bengio, *The
    Turkish–Israeli Relationship: Changing Ties of Middle Eastern Outsiders*, London:
    Palgrave Macmillan, 2004, p. 53; Shmuel Segev, *The Iranian Triangle: The Untold
    Story of Israel's Role in the Iran-Contra Affair*, New York: Free Press, 1988, p. 36;
    Schonmann, 'The Phantom Pact: Israel's Periphery Policy in the Middle East'.

52. ISA/RG93.8/6530/9: 'Israel–Turkey 1962', Sep. 1962.

53. ISA/RG130.23/3448/20: Moshe Sasson to Levavi, 22 July 1963; ISA/RG130.23/
    3559/31: Moshe Sasson to Elizur, 9 June 1965; ISA/RG130.23/3604/4: Shek
    to Moshe Sasson, 20 June 1965; ISA/RG130.23/3604/4: Moshe Sasson to Shek,
    30 June 1965; ISA/RG130.23/3604/4: Elizur to Moshe Sasson, 11 July 1965;
    ISA/RG130.23/3604/4: Moshe Sasson to Shek, 20 July 1965; ISA/RG93.18/
    267/1: Moshe Sasson to Eliachar, 15 Feb. 1966; Bengio, *The Turkish–Israeli
    Relationship*, pp. 61–2.

54. ISA/RG130.23/3604/4: Moshe Sasson to Shek, 17 Nov. 1965; ISA/RG93.18/
    267/1: Moshe Sasson to Eliachar, 15 Feb. 1966; ISA/RG93.18/267/1: Moshe
    Sasson to Eliachar, 27 Feb. 1966; ISA/RG93.18/267/1: Moshe Sasson to
    Eliachar, 2 Mar. 1966; ISA/RG93.8/6555/41: 'Background Paper: Israel–Turkey
    Relation', 18 Dec. 1966.

55. ISA/RG43.4/6266/3: Prime Minister's Office to Lubrani, 2 July 1964; ISA/
    RG43.4/7229/28: Shek to Moshe Sasson, 30 Aug. 1964; ISA/RG130.2/4322/3:
    Moshe Sasson to Yahil, 15 Aug. 1964; ISA/RG93.18/267/1: Moshe Sasson to
    Eliachar, 15 Feb. 1966.

56. ISA/RG93.8/6555/41: 'Background Paper: Israel–Turkey Relation', 18 Dec.
    1966.

57. ISA/RG130.23/3604/4: Moshe Sasson to Shek, 31 Mar. 1965; ISA/RG130.23/
    3604/4: Moshe Sasson to Shek, 30 June 1965; ISA/RG130.23/3604/4: Moshe

Sasson to Shek, 17 Nov. 1965; ISA/RG93.18/267/1: Moshe Sasson to Eliachar, 2 Mar. 1966; ISA/RG93.18/267/1: 'Israel–Turkey Relations', 10 Mar. 1966.

58. ISA/RG130.23/4075/26: Gilboa to Yariv, 10 June 1966; Rabin to Tural, early June 1966; ISA/RG130.23/4075/26: 'An Expression of Ecumenical Concern', *New York Times*, 10 Apr. 1966, p. 154; ISA/RG93.8/6555/41: Bitan to Harman, 5 May 1966; Bengio, *The Turkish–Israeli Relationship*, pp. 64–7.

59. Klieman, *Statecraft in the Dark*, p. 42.

60. Ibid., pp. 40, 75.

61. In this chapter I adopt Elie Podeh's felicitous phrase 'Mistress Syndrome' while adapting it to capture a slightly different phenomenon in Israel's external relations. Podeh used the term 'mistress syndrome' to describe a condition afflicting Israel's relations with the Western powers, whereby they came to perceive the Arab states as the legal wife, while Israel was treated as a desirable, but hidden, ally. In his article, Podeh sought to explain Israel's failure to associate itself with Western defence schemes for the Middle East in the early 1950s, by calling attention to what he considered to be mistakes made by Israel during the negotiation process. He argued that Israeli policy-makers prematurely conveyed the impression that their wartime cooperation was assured. Consequently, the Western powers saw no reason to upset the Arab states by offering Israel the formal defence arrangement it desired. Elie Podeh, 'The Desire to Belong Syndrome: Israel and Middle-Eastern Defense, 1948–1954', *Israel Studies*, 4, 2 (1999), pp. 122, 144. The term was first used by Haggai Eshed, also in the context of Israel's relations with the Western powers in the 1950s. Eshed observed that Israel 'could not get away from the syndrome of "the mistress who would be a wife"—the semi-covert ally, weak and vulnerable, lacking solid guarantees for its survival or a clear declaration by the West of its commitment to its defense'. Haggai Eshed, *Reuven Shiloah: The Man Behind the Mossad: Secret Diplomacy in the Creation of Israel*, London: Frank Cass, 1997, p. 273. The use of the mistress analogy in this context could be traced back to 1949, when Joseph Linton, political secretary at the London office of the Jewish Agency, expressed his bitterness at the British decision to postpone de jure recognition of Israel. He told the British it reminded him of Heinrich Heine's poem '*Blamier mich nicht, mein schönes Kind*' about the lover who asks his mistress not to greet him when they meet in public, strolling down the main avenue. Cited in Mordechai Bar-On, *Of all Kingdoms: Israel's Relations with the United Kingdom During the First Decade After the End of the British Mandate in Palestine 1948–1958* [in Hebrew], Jerusalem: Yad Ben-Zvi, 2006, p. 53.

62. ISA/RG43.3/7225/12: Moshe Sasson to Eliahu Sasson, 25 May 1959; ISA/RG43.4/7225/12: Eliahu Sasson to Moshe Sasson, 28 May 1959.

6. CONFRONTING CAIRO: ISRAELI PERCEPTIONS OF NASSER'S EGYPT, 1960–6

1. This chapter is based on a work-in-progress which examines the role of early warning in the Israeli perception of national security between 1948 and 1973.

2. Yigal Sheffy, 'Early Warning of Intentions or of Capabilities? Revisiting the Israeli–Egyptian Rotem Affair, 1960', *Intelligence & National Security* (forthcoming); Sheffy, *Early Warning Countdown: The 'Rotem' Affair and the Israeli Security Perception, 1957–1960* [in Hebrew], Tel Aviv: Ma'arachot, 2008.

3. On the 'war over the water' see Avi Cohen, *Defending Water Resources*, History of the Israeli Air Force Series, vol. 3 [in Hebrew], Tel Aviv: Ministry of Defence Publishing House, 1992; Moshe Shemesh, 'Prelude to the Six-Day War: The Arab–Israeli Struggle over Water Resources', *Israel Studies*, 9, 3 (2004), pp. 1–45; Ami Gluska, '"The War Over the Water" during the 1960s', in Mordechai Bar-On (ed.), *Never-Ending Conflict: A Guide to Israeli Military History*, Westport, CT: Praeger, 2004, pp. 109–31.

4. Michael Bar-Zohar, *Ben Gurion: A Political Biography* [in Hebrew], Tel Aviv: Am Oved, 1977, vol. 3, pp. 1526–8.

5. Until 1968 the IDF military ranks higher than *aluf mishne* (colonel) were *Aluf* (brigadier general) and *rav aluf* (major general), the latter borne only by the chief of the General Staff. In 1968 a rank of *tat aluf* was created between *aluf mishneh* and *aluf*, making *aluf* equivalent to major general and *rav aluf* to lieutenant general. For the sake of simplicity, ranks mentioned in this article are referred to by their post-1968 British equivalents.

6. Amit was the director of IDF military intelligence (AMAN) from January 1962 to January 1964, and director of the Mossad from March 1963 to September 1968. Between March 1963 and January 1964 he served as director of both agencies.

7. IDF and Defence Establishment Archives, IDFA/31/281/2010, Office of Minister of Defence, weekly staff meeting (hereafter: MOD weekly staff meeting), 5 July 1963. All archival documents cited are in Hebrew and held at the IDF and Defence Establishment Archives (hereafter: IDFA), Kiryat Ono, Tel Hashomer military base. For the sake of simplicity, their references appear here in English only.

8. Major General Meir Amit to Prime Minister Levi Eshkol, Feb. 1966, cited in Meir Amit, 'Secret Contacts for Peace: A Lost Opportunity', in Hesi Carmel (ed.), *Intelligence for Peace: The Role of Intelligence in Times of Peace*, London: Frank Cass, 1999, p. 242.

9. Ibid., pp. 226–57; Meir Amit, *Head on: A Personal Observation on Major Events and Hidden Episodes* [in Hebrew], Or Yehudah: Hed arzi, 1999, pp. 204–28; Zaki Shalom, 'A Missed Opportunity' [in Hebrew], *ha-tziyonot*, 22 (2001), pp. 321–53; IDF, Chief of the General Staff diary, 9 Feb. 1966.

10. Eitan Haber, *'Today War Will Break Out': The Reminiscences of Brig. Gen. Israel Lior, Aide-de-Camp to Prime Ministers Levi Eshkol and Golda Meir* [in Hebrew], Tel Aviv: Edanim, 1987, pp. 64–5.

11. IDFA/1230/535/2004, AMAN, Intelligence Survey 50/61, 'Nasser's Speech on 23/12/61', 28 Dec. 1961.

12. IDFA/1547/535/2004, AMAN, Annual Intelligence Assessment, Jan. 1963; Ami Gluska, *Eshkol. Give the Order! The IDF and the Israeli Government on the Road to the Six-Day War, 1963–1967* [in Hebrew], Tel Aviv: Ma'arachot, 2004, pp. 46–7.

13. IDFA/191/117/1970, IDF General Staff meeting, 2 Dec. 1963.

14. IDFA/94/764/2004, AMAN, Semi-Annual Intelligence Assessment, 1964.

15. AMAN, Annual Intelligence Assessment, 1 Oct. 1964.

16. General Staff meeting, 8 Mar. 1965, cited in Gluska, 'The War Over the Water', pp. 101–2.

17. Shemesh, 'Prelude to the Six-Day War', pp. 29–30; Michael B. Oren, *Six Days of War: June 1967 and the Making of the Modern Middle East*, Oxford: Oxford University Press, 2002, p. 40.

18. IDFA/2/335/2006, IDF General Staff meeting, 6 Mar. 1967.

19. Sheffy, *Early Warning Countdown*, pp. 263–64.

20. IDFA/117/70/2006, General Staff meeting, 24 Apr. 1967. On Rabin's view regarding Nasser's intentions in Apr. 1967, see Yitzhak Rabin, *Rabin's Memoirs*, Boston: Little, Brown, 1979, p. 66.

21. IDFA/1943/535/2004, AMAN, Annual Intelligence Assessment, 31 Dec. 1965.

22. Yitzhak Greenberg, *Account and Power: Defence Budget from War to War 1957–1967* [in Hebrew], Tel Aviv: Ministry of Defence Publishing House, 1997, pp. 116–32; Greenberg, 'The Planning of the IDF Order of Battle between the 6 Day War and Yom Kippur War' [in Hebrew], *Iyyunim be-tekumat Yisrael*, 14 (2004), pp. 393–4; Amiad Drezner, 'The Buildup of the Armoured Force, 1956–1967', in Haggai Golan and Shaul Shai (eds), *Pioneers: 40th Anniversary to the Six Day War* [in Hebrew], Tel Aviv: Ma'arachot, 2007, pp. 77–103.

23. IDFA/195/117/1970, General Staff meeting, 6 Nov. 1966.

24. Ami Gluska, *The Israeli Military and the Origins of the 1967 War: Government, Armed Forces and Defence Policy 1963–67*, London: Routledge, 2006, pp. 74–6. This is an abridged edition of the book in Hebrew (see ref. 12). References below are to the English edition, unless otherwise noted.

25. Matitiahu Mayzel, *The Golan Heights Campaign: June 1967* [in Hebrew], Tel Aviv: Ma'arachot, 2001, pp. 22–4; Hanoch Bartov, *Dado, 48 Years and 20 Days: The Full Story of the Yom Kippur War and of the Man Who Led Israel's Army*, Tel Aviv: Ma'ariv Book Guild, 1981, pp. 83–8. See also, Oren, *Six Days of War*, pp. 23–4.

26. Clive Jones, *Britain and the Yemen Civil War, 1962–1965*, Brighton & Port-

land: Sussex Academic Press, 2004, pp. 136, 148–50; Duff Hart-Davis, *The War that Never Was*, London: Century, 2011, pp. 138 ff.; Yael Bar and Lior Asterline, 'The Secret Ingredient of the Sauce' [in Hebrew], *bite'on heil ha-avir*, 180 (2008), pp. 22–9.

27. On the Israeli–Kurdish connections: Shlomo Nakdimon, *The Crushed Hope: Israeli–Kurdish relations, 1963–1975* [in Hebrew], Tel Aviv: Sifre Hemed, 1996; Eliezer Tsafrir, *I am a Kurd* [in Hebrew], Or Yehudah: Hed Arzi, 1999. On the Israeli–Sudanese connection: Benjamin Beit Hallahmi, *The Israeli Connection: Who Israel Arms and Why*, New York: Pantheon Books, 1987, pp. 47–9; Robert O. Collins, *A History of Modern Sudan*, Cambridge: Cambridge University Press, 2008, pp. 103–7; Zvi Zamir and Efrat Mass, *With Open Eyes* [in Hebrew], Or Yehuda: Kinneret, 2001, pp. 86–9.

28. IDFA/39/281/2010, MOD weekly staff meeting, 19 Mar. 1965; Jewish Telegraph Agency, Daily News Bulletin, 32, 69, 29 Mar. 1965, www.archive.jta.org, accessed 15 Sep. 2011.

29. Bar and Asterline, 'The Secret Ingredient', p. 28.

30. Rabin, pp. 61–4; Gluska, *The Israeli Military and the Origins of the 1967 War*, pp. 74–91.

31. Gluska, ibid., p. 83; IDFA/1943/535/2004, Annual Intelligence Assessment, 31 Dec. 1965. I am indebted to Prof. Uri Bialer for drawing my attention to the issue of the dichotomy.

32. IDFA/7/120/2009, IDF General Staff meeting, 8 Mar. 1965.

33. See, for example, Shlomo Aronson, *The Politics and Strategy of Nuclear Weapons in the Middle East: Opacity, Theory and Reality, 1960–1991*, Albany: State University of New York Press, 1991; Ariel Levite and Emily Landau, 'Arab Perceptions of Israel's Nuclear Posture, 1960–1967', *Israel Studies*, 1, 1(1996), pp. 34–59; Avner Cohen, 'Cairo, Dimona and the June 1967 War', *Middle East Journal*, 50, 2 (1996), pp. 190–210; Cohen, *Israel and the Bomb*, New York: Columbia University Press, 1998.

34. Levite and Landau, 'Arab Perceptions of Israel's Nuclear Posture', p. 34.

35. IDFA/95/764/2004, IDF General Officers' Symposium, 16 Mar. 1961. For Nasser's reaction, see, for example, William B. Bader, *The United States and the Spread of Nuclear Weapons*, New York: Pegasus, 1968, p. 96.

36. IDFA/1547/535/2004, AMAN, Annual Intelligence Assessment, Jan. 1963.

37. Michael Bar Zohar, *The Hunt for the German Scientists*, London: Barker, 1967; Zohar, *Ben Gurion*, pp. 1529–45; Isser Harel, *The German Scientists crisis, 1962–1963* [in Hebrew], Tel Aviv: Sifriyat Ma'ariv, 1982; Owen Sirrs, *Nasser and the Missile Age in the Middle East*, Abingdon: Routledge, 2006; Shlomo Aronson, *The Politics and Strategy of Nuclear Weapons in the Middle East: Opacity, Theory and Reality, 1948–1993* [in Hebrew], Jerusalem: Academon, 1993, pp. 308–17.

38. Cohen, *Israel and the Bomb*, p. 256; Moshe Shemesh, *Arab Politics, Palestinian*

Nationalism and the Six Day War, Brighton and Portland, OR: Sussex Academic Press, 2008, p. 148; IDFA/514/765/2004, AMAN translation of Haykal's article, 24 October 1965.

39. Levite and Landau, 'Arab Perceptions of Israel's Nuclear Posture', p. 46; Shemesh, *Arab Politics*, pp. 147–51; Shlomo Aronson, *Levi Eshkol: From Pioneering Operator to Tragic Hero—A Doer*, London and Portland, OR: Vallentine Mitchell, 2011, pp. 150–2.

40. IDFA/513/765/2004, AMAN, Intelligence Survey, 56/65, 8 Oct. 1965; IDFA/42/281/2010, MOD weekly staff meeting, 29 Oct. 1965.

41. IDFA/1943/535/2004, AMAN Annual Intelligence Assessment, Dec. 1965.

42. Gluska, '"The War Over the Water"', pp. 33–4.

43. IDFA/268/764/2004, AMAN, Intelligence Assessment, Feb. 1966.

44. Private source.

45. For a brief account: Ephraim Lapid, 'Collecting Information in Preparation for the Six-Day War', in Amos Gilboa and Ephraim Lapid (eds), *Israel's Silent Defender: An Inside Look at Sixty Years of Israeli Intelligence*, Jerusalem and Springfield, NJ: Gefen Books, 2011, pp. 65–70.

46. Interview with Brigadier General (ret.) Ephraim Lapid, 14 Sep. 2011, Tel Aviv.

47. Yigal Sheffy, *Early Warning and the 1967 War* (see above, n. 2).

48. For example: Gluska, '"The War Over the Water"', p. 261; Aryeh Shalev, *Israel's Intelligence Assessment before the Yom Kippur War: Disentangling Deception and Distraction*, Portland, OR: Sussex Academic Press, 2010, pp. 13–21.

49. For different views, see Richard B. Parker, *The Politics of Miscalculation in the Middle East*, Bloomington, IN: Indiana University Press, 1993, pp. 59–98; Yair Evron, *Israel's Nuclear Dilemma*, Ithaca, NY: Cornell University Press, 1994, pp. 47–9; C.L. Brown, 'Nasser and the June War: Plan or Improvisation', in Samir Seikaly et al. (eds), *Quest for Understanding: Arabic and Islamic Studies in Memory of Malcolm H. Kerr*, Beirut: American University of Beirut, 1991, pp. 119–35; Aharon Yariv, *Cautious Assessment: A Collection of Essays* [in Hebrew], Tel Aviv: Ma'arachot, 1998, pp. 154–6; Laura James, 'Nasser and his Enemies: Foreign Policy Decision Making in Egypt on the Eve of the Six-Day War', *Middle East Review of International Affairs*, 9, 2 (2005), pp. 23–44; Moshe Gat, 'Nasser and the Six Day War, 5 June 1967: A Premeditated Strategy or An Inexorable Drift To War?' *Israel Affairs*, 11, 4 (2005), pp. 608–35; Ronald Popp, 'Stumbling Decisively into the Six-Day War', *Middle East Journal*, 60, 2 (2006), pp. 281–309; Shimon Golan, *A War on Three Fronts* [in Hebrew], Tel Aviv: Ma'arachot, 2007, pp. 338–42; Shemesh, *Arab Politics, Palestinian Nationalism and the Six Day War* (n. 38), Chapter 7.

7. THE LIMITS OF PUBLIC DIPLOMACY: ABBA EBAN AND THE JUNE 1967 WAR

1. Cited in Eytan Gilboa, 'Public Diplomacy: The Missing Component in Israel's Foreign Policy', in Efraim Inbar (ed.), *Israel's Strategic Agenda*, London: Routledge, 2007, p. 122.
2. Some of the earliest accounts of the war include Michael Bar-Zohar, *The Longest Month*, Tel Aviv: Levin Epstein, 1968, and *Embassies in Crisis: Diplomats and Demagogues Behind the Six-Day War*, Englewood Cliffs, NJ: Prentice Hall, 1970; Tim Hewat (ed.), *War File: The Voices of the Israelis, Arabs, British and Americans, in the Arab–Israeli War of 1967*, London: Panter Books, 1967; David Kimche and Dan Bawly, *The Sandstorm: The Arab–Israeli War of June 1967: Prelude and Aftermath*, London: Secker & Warburg, 1968; Walter Laqueur, *The Road to Jerusalem: The Origins of the Arab–Israeli Conflict, 1967*, New York: Columbia University Press, 1968; Shabtai Teveth, *The Tanks of Tammuz*, London: Sphere Books, 1969.
3. Avi Shlaim, *The Iron Wall: Israel and the Arab World*, London: Penguin, 2000, p. 236.
4. See for example Ahron Bregman, *Israel's Wars: A History Since 1947*, London: Routledge, 2002; L. Carl Brown, 'Origins of the Crisis', in Richard B. Parker (ed.), *The Six Day War: A Retrospective*, Gainesville: University Press of Florida, 1996, pp. 13–73; Moshe Gat, 'Nasser and the Six Day War, 5 June 1967: A Premeditated Strategy or Inexorable Drift to War?' *Israel Affairs*, 11, 2 (2005), pp. 608–35; W. Roger Louis and Avi Shlaim (eds), *The 1967 Arab–Israeli War: Origins and Consequences*, Cambridge: Cambridge University Press, 2012; Benny Morris, *Righteous Victims: A History of the Zionist–Arab Conflict, 1881–2001*, London: Verso, 2001; Michael Oren, *Six Days of War*, Oxford: Oxford University Press, 2002; Tom Segev, *1967: Israel, the War, and the Year that Transformed the Middle East*, New York: Metropolitan Books, 2005, Shlaim, The Iron Wall; Patrick Tyler, *A World of Trouble: The White House and the Middle East—from the Cold War to the War on Terror*, New York: FSG, 2009.
5. Isabella Ginor and Gideon Remez, *Foxbats Over Dimona: The Soviets' Nuclear Gamble in the Six-Day War*, New Haven, CT: Yale University Press, 2007, and 'Un-Finished Business: Archival Evidence Exposes the Diplomatic Aspect of the USSR's Pre-planning for the Six Day War', *Cold War History*, 6, 3 (2006), pp. 377–95. See also Roland Popp, 'Stumbling Decidedly into the Six-Day War', *The Middle East Journal*, 60, 2 (2006), pp. 281–309.
6. Abba Eban, *An Autobiography*, New York: Random House, 1977, p. 199.
7. Author's interview with Moshe Raviv, 12 May 2009.
8. Segev, 1967, p. 267; M. Golan, *The Secret Diaries of Henry Kissinger*, New York: Quadrangle, 1975.

9. Author's interviews with Suzy Eban (wife, 17 Mar. 2010), Raphael Eban (brother, 7 July 2010), Oliver Sacks (cousin, 23 Feb. 2010) and Rachel Gordon (aide at the Ministry of Foreign Affairs, 27 July 2010).

10. Michael Brecher, *The Foreign Policy System of Israel: Setting, Images, Process*, London: Oxford University Press, 1972, p. 328.

11. Testimony to Eban's view that words are superior to deeds is found in an exchange of letters with Ben-Gurion on the subject of the deterioration of relations with France under de Gaulle. Posing the question who was the greatest Frenchman of their generation, Eban wrote to Ben-Gurion: 'In my opinion Jean Monnet—and not De Gaulle—is the greatest Frenchman of our generation because the actions of men are ephemeral but noble ideas are immortal.' Cited in R. Adam (ed.), *Abba Eban: A Statesman and a Diplomat*, Jerusalem: Ministry of Foreign Affairs, Hebrew, 2003, p. 138.

12. Ahron Klieman, 'Israel: Succumbing to Foreign Ministry Declinism', in B. Hocking (ed.), *Foreign Ministry: Change and Adaptation*, Basingstoke: Palgrave, 1999, pp. 86–7.

13. Elinor Burkett, *Golda*, New York: Harper Collins, 2008, p. 186.

14. Ibid., p. 182.

15. Avi Shlaim, *Lion of Jordan: The Life of King Hussein in War and Peace*, London: Penguin, 2007, p. 253.

16. Brecher, *The Foreign Policy System of Israel*, p. 247.

17. 'Statement to the Security Council by Foreign Minister Eban—6 June 1967', *Israel's Foreign Relations Selected Documents*, vols 1–2: 1947–74, doc. 19.

18. Burkett, *Golda*, p. 220.

19. Telegram 196541, 'Telegram from the Department of State to the Embassy in Israel', 17 May, 1967. Foreign Relations of the United States (hereafter FRUS) *Volume XIX, The Arab–Israeli Crisis and War, 1967*, doc. 8.

20. Golda was undergoing cancer treatment at the time and wasn't fit to travel in any case. Burkett, *Golda*, p. 219; Michael Bar-Zohar, *The Longest Month*.

21. Zaki Shalom, 'Lyndon Johnson's Meeting with Abba Eban, 26 May 1967: An Introduction', *Israel Studies*, 4, 2 (1999), p. 223.

22. CIA Office of Current Intelligence (OCI), 'Overall Arab and Israeli Military Capabilities', 23 May 1967, FRUS XIX, doc. 44.

23. Cited in Bar-Zohar, *Embassies in Crisis*, p. 116.

24. 'Memorandum of Conversation', 26 May 1967. FRUS XIX, doc. 77.

25. Board of National Estimates, 'Military Capabilities of Israel and the Arab States', 26 May 1967, FRUS XIX, doc. 76; J.L. Freshwater [pseudonym], 'Policy and Intelligence: The Arab–Israeli War', *Studies in Intelligence*, 13, 1 (1969), p. 6.

26. 'Memorandum of Conversation', op. cit.

27. Segev, *1967*, p. 267; Eban, *An Autobiography*, p. 359; Michael Oren, 'Did Israel Want the Six Day War?' *Azure*, 7 (1999), p. 67.

28. William. B. Quandt, 'Lyndon Johnson and the June 1967 War: What Color Was the Light?' *Middle East Journal*, 46, 2 (1992), p. 214.

29. Lyndon Johnson Presidential Library (hereafter LBJ), President's Daily Diary, 4/16/67-6/30/67, Box 11: Daily Diary May 16–31, 1967 (26 May 1967).

30. Ibid.

31. Jon Kimche, *Palestine or Israel: The Untold Story of Why We Failed, 1917–1923: 1967–1973*, London: Secker & Warburg, pp. 257–8.

32. Segev, *1967*, p. 329.

33. Eban, *An Autobiography*, pp. 384–5.

34. Amit recounted this view in several interviews and in his memoir, *A Life in Israel's Intelligence Service: An Autobiography*, London: Vallentine Mitchell, 2009. However, according to Patrick Tyler, Amit's version 'is so at variance with the facts that it raises the question of whether the Mossad chief fabricated his most prominent account, published in Hebrew, to justify the pre-emptive war decision for a domestic Israeli audience'. To compare, see Tyler, *A World of Trouble*, pp. 94–5, against Amit's own account in Parker, *The Six-Day War*, pp. 136–52.

35. The National Security Archive, from private collection, 'Memorandum for: The President, From Richard Helms, CIA Director', 2 June 1967. Available at http://www.gwu.edu/~nsarchiv/NSAEBB/NSAEBB265/19670602.pdf

36. Oren, *Six Days of War*, p. 147.

37. Michael Brecher, *Decision in Crisis: Israel, 1967 and 1973*, Berkeley: University of California Press, 1980, p. 157 (n. 159).

38. Segev, *1967*, p. 332.

39. 'Telegram from the Embassy in the United Arab Republic to the Department of State', Cairo 4 June 1967, 1925Z. FRUS XIX, doc.145. The American telegram to Cairo from 3 June states that Johnson would welcome the visit, adding, 'we hope it will be possible for him [Mohieddin] to come without delay'. The report also adds that Avraham Harman has been informed about the possibility of the visit. FRUS XIX, doc. 134 (n. 2); National Archives and Records Administration, RG 59, Central Files 1967–69, POL ARAB–ISR; LBJ Library, National Security File, Country File, Middle East Crisis, Anderson Cables.

40. Bar-Zohar, *The Longest Month*, p. 196.

41. Suzy Eban, *A Sense of Purpose: Recollections*, London: Halban, 2008, p. 285.

42. Cited in Shlomo Gazit, *The Carrot and the Stick: Israel's Policy in Judea and Samaria, 1967–1969*, Washington, DC: B'nai Brith Books, 1995, p. 135.

43. Cited in D. Bavly, *Dreams and Missed Opportunities: 1967–1973*, Jerusalem: Carmel, 2002, p. 47.

44. A. Eban, *Personal Witness: Israel Through My Eyes*, New York: G.P. Putnam's Sons, 1992, p. 450.

8. ISRAEL IN SUB-SAHARAN AFRICA: THE CASE OF UGANDA, 1962–72

1. ISA 1047/35: Embassy in Kampala to Africa Division, 1 Jan. 1965.
2. Arye Oded, 'Israeli–Ugandan Relations in the Time of Idi Amin', *Jewish Political Studies Review*, 18/3, 4 (2006).
3. Amos Ettinger, *My Land of Tears and Laughter*, New York: Cornwall Books, 1994, p. 203.
4. Amii Omara-Otunnu, *Politics and the Military in Uganda, 1890–1985*, London: Palgrave Macmillan, 1987, p. 51.
5. James H. Mittelman, *Ideology and Politics in Uganda: from Obote to Amin*, Ithaca: Cornell University Press, 1975, pp. 92–3.
6. ISA 1568/35: Embassy in Kampala to Prime Minister, 10 June 1966.
7. ISA 1047/35: Embassy in Kampala to Africa Division, 13 Aug. 1963.
8. Kenneth Ingham, *Obote: A Political Biography*, London: Routledge, 1994, p. 91.
9. Ibid., pp. 92–3.
10. Omara-Otunnu, *Politics and the Military in Uganda*, pp. 43, 58–62.
11. National Archives at College Park, MD (hereafter NAII), RG (Record Group) 59, DEF 19 ISR: Uganda, Embassy in London to Department of State, 28 July 1964; TNA FO/371 175812 ER1073/2: Morris to Beith, 27 July 1964.
12. Ettinger, *My Land of Tears*, pp. 204–7.
13. Omara-Otunnu, *Politics and the Military in Uganda*, p. 66.
14. *The Arms Trade Registers*, Stockholm International Peace Research Institute (SIPRI), Cambridge, MA: MIT Press, 1975, p. 89.
15. Mittelman, *Ideology and Politics in Uganda*, pp. 106–10.
16. Ingham, *Obote*, p. 91.
17. ISA 1047/34: Embassy in Kampala to Africa Division, 19 Oct. 1964.
18. ISA 1047/35: Shaham to Africa Division and Ministry of Defence, 4 Oct. 1963.
19. Ibid.
20. ISA 1047/34: Embassy in Kampala to Africa Division, 24 Nov. 1965; Oded, *Uganda and Israel*, p. 52.
21. Mittelman, *Ideology and Politics in Uganda*, pp. 104–5.
22. Omara-Otunnu, *Politics and the Military in Uganda*, pp. 67–8.
23. Ibid.
24. ISA 1047/35: Embassy in Kampala to Africa Division, Ministry of Defence, 8 Sep. 1965.
25. ISA 1047/34: Embassy in Kampala to Africa Division, 21 Sep. 1965.
26. ISA 1047/35: Lubrani to Avriel, 13 Oct. 1965.
27. ISA 1047/35: Embassy in Kampala to Africa Division, 17 Nov. 1965.
28. ISA 1047/34: Embassy in Kampala to Africa Division and Ministry of Defence, 1 Dec. 1965.
29. Omara-Otunnu, *Politics and the Military in Uganda*, pp. 75–6.

30. Mittelman, *Ideology and Politics in Uganda*, p. 81.
31. ISA 3981/7: Africa Division to Embassy in Kampala, 12 Apr. 1966.
32. ISA 1568/35: Embassy in Kampala to Prime Minister, 10 June 1966.
33. ISA 3158/1: Consultations on Africa, 7 July 1966.
34. TNA FO/371 187697 J1075/1/A: Hadow to Morris, 7 Apr. 1966.
35. ISA 3993/17: Bitan to Eban, 27 Sep. 1966.
36. ISA 3981/7: Embassy in Kampala to Africa Division, 5 Oct. 1966.
37. ISA 3993/17: Sofer to Shek, 11 Feb. 1966.
38. ISA 3981/7: Embassy in Kampala to Foreign Ministry, 6 Oct. 1966.
39. ISA 3981/2: Embassy in Kampala to Africa Division, 2 Aug. 1967.
40. ISA 3981/2: 'Uganda', Report of Foreign Ministry, 14 Sep. 1967.
41. NAII, RG59, SNF, DEF 19–9: Isr-Uganda, Embassy in Kampala to Department of State, 27 June 1967.
42. Ingham, *Obote*, p. 134.
43. ISA 3981/2: Embassy in Kampala to Africa Division, 23 Aug. 1967; ISA 3981/2, 'Uganda', Report of Foreign Ministry, 14 Sep. 1967.
44. ISA 3981/2: Embassy in Kampala to Africa Division, 11 Oct. 1967; *The Arms Trade Registers*, p. 89.
45. ISA 4161/6: Foreign Ministry report, 15 June 1969.
46. NAII, RG59, SNF, DEF 12–5: Uganda, Embassy in Kampala to Department of State, 8 Oct. 1969.
47. Ronen Bergman, 'Israel and Africa: Military and Intelligence Liaisons', unpublished PhD dissertation: University of Cambridge, 2007, p. 118.
48. ISA 4551/23: Ofri's report: 'Uganda 1969', dated Jan. 1970.
49. Omara-Otunnu, *Politics and the Military in Uganda*, pp. 88–91.
50. Peter Woodward, 'Uganda and Southern Sudan', in Bernt Hansen Hölger and Michael Twaddle (eds), *Uganda Now: Between Decay and Development*, London: James Currey, 1988, p. 231.
51. Tony Avirgan and Martha Honey, *War in Uganda: The Legacy of Idi Amin*, Westport, CT: Lawrence Hill and Company, 1982, p. 10.
52. Mittelman, *Ideology and Politics in Uganda*, pp. 212–13.
53. ISA 4551/30: Bar-Lev and Boneh to Foreign Ministry, Defence Ministry and Mossad, 26 Jan. 1971. In fact there is no evidence that Amin planned his coup months earlier.
54. ISA 5299/30: Oded to Africa Division 'A', 12 Apr. 1972.
55. ISA 4551/30: Bar-On to Embassy in Kampala, Mossad, Defence Ministry, 27 Jan. 1971.
56. ISA 5299/30: Oded does not name those who were to be 'eliminated'. Oded to Africa Division 'A', 12 Apr. 1972.
57. ISA 4551/31: Embassy in Kampala to Africa Division and Mossad, 26 Feb. 1971.

58. ISA 4551/31: Oded to Africa Division, 1 Feb. 1971; ISA 4551/31, Embassy in Kampala to Africa Division, 19 Feb. 1971.
59. ISA 4551/31: Foreign Ministry to Embassies in Lusaka and Nairobi, 24 Feb. 1971.
60. ISA 4551/23: Ofri to Bar-On, 11 Feb. 1971.
61. ISA 4551/12: Ofri to Aynor and Shimoni, 5 Mar. 1971.
62. Arye Oded, *Uganda and Israel* [in Hebrew], Jerusalem: 2002, p. 72.
63. ISA 4551/12: Aynor to Shimoni, 4 Apr. 1971.
64. ISA 4551/12: Embassy in Kampala to Foreign Ministry, 22 Apr. 1971.
65. ISA 4551/12: Foreign Ministry to Embassy in Kampala, 3 May 1971.
66. ISA 4551/23: Ofri to Rafael and Shimoni, 25 June 1971.
67. Oded, *Uganda and Israel*, p. 67.
68. ISA 4551/20: Oded to Aynor, 11 July 1971. The Jet Commander carried ten passengers with a range of 4,430km.
69. Oded, *Uganda and Israel*, pp. 70, 84.
70. Golda Meir, *My Life*, New York: G.B. Putnam's Sons, 1975, pp. 335–6.
71. ISA 4551/20: Bar-On to Rafael, Shimoni and Shalev, 14 July 1971.
72. ISA 4551/20: Bar-On to Embassy in Kampala, 30 Sep. 1971. Uganda never signed the contract.
73. ISA 4551/23: Laor to Shalev, 20 Oct. 1971.
74. Judith Listowel, *Amin*, London: IUP Books, 1973, p. 102; Mittelman, *Ideology and Politics in Uganda*, pp. 207–8.
75. ISA 4551/23: Special Report of Mossad Research Division, 26 Oct. 1971.
76. Oded, *Uganda and Israel*, p. 85.
77. ISA 4551/19: Embassy in Kampala to Foreign Ministry, 15 Nov. 1971.
78. ISA 8747/4: UN Division to Legation and Division Heads, 7 Jan. 1974.
79. ISA 4551/19: Embassy in Kampala to Foreign Ministry, 24 Nov. 1971.
80. ISA 4551/19: Embassy in Kampala to Africa Division, 9 Dec. 1971.
81. ISA 4551/19: Shalev to Laor, 22 Dec. 1971.
82. Oded, *Uganda and Israel*, p. 82.
83. ISA 4551/12: Bar-Lev's letter to Amin, 17 Dec. 1971.
84. Jan Jelmert Jorgensen, *Uganda: A Modern History*, New York: St. Martin's Press, 1981, p. 273; ISA 5298/4: Shalev to Bar-On, 16 Jan. 1972.
85. ISA 5298/8: Embassy in Kampala to Africa Division, 3 Feb. 1972.
86. Oded, *Uganda and Israel*, p. 91.
87. ISA 5298/4: Laor to Tsur, 10 Feb. 1972.
88. David Martin, *General Amin*, London: Sphere, 1978, pp. 162–3.
89. ISA 7314/3: Oded to Shimoni, 17 Feb. 1972.
90. ISA 5298/8: Consultations at Foreign Ministry, 18 Feb. 1972.
91. Omara-Otunnu, *Politics and the Military in Uganda*, p. 114.
92. ISA 7314/3: Laor to Shalev, 24 Feb. 1972.

93. Oded, *Uganda and Israel*, pp. 95–7.

94. Ibid., pp. 98–103.

95. Listowel, *Amin*, pp. 135–6; Oded, *Uganda and Israel*, p. 98.

96. ISA 5299/31: Africa Division to Embassies, 26 Mar. 1972.

97. ISA 5298/4: (Lt Colonel) A. Raz to Ministry of Defence, 25 Mar. 1972.

98. Oded, *Uganda and Israel*, p. 99.

99. ISA 5299/31: Embassy in Kampala to Foreign Ministry, 26 Mar. 1972.

100. Ibid.

101. Ibid.; Listowel, *Amin*, p. 137.

102. ISA 5299/31: Meeting at the Foreign Ministry, 28 Mar. 1972.

103. ISA 5299/31: Foreign Ministry to Embassy in Rome, 30 Mar. 1972.

104. ISA 5299/31: Embassy in Kampala to Foreign Ministry, 2 Apr. 1972; ISA 5299/31, Amir to Shimoni, 2 Apr. 1972.

105. Oded, *Uganda and Israel*, p. 100.

106. ISA 4551/22: Oded to Shalev, 27 Mar. 1972.

107. ISA 5298/6: Hareven to Meir, 9 Apr. 1972.

108. ISA 5299/31: Amir to Shalev, 4 Apr. 1972.

109. ISA 5299/31: Africa Division to Legations in Africa, 30 Mar. 1972.

110. ISA 5299/31: Bar-On to Shalev, 3 Apr. 1972.

111. ISA 5299/31: Tene to Haran, 2 Apr. 1972.

112. Oded, *Uganda and Israel*, p. 110.

113. ISA 5298/6: Dafni to Gazit, 4 Apr. 1972.

114. ISA 5298/6: Oded to Naot (Embassy in Freetown), 7 Apr. 1972.

115. ISA 5298/6: Dafni to Gazit, 4 Apr. 1972.

116. ISA 5299/31: Engel (Mossad) to Shimoni, 31 Mar. 1972.

117. ISA 5298/6: Golan's letter to Shimoni, Africa Division, 19 Apr. 1972.

118. ISA 7314/5: 'Visits to Africa', Meeting at Foreign Ministry, 14 June 1972.

119. ISA 5298/7: Director General's Office, Foreign Ministry, 6 Nov. 1972.

120. ISA 8526/15: Bein to Milo, 13 Oct. 1975.

121. ISA 4779/6: 12 July 1976, Herzog to Foreign Ministry.

9. ISRAEL'S CLANDESTINE DIPLOMACY WITH SUDAN: TWO ROUNDS OF EXTRAORDINARY COLLABORATION

1. A telegram sent to Sudan by Israel's Minister of Foreign Affairs Moshe Sharrett on 3 Jan. 1956. The Israel State Archives (ISA), Prime Minister's Office, Jerusalem. ISA/RG 130/MFA/2454/14. I would like to express my gratitude to the staff of the Israel State Archives for their kind and efficient help.

2. ISA/RG 43/G/5573/2.

3. Ethiopia, like Sudan, was alarmed by Egypt's Gamal Abd al-Nasser, whose militant philosophy encouraged the Eritrean separatists to fight for their indepen-

dence. In fact, the Eritrean Liberation Front 'was born in the bosom of Nasser', who 'privately' saw the Ethiopian Emperor Haile Selassie as an enemy. Haggai Erlich, *Ethiopia and the Middle East*, Boulder, CO: Lynne Rienner, 1994, pp. 130–3. This further nourished Ethiopia's historical 'image of itself … [as] a beleaguered country surrounded mostly by hostile or potentially hostile countries with no natural friends in its immediate vicinity'. This point of commonality with Israel paved the way for the strategic affinity between Jerusalem and Addis Ababa, projecting also on the contacts between Jerusalem and Khartoum. Michael B. Bishku, 'Israel and Ethiopia: From a Special to Pragmatic Relationship', *Conflict Quarterly*, 14, 2 (1994), pp. 41–2. See also Haggai Erlich, *Ethiopia and the Challenge of Independence*, Boulder, CO: Lynne Rienner, 1986, pp. 219–20 and 154–5; and Haggai Erlich, *The Struggle Over Eritrea, 1962–1978: War and Revolution in the Horn of Africa*, Stanford, CA: Hoover Institution Press, 1983, p. 62.

4. For details on the periphery doctrine see Michael Bar Zohar, 'David Ben-Gurion and the Policy of the Periphery 1958: Analysis', in Itamar Rabinovich and Jehuda Reinharz (eds), *Israel in the Middle East: Documents and Readings on Society, Politics, and Foreign Relations, pre-1948 to the Present*, Waltham, MA: Brandeis University Press, 2008, pp. 191–7.

5. For the roots and course of Sudan's civil war, see Mohamed Omer Beshir, *The Southern Sudan*, Khartoum: Khartoum University Press, 1970; Edgar O'Ballance, *The Secret War in the Sudan, 1955–1972*, Hamden, CT: Archon Books, 1977; Mom K.N. Arou et al. (eds), *North–South Relations in the Sudan Since the Addis Ababa Agreement* [of 1972], Khartoum: Institute of African & Asian Studies, University of Khartoum, 1988; John Voll (ed.), *Sudan: State and Society in Crisis*, Bloomington: Indiana University Press, 1991; Mansour Khalid, *War and Peace in Sudan: A Tale of Two Countries*, London: Kegan Paul, 2003; and Yehudit Ronen, *Sudan in a Civil War: Between Africanism, Arabism and Islam*, Tel Aviv: Ha-Kibutz Ha-Mehuhad and Tel Aviv University, 1995.

6. Most of the relevant Israeli documents relating to these two chapters of clandestine diplomacy are still under the cover of state censorship.

7. In fact, this slogan was central to Egyptian nationalism since the beginning of the twentieth century. The Egyptian King Farouq (1937–52) even declared himself 'the King of Egypt and Sudan'.

8. ISA/RG 130/mfa/2454/14. Quoted in a letter sent by an unidentified Israeli official to the Foreign Affairs Ministry in Jerusalem, 28 Sep. 1956.

9. Addis Ababa became the headquarters of Israeli clandestine diplomacy vis-à-vis Sudan and other sub-Saharan African countries.

10. France was a prominent colonial power in Africa, being deeply entrenched strategically, militarily, politically and economically in many of the countries in the continent, including Sudan's neighbouring states. The convergence of the French

anti-Nasser position, which reached a peak following his nationalisation of the Suez Canal on 26 July 1956, with Sudan's conflicting interests with Nasser, increased French interest in Khartoum.

11. ISA/RG 130/MFA/2454/14. This was disclosed by the Israeli official in a report he sent to Jerusalem on 28 Aug. 1956. No follow-up documents were available in the Ganzah Hamedina in July 2011.

12. The Arab League (Jamiat al-Duwal al-Arabiyya) was founded in Cairo in Mar. 1945 as a realisation of the Arab Unity vision. Sudan joined the Arab League in 1956.

13. ISA/ RG 43/G/5573/2. In a report addressed by an Israeli official to the Ministry of Foreign Affairs on 11 May 1956.

14. Dan Raviv and Yossi Melman, *Every Spy a Prince: The Complete History of Israel's Intelligence Community*, Boston: Houghton Mifflin Company, 1990, p. 84.

15. Moshe Sharett, *Personal Diary*, Tel Aviv: Maariv, 1978, p. 1160.

16. For more details on the dynamics relevant to the contacts in 1956, see Mahmoud Muhareb, *Israeli Interference in Sudan*, Doha: Arab Center for Research & Policy Studies, 2011, pp. 3–6.

17. ISA/ RG 130/MFA/2454/14, quoting a report by an Israeli Foreign Ministry official. See also *Ruz al-Yusuf* (Cairo, daily), 28 Apr. 1958 and ISA/RG 43/G/5573/2.

18. On 27 Sep. 1955 the Soviets signed their first arms deal with Egypt, becoming Cairo's foremost military supporter.

19. Raviv and Melman, *Every Spy a Prince*, p. 84 and Avner Yaniv, *Politics and Strategy in Israel*, Tel Aviv: Sifriat Poalim, 1994, p. 177.

20. Ben-Gurion asked the American assistance not only for Sudan but also to the 'outer ring' countries surrounding the anti-Israeli Arab core. These included Ethiopia, Turkey and Iran.

21. Ben-Gurion to Eisenhower, 24 July 1958, Bishku, *Israel and Ethiopia*, p. 44.

22. Avraham Sela (ed.), *The Continuum Political Encyclopedia of the Middle East*, New York: Continuum, 2002, pp. 160–1. This unionist framework collapsed in the autumn of 1961.

23. Bishku, 'Israel and Ethiopia', p. 44.

24. Raviv and Melman, *Every Spy a Prince*, p. 85.

25. Among Sudan's explicit anti-Israeli moves were the breaking off of its diplomatic relations with the German Federal Republic following Bonn's establishment of diplomatic relations with Israel in 1965; joining the warring Arab camp in the war in June 1967, sending an infantry battalion to Egypt; cutting off its diplomatic relations with the United States in a protest against what Khartoum claimed to be active support of Israel in the war; and hosting the Arab Summit conference in Khartoum in the aftermath of the 1967 war, during which the 'three no's' strategy was defined (no peace with Israel, no negotiation with Israel and no recognition of Israel).

26. Tom Segev, 'The Exodus from Ethiopia', *Haaretz*, 19 Mar. 2010.

27. Exiled to Assyria by Tiglath Pilser in 722 BC. For a detailed survey of the origins of the Jews of Ethiopia, see Steven Kaplan, *The Beta Israel (Falasha) in Ethiopia: From Earliest Times to the Twentieth Century*, New York: New York University Press, 1992. Haggai Erlich et al., *Ethiopia—Christianity, Islam, Judaism*, Tel Aviv: The Open University, 2003, pp. 272–6. Tudor Parfitt and Emanuela Trevisan Semi (eds), *Jews of Ethiopia: The Birth of an Elite*, New York: Routledge, 2005.

28. See e.g., Ahmed Karadawi, 'The Smuggling of the Ethiopian Falasha to Israel through Sudan', *African Affairs*, 90, 23 (1991). For a discussion of the origins of the 'Jewishness' of the Ethiopian Jews, see also David Kessler and Tudor Parfitt, 'The Falashas: Jews of Ethiopia', *Minority Rights Group*, 67 (1985) and *Operation Moses*, London: Weidenfeld and Nicolson, 1985.

29. 'The History of the Ethiopian Jews', Jewish Virtual Library, accessed 31 July 2011, http://www.jewishvirtuallibrary.org/jsource/Judaism/ejhist.html

30. The interim European stations were Belgium, Switzerland and Italy. 'Sudan-Falasha staging post', *Africa Now* (London, monthly), Jan. 1985, 13. Since the operations themselves are not the subject of this chapter I intentionally avoided entering details which are not relevant to the clandestine operation.

31. 'The History of the Ethiopian Jews'.

32. Hagar Salmon (ed.), *Ethiopia: Israel Communities in the East throughout the 19th and 20th Centuries*, Jerusalem: Ben-Tzvi Institute, 2007, p. 7; and Israel Association for Ethiopian Jews, accessed 23 Feb. 2011, http://iaej-english.org/

33. Mengistu came to power in a military coup in 1974, ending the rule of Emperor Haile Selassie. Mengistu found it expedient to maintain close military links with Israel, which was interested in preventing the Arab countries from succeeding in gaining complete control over the Red Sea through the secession of Eritrea. These military contacts were cut however by Mengistu in 1978 following the public exposure by Israel's Foreign Minister Moshe Dayan who spoke of Israel's support for Ethiopia. See Colin Legum, 'Africa and the Middle East', in *Middle East Contemporary Survey 1977–78*, New York: Holmes & Meier, 1979, p. 70.

34. Michael Bar-Zohar and Nissim Mishal, *The Mossad*, Tel Aviv: Yediot Ahronot Books, 2010, pp. 305–17.

35. Yuval Arnon-Ohana (ed.), *Hagadat Yetziat Mitzraim*, Tel Aviv: Misrad Ha-Bitachon, 2005.

36. Mahmoud Muhareb, *Israeli Interference*, pp. 9–10.

37. Gad Shimron, *The Mossad and its Myth*, Jerusalem: Keter, 2011, p. 211, referred to earlier clandestine cooperation between Israel and Marxist Ethiopia, which have well served Israel by providing it with the essentially needed logistics in the ports along the Eritrean coast on the Red Sea while transferring oil from Iran to Israel.

38. 'The History of the Ethiopian Jews'. 'I am Oassa Obbada', *Yediot Ahronot* (Tel Aviv, daily), 27 May 2001, and Shahar Genosar, 'Last Station, Sudan', *Yediot Ahronot*, 27 June 2003, 20.

39. Bishku, *Israel and Ethiopia*, p. 49.

40. Since the issues relating to Israel's clandestine diplomacy with Ethiopia and the transfer of the Beta Israel to Israel are not germane to the subject of this research work, the discussion does not deal with them.

41. Partiff, 'Operation Moses', p. 43.

42. Gad Shimron, *The Mossad*, pp. 215–16.

43. 'Falasha Airlift Fuels Regional Tension', *Africa Economic Digest* (London, weekly), 11 Jan. 1985.

44. Thomas L. Friedman, 'Israel-Run Airlift of Ethiopia's Jews from Sudan', *The New York Times*, 7 Jan. 1985, 1.

45. 'Out of Africa', *Jerusalem Post*, 31 Oct. 1986, pp. 17–18.

46. Friedman, 'Israel-Run Airlift of Ethiopia's Jews from Sudan'.

47. *Africa Economic Digest*, 11 Jan. 1985.

48. See e.g., Sudanese News Agency (SUNA, Khartoum), 6 Jan. 1985 (Daily Report [DR], 7 Jan. 1985). See also an interview with Umar Muhammad al-Tayyib, head of Sudan's Security Organisation and first vice president in *al-Hawadith* (London, weekly), 8 Feb. 1985.

49. SUNA, 6 Jan. 1985 (DR, 7 Jan. 1985).

50. *Africa Economic Digest*, 11 Jan. 1985.

51. For the repeated claims by the Sudanese, denied, however, by Ethiopia, see e.g., R. Omdurman, 13 Apr. 1985 (BBC Summary of World Broadcasts [SWB], 15 Apr. 1985); *Arabia and the Gulf*, 11 July 1977 and R. Omdurman, 2 Feb. 1984 (BBC SWB, 13 Feb. 1984). For more on these two countries' hostile relations at that time see Yehudit Ronen, 'Ethiopia's Involvement in the Sudanese Civil War: Was it as Significant as Khartoum Claimed?' *Northeast African Studies*, 9, 1 (2002), 103–26. Haggai Erlich, *Islam and Christianity in the Horn of Africa*, Boulder, CO: Lynne Rienner, 2010, pp. 11–43.

52. For background details on the roots and course of Sudan's civil war, see Mohamed Omer Beshir, *The Southern Sudan*, Khartoum: Khartoum University Press, 1970; Edgar O'Ballance, *The Secret War in the Sudan, 1955–1972*, Hamden, CT: Archon Books, 1977; Arou et al., *North–South Relations in the Sudan Since the Addis Ababa Agreement*; Mansour Khalid, *War and Peace in Sudan: A Tale of Two Countries*, London: Kegan Paul, 2003; and Yehudit Ronen, *Sudan in a Civil War: Between Africanism, Arabism and Islam*, Tel Aviv: Ha-Kibutz Ha-Mehuhad and Tel Aviv University, 1995.

53. SUNA, 6 Jan. 1985 (DR, 7 Jan. 1985).

54. *New York Times*, 24 Mar. 1985.

55. 'The History of the Ethiopian Jews'.

56. Sudan's ambassador in Kuwait, Kuwait News Agency (KUNA), 24 Mar. 1985 (DR, 25 Mar. 1985); Sudan's foreign minister in a press statement, SUNA, 30 Mar. 1985 (DR, 3 Apr. 1985).

57. For a detailed survey on Sudan's failed economy and bloody civil war during the mid-1980s, see Yehudit Ronen, 'The Democratic Republic of Sudan', in Itamar Rabinovich et al. (eds) *Middle East Contemporary Survey 1984–85*, Tel Aviv: The Moshe Dayan Center, Tel Aviv University, 1987, pp. xi, 616–20.

58. John O. Voll (ed.), *Sudan: State and Society in Crisis*, Bloomington and Indianapolis: Indiana University Press, 1991, p. viii.

59. R. Omdurman (Khartoum), 23 Nov. 1977 (BBC SWB, 24 Nov. 1977).

60. The 'pan-Arab Front of Steadfastness and Resistance', which included Syria, Libya, Algeria, the People's Democratic Republic of Yemen (South Yemen) and the Palestine Liberation Organization (PLO) spearheaded the rejection of the peace process with Israel.

61. *Arab Report and Record* (London, bi-weekly), 1–15 June 1977, p. 458.

62. R. Cairo, 14 Sep. 1976 (BBC SWB, 15 Sep. 1976); SUNA, 20–1 Dec. 1983 (DR, 21–2 Dec. 1983). See also Numayri's interview with *al-Hawadith*, 11 May 1983. See also *Sudanow* (Khartoum, monthly), Dec. 1983.

63. Raviv and Melman, *Every Spy a Prince*, p. 84.

64. *New York Times*, 24 Mar. 1985.

65. Dahab fulfilled his commitment to lead the country during one transitional year in order to smooth the way for the renewal of democratic life in Sudan. In Apr. 1986, Sudan's democratically elected Constituent Assembly convened in Khartoum for its first session. A short while later, Sadiq al-Mahdi's Umma leader, who had won the elections, established a new government, leading the country until 30 June 1989, when a new military and Islamist regime ascended to power under Umar Hasan Ahmad al-Bashir.

66. Gideon Rafael, *Destination Peace: Three Decades of Israeli Foreign Policy*, New York: Stein and Day, 1980, p. 78.

67. Geoff Berridge and Thomas G. Otte, *Diplomatic theory from Machiavelli to Kissinger: Studies in Diplomacy*, New York: Palgrave Macmillan, 2001, pp. 198–9.

10. SHADOWY INTERESTS: WEST GERMAN–ISRAELI INTELLIGENCE AND MILITARY COOPERATION, 1957–82

1. Much of the information contained in this chapter, unless otherwise cited, was obtained through a series of over fifty interviews with former German and Israeli intelligence officials, diplomats and decision-makers, conducted in the years 1995–2010. Most interviewees requested, and were promised, anonymity.

2. The subject of former Nazis in the BND has for decades been a taboo theme within the organisation. Only in 2011, responding to public pressure and a series

of revealing newspaper articles, did the BND appoint a commission of four historians to investigate the organisation's employment and association with Nazi war criminals.

3. Over the past decade a rich body of literature has emerged on the OG, fuelled by the release of thousands of US intelligence files dealing with the early years of West German intelligence. Perhaps the most comprehensive are James Critchfield, *Partners at the Creation: The Men Behind Postwar Germany's Defense and Intelligence Establishments*, Annapolis: US Naval Institute Press, 2003, and Jens Wegener, *Die Organisation Gehlen und die USA*, Berlin: Lit Verlag, 2008.

4. In his typical style of understatement Gehlen wrote 'After the Suez war of 1956 we began to take a more professional interest in the Israelis.' Reinhard Gehlen, *Der Dienst*, Meinz: Hase & Koehler, 1971, p. 287.

5. Isser Heral, born in Vitebsk, Poland, immigrated to Palestine in Jan. 1930. For his biography see Michael Bar-Zohar, *HaMemune* (*The One In Charge*), Tel Aviv, 1970, pp. 1–7.

6. Until 1965, Israel did not have an embassy in Germany. Israeli interests were represented by a liaison office known as the 'Israeli mission' in Cologne, conveniently located outside but in the vicinity of the capital Bonn.

7. BND personnel were assigned cover names for operational use. These cover names often began with the same letter as the person's real surname. Many Mossad officers never knew the real names of their BND counterparts, even after years of working together, since cover names were used even on social occasions. For 'Holten' see Frank Heigl and Jurgen Saupe, *Operation EVA: Die Affaere Langemann*, Berlin: Konkret Literatur Verlag, 1982, p. 81.

8. Wolfgang Langkau, born 1903, served during the Third Reich as an artillery officer and after the end of the war joined the OG. In 1957 he was appointed to head the 'Strategic Office', which he headed until his retirement in 1968. Partially as a mark of success to his relations with Israel he was promoted in 1962 to the rank of brigadier general. See Heinz Hoehne and Hermann Zolling, *Network*, London: Secker & Warburg, 1971, p. 207.

9. Ibid.

10. There are several versions regarding the unmasking of Felfe as a traitor. One version maintains that clues were provided by the Soviet KGB defector Anatoli Golytzin, who defected to the West five weeks before Felfe's arrest. This version is, however, somewhat in question due to the fact that the investigation against Felfe began many months before Golytzin's defection. Gehlen, who at first objected to his close friend Felfe being suspected, later claimed in his autobiography that he himself had initiated Felfe's investigation. This is, however, disputed by many former BND officers who knew that Gehlen was not ready to believe, almost until the last moment, that his protégé Felfe was in fact a Soviet spy. See Hoehne and Zolling, *Network*, pp. 229–49. Felfe was released in 1969;

see also 'Bonn Trades Top Soviet Agent For Three Students Jailed as Spies', *The New York Times*, 15 Feb. 1969.

11. Assessment of the damage caused by Felfe's treachery is detailed in CIA files released in response to the Nazi War Crimes Disclosure Act. See Name File 'Felfe, Heinz', 4 vols, National Archives and Records Administration [NARA], Record Group [RG] 263 (Records of the Central Intelligence Agency), CIA Name Files, Second Release, Boxes 22–3; 'Felfe, Heinz: Damage Assessment', NARA, RG 263, CIA Subject Files, Second Release, Box 1; 'KGB Exploitation of Heinz Felfe: Successful KGB Penetration of a Western Intelligence Service', Mar. 1969, NARA, RG 263, CIA Subject Files, Second Release, Box 1.

12. The BND daily report to the Kanzler is among the highest-classified of all documents in the German government and is restricted to a small circle of officials at the Kanzler's Office (Bundeskanzleramt).

13. Harel openly opposed that policy and resigned in 1963 as a result of arguments with Ben-Gurion over Germany.

14. The author is in possession of a short film made during the tank experiments attended by Held, and an interview Held gave to British television detailing his discovery.

15. Shpiro Shlomo, 'Cold War Radar Intelligence: Operation Cerberus', *Journal of Intelligence History*, 6, 2 (2006), pp. 61–74.

16. See Yaacov Erez and Ilan Kfir, *The Israeli Air Force*, Tel Aviv: Revivim Publishers, 1981, p. 60.

17. Shpiro, 'Operation Cerberus', pp. 61–74.

18. For Penkovsky's career see Jeffery Richelson, *A Century of Spies*, New York: Oxford University Press, 1995, pp. 274–9.

19. After Penkovsky's death the CIA leaked a small part of the information he provided to journalist Frank Gibney, who published them under the title *The Penkovsky Papers*. These, however, were just a few of the over 10,000 pages of reports gleaned from Penkovsky's various debriefings, rolls of film and written reports.

20. Most of the relatively few Israeli aircraft losses were due to fire from the ground, mainly by SAM missiles. See Zeev Shiff, *Phantom over the Nile*, Haifa: Shikmona Publishing, 1970, p. 98.

21. Chaim Herzog, *The War of Atonement*, Jerusalem: Idanim Publishers, 1983, pp. 181–9.

22. Itzhak Shoshan, *The Last Battle of I.N.S. 'Eilat'*, Tel-Aviv: Maariv, 1993, pp. 156–9, 246.

23. Some experts thought this would only be possible in projecting a small, defused image, but not one which could precisely emulate a ship or aircraft. Ibid., pp. 156–9.

24. Ibid., p. 246.

25. Leber instructed that the people indoctrinated with the CERBERUS project

must 'observe the highest possible discretion in every aspect (auf strengste Diskretion in allen Bereichen achten)'. Quoted in a confidential report to the German minister of defence, Bonn, 8 Aug. 1990.

26. German Ministry of Defence, *BMVg Bericht—Ablauf und Stand des Vorhabens Stoer- und Taeuschsenders CERBERUS/TSPJ*, p. 92.

27. Ibid., pp. 83–5.

28. The issue of Soviet radar frequencies played a major role in US intelligence activities against the Soviet Union. As early as 1950, the CIA set up various electronic 'radar listening posts' in Europe to identify radar signals, and later also tried to obtain Soviet radar readings by using specially modified Liberty ships stationed off Soviet coasts. See William Burrows, *Deep Black—The Secrets of Space Espionage*, London: Bantam, 1988, pp. 56–8.

29. Israeli military intelligence had already possessed an older version of this radar, P-30, but this system was incapable of detecting low-flying aircraft and that is why it was being replaced by the Egyptians with the vastly superior P-12. Schiff, *The Israeli Airforce*, p. 121.

30. Ibid.

31. Husum has long been used as a base for both BND and Bundeswehr intelligence activities. See Erich Schmidt-Eenboom, *Der BND*, Dusseldorf: Econ, 1993, pp. 225, 237.

32. Shpiro, 'Cold War Radar Intelligence', 2006, pp. 61–74.

33. Richelson mentioned the CIA side of the agreement but does not refer to the BND's role in this arrangement. Jeffrey Richelson, *The US Intelligence Community*, Boulder: Westview, 1995, p. 280.

34. Erich Schmidt-Eenboom, *Der BND*, Duesseldorf: Econ, 1993, p. 245.

35. In public, the CERBERUS system was presented as having been developed by the German firm of AEG. See *International Defence Review*, 18, 18 (1985), p. 174.

36. For the process of planning and formulation of strategy at the West German Ministry of Defence and Bundeswehr see Werner von Scheven and Hartmut Schmidt-Petri, *Die Bundeswehr*, Mannheim: Meyers, 1987, pp. 96–7.

37. This strategy meant a NATO nuclear response proportional to the level of attack launched against it. Such a strategy required more diverse nuclear weapon delivery methods which could survive a Soviet nuclear attack and still maintain such a response (second-strike capability) so as to deter attack in the first place. See Karl-Heinz Kamp, *Die Nuklearen Kurzstreckenwaffen der NATO 1945–1991: Strategie und Politik*, Sankt Augustin: KAS, 1993, pp. 121–84.

38. There is a wide body of literature on NATO nuclear strategy of that period. For detailed analyses see John Baylis and John Garnett, *Makers of Nuclear Strategy*, London: Palgrave MacMillan, 1991; Daniel Charles, *Nuclear Planning in NATO*, Cambridge: Ballinger, 1987; Donald Cotter, *The Nuclear Balance in Europe*,

Washington, DC: United States Strategic Institute, 1987; Michael Legge, *Theater Nuclear Weapons and NATO Strategy of Flexible Response*, Santa Monika: Rand, 1983.

39. Mechtersheimer, *MRCA TORNADO*, Bad Honnef: Osang Verlag, 1977, pp. 99–108.
40. For the issue of US–German command sharing over nuclear weapons, often referred to as 'dual-key systems', and problems of sharing the control of nuclear weapons in wartime see Kamp, *Die Nuklearen Kurzstreckenwaffen*, 1993, pp. 200–5, 222–33.

11. PUBLIC TENSIONS, PRIVATE TIES: IRELAND, ISRAEL AND THE POLITICS OF MUTUAL MISUNDERSTANDING

1. National Archives of Ireland (hereafter NAI) Department of the Taoiseach (hereafter DT) S/14330. Telegram from Moshe Shertok, Ministry of Foreign Affairs, Jerusalem, to Minister for External Affairs, Dublin, 27 May 1948.
2. NAI DT S/14330. Telegram from James J Comerford, Sean Keating, Paul O'Dwyer and Joseph McLaughlin to John A Costello, Taioseach, 2 June 1948.
3. See Michael Brecher, *The Foreign Policy of Israel: Setting, Images, Process*, London and Oxford: Oxford University Press, 1972, p. 440.
4. See Fintan O'Toole, 'The other side of Arthur Griffith', *Irish Times*, 15 Aug. 1992; Brian Maye, 'Griffith was an Irish nationalist and not fascist', *Irish Times*, 28 Aug. 1992.
5. For Irish responses to the Balfour Declaration see *Supplement to Zionist Review*, 1, 8 (Dec. 1917), pp. 3–14.
6. Chaim Herzog, *Living History: A Memoir*, London, New York: Pantheon, 1996, p. 12.
7. See Shulamit Eliash, *The Harp and The Shield of David: Zionism and the State of Israel*, London: Routledge, 2007, p. 43.
8. David Vital, *A People Apart: The Jews in Europe, 1789–1939*, Oxford: Oxford University Press, 1999, pp. 296–7, n. 18.
9. Conor Cruise-O'Brien, *The Siege: The Story of Israel and Zionism*, London: Paladin Books, 1988, pp. 331–2, p. 14.
10. Richard P. Stevens, 'The Vatican, the Catholic Church and Jerusalem', *Journal of Palestine Studies*, X, 3 (Spring 1981), pp. 100–10, p. 107.
11. Joseph Morrison Skelly, *Irish Diplomacy at the United Nations*, Dublin: Irish Academic Press, 1997, p. 39.
12. See Secretary, DT, to Con Cremin, DEA, 17 Jan. 1959 and memorandum from Leo T. McCauley, Irish Ambassador to the Holy See, to the Secretary, DEA, 12 Nov. 1958, NAI DT/S 16583.
13. Walter Eytan, *The First Ten Years: A Diplomatic History of Israel*, New York: Simon and Schuster, 1958, p. 14.

14. *Dáil Debates*, vol. 171, col. 970, 26 Nov. 1958.

15. Boland eventually won this election, beating Icelandic and Czech candidates and gaining the support of most of the Western bloc of nations as well as many of the old Commonwealth states.

16. NAI Department of Foreign Affairs (hereafter DFA) 2001/43/119. Ambassador in London to Secretary, DEA, 13 Sep. 1960.

17. NAI DFA PS35/1. Cremin to Boland, 17 June 1961.

18. Ibid.

19. Oral History Project, Institute of Contemporary Jewry, Hebrew University of Jerusalem, Project 1 (82). See Nurock Interview, State Administration in Palestine, 30 Aug. 1970, p. 2.

20. NAI DFA 2001/43/119. Minutes of Nurock's meeting with Aiken, 31 Jan. 1962.

21. NAI DFA 438/21/21. DFA minutes attached to discussion on Gifts to the Hebrew University, 26 June 1962.

22. See DEA to DT, 30 July 1965, NAI DFA 98/6/219.

23. See report on German Diplomatic Relations with Israel, by Ambassador Kennedy, Bonn, 24 May 1965, NAI DFA 2001/43/119. Moreover, none of the Arab states had retaliated against West Germany by granting recognition to East Germany, a concern that had long preoccupied Bonn.

24. *Irish Press*, 4 Mar. 1963.

25. See, for example, *Europe Agency Reports*, 8 Feb. 1964, 19 Feb. 1964 and 16 Apr. 1964.

26. *Financial Times*, 5 Oct. 1966.

27. See Brendan Dillon, Irish Mission, Brussels, to O'Sullivan, Assistant Secretary, DEA, 11 Oct. 1966, NAI DFA 98/3/337.

28. Report from MJ Quinn, Irish Embassy London to DEA, 24 Mar. 1966, NAI DFA 99/1/207.

29. See DEA to Mr R. Cuffe, Department of Agriculture, 23 Mar. 1965 and memorandum on Review Conference of Commonwealth Agricultural Bureaux, DEA, 17 June 1965, NAI 2001 DFA 43/119.

30. Gideon Rafael, *Destination Peace: Three Decades of Israeli Foreign Policy, A Personal Memoir*, New York: Stein and Day, 1981, p. 359.

31. See Alfred Joachim Fischer, 'Eire and Israel Establish Diplomatic Relations: Background Information on the Exchange of Ambassadors', *Contemporary Review* (1975), pp. 285–9

32. Ambassador Shlomo Argov, 'The Choice Before Europe', Address before the Diplomatic and Commonwealth Writers Association of Britain, London 15 June, 1981, reprinted in *An Ambassador Speaks Out: Speech and Writing*, London and Jerusalem: Weidenfeld & Nicolson and the Van Leer Jerusalem Foundation, 1983, p. 203.

33. Rafael, *Destination Peace*, p. 359.
34. See statement by Minister Cosgrave at UNGA Plenary meeting 603, 30 Nov. 1956, *Official Records of the General Assembly, 11th Session*, New York: United Nations, vol. 1, p. 452.
35. Ibid., p. 454.
36. NAI DFA 2001/43/119. Minutes of a meeting between Max Nurock, Israeli Foreign Ministry and Frank Aiken, the Minister for External Affairs, Dublin 24 Jan. 1962, 31 Jan. 1962.
37. NAI DFA 2001/43/872. Statement by Mr Frank Aiken, T.D., Tanaiste and Minister for External Affairs of Ireland on the Question of Palestine Arab Refugees, in the Special Political Committee of the 22nd Session of the General Assembly of the United Nations, 14 Dec. 1967.
38. Arthur Lall, *The UN and the Middle East Crisis*, New York: Columbia University Press, 1968, pp. 151–2.
39. NAI DFA 2001/43/99. Cremin to McCann, 11 July 1967.
40. See, for example, Alain Dieckhoff, 'Europe and the Arab World: The Difficult Dialogue', in Ilan Greilsammer and Joesph HH Weiler (eds), *Europe and Israel, Troubled Neighbours*, Berlin and New York: Walter De Gruyter, 1988, p. 273.
41. Israeli Foreign Ministry statement on UNGA Resolution 3210, 15 Oct. 1974, *Israel's Foreign Relations: Selected Documents*, (hereafter *Israel Documents*), Jerusalem: Ministry of Foreign Affairs, vol. 3, p. 104.
42. Avi Beker, *The United Nations and Israel: From Recognition to Reprehension*, Lexington, MA and Toronto: Lexington Books, 1988, p. 82.
43. Statement by Deputy Prime Minister and Foreign Minister Allon to Heads of Diplomatic Missions in Israel, 14 Nov. 1974, *Israel Documents*, vol. 3, p. 128; Rafael, *Destination Peace*, p. 359.
44. Garret Fitzgerald, *All in a Life: An Autobiography*, London: Macmillan, 1991, pp. 159–61.
45. See 'Dr Fitzgerald visits Middle East' and 'EEC Ministers in Dublin' in *Bulletin of the Department of Foreign Affairs*, 866, 9 June 1975, pp. 7–8.
46. TNA, FCO 30/3028. Minister of State Report on Euro-Arab Dialogue at Dublin Meeting, 28 May 1975.
47. *Seanad [Irish Senate] Debates*, vol. 125, col. 873, 7 June 1990.
48. Irish Government Communique, 10 Feb. 1980, Irish Government Information Service. See also *Irish Times*, 20 Feb. 1980.
49. See *Bahrain Declaration: Ireland's Definitive Official Commitment to an Independent Palestine*, Dublin: Eurabia Irish Office, 1980.
50. See, for example, *Ma'ariv*, 12 Feb. 1980.
51. See *New York Times*, 21 Apr. 1980; *London Times*, 28 Apr. 1980.
52. Summary of a meeting between Foreign Minister Peres and Minister for Foreign Affairs Spring of Ireland, 18 June 1995, *Israel Yearbook*, vol. 15, 1995–6,

p. 27. Interview with Ambassador Oded Eran, 'Middle East Conflict: Counting the Cost', *Business & Finance*, 14 Dec. 2000.

53. Address by PLO chairman Arafat to Oireachtas Joint Committee on Foreign Affairs, 16 Dec. 1993. See also *Irish Times*, 4 May 1999.

54. Israel Eldad, 'Dis-Orient House', *Yedioth Ahronoth*, 23 June 1995.

55. *Irish Times*, 21 and 22 Jan. 1999.

56. See *Jerusalem Post*, 3 May 1999 and 'Eight States to Upgrade Relations with Palestinians', *The Israel Report* (May–June 1999), p. 5.

57. *ArabicNews.com*, 9 May 1998.

58. *Irish Times*, 22 Sep. 1999 and 9 Nov. 2001. See also opinion piece by Palestinian delegate-general to Ireland, Ali Halimeh, 'Palestine's Future', *Irish Times*, 15 Mar. 2003.

59. *Irish Times*, 16 Oct. 2001.

60. *Irish Independent*, 15 Dec. 2001.

61. Dáil Debate, vol. 552, col. 169, 17 Apr. 2002. See also statement by UN Ambassador Richard Ryan in the Security Council on the situation in the Middle East, including the question of Palestine, Department of Foreign Affairs (hereafter DFA) press release, 29 Mar. 2002 and also *Irish Times*, 30 Mar. 2002.

62. *Irish Times*, 10 Apr. 2002.

63. *Irish Times*, 27 June 2003.

64. See Estimates: Public Services 2001—vote 38, Department of Foreign Affairs (revised), Oireachtas Select Committee on Foreign Affairs, 20 June 2001.

65. www.aertel.ie/news, 10 Sep. 2001 (accessed on 5 July 2010).

66. *Dáil Debates*, vol. 524, col. 883, 19 Oct. 2000.

67. *Irish Times*, 16 Oct. 2001.

68. Taoiseach condemns killing of Israel's minister of tourism, Department of Taoiseach press release, 17 Oct. 2001.

69. *Ha'aretz* [English Edition], 23 Oct. 2001; *Irish Times*, 29 Oct. 2001.

70. *Irish Times*, 28 Feb. 2002.

71. Statement by UN Ambassador Richard Ryan in the Security Council on the situation in the Middle East, including the question of Palestine, DFA press release, 29 Mar. 2002.

72. Minister Cowen calls for immediate implementation of Security Council resolution on the Middle East, DFA press release, 30 Mar. 2002.

73. See, for example, statements by Ambassador Richard Ryan on the situation in the Middle East, including the question of Palestine, 15 Mar. and 20 Aug. 2001, http://www.un.int/ireland/scstatements/sc32.htm

74. *Irish Times*, 14 Mar. 2002

75. Possible links between republican paramilitaries and Palestinian terror groups were raised in the context of rising Irish–PLO ties by supporters of Israel in the Dáil. Other than that the matter rarely gained a mention. This is in sharp con-

trast to the widespread controversy aroused by Libya's relationship with the IRA during the 1980s.

76. *Irish Times*, 11 Sep. 2001.

77. Ibid. Cowen repeated this in his subsequent address to the National Committee on American Foreign Policy, New York, 30 Oct. 2001, DFA press release, 30 Oct. 2001.

78. *Irish Times*, 22 Apr. 2002.

79. Minister Cowen condemns suicide bombings 'outrage' in Israel, DFA press release, 8 May 2002.

80. See statement by Prime Minister Barak to London press conference, Israeli Foreign Ministry press release, 23 Nov. 1999.

81. *Irish Times*, 26 June 2003.

82. *Irish Times*, 15 Dec. 2003

83. Speech by Minister for Foreign Affairs, Mr Brian Cowen, TD, Tel Aviv University, 15 Jan. 2004, http://www.irlgov.ie/iveagh (accessed 16 July 2010).

84. *Ha'aretz Online* [English edition], 23 May 2004

85. Ambassador Zvi Gabay, 'Providing a home for every Jew who requires a haven', *Irish Times*, n.d.

12. ISRAELI TRACK II DIPLOMACY: THE BEILIN–ABU MAZEN UNDERSTANDINGS

1. The Palestinian academics involved prefer the term 'the Stockholm document' since the talks primarily took place in and around the Swedish capital. In this chapter, the document is referred to as 'the Understandings'.

2. Agha et al., *Track II Diplomacy: Lessons from the Middle East*, Cambridge, MA: MIT Press, 2003, p. 1.

3. Menachem Klein and Riad Malki, 'Israeli–Palestinian Track II Diplomacy', in Edy Kaufman, Walid Salem and Juliette Verhoeven (eds), *Bridging the Divide: Peace building in the Israeli–Palestinian Conflict*, London: Lynne Rienner, 2006, p. 113.

4. Agha et al., *Track II Diplomacy*, p. 4–5.

5. Ari Shavit, 'Beilin–Abu Mazen and no further', *Ha'aretz*, 2 Nov. 2001.

6. Aaron Klieman, *Israeli Diplomacy in the Back-Channel*, Davis Occasional Papers, no. 80, Jerusalem: The Leonard Davis Institute for International Relations, 2000, p. 10.

7. Uri Savir, *The Process: 1100 days that Changed the Middle East*, New York: Random House, 1998, p. 80.

8. Khalil Shikaki, 'Ending the Conflict: Can the Parties Afford It?' in Robert Rothstein, Moshe Ma'oz and Khalil Shikaki (eds), *The Israeli–Palestinian Peace Process: Oslo and the Lessons of Failure*, Brighton: Sussex Academic Press, 2002, pp. 40–6; Interview with Ron Pundak, Tel Aviv, 7 May 2009.

9. Interview with Yair Hirschfeld, Tel Aviv, 17 May 2009.

10. Interview with Ron Pundak, Tel Aviv, 7 May 2009. This argument is echoed in Robert Rothstein, 'Fragile Peace and Its Aftermath', in Robert Rothstein (ed.), *After the Peace: Resistance and Reconciliation*, Boulder, CO: Lynne Rienner Publishers, 1999, pp. 223–5, and Aaron Miller, 'The Pursuit of Israeli–Palestinian Peace: A Retrospective', in Robert Rothstein, Moshe Ma'oz and Khalil Shikaki (eds), *The Israeli–Palestinian Peace Process: Oslo and the Lessons of Failure*, Brighton: Sussex Academic Press, 2002, p. 32.

11. Interview with Yossi Beilin, Tel Aviv, 12 May 2009.

12. Interview with Ron Pundak, Tel Aviv, 7 May 2009.

13. Interview with Yair Hirschfeld, Tel Aviv, 17 May 2009.

14. Interview with Ahmad Khalidi, London, 9 Sep. 2010; Agha et al., *Track II Diplomacy*, p. 72.

15. Interview with Yair Hirschfeld, Tel Aviv, 17 May 2009.

16. Interview with Ron Pundak, Tel Aviv, 7 May 2009.

17. Interview with Yair Hirschfeld, Tel Aviv, 17 May 2009.

18. Yossi Beilin, *Touching Peace: From the Oslo Accord to a Final Agreement*, London: Weidenfeld & Nicolson, 1999, p. 181; Agha et al., *Track II Diplomacy*, p. 80.

19. Beilin, *Touching Peace*, pp. 71–2

20. Ibid., p. 74

21. Klieman, *Israeli Diplomacy*, p. 14.

22. Savir, *The Process*, p. 96; interview with Yair Hirschfeld, Tel Aviv, 17 May 2009.

23. Agha et al., *Track II Diplomacy*, p. 81

24. Swedish Labour Movement Archives, Sten Andersson's Archive, Series 4.2: Vol. 6. Letter from Schori to Andersson, 'Breakfast with Beilin in Jerusalem, 11/04/1995'.

25. Interview with Yossi Beilin, Tel Aviv, 12 May 2009.

26. Interviews with Ahmad Khalidi, London, 9 Sep. 2010, and Hussein Agha, London, 13 Sep. 2010.

27. Interview with Ron Pundak, Tel Aviv, 7 May 2009.

28. Interview with Yossi Beilin, Tel Aviv, 12 May 2009.

29. Interview with Ahmad Khalidi, London, 9 Sep. 2010.

30. Agha, *Track II Diplomacy*, pp. 82–3; interview with Ann Dismorr, Stockholm, 17 Apr. 2009.

31. Interviews with Ron Pundak, Tel Aviv, 7 May 2009, and Yair Hirschfeld, Tel Aviv, 17 May 2009; Agha et al., *Track II Diplomacy*, pp. 72, 82–3.

32. Interview with Ron Pundak, Tel Aviv, 7 May 2009.

33. Interview with Yossi Beilin, Tel Aviv, 12 May 2009.

34. Beilin, *Touching Peace*, p. 183.

35. 'Documents and Source Material', *Journal of Palestine Studies*, 26, 1 (1996), pp. 148–52.

36. Interview with Yossi Beilin, Tel Aviv, 12 May 2009.

37. Ibid.

38. Beilin, *Touching Peace*, p. 184

39. Interviews with Yossi Beilin, Tel Aviv, 12 May 2009, and Ahmad Khalidi, London, 9 Sep. 2010.

40. Neil Lochery, *The Difficult Road to Peace: Netanyahu, Israel, and the Middle East Peace Process*, Reading: Ithaca Press, 1996, p. 104.

41. Gerald Steinberg, 'Peace, Security and Terror in the 1996 Elections', in Daniel Elazar and Shmuel Sandler (eds), *Israel at the Polls, 1996*, London: Frank Cass, 1998, pp. 219–20.

42. Ari Shavit, 'Beilin–Abu Mazen and no further,' *Ha'aretz*, 2 Nov. 2001.

43. Klieman, *Israel Diplomacy in the Back Channel*, pp. 24–5.

44. 'Documents and Source Material', pp. 148–52.

45. Interview with Yossi Beilin, Tel Aviv, 12 May 2009; Giora Goldberg, 'The Electoral Fall of the Israeli Left', in Elazar and Sandler (eds), *Israel at the Polls, 1996*, p. 57.

46. 'Suicide and Bombing Attacks since the DoP (Sept. 1993)', http://www.mfa.gov.il/MFA/Terrorism-+Obstacle+to+Peace/Palestinian+terror+since+2000/Suicide+and+Other+Bombing+Attacks+in+Israel+Since.htm, accessed on 15 Oct. 2011.

47. Barry Rubin, 'External Influences on the Israeli Elections', in Elazar and Sandler (eds), *Israel at the Polls*, p. 158.

48. Ibid., pp. 159–62.

49. Steinberg, 'Peace, Security, and Terror', pp. 215–16, 218.

50. Daniel Elazar and Shmuel Sandler, 'Introduction: The Battle over Jewishness and Zionism in the Post-Modern Era', in Elazar and Sandler (eds), *Israel at the Polls, 1996*, p. 9

51. 'Documents and Source Material', p. 149.

52. Yossi Beilin, *The Path to Geneva: The Quest for a Permanent Agreement, 1996–2004*, New York: RDV Books, 2004, p. 98.

53. Goldberg, 'The Electoral Fall of the Israeli Left', p. 55.

54. Jonathan Mendilow, 'The Likud's Double Campaign: Between the Devil and the Deep Blue Sea', in Asher Arian and Michal Shamir (eds), *The Elections in Israel, 1996*, Albany, NY: State University of New York Press, 1999, p. 198.

55. Interview with Yossi Beilin, Tel Aviv, 12 May, 2009.

56. 'Documents and Source Material', p. 149.

57. Beilin, *Path to Geneva*, pp. 94–6.

58. Agha et al., *Track II Diplomacy*, p. 75.

59. Ibid., p. 86.

60. Interviews with Ahmad Khalidi, London, 9 Sep. 2010, and Hussein Agha, London, 13 Sep. 2010.

61. Ibid.
62. Interview with Hussein Agha, London, 13 Sep. 2010.
63. Beilin, *Path to Geneva*, pp. 153–4.
64. Interview with Yossi Beilin, Tel Aviv, 12 May 2009.
65. Klieman, *Israeli Diplomacy in the Back-Channel*, pp. 15–16.
66. Ibid., pp. 26–7.
67. Interview with Hussein Agha, London, 13 Sep. 2010.

13. THE DEAL THAT NEVER WAS: ISRAEL'S CLANDESTINE NEGOTIATIONS WITH SYRIA, 1991–2000

1. On the Madrid Conference and particularly on the Israeli–Syrian negotiations that took place there see Ahron Bregman and Jihan el Tahri, *The Fifty Years War: Israel and the Arabs*, London: BBC Books/Penguin, 1998, pp. 218–21.
2. Interview with Ambassador Itamar Rabinovich for *The Fifty Years War*, London, no date, Liddell Hart Archive, King's College London.
3. This and the following are based on Ahron Bregman's interview with Warren Christopher, Los Angeles, 23 Jan. 1998, in the author's archive.
4. Yitzhak Rabin–Warren Christopher transcript of conversation, Jerusalem, 3 Aug. 1993, private source, in the author's archive.
5. Private source; also Patrick Seale in *Al-Hayat*, London, 22 Nov. 1999.
6. Ibid.
7. Private source.
8. Bregman and el Tahri, *The Fifty Years War*, pp. 253–5.
9. Patrick Seale in *Al-Hayat*, London, 21 Nov. 1999.
10. This and the following are based on a transcript of a Rabin–Christopher conversation, 18 July 1994, private source, in the author's archive.
11. From transcript of conversation Christopher–Assad, Damascus, 19 July 1994, in author's archive.
12. Interview with Ehud Barak, Tel Aviv, 17 Nov. 1997, in the author's archive.
13. On the Barak–Shihabi Washington meeting see Bregman and el Tahri, *The Fifty Years War*, pp. 265–6.
14. On this period, see Bregman and el Tahri, *The Fifty Years War*, Chapter 35, pp. 266–72.
15. On this see, Uri Sagie, *The Frozen Hand*, Tel Aviv: Yedioth Ahronoth Books, 2011, pp. 33–4 [in Hebrew].
16. Private source and also Martin Indyk, *Innocent abroad: An Intimate Account of American Peace Diplomacy in the Middle East*, New York: Simon & Schuster, 2009, p. 250.
17. Interview with Madeleine Albright for *Elusive Peace*, Washington, 19 Jan. 2005, in the author's archive.

18. Interview with Ehud Barak, for *Elusive Peace*, Tel Aviv, 1 Nov. 2004, in the author's archive and at the Liddell Hart Centre, King's College, London.

19. Ibid.

20. Martin Indyk, *Innocent Abroad*, p. 268.

21. The following points are based on the original March document ('The Script'), private source.

22. This and the following quotes are from a transcript of a Clinton–Barak telephone conversation, 26 Mar. 2000, 13:10, private source. The full text appears in Ahron Bregman, *Cursed Victory: A History of Israel and the Occupied Territories*, London: Penguin, 2013.

23. The above is based on a transcript of Clinton–Barak telephone conversation, 26 Mar. 2000, 20:45, private source.

CONCLUSION

1. Mark Perry, 'Israel's Secret Staging Ground', *Foreign Policy*, 28 Mar. 2012. www.foreignpolicy.com/articles/2012/03/28/israel_s_secret_staging_ground? (accessed 3 Apr. 2012).

2. Malcolm H. Kerr, *The Arab Cold War: Gamal 'Abd al-Nasir and His Rivals*, London: Oxford University Press, 1967.

3. Vance to Carter, 'The US Relationship with Iran', 10 Nov. 1977, NLC-5-5-7-12-1, Jimmy Carter Library, Atlanta, Georgia.

4. Bill Clinton, *My Life*, New York: Knopf Publishing Group, 2004, p. 739.

5. American embassy Manama to State Department, 8 Mar. 1978, JCL.

6. TNA FCO 8/3536/NBL 020/1, Memorandum of conversation of UK officials with Qaboos and Zawawi, 16 Oct. 1980, Foreign and Commonwealth Office.

INDEX

Abbas, Mahmoud (Abu Mazen): 214,
218, 221–2; member of PLO, 210,
213; Palestinian Prime Minister,
204

Abbud, General Ibrahim: rise to
power (1958), 159

Abdullah I, King: 7, 40, 42, 44;
background of, 34–5; family of,
34–5, 37; political engagement
with Zionists, 32–6, 40–1, 43–7;
property owned by, 36; reign of, 45

Abujaber, Sa'id Pasha: 39

al-'Adwan, Sultan: 39

Afghanistan: Operation Enduring
Freedom, 177; Soviet Invasion of
(1979–89), 183

Africanisation: 139; concept of, 138

Agha, Hussein: 216; role in Beilin-
Abu Mazen Understandings, 210

Agranat Commission: 19

Ahdut Ha-Avoda: merger with Mapai
(1965), 16

Ahern, Bertie: meeting with Yasser
Arafat, 203–5; Taoiseach of Republic of Ireland, 203

Aiken, Frank: 194; Irish Foreign Minister, 193, 198–9

Ala, Abu: Palestinian negotiator for
Oslo I Accords, 216

Albania: 65

Albright, Madeline: US Secretary of
State, 222–3, 233; visit to Syria, 233

Ali, General Ahmed Ismail: Egyptian
Defence Minister, 179; visit to
USSR (1972), 179

bin Ali, Sharif Hussein: family of, 35,
37

Aliyev, Ilham: President of Azerbaijan,
241

Alon, Moshe: 90, 92, 96; background
of, 125

Allon, Yigal: 127, 134; Israeli Deputy
Prime Minister, 127; Israeli Foreign
Minister, 152, 201

Amer, Abd al-Hakim: Egyptian
Defence Minister, 107

Amin Dada, Idi: 10, 143, 147, 150;
military career of, 143–4; political
opponents of, 145–6; severance
of diplomatic relations with Israel
(1972), 137–8, 149–50, 152; rise
to power (1971), 138, 144–5

Amit, Meir: 128, 133–4; head of
Mossad, 3, 9, 107, 132, 173; Israeli
Director of Military Intelligence,
107

Amir, Yigal: role in assassination of
Yitzhak Rabin (1995), 216

INDEX

INDEX

INDEX

Lieberman, Avigdor: nomination for Israeli Foreign Minister, 27

Likud Party: 15, 20–1, 24, 26, 217; electoral campaign of (1996), 220–1, 230; members of, 221, 225

Lissak, Moshe: concept of 'regimented voluntarism', 16

Livni, Tzipi: Israeli Foreign Minister, 1

Lochery, Neill: *The Difficult Road to Peace*, 218

Lourie, Arthur: Israeli Ambassador to UK, 194

Lubrani, Uri: Israeli Ambassador to Uganda, 140, 143

MacMichael, Sir Harold: British High Commissioner in Palestine, 59

Madrid Conference (1991): 225

Maher, Ahmed: Egyptian Foreign Minister, 207

Mahjoub, Muhammad Ahmad: 159

Mali: 152

mamlachtiyut: 6–7, 18–19; concept of, 16; influence over Israeli foreign policy, 21; weakening of, 19–20, 27

Mapai: 16–17; members of, 16, 127, 135; merger with Ahdut Ha-Avoda (1965), 16

McLaughlin, Joseph: 190

McNamara, Robert: 132, 134; US Secretary of Defense, 123, 130

Menderes, Adnan: 91–2, 95–6; arrest and execution of (1961), 98; Turkish Prime Minister, 90

Meir, Golda: 94, 96–7, 129, 136, 146; administration of, 126; background of, 125; general secretary of Mapai Party, 135; Israeli Foreign Minister, 91, 127, 142, 158; view of diplomacy, 127

Mengitsu, Haile Mariam: 161

Mexico: oil exports from, 79

Middle East Peace Summit at Camp David (2000): 222; attendees of, 4

Minerbi, Sergio: Israeli Ambassador to EEC, 197

Mordechai, Yitzhak: 231

Morocco: 196

Mossad: 10, 73, 75–6, 146–7, 171–3, 175, 183, 216; personnel of, 1, 3, 8–9, 74, 76–7, 83, 107, 113, 132–3, 141, 143, 150, 171, 175, 187, 236; relationships with BND, 170, 174–6, 180, 182–3, 185, 187; Tevel, 3; training of Ugandan security services, 141, 150

Mossad Le'Aliyah Bet: 52

Mossadegh, Mohamed: leader of National Front Party, 77; nationalisation of assets of AIOC (1951), 70, 80–1; Prime Minister of Iran, 70

Moualem, Walid: Israeli Ambassador to USA, 229

Nahal: 138

al-Nasser, Gamal Abd: 93, 96, 107, 114–15, 119, 128, 156, 159, 245; associates of, 115–16; death of, 144; influence of, 159; *Le Monde* interview (1963), 106; President of Egypt, 9, 104, 139

National Iranian Oil Company (NIOC): 82; establishment of, 81

nationalism: 17, 66; Arab, 9, 38, 40–1, 46, 93; ethnic, 7, 13, 15, 18–19, 22, 28, 30; Irish, 189, 191; religious, 26–7

Netanyahu, Binyamin: 1, 207, 219, 223; *A Place Among the Nations*, 28; electoral performance of (1996), 220–1; foreign policy of, 230–1;

302

Tunisia: 196; Tunis, 212

Turkey: 62, 76, 92, 159; Ankara, 85, 88, 90, 92, 94, 242; diplomatic relationship with Israel, 8, 73, 78, 85–90, 96–8, 100–1; Justice Party, 99; member of NATO, 89; military coup (1960), 98; Ministry of Foreign Affairs, 89; recognition of Israel (1949), 78

Uganda: 141, 151; Acholi tribe, 144; Air Force, 147; borders of, 146; diplomatic relationship with Israel, 9, 140–1, 144–5, 149–52, 244; independence of (1962), 137; Kampala, 10, 138, 141, 143, 148, 152, 244; military of, 139–41, 143, 147; military procurement from Israel, 142–3, 145–6; Muslim population of, 140

af Ugglas, Margareta: Swedish Foreign Minister, 213

Ukraine: Sevastopol, 61

United Arab Emirates (UAE): 1

United Arab Republic (UAR): 131; collapse of (1961), 108; establishment of (1958), 92–3, 159; members of, 92–3, 104

United Kingdom (UK): 3, 77, 139, 144, 180, 184; Colonial Office, 49, 53; Directorate of Military Intelligence Section 9 (MI9), 51–2, 61–2, 64, 66; Foreign and Commonwealth Office, 49, 55, 113, 190; government of, 34–5, 50, 68, 113, 201, 206; Jewish population of, 190; Labour Party, 113; London, 11, 33, 35, 39, 49, 53, 69, 71, 93, 112–13, 129, 139, 157, 192, 194, 197–8, 210, 212; military of, 50–1, 60, 125, 177; Secret Intelligence Service (MI6/SIS), 51,

53–4, 57, 61–2, 157, 178; Security Service (MI5), 51; Special Air Service (SAS), 112; Special Operations Executive (SOE), 51–2, 55, 58–60, 62, 66; War Office, 63

United Nations (UN): 86, 92, 107, 133–4, 136–7, 147, 192, 198–9, 208, 244; Emergency Force (UNEF), 128; General Assembly, 95–7, 147, 194, 198–200; Interim Force in Lebanon (UNIFIL), 201–2; members of, 193–4; personnel of, 152; Security Council, 96–7, 122, 124, 195, 200–2, 205–6; Special Committee on Palestine, 124

United States of America (USA): 128, 144, 152, 161, 192, 199; Central Intelligence Agency (CIA), 75, 123, 130, 164, 172, 177–8; Congress, 131; diplomatic relationships with Israel, 3–4, 22–3, 72, 122, 125, 134, 247; military of, 177; New York, 53, 97, 124, 192; Office of Strategic Services (OSS), 75; Pentagon, 123, 130; State Department, 75, 247; Washington DC, 1, 3–5, 10, 21, 23, 69, 71, 89–90, 93, 96, 124–5, 127–9, 132, 155, 162, 166, 203, 225, 233, 239, 245

al-Unsi, Muhammad: 40, 43

de Valera, Eamon: Taoiseach of Republic of Ireland, 193

Vance, Cyrus: US Secretary of State, 243

Venezuela: 70; oil exports from, 79–80

Vered: building projects of, 150

Waiyaki, Munyua: Israeli Foreign Minister, 152